The Mirage Shall Become a Pool

The Mirage Shall Become a Pool
A New Testament Theology of Social Justice and Charity

ONDREJ HRON

◆PICKWICK *Publications* • Eugene, Oregon

THE MIRAGE SHALL BECOME A POOL
A New Testament Theology of Social Justice and Charity

Copyright © 2012 Ondrej Hron. All rights reserved. Except for brief quotations in critical publications or reviews, no part of this book may be reproduced in any manner without prior written permission from the publisher. Write: Permissions, Wipf and Stock Publishers, 199 W. 8th Ave., Suite 3, Eugene, OR 97401.

Pickwick Publications
An Imprint of Wipf and Stock Publishers
199 W. 8th Ave., Suite 3
Eugene, OR 97401

www.wipfandstock.com

ISBN 13: 978-1-60608-640-7

Cataloguing-in-Publication data:

Hron, Ondrej.

    The mirage shall become a pool : a New Testament theology of social justice and charity / Ondrej Hron.

        xviii + 388 pp. ; 23 cm. Includes bibliographical references and indexes.

        ISBN 13: 978-1-60608-640-7

    1. Social Justice—Biblical teaching. 2. Charity—Biblical teaching. 3. Poor—Biblical teaching. I. Title.

BS680 P47 H75 2012

Manufactured in the U.S.A.

This publication is the result of research conducted under the Grant Agency of the Academy of Sciences of the Czech Republic research grant number KJB901830703—*Pursuing Sin: Hamartiological Heuristics as a Guide to the Ethics of Justice and Mercy*—and appears with its financial support.

Scripture quotations taken from the New American Standard Bible®, Copyright © 1960, 1962, 1963, 1968, 1971, 1972, 1973, 1975, 1977, 1995 by The Lockman Foundation. Used by permission. (www.Lockman.org)

New Revised Standard Version Bible, copyright 1989, Division of Christian Education of the National Council of the Churches of Christ in the United States of America. Used by permission. All rights reserved.

Scripture quotations marked NLT are taken from the Holy Bible, New Living Translation, copyright 1996, 2004. Used by permission of Tyndale House Publishers, Inc., Wheaton, Illinois 60189. All rights reserved.

Scripture quoted by permission. Quotations designated (NET) are from the NET Bible® copyright ©1996-2006 by Biblical Studies Press, L.L.C. http://bible.org. All rights reserved.

for
HEINZ & LUCIE
LEOŠ & ESTER
SIMEON & SHALOMI

וְהָיָה הַשָּׁרָב לַאֲגַם

Isaiah 35:7

(Isa 35:5–7; 41:17–18; 58:10–11; Ps 107:35–43)

πᾶσα ἀδικία ἁμαρτία ἐστίν

1 John 5:17

Contents

List of Figures x

Abbreviations xi

Preface xv

Introduction 1

PART ONE: Whose Justice, Which Charity? Issues in Seeking and Finding

1 Mutual Confessions of Particularity 15

2 Seeing Eye to Eye on Poverty 43

3 What's Hermeneutics Got to Do with It? 58

PART TWO: Lowering the White Flag: A Hermeneutical Methodology

4 The Hermeneutics of Demarcating Biblical Justice 91

PART THREE: New Testament Contours: An Analysis of the Data

5 Everything the NT Says about Helping the Poor 121

6 Hearing the Witness: Data Integration 241

7 Drawing Conclusions, Sketching Extrapolations 276

Appendix 343

Bibliography 347

Index of Names 369

Index of Scripture 375

Figures

1. Justice as a Function of Need   21
2. Social Games   32
3. Main Resolution Levels   85
4. Differentiation Indicators Legend   123
5. The Purposive Component of Interhuman Love   240
6. NT Justice as a Function of Need   269
7. "Parallel"-Generated Extrapolation   330

Abbreviations

//	textual parallel
AB	Anchor Bible
ABD	*Anchor Bible Dictionary*
AD	*anno Domini*, in the year of our Lord
ANF	*Ante-Nicene Fathers*
ASV	American Standard Version
BBE	Bible in Basic English
BC	before Christ
BDAG	Bauer, W., F. W. Danker, W. F. Arndt, and F. W. Gingrich, *Greek-English Lexicon of the New Testament and Other Early Christian Literature*
BDB	Brown, F., S. R. Driver, and C. A. Briggs. *A Hebrew and English Lexicon of the Old Testament*
BECNT	Baker Exegetical Commentary on the New Testament
BHS	*Biblia Hebraica Stuttgartensia*
CEV	Contemporary English Version
ChrCent	*Christian Century*
CV	*Communio viatorum*
DARBY	J. N. Darby Translation
DÉLG	*Dictionnaire étymologique de la langue grecque*
DOUAY-RHEIMS	Douay-Rheims Translation (of the Vulgate)
EDBT	*Evangelical Dictionary of Biblical Theology*
EDNT	*Exegetical Dictionary of the New Testament*
ed(s).	editor(s), edition
EGT	Expositor's Greek Testament
ERV	English Revised Version (1885)
ESV	English Standard Version
et al.	*et alii*, and others

HALOT	*Hebrew and Aramaic Lexicon of the Old Testament*
HCSB	Holman Christian Standard Bible
ibid.	*ibidem*, in the same place
ICC	International Critical Commentary
Int	*Interpretation*
ISBE	*International Standard Bible Encyclopedia*
JBL	*Journal of Biblical Literature*
JETS	*Journal of the Evangelical Theological Society*
JPS	Jewish Publication Society, *The Holy Scriptures according to the Masoretic Text*
KBL	Koehler, L., and W. Baumgartner, *Lexicon in Veteris Testamenti libros*
KJV	King James Version
LXX	Septuagint (the Greek OT)
MM	Moulton, J. H., and G. Milligan, *The Vocabulary of the Greek Testament*
MOFFATT	J. Moffatt, *The New Testament: A New Translation*
MT	Masoretic Text (of the OT)
NA^{27}	Nestle-Aland, *Novum Testamentum Graece*, 27th ed.
NAB	New American Bible
NAC	New American Commentary
NASB	New American Standard Bible (1995 Update)
NBD^2	*New Bible Dictionary*, 2nd ed.
NCV	New Century Version
n.d.	no date
NET	New English Translation
NETS	New English Translation of the Septuagint
NIBCNT	New International Biblical Commentary on the New Testament
NICNT	New International Commentary on the New Testament
NICOT	New International Commentary on the Old Testament
NIDNTT	*New International Dictionary of New Testament Theology*
NIDOTTE	*New International Dictionary of Old Testament Theology and Exegesis*

NIGTC	New International Greek Testament Commentary
NIV	New International Version
NJPS	*Tanakh: The Holy Scriptures: The New JPS Translation according to the Traditional Hebrew Text*
NKJV	New King James Version
NLT	New Living Translation
NPNF[1]	*Nicene and Post-Nicene Fathers*, Series 1
NRSV	New Revised Standard Version
NT	New Testament
OT	Old Testament
OTL	Old Testament Library
repr.	reprinted
rev.	revised
RSV	Revised Standard Version
TDNT	*Theological Dictionary of the New Testament*
TDOT	*Theological Dictionary of the Old Testament*
TEV	Today's English Version (Good News Bible)
TNTC	Tyndale New Testament Commentaries
TS	*Theological Studies*
TWOT	*Theological Wordbook of the Old Testament*
vol(s).	volume(s)
v(v).	verse(s)
WBC	Word Biblical Commentary
YLT	Young's Literal Translation

Preface

How does one get mixed up in a gang turf war? Usually by spending too much time in the wrong neighborhood. Tripping into deeply-held theological conflicts is sometimes not that much different. I have been captivated by the plight of the world's poor for a long time—almost a quarter of a century. The uncomfortable passages of Scripture are probably most to blame. But the rundown places of the world have taken their toll too. These can be found most anywhere—all it takes is wandering off the beaten tourist track in Peru, Bolivia, Brazil, or even the Ukraine. Sometimes one does not even have to wander—for some places are the conspicuous equivalents of economic gulags. I am grateful for the opportunity I have had to become intimately familiar with the situation of the homeless and the refugee. With the existential circumstances of those sleeping in boxes as well as those fleeing with only the clothes on their backs. Confronted with both self-respecting and "entitled" poverty—the kind that motorcycles by and rips brass earrings out of ladies' ears in the mistaken notion that they might be worth something—what does one do with the questions that such experiences bring?

For a believer this means pulling out the cheat sheet. But it is hard to benefit much from it if one does not trust its answers. So some put the stigma to such cheating and trust their intuition more. As much as it can be helped, that will not be the case here. In pursuing a NT theology of social justice and charity, our main assumption will be the appropriateness of keeping with what theologian Richard Hays refers to as a "hermeneutic of trust."[1] With adhering to a high view of Scripture. With giving in to the hope that: "All scripture is inspired by God and is useful for teaching, for reproof, for correction, and for training in righteousness, so that everyone who belongs to God may be proficient, equipped for every good work" (2 Tim 3:16–17 NRSV). Though here asserted of the Hebrew Bible, what is often referred to as the OT, we have good

---

1. This terminology was popularized and brought into modern theological parlance by Hays during his much acclaimed Society of Biblical Literature address at its annual conference of 1996 (R. Hays, "Salvation by Trust?" 218–23).

reason to trust that it ultimately applies equally to the New. And helping the poor, whether it be justice or charity, is certainly subsumed under a proficiency in "righteousness" and "every good work." And if Scripture is sufficient for creating in us such proficiency, then it is surely not ineffable concerning our obligations to the poor. And so trust leads to hope, and hope to abandoning all cultured agnosticism about our treatment of the poor. So, abandon the easy deflections all ye who enter here!

My views have changed during this study. Both my understanding of justice, in terms of what it all demands, and the relative prioritization of the poor, in terms of who is to be helped first, have been altered. I think this was as surprising to me as it would be for anyone. Though cheerfully suffering from a substantial expansion and revision, the present book was born in my doctoral dissertation. But the gestation has taken longer still—already causing morning sickness during my master's thesis work. Both of these former endeavors contribute—as do the *urtexts* of this book that were presented, in their shorter recensions, at the recent annual meetings of the Evangelical Theological Society. I am very grateful for the interaction and feedback this has allowed me to receive.

I am indebted to many. I owe much thanks to Miroslav Volf for being willing to be the primary evaluator for this research project. To Kenneth Radant who kindly provided the secondary evaluation. And to the *Grant Agency of the Academy of Sciences of the Czech Republic* for accepting their recommendations and generously funding this endeavor. Nicholas Wolterstorff's genial interaction with the material has had a substantial impact on its final form. His thoughtful comments and critiques on various points were invaluable—they have indeed made this a much better book than it would otherwise have been. I am also grateful for the feedback received from theologians Jakub Trojan and Petr Macek—for their careful attention to detail. For philosopher Thomas K. Johnson's academic friendship and many kind offers of timely assistance. Kenneth Radant also deserves much credit and thanks for assisting me in processing my early thoughts on these thorny issues—along with Paul Chamberlain. As does Daniel R. Nicholson for his focused encouragement—which was so consequential for me during the early stages of my infection with these matters. I must also thank Kevin Peacock for providing valuable advice when my forays into the OT became particularly ambitious. Nor can I forget to acknowledge Robert Overgaard for his early stylistic suggestions. Stephen J. Wellum is to be thanked for his encouragement and being willing to render an evaluation of my research. As are the other American theologians who were kindly ready to make time to provide feedback. I am very grateful for all of the advice and assistance I received from my editor, Chris Spinks, my typesetter, Patrick Harrison, and for all of my interaction with the friendly people at Wipf and Stock Publishers. Nor can I forget all those who prayed.

Soli Deo Gloria.

Introduction

THE UNBEARABLE ELUSIVENESS OF SOCIAL JUSTICE

IT SEEMS THAT SOCIAL justice leads an epically tragic existence. She is both irresistibly beautiful and yet scarcely approachable. She multiplies her paradoxes. She is at once Helen of Troy and Medusa. We would pursue her—but a distorted reflection on our polished shields is all we seem capable of bearing.

Few issues are as practically relevant and yet so consistently controversial. What believer wants to be unjust to the poor? So why is social justice, despite its unassailable worth, so wildly untamable?

We are particular. That is another way of saying that we are provincial, perspectival, and subjective in our perceptions of social justice. We have no readymade access to social justice and thus our assumptions hold an almost unbreakable spell over us. The claim that we are particular has become somewhat common currency of late. But one does not have to be out dating the postmodern condition to perceive particularity's effects—particularly when it comes to social justice. Theological disagreement and dissonance is present even among evangelical thinkers—Christians who otherwise share a great deal of theological concurrence. We do not have to read widely before we are confronted with mutually exclusive understandings of social justice. The disagreements are not well hidden.

We are particular and we read our preconceptions into the text. Our plight is aggravated by our tendency to construct and synthesize our understandings of social justice higher up the ladder of abstraction. When we birth our conceptions several strides from the biblical text, each step inadvertently serves to make our presuppositions safer. Each rung lets them quietly seep in. And so we produce dissonant theologies of social justice with little grounds for mutual evaluation. As disconcerting as the plight of the Dalits in India, our assumptions have become the untouchables.

Yet a deep concern for helping the poor is evident in both Christian testaments. We are confronted by an apparent mystery but with no scarcity of clues. We are always particular in initially coming to Scripture, but usually the text—if we let it—acts on us to reduce our particularity—functioning to eliminate certain preconceptions. So why do we seem to catch only mirrored glimpses of our obligations toward the poor? When I claimed earlier that we have no readymade access to social justice I did not mean that the Bible has little to say about justice or social concern. This is certainly not the case. I meant rather that social justice is a slippery entity and we profoundly differ over its beginning and end.

Social justice carries all the markings of a maverick. Philosophers recognize it to be a "special obligation": an obligation which is not owed equally to all persons as justice generally is. Social justice is only owed to the poor—the subset of persons frequently distinguished from all others by the lone virtue of their poverty.

So some are filled with doubt. Perhaps while participating in the Greek theater, social ethics has put on the wrong mask. Thus, despite all appearances, the voice we hear calling is rather merciful charity and not justice after all. What if the special obligation of social justice is an imposter? For if she really is Medusa, we should do the heroic deed and be done with her.

But others are certain that social justice can nowise suffer a case of mistaken identity. She is irresistibly apparent and will not be diluted with notions of charity and mercy. If she is a Siren, we should fearlessly unbind ourselves from the mast of charity and abandon ourselves to her. Perhaps the tales of impending doom—if we surrender to her seductive song—are greatly exaggerated.

Still others desire neither her death nor are set on her alone. Perhaps the biblical call to help the poor circumscribes social justice and leaves a place for merciful charity. Perhaps both can coexist without diluting or subverting each other. This is certainly the more complicated route. If social justice is Helen, we should seek both her and the spoils of Troy at once. It certainly has a practical air to it.

So we come to Scripture looking for her name. But while we find a great many passages calling us to help the poor, too few of them explicitly identify their call as a matter of justice obligation or mercy. And even texts which do contain such terminology are, as we shall see, contested. Calls unto justice and mercy come in the same grammatical and syntactical forms. With no facile way to tell biblical justice and mercy apart, our preconceptions are left to run free and unhindered. This is the nexus of the problem of social justice—the mathematical origin where all of the axes of contention converge. Thus in the case of social justice our security clearance to the Bible has been revoked because we have misplaced our access card. And we wonder if we ever really had it.

So we solemnly greet the midwife of cynicism and wonder if social justice is after all ineffable. Perhaps the famous complaints of George Tyrrell and Albert Schweitzer against the First Quest for the historical Jesus—that theologians looking down a dark well are very likely to see little more than a blurry image of their own faces—apply here as well. Perhaps our theological conceptions of social justice are merely a reflection of us.

In asking why social justice is so contested among believers, that is the short answer. A more detailed response will be provided in part 1 as a way of critically reflecting on our variously conditioned preconceptions. There is a lot that we need to be prepared to leave behind—or at least to cache away in suspended animation.

RECOUPING OUR LOSSES

Cynicism is a shiny toy—sometimes it is a lot of fun to play with. But we have a lot to lose if we let it into the nursery of social justice. For a believer, justice is no abstract thing, it is a line not to be crossed. If we transgress it, we are constrained to make things right. We know that we cannot hope to enjoy God's favor unless we "let justice [מִשְׁפָּט, *mishpat*] roll down like waters And righteousness [צְדָקָה, *tsedaqah*] like an ever-flowing stream" (Amos 5:24).[1] To whatever extent helping the poor is a

---

1. Those in positions of societal responsibility receive special attention in the broader context of this verse. Individuals in a position to pervert or uphold judicial justice are addressed in verses 12 and 15. Whether verse 11 condemns the levying of heavy taxes or high land rent is uncertain. The former would implicate rulers while the latter the rich for demanding a degree of tribute which God deems worthy of punishment. The consequences of these transgressions affect the whole remnant (vv. 15, 21–23). Their corporate worship becomes detestable to God. The responsibility to seek good and hate evil, as emphasized in verses 14–15, sends echoes beyond the palaces and the judiciaries. So while only some may be in a position to accomplish judicial justice (מִשְׁפָּט, *mishpat*), the call to act in accordance with prescriptive justice (צְדָקָה, *tsedaqah*) is less contained.

Unless otherwise indicated, all biblical quotations are taken from the NASB. For the sake of accessibility, original language terms will be provided in their lexical form

matter of justice, to that extent we are fully bound. Indeed, the primary benefit of resisting the ambiguity is uncovering our comprehensive constraint obligations toward the poor—what biblical justice demands. We dare not lose that—who wants to court God's recompense for injustice? There are consequences to society, to local churches, and to us personally if we do injustice. If we love God we cannot help but want to know where the lines fall.

This is the biggest win to be had if we can but gain access—confidence concerning the domain of social justice. What is the set of a believer's morally binding obligations to the poor? We want to know where its boundaries lie or to be sure if it is, after all, a null set. Finding where social justice ends also clarifies where merciful charity begins. The domain of charity—its proper limits—comes into reach. Tempting treatments of the poor which do not find a home in either domain can be identified and resisted. We must pursue the boundaries of these domains if we want to hold on to the hope of breaking through the present theological impasse. It is necessary for making our disparate conceptualizations evaluable.

The practical implications of isolating the domains of social justice and charity will not let themselves be left behind. A few of these bear mentioning. Help competition exists in most Western urban contexts. Often churches and para-church urban missions offer competing sources of help. Ministries with greater incentives and fewer disincentives will naturally attract more participants to their brand of the same service. Wherever overlap exists, ministries that seek to encourage lifestyle change among the indolent will be marginalized by those that do not. A handout can price out every other form of competition. Meaningful cooperation can only exist where there is substantial ethical agreement or mutually exclusive specialization. Greater ethical agreement becomes a valuable asset. So we come to the other side. If helping the poor is an issue of social justice no matter the poverty's origin, then placing any conditions or requirements upon our assistance is morally wrong. At the very least any such conditions become a form of patronizing and, perhaps much worse, may just be another ironically twisted manifestation of the oppression of structural evil. Who wants to have their hand

---

(lemma) and transliterated—except where the original language text is being directly quoted. When making an exception for the occasional plural noun (as appropriate), the reader will be suitably informed.

in that? To the extent to which helping the poor is a matter of justice, to that extent our aid should be immediate and practically without condition. To that extent it is comprehensively owed to the poor. Thus the disambiguation of the domains of justice and mercy determines what, if anything, may be demanded of believers by the indolent.

Finding the boundaries on the map of social justice also allows us to prioritize our treatments of the poor. When resources are limited, as is very often the case, instances of justice obligation must take priority over matters of mercy. When mutually exclusive choices must be made, justice must be fulfilled before any of the remainders are allotted for mercy. Doing the good of mercy can never overcome the evil of perpetrating injustice by withholding its dues for the sake of accomplishing the mercy. Giving to charity so as to renege on our just debts is morally culpable. Justice rightly demands our foremost attention.

What else does demarcating the proper domains of justice and mercy do for us? The isolation of these two domains also determines whether believers may consider the goals and values of each helping context without being comprehensively constrained by every need on a "first come, first serve" basis. Only within the domain of mercy can the best approach and assistance distribution be sought without fear that such discernment constitutes immediate moral transgression.

The differentiation of social justice and charity also establishes whether the un-hypocritical ownership of possessions is morally possible. Because the Bible mandates giving to the poor, the obligation level of this mandate determines whether believers can retain possessions—at least as long as there are any poor within our reach. This differentiation therefore arbitrates what constitutes consistent Christian living. While the answer to this seems obvious to first world believers because we have generally conflated it with our lifestyle, it is not so clear elsewhere.[2] And who is immune from fudging consistency in their own favor?

The sought isolation of justice and mercy also regulates which ends of social activism are justified and validated by justice. "We demand mercy" does not sit well on a placard. It makes for a limp rallying call.

---

2. The Cold War meaning is not intended in my referrals to the first and third worlds. The delineation rather highlights the socioeconomic differences between the developed and the developing nations. Thus the third world becomes a synonym for what is sometimes called the two-thirds world—but even more so for the world's poorer places. And the first world signifies the world's wealthy nations.

As such, the distinction we are seeking furnishes the moral ground for social change.

With so much at stake, it is no surprise that social justice and charity are so relentlessly contested. We have so much to gain if we could but demarcate them, and so much to lose if we do not. To the best of the author's knowledge, the present work is the first of its kind in seeking out a passage level, biblically generated differentiation. A way down from the ladder. A means to making our presuppositions more open to evaluation on the basis of Scripture itself. I gather that access to biblical justice and charitable mercy is available to us. That cynicism need not be our Christian realism. That we can push forward and enable a text-driven discussion. Perhaps a North Star can be found. Perhaps we can change the conversation.

OF EMPERORS AND NEW CLOTHES

Just as we were breathing a sigh of relief that we had indeed only invited our most polite friends to our little baby shower, one colleague—who had up until now been quietly listening to everyone's well-wishes—crushed his Styrofoam cup and agitatedly made his way to the foot of the crib. Turning his back to the infant he sized up the silence that had quickly settled on the room. "Why," he demanded, "is everyone so easily taken in? Surely this baby was completely unnecessary. In this world, to be loved is to be needed—surely any love this infant receives is naught but cruel pretense." Impervious to the shock and discomfort rippling among his audience, he said his piece. A passage level differentiation of social justice and charity already existed, did it not? Why could we not say, as others had done, that whenever we encounter a command in Scripture it signifies a justice obligation and all other comers are instances of mercy? Why bother throwing a shower for anything more complicated?

Recovering at the speed of parental defensiveness, I offered my protest. Would my colleague agree that forgiveness is an instance of mercy? Most people would have no reservations in agreeing that to be the case—this is generally, if not unanimously, agreed. Forgiveness is, for example, linked to mercy in Matt 18:33. Yet forgiveness is also commanded (Mark 11:25; Luke 17:3–4). Worse still, mercy itself is commanded in various passages (Luke 10:37; Jude 1:22–23). Making commands harbingers of justice simply will not do.

Always the peacemaker, my colleague's fiancée went to join him by the crib. Perhaps my colleague had spoken too quickly she consoled, but he may not be altogether incorrect. What if it was that all negatively phrased commands—rather than all commands—were the true signposts of justice obligation? Positive commands, like those concerning having mercy and granting forgiveness, can be mercy imperatives while the "shall not" commands might nevertheless herald justice. Perhaps this is where the honor is due.

Presently my wife—who had squeezed all the blood out of my hand with her own in the preceding moments—recovered her voice. Clearing her throat quietly she began to question whether positive and negative phrasing could really be allotted so much significance. Is it not more likely that such formulation differences are largely in the semantic domain and conceptually interchangeable? Is it not true that the same command can be given both positively and inversely? Is not the positive command to love one another in Rom 13:8 a summary command for its negatively phrased subcomponents in Rom 13:9? Do not all imperatives of the form "do not do this, but do its opposite" militate against such a differentiation (Num 30:2; Matt 5:39; Rom 12:16)? Are not such positive and negative formulations correlated throughout Scripture as in Deut 23:21, 23? Colossians 3:9 commands "do not lie to one another," while Eph 4:25 mandates "therefore, laying aside falsehood, SPEAK TRUTH EACH ONE *of you* WITH HIS NEIGHBOR, for we are members of one another." The conceptual overlap is clear—as with Zech 8:16 from which Eph 4:25 is quoted—the phraseology has come to no avail.

Furthermore, she noted while transitioning her gaze to my colleague, why should we be satisfied with a differentiation limited to imperatives? Had not Richard Hays repeatedly warned that narrative must not be forgotten when seeking the moral vision of Scripture? Does he not even claim that it should be allotted primacy in identifying our moral obligations?[3] A differentiation constrained to commands is condemned to a textual poverty of its own making. What compels you into self-imposed exile? While differences in syntax and genre provide no raw material for a passage level isolation of social justice, why should they be permitted to filter the data set? Are we to ignore all other revelations of God's moral evaluation? Such impoverishment is deeply undesirable, and will almost certainly be challenged as theologically motivated or

---

3. R. Hays, *The Moral Vision of the New Testament*, 310.

receive some such abuse. Thankfully by now the hour had grown late and, as our guests said their goodbyes, I assured my wife that everything would be okay—I had fitted the baby with her best earplugs.

And so my contention remains. We need that elusive access—a *discrimen* evident at the textual level. A means to moral insight present at the passage level, a clarion against seeking confirmation in comfortable abstractions. We need to identify something heuristically present in a large portion of the passages concerning the treatment of the poor. We must defend our theological constructs by showing *how* we identify mandated treatments as matters of justice or not. We must prove that more than just assumptions are in play. Developing such a hermeneutical *discrimen* will be the focus of part 2.

But two objections simply will not wait. What if pinning one's hopes on any such textual level *discrimen* is like sheltering oneself in the warmth of the emperor's new clothes? Does not biblical theology positively forbid any such endeavor? With each section of Scripture developing its own unique themes, how can seeking any such commonality be anything other than artificial superimposition against the grain of the text itself? Accordingly, some biblical theologians may object that no such trans-human author continuity may be pursued on principle.[4] In some senses the issue need not detain us too long. Those that deny this possibility categorically are not likely to be reading this book. Nevertheless, the author would invite any who are on the fence to suspend their judgment until after having assessed the textual data. God's ethical evaluation of human behavior is a concern apparent throughout Scripture. It is, at minimum, theoretically possible for a consistent pattern to emerge. Most systematic theologians will provide a defense of the possibility of systematic theology.[5] After all, they too are commanded to work quietly and earn their own bread.

---

4. Theology, like other contemporary disciplines, inspires divisions of labor. I refer here to one of these: that which tends to exist between biblical and systematic theologians. A few polymaths notwithstanding, biblical theologians tend to become specialists in detail (the unique texture of each brick) while systematic theologians specialize in the grand composite (the impact of the final edifice).

5. The argument often ends up revolving around a discussion of God's authorial intent—the extent to which He intended Scripture to function as a coherent witness. Systematic theologians are not the only interested party—it is hard for anyone seeking leading from the Bible to dodge this subpoena. As theological treatments are virtually innumerable, permit me to mention but one philosophical witness: Wolterstorff, *Divine Discourse*; Wolterstorff, "The Unity behind the Canon," 217–32.

Nevertheless, my claim is simultaneously bolder and more timid than what generally functions as the systematic common ground among Evangelicals. In addition to denying that Scripture is a kaleidoscope of irreconcilably different pictures, I recklessly contend that at least some common threads are discernable at the biblical passage level. But cautiousness has its place too. David Kelsey has influentially argued that all systematic theologians engage in an imaginative synoptic judgment regarding "God's presence in, through, and over-against the activities comprising the church's common life."[6] For Kelsey, this synoptic construal concerning the mode of God's presence is a pre-textual preconception. It casts the die. This synoptic verdict concerning "what Christianity is basically all about" subsequently determines how we "construe and use particular passages of Scripture."[7] Richard Hays develops this latter insight by transposing Kelsey's synoptic judgment from a focus on Scripture's *aim* (what it is meant to accomplish as a mediator of God's presence) into an imaginative construal concerning Scripture's *content*.[8] The hub of the claim becomes that all systematic theologians engage in an imaginative synoptic judgment concerning the main themes of Scripture. These synoptic construals then go on to provide the theologian's systematization with its conceptual glue and controlling motifs.

In terms of social justice and charity, I think we might want to be more cautious—to make a foolhardy attempt to sneak in under Hays's radar. Not seeking a theological "theory of everything" allows us some maneuverability. More important than questioning whether Scripture allows us to helpfully grasp it in single synoptic judgments, we can strive to consciously place some of our cherished motifs into synoptic limbo. To whatever extent we are uncomfortable with theological subjectivism, Hays's and Kelsey's observations should make us timid. Perhaps we can observe recurrent patterns at the textual level *asynoptically* and summon a concerted effort to postpone synoptic considerations until the last possible moment. The more data we amass *asynoptically* (while retaining mental blindness toward the big picture), the less imagination

---

6. Kelsey, *Proving Doctrine*, 163.

7. Ibid., 159, 167.

8. R. Hays, *The Moral Vision of the New Testament*, 194–95. Interestingly, Kelsey's emphasis on the role of the imaginative construal has garnered noticeable favor even among biblical scholars—though often more so in its transposed form. See, for example, Brueggemann, *Theology of the Old Testament*, 731–32.

will be required of us in evaluating the plausibility of the existence of a textual *discrimen*. This is why part 3 will go to great lengths to present the textual data of the NT to the reader to judge which patterns may be present. Despite the vivacious play of nuance, perhaps there is a pattern to the polyphony.

Even if we tentatively grant the possibility of success, a second objection immediately springs to the fore. Earlier I had compared social justice to Medusa, a Siren, and Helen of Troy—as either worthy of elimination, as worthy of complete submission, or as one worthy goal of two. So some say there is no biblical social justice but only charity, others say there is only social justice and no charity, and some argue that you can have both without either one diminishing or compromising the other. And some say this is a false trichotomy. Another possibility emerges. Perhaps as the Greek goddess Artemis gave way to the Roman goddess Diana, social justice and mercy are merely points on a continuum—broaching no practical need for a differentiation. What if there is no hard line between justice and mercy? Do we not occasionally witness an overlap in biblical terminology—with righteousness or justice (צְדָקָה, *tsedaqah*) being translated as pity or merciful kindness (ἐλεημοσύνη, *eleēmosynē*) in the Septuagint (Isa 1:27)? Does not Matt 6:1–4 refer to almsgiving or mercy unto the poor (ἐλεημοσύνη, *eleēmosynē*) as an instance of righteousness or justice (δικαιοσύνη, *dikaiosynē*)?[9] Despite this overlap—which will receive attention during the discussion of the *discrimen* in part 2—I would venture to say that very few people, upon reflection, actually believe this claim. Even fewer people attempt to live it consistently. For even when we seek to avoid such a boundary we still assume that some of the good we could do for others is voluntary on our part. And so our practice refutes our doubts and we delimit and curtail the domain of justice.

There are a number of additional reasons for not surrendering the border. For the present let us consider one more. This contention is both more ethically grave and wider reaching than the first—for it claims that affirming the location as well as the involatility of the boundary matters. Why? Because fuzzy continuums lead to injustice. Examples abound. Recalling a 1976 conference in South Africa, Nicholas Wolterstorff

---

9. Not to be left out, the same overlap is likewise present in the intertestamental literature (Tobit 2:14; 12:9; 14:11; and Baruch 5:9).

recounts the plight of the "black" and "colored" South Africans under apartheid:

> They told in slow quiet tones of the many ways in which they were wronged. The Afrikaners responded by saying that it was all for the sake of the future good. Some told of the charity that they and their families had extended to blacks and coloreds: cast-off clothing given to families living in huts in the back yards, Christmas trinkets given to the children, and so forth. They charged that the strategies of resistance and the words of criticism employed by some blacks and coloreds were hurtful and not loving. And they assured their black and colored "brothers," as they called them, that if they just behaved, they would see what a generous people the Afrikaners were at heart. I saw, as never before, the good overwhelming the just, and benevolence and the appeal to love being used as instruments of oppression.[10]

What Wolterstorff and others have noticed is that matters of justice readily become matters of mercy in the perspective of the perpetrators. What better way to make the requirements of justice optional? The observation is profound: even otherwise morally sensitive persons are able to perpetuate injustice if they can self-defensively reclassify it as an instance of mercy. Such confusions continue on in Palestine and elsewhere. A continuum approach to justice and mercy contains in itself no antidote against injustice. For it readily makes border region justices seem voluntary. When mixed with human depravity, the results are tragic—heartbreaking and maddening at the same time. The false trichotomy stands.

The present engagement confines itself to a focus on the NT theology of helping the poor. There are a number of reasons for this. The *discrimen* itself was extrapolated from a consideration of all of canonical Scripture. Nonetheless, while it would be preferable to address the Hebrew Bible simultaneously, several factors make the present focus desirable. As with mathematical proofs, so in theology it is wise to proceed from the simple to the complex. The writings of the NT span a comparatively much smaller range of time and culture than those of the OT. This simplifies things tremendously as socioeconomic and political-cultural differences—and the considerations they entail—are more contained. There is also a practical impetus to beginning with the NT. Whereas

---

10. Wolterstorff, *Justice*, vii.

all evangelical believers generally affirm the continued moral applicability of the NT, the continued prescriptiveness of the OT is significantly contested. Any treatment of the Hebrew Bible necessarily embroils its author in defending a particular understanding of the relation of the testaments. Happy is he who is able to avoid this. It is nevertheless clear that the New assumes the Old and so whenever the NT data quotes or alludes to the OT, the latter will be considered to have been "brought forward" to participate in the NT discussion. Hopefully there is not too much shame, and something to gain, even in starting with what OT scholar Walter Kaiser lightheartedly calls the Bible's appendix.

So armed with a hermeneutic of trust and a parallel distrust of methodological indeterminism, we are ready to begin. In part 1 we will endeavor to shake out the relevant issues. Part 2 will follow with the development of a *discrimen* capable of addressing them. Part 3 will then engage the NT data and proceed to integrate it into a NT theology of helping the poor. Perhaps what taunted us as an evanescent play of desert heat and light can become a place of succor after all. The mirage, a pool.

PART ONE

Whose Justice, Which Charity?
Issues in Seeking and Finding

ONE

Mutual Confessions of Particularity

TIME TO PACE AROUND the target a little. Social justice is a special obligation. It refers, as I have been using the expression, to justice unto the poor. It is not the set of all justices due to the poor but rather the exclusive set of all justices due to them *alone*. Most justice obligations extend to benefit everyone. We are in pursuit of those which make the poor their exclusive recipients—a preferential option of sorts. Maybe an example will be helpful. Precisely because not murdering the poor is a matter of justice generally, it is, correspondingly, not a matter of social justice. General justice is not nearly as contentious.

So, to what extent is justice a function of need? The reply is to be found in the domain of social justice. This heuristic notion of social justice therefore subsumes the common philosophical notions of economic or distributive justice—the moral constraints intended to govern the allocation of the burdens and benefits of a society's economic activity. How is it larger? Biblically, justice unto the poor may envelop special obligations which are wider-reaching than solely economic adjustment or assistance. It is at least theoretically possible that justice obligations tied to need, if such exist, may address more than the need itself. Perhaps these obligations may extend to mitigating the side effects of need. Perhaps obligations such as special protection or impartiality in allotting respectful treatment are patiently awaiting their excavation.

All of these potential obligations deservedly garner evangelical concern. Justice has resurfaced as a significant focus in evangelical social and missiological thought. To the extent that statistics are capable of approximating reality, Evangelicals by and large appear to possess a great concern for helping the poor.[1] Unfortunately this commendable passion

---

1. Sociological research conducted by Mark Regnerus, Christian Smith, and David Sikkink asserts that Evangelicals, at least in the United States, are more generous to the poor, per capita, than any other religious or non-religious social group (Regnerus et al., "Who Gives to the Poor?" 481–93).

has not translated into theological agreement concerning a believer's justice obligations toward the world's poor. The domains of social justice and charity remain elusively intertwined with our particularities.

Earlier I claimed that we read our preconceptions into the text—and that this is a pandemic-grade infection. It is only healthy to take a long solemn look at our variously conditioned presuppositions before we seek to lower them into a casket. They need both our self-conscious respect—for all their formative influences upon us—and our willingness to lay them to rest. We cannot buffer what we do not readily acknowledge.

We are all particular in a number of ways. In terms of our interpretation of the biblical testimony concerning social justice and charity, the permeative influence of our situatedness can be laid out along several trajectories. We can broadly classify these trajectories into three hermeneutical moments. Some are pre-hermeneutical and not readily evaluable on the basis of Scripture, others are pre-hermeneutical and comparatively evaluable, while others still are manifestly hermeneutical in nature.

Preconceptions of the first type encompass our ideological perspectivalness, our sociocultural subjectivity, and our psychological particularity. All of these variously conditioned particularities are our pre-hermeneutical companions—close friends who influence us even before we come to Scripture to interpret it. They are the reason that our intuitions cannot be trusted—why our horse sense has become an unfruitful gelding. Though they have developed an immunity to the effects of Scripture, they must nonetheless be made evaluable by any hermeneutical methodology that proposes to move beyond them. These presuppositions, and the contentions they generate, will receive our attention shortly.

Only one significant preconception—our preferred definition of poverty—bears the characteristics of the second hermeneutical moment. Our pre-hermeneutical assumptions concerning who all is to be considered poor are comparatively evaluable on the basis of Scripture. The chapter to follow aims to provide such a NT evaluation.

The third preconception type encompasses theological particularities that must be evaluated on additional grounds due to their complex systematic nature. These contentions, in contrast to the first two types, are ultimately hermeneutical in scope due to their prospective filtering of the biblical data set. They include our disparate approaches to the continuity of the covenants, the modes of ethical appropriation, the human/divine ethical disjunction, cultural specificity, and data post-processing. These cardinal disagreements revolve around determining the domain of the biblical data which constitutes the relevant data set concerning helping the poor. They will receive the attention they merit right after the chapter concerning poverty.

Contemplating our variously conditioned particularities does more than merely make us aware of what we must hold lightly. Our mutual particularities, particularly our pre-hermeneutical ones, are the argument for the sort of methodology that is needed. They demonstrate that a passage level hermeneutical methodology is necessary and reveal the capabilities that it must possess.

IDEOLOGICAL PARTICULARITY

Political conceptions of justice are rooted in the philosophical understandings that serve to undergird the public-square manifestation. The intimate intertwining of these two conception spheres allows a consideration of the philosophical realm to suffice as a consideration of both.

Our political and philosophical leanings comprise our most self-evident set of justice presuppositions. Where along the continuum between complete societal or community responsibility and complete individual responsibility do we feel most comfortable? When Lev 25:35 mandates: "Now in case a countryman of yours becomes poor and his means with regard to you falter, then you are to sustain him, like a stranger or a sojourner, that he may live with you," is providing the interest-free loan mentioned here an instance of justice or mercy? Is visiting "orphans and widows in their distress" (Jas 1:27)—so as to provide material and other practical assistance—an issue of justice level obligation or charity? Our answers to these questions are naturally conditioned by political values.

History has yielded no shortage of philosophical approaches to justice. These various historically extant approaches can be categorized along a number of axes. The most interesting of these, for our purposes, will be the axis along which we experience the greatest divergence over the nature of justice—particularly justice unto the poor. For it is not too presumptuous to expect that the continuum which highlights our differences most starkly is closest to the heart of the dissonance.

This axis, and the core contention it highlights, can be expressed in a number of ways. Kim Hawtrey, in considering economic justice, has helpfully described the opposing poles of this spectrum.[2] While one pole argues that justice is best understood as a regulator of means, the other contends that justice is ultimately a regulator of ends. The former pole represents the commutative approach to economic justice and contends that justice is about fairness of procedures. Justice has been served when economic transactions are uncoerced and both parties are satisfied with their exchange. Justice is a regulator of the rules of the game—but not of its results. So justice regulates procedures rather than outcomes. The less intervention concerning ends, the better. The latter pole exemplifies the distributive approach to economic justice and argues the opposite—that justice is about fairness of outcomes. Justice is transgressed whenever the results of the game are large (or increasing) disparities in the distribution of economic benefits. In the face of such inequitable outcomes, ends-oriented justice must demand intervention. We can meaningfully refer to what resides at the tips of these two poles as the strict libertarian (means-based) and strict egalitarian (ends-based) conceptions—and acknowledge that a continuum of positions exists between them.

This spectrum unfurls the watershed question—our core contention concerning social justice. To what extent is justice a regulator of means and to what extent is it a regulator of ends? Where is the proper locus of the applicability of justice? What is its rightful jurisdiction? To what extent, if any, is justice a function of need? Is justice ever rightly concerned with the results of the game?

If the question sounds familiar it is because it finds an analogy in the broader sphere of ethics itself. Deontological approaches to ethics assert that the rightness or wrongness of an "action" is intrinsic to the act itself and extrinsic to the results of the act. Consequentialist approaches claim the opposite.[3] That "actions" are to be judged right or wrong on the basis of their results alone and not on the basis of their means. So what jurisdiction should ethics regulate? Maybe we can resolve our dissonance at this level. Recognition of this analogousness unfortunately does not, as we shall see, help us arbitrate our core contention over justice. A clear

---

2. Hawtrey, "Economic Justice," 98–105.

3. For simplicity's sake, *aretaic* or virtue approaches will be passed over at present. These ethical trajectories assess moral acts on the basis of their compatibility with the kind of character a person ought to possess. Such approaches do not ultimately provide a way of escape from the issue at hand. If people ought to do what is in line with creating and keeping virtue, ought they to regulate, as the proper outplay, their actions or the results of their actions?

winner in the ethical realm would have been a nice hint. Evangelicals do tend to favor deontological approaches because consequentialist theories have often tended to identify their ends in broad strokes—strokes that aim at a general value or set of values such as happiness, pleasure, or general welfare. Strokes that often lead to scenarios where "the ends justify the means."

Consequentialism, however, becomes less biblically disconcerting when it is transitioned from the macro realm to the realm of micromanaging. Biblical mandates have often been philosophically translated from a deontological formulation into a consequentialist one and vice versa. Does not the command to not murder mean that we are not willfully to engage in any willful means that would bring about the death of an innocent noncombatant?[4] In this sense the issue reduces itself to a matter of semantics and phraseology since acts and their intended results are deeply intertwined. Such a micromanaging of ends has sometimes been referred to as *indirect consequentialism*. It is indirect because it regulates rules by way of their consequences rather than acts generally.

While we may tend toward a deontological understanding, additional factors quickly surface to buttress our suspicions that no clear-cut winner will emerge. Some biblical mandates—such as our moral responsibility to not cause other believers to stumble—are inspired for us in a consequentialist formulation (Matt 18:6 // Mark 9:42 // Luke 17:2; 1 Cor 8:12–13). Such texts concentrate their gaze toward the desired ends rather than the means. The result being sought determines which concrete treatments are right or wrong. Moreover, if we acquiesce that moral dilemmas do in fact occur, a consequentialist understanding appears to address the issues raised by them most naturally. The classic example of lying to Nazi soldiers regarding the Jews one is hiding illustrates the point. In all such situations the rightness or wrongness of the "action" is extrinsic to the act and intrinsic to the consequences of the act. Even the approach of *tragic morality*—which believes that the lesser evil, though it remains an evil, must be chosen—requires a shift of focus toward evaluating the consequences of our actions in order to discern which mandates are jostling for our obedience. The results of the game become the nexus of our moral decision making.

---

4. The consequentialist formulation given here is in the form of a pragmatic common minimum. Some believers contend that capital crimes and just war no longer mediate the imperative to not kill and so would favor a less restricted formulation.

This is not enough to prove that indirect consequentialism is to be preferred to a deontological approach. Nor does it ascertain the width of the divide or the degree of complimentary coexistence possible between these two approaches. For while the Bible does not itself furnish a deontological rule for managing moral dilemmas, one could be manufactured on the basis of inference. All biblical texts suggesting a consequentialist formulation can be reconstituted—due to the close relation between acts and their intended results—as expressing unusually broad deontological principles concerning acts. Our lingering suspicions are however enough to contend that seeking a resolution concerning the proper jurisdiction of justice via the proxy of ethics does not succeed. Whatever nascent hope we may have had is crushed. Retreating to the depths of normative ethical theory does not uncover a clear precedent for an exclusive preference for adjudicating means rather than ends.

So the core contention remains unblinking before us. To what extent is justice a regulator of means and to what extent is it a regulator of ends? To what degree is biblical justice libertarian and to what degree is it egalitarian? Our philosophical particularity suffers no shortage of champions.

Robert Nozick is a recent representative of the means-oriented trajectory.[5] He argues that justice is non-patterned. That justice has no ends in mind—no pattern that it hopes to attain. That it can endure no fixed correlation between means and ends. We pay sports stars their market value—not what they somehow objectively deserve. And we do this because the same market allows us to make similarly disproportionate amounts of money on them. The only "pattern" is the chaotic whimsy of the market.

In contradistinction, the recent "veil of ignorance" approach of John Rawls—that people would choose egalitarian societies if they did not know in advance what their economic status would be—heads toward the ends-oriented pole of the spectrum.[6] Rawls contends that people would certainly think about ends in contemplating their preferred society if they could not foresee their own place in it—if they did not know whether they would end up an intellectual or handicapped, gifted or plagued by disorders, secure or a pauper. That they would adopt a "difference principle" that would favor the poorest whenever the creation

---

5. Nozick, *Anarchy, State, and Utopia*, 150–59.
6. Rawls, *A Theory of Justice*, 12, 19, 136–42.

of disparities would prove beneficial to increasing the overall welfare of their society.[7] So if more wealth were to be created by allowing inequalities, inequalities could be pursued only to the extent that they raised the absolute economic position of the most poor. Justice is a function of ends. Patterned to needs. The strategy of both trajectories is to move our attention toward scenarios where means cannot but override ends and vice versa. And to hope that we ascribe justice there.

Biblically, the situation may be more complex. Perhaps broad ranging principles are not welcome. It may be that ends-oriented justice regulates only very specific contexts of great need. Perhaps this was implied in John the Baptist's concern for the fruits of repentance in Luke 3:11: "Let the man who has two tunics share with him who has *none*; and let him who has food do likewise" (italics added). Perhaps a visualization of some of the main options along this significant philosophical continuum will prove helpful.

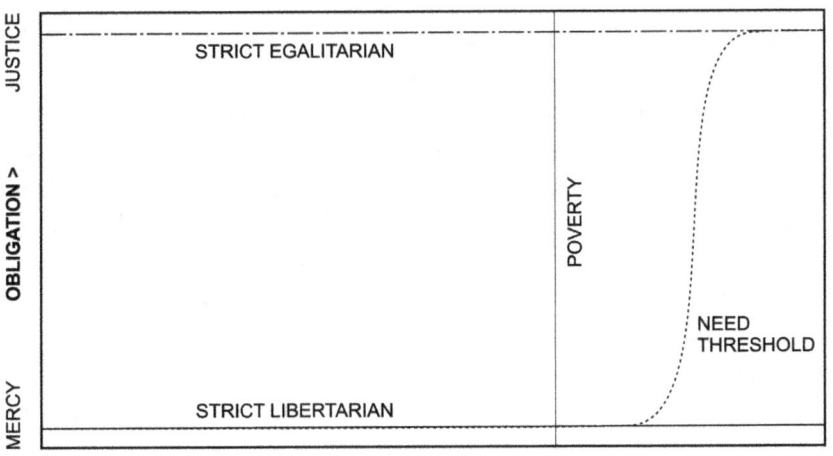

FIGURE 1: Justice as a Function of Need

"From each according to his ability, to each according to his needs!"[8] leads to the strict egalitarian relation that could be considered, at least in tendency, as broadly Marxist—at least in the theorized higher phase of communist society. Karl Marx thought that the first phase of commu-

---

7. Ibid., 75–83.

8. The quotation is the author's translation of "Jeder nach seinen Fähigkeiten, jedem nach seinen Bedürfnissen!" as found in Marx and Engels, "Kritik des Gothaer Programms," 21.

nism would allot to everyone according to their labor contribution. He believed that the higher phase would come about naturally and did not speak of it in justice terms—beyond employing the classic phraseology of "to each according to something." So Marx does seek strict egalitarianism but avoids technically labeling it a matter of justice.

Marx's avoidance of stating his case in terms of moral principles may have been wise. Strict egalitarianism has proven somewhat difficult to achieve. During their sojourn behind the iron curtain, a form of humor spread among the Slavic countries which juxtaposed what the system taught with the untaught reality. So the disenchanted would quip that "we are all equal; but some are more equal than others." They would happily add to what they had been well taught and contend that "capitalism is the exploitation of man *by* man; communism is the *exact* opposite" (in the precise inverse sense). But perhaps this is just the perspective of those who, having started with an industrialized state, saw the economies (and wellbeing) of their countries dwindle. For many in underdeveloped nations, stricter egalitarianism appears to hold out the possibility of immediate personal improvement.

Strict egalitarians argue that justice does not fluctuate with need—for it always seeks ends-oriented equality for all. Strict libertarians such as Friedrich Hayek would agree—but only as far as the first claim. Strict libertarians contend that justice never addresses ends and therefore consider the meeting of all resultant needs a matter of mercy. Milton Friedman is perhaps less strict. He advocated a "negative income tax," which would supplement the income of the most poor as an alternative to the welfare system in the United States. Debate exists regarding whether this proposal was, in Friedman's mind, a matter of justice, mercy, or economic pragmatism.

Some have proposed a "need threshold" relation. For Rawls, any departure from strict egalitarianism—a partial stepping down from ends-oriented justice toward mercy—must be regulated by ends-oriented justice itself in that it must raise the absolute position of the most poor. So the determination of where properly to place the step function is a matter of justice and is guided by the "difference principle." The breadth of the most poor determines the minimum (rightmost) possible location of the step function. Starting with the maximum of strict egalitarianism the step function may move rightward—decreasing the domain of justice—but only so far as the most poor continue to become absolutely better off. Thus the step function finds its home at the point where any further decrease in the domain of ends-oriented justice would not provide an absolute benefit to the most poor.

Rawls is not the only one who has proposed that perhaps at some need threshold ends become a matter of justice. The location of the step function is readily adjusted with respect to some economic mean or some minimum needs level. The location of the poverty line is also contested. Both could be moved to the left or to the right. If, in the end, the step function is to be found on or leftward of the poverty line we should heed the Siren's song. If the step function never rises then social justice is Medusa. If the curve is to be found somewhere below the poverty line, then we are right to pursue Helen and Troy. And so the new wineskins have begun to resemble the old.

So what is justice rightfully concerned with—means or ends? Where all does justice rightfully speak up? To what extent is justice a function of need? What is the proper domain of social justice? Our philosophical particularities never disappoint. They always put on a great show—and are with us until the last act.

RECENT THEOLOGICAL INFLUENCES

Philosophical leanings readily find their way into the theological arena, both in their egalitarian forms and in their more libertarian varieties. Nevertheless, the theological "movements" that have initiated much of the theological reflection in the twentieth century have been indebted to broadly egalitarian conceptions.[9] So our present summary will focus on the ends-oriented side of the continuum. The social gospel, liberation theology, and sustenance rights "movements" do not find complete acceptance within evangelical theology. Nonetheless they exert a measured to significant influence on evangelical thinkers such as Anthony Hoekema, Ronald Sider, and the many who find Nicholas Wolterstorff's vision of *shalom* deeply sympathetic.

---

9. Many practical level guidebooks concerning biblical justice and mercy toward the needy have likewise been produced within this recent timeframe. These works however do not readily address their theological presuppositions nor is it their purpose to engage the issues at a scholarly level. Some popular examples include Nouwen, *Out of Solitude*; Nouwen, *The Wounded Healer*; McNeill et al., *Compassion*; Olasky, *The Tragedy of American Compassion*; Olasky, *Renewing American Compassion*; Keller, *Ministries of Mercy*.

The social gospel made its public appearance in early-twentieth-century North America, whereas liberation theology began its ascent in South America in the latter half of the century. The sustenance rights approach is the most recent. While the first two approaches are fairly well defined and are generally understood to have passed the apex of their influence, sustenance rights is a nascent idea that has not as yet emerged as a defined movement. Sustenance rights, despite its transatlantic influence, may never become a readily identifiable movement in the same way that the other two have. Even so, it has already gained recognizable mindshare within contemporary theological and missiological thinking among Evangelicals.

Our theological discourse is as perspectival and variously conditioned as its philosophical counterpart. Whether means-oriented or ends-oriented, our philosophical particularities can quote Scripture too.

The Social Gospel

Walter Rauschenbusch, the maternal grandfather of Richard Rorty, is deservedly known as the father of the social gospel. This movement, which included Samuel Z. Batten and Washington Cladden among its leaders, nonetheless owes a significant debt to the foundation laid for it by the vehemently practically-oriented theology of Albrecht Ritschl. Rauschenbusch's "Christian Socialism" entailed both a rejection of Marxism as well as the criticism of capitalism on the basis of its greed.[10]

Rauschenbusch pressed for a "cooperative commonwealth"—both regarding labor and in terms of the notion that some property should be owned collectively. In confronting "parasitism"—particularly among the comfortable rich—he stressed that "idleness is active selfishness; it is not only unethical, but a sin against the Kingdom of God."[11] Productive labor in accordance with one's ability was for Rauschenbusch "one of 'the conditions of salvation.'"[12] In parallel he argued that natural resources and some of the property associated with "the means of production" should be held in common.[13]

---

10. Rauschenbusch, *Christianizing the Social Order*, 241–51; Murphey, *Liberal Thought in Modern America*, 60.

11. Rauschenbusch, *A Theology for the Social Gospel*, 55, 56.

12. Ibid., 56.

13. Ibid., 143; Rauschenbusch, *Christianity and the Social Crisis*, 388–400.

"The Brotherhood for the Kingdom" was founded in order to reemphasize the present nature of the kingdom of God among Christians.[14] In envisioning God's present kingdom as a higher moral order, Rauschenbusch nonetheless viewed the kingdom's outworking in very socialist and structural terms. In keeping with this trajectory, Rauschenbusch is commonly credited for being the first in North America to develop the notion of "institutionalized sin"—what is otherwise known as structural or systemic evil.[15] Seeking a solution, Rauschenbusch came to believe that salvation was best understood as a voluntary socialization of the soul away from its primary sin of selfishness.[16]

Rauschenbusch adopted the then common notion that evolutionary theory entails that everything is getting better. Believing the social gospel to be a higher Hegelian synthesis of history and theology, he asserted that the coming socialistic evolution of society would be the kingdom of God—as best as could be expected on earth.[17] It is helpful to consider that Rauschenbusch's early writings predated the gradual formation of a substantial middle class in America—which was not a safety-net state at the time.

Rauschenbusch's influence has not ceased to be felt. Anthony Hoekema is among the Evangelicals who, in their concern to address social issues, have separated the theology of the social gospel from the ethics of the social gospel in order to preserve the latter.[18] Because these ethical convictions are widely articulated among Evangelicals, the hermeneutical methodology we are seeking must assist us in isolating the biblical concept of oppression and systemic evil—as well as its remedies. Our methodology must also identify notions of common property and evaluate whether such notions are subsumed under biblical justice. A biblical evaluation of idleness also merits our interest.

---

14. Rauschenbusch, *Christianizing the Social Order*, 23–24, 94–95.
15. Balanoff, "Norman Thomas," 101.
16. Handy, ed., *The Social Gospel in America*, 262.
17. Rauschenbusch, *Christianizing the Social Order*, 405.
18. Hoekema, "Two Poles or One Goal?" 4–6.

Liberation Theology

Seeking to liberate an oppressed people group is the driving focus of theologies of liberation. Three major types are generally isolated. "Black liberation theology" tackles injustice toward those of African origin, "feminist liberation theology" focuses on liberating women, and "liberation theology" targets the socioeconomic oppression of the poor. Naturally, it is "liberation theology," which seeks to address the plight of the poor, that is most pertinent here.

This theology of liberation originated in South and Central America through the efforts of the likes of José Porfirio Miranda, Juan Luis Segundo, José Míguez Bonino, Hugo Assmann, and Gustavo Gutiérrez.[19] With so many thinkers subsumed under this banner, some disparity exists concerning particulars as well as which societal model, if any, is presented as liberation theology's revolutionary goal. Nevertheless, it is widely held that Gutiérrez's *A Theology of Liberation* functions as the *Magna Carta* of the movement.[20]

Gutiérrez's theology can be summarized around four cardinal convictions. His first assertion is that hermeneutics must be made dependent upon praxis and the theologian's social context. So Gutierrez argues for contextual particularity. For embracing it. He thus eschews the Bible as a primary guiding authority for the development of theology in favor of the contextual practices of the church in pursuing economic justice for the poor. Marxist political and macroeconomic assumptions are pragmatically accepted as the proper roots of theology in his context. Gutiérrez's second affirmation is that God maintains a special concern and love for the poor—a "preferential option" which does not extend to the rich, free, and fed. The church, Gutiérrez contends, ought to mimic God in this regard. Gutiérrez's third contention is that sin is pervasive and must never be perceived as solely privatized. Existing primarily as alienation and partially as self-centeredness, sin invades all aspects of human social life so as to constitute an enveloping "hamartiosphere."[21] For Gutiérrez, all forms of alienation are themselves sin—rather than

---

19. Miranda, *Marx and the Bible*; Segundo, *Liberation of Theology*; Bonino, *Doing Theology in a Revolutionary Situation*; Assmann, *Theology for a Nomad Church*; Gutiérrez, *A Theology of Liberation*.

20. Ferm, *Contemporary American Theologies*, 64; Enns, *The Moody Handbook of Theology*, 596.

21. Gutiérrez, *A Theology of Liberation*, 103.

merely the result of sin. Exodus 1–3 (the exodus out of Egypt) replaces Genesis 1–3 (the account of creation) as the ultimate exemplar of the origin of sin and its proper solution. Due to his emphasis on alienation, structural evil becomes the principal sin in Gutiérrez's hamartiology. The biblical connection between the issues of sin and salvation require Gutiérrez to transform the traditional concept of salvation into liberation. This fourth conviction conceptualizes liberation as consisting of three interrelated components. Gutiérrez consistently mentions political and socioeconomic liberation first, inner liberation in the form of peace for those struggling against servitude second, and, last of all, liberation from personal sin.[22] Building on Jürgen Moltmann's *Theologie der Hoffnung* (*Theology of Hope*), Gutiérrez sets his three-fold salvation within an eschatological framework wherein the desire for hope creates within people the will to liberation.[23]

Michael Novak has characterized Latin American socioeconomic systems as "mercantilist and quasi-feudal . . . statist . . . privilege-centered, not open to the poor but protective of the rich."[24] In light of such a context, Gutiérrez's downplaying of the importance of personal sin in comparison to structural sin becomes easier to apprehend. His setting also helps to illuminate why he makes no distinctions among the poor and why "the poor" are always deemed synonymous with "the oppressed." In engaging with liberation theology, evangelical thinkers have sometimes gleaned its assumptions and principles. Ronald Sider, to take but one prominent example, adopts the notion that Exodus 1–3 deserves to take precedence over Genesis 1–3 as the beginning of God's self-revelation.[25] Liberation theologians—in slowly warming toward democracy—have significantly modified their politico-economic views in recent years.[26] Gutiérrez's approach nonetheless continues to provide a seminal theological backdrop for contemplating ends-oriented justice. Due to liberation theology's wide-reaching influence, our approach must

---

22. Ibid., xxxviii.

23. Ibid., 124–25.

24. Novak, *Will It Liberate?* 5.

25. Sider, *Lifestyle in the Eighties*, 13–19. Sider has changed some of his views in recent years and is no longer as concerned with income and wealth disparity between different groups. See Sider, *Rich Christians in an Age of Hunger*, xiii–xiv.

26. McGovern, *Liberation Theology and Its Critics*, 230; Sigmund, *Liberation Theology at the Crossroads*, 40; C. Smith, *The Emergence of Liberation Theology*, 231–32.

be able to investigate what qualifies as unjust alienation and whether all of the poor are necessarily so due to oppression.

Sustenance Rights

Human rights not only provide the moral foundation for organizations such as Amnesty International but also receive their fair share of philosophical attention. While the Bible generally avoids presenting moral responsibility in terms of rights-based language—except perhaps with respect to conjugal rights (Exod 21:10; 1 Cor 7:4) and supporting pastors (1 Cor 9:4–6, 12, 18)—it is not uncommon for theologians and philosophers to attempt to translate biblical prescriptions into rights language.[27] Pursuing one such translation effort, Christopher Wright defines individual rights in terms of what people are made responsible for with respect to others in the Bible.[28] Pursuing this trajectory in *Until Justice and Peace Embrace*, Nicholas Wolterstorff was among the first evangelical philosophers to translate biblical prescriptions concerning helping the poor into the notion of sustenance rights.[29]

Though the sustenance rights approach has gained considerable mindshare among Christian scholars, it appears to lack the formal organization required for it to be considered a movement. Nonetheless, general characteristics can be distinguished.

Wolterstorff formulates the concept of sustenance rights from within his much acknowledged articulation of *shalom* as holistic wellbeing, harmony, and rest. His premise is that, in order to achieve *shalom*, "piety and charity are not sufficient."[30] Wolterstorff's notion of sustenance rights is complicated by his concern for both architectonic or structural "social arrangements" as well as individual responsibility.[31]

---

27. Nicholas Wolterstorff, for example, contends that "the recognition of natural human rights is a gift of the Hebrew and Christian Scriptures to the world" for "the recognition of human rights cannot, over the long haul, float free of its theistic foundations" (Wolterstorff, "How Social Justice Got to Me and Why it Never Left," 673, 675). Sometimes דִּין (*din*) and מִשְׁפָּט (*mishpat*) are also translated as indicating rights. Nevertheless, such translations frequently deserve to be understood in light of their contextual focus upon receiving proper judgment in judicial contexts (as in Prov 31:5–9 for instance).

28. Wright, *Walking in the Ways of the Lord*, 253.

29. Wolterstorff, *Until Justice and Peace Embrace*, 81–83.

30. Ibid., 81.

31. Ibid.

Sustenance rights entail that people possess a legitimate moral claim to being "adequately sustained in existence" and that the actual enjoyment of this good be socially guaranteed against threats which are serious, remediable, and ordinary.[32] Wolterstorff considers these rights to be basic or cardinal. Sustenance rights may only be abrogated in situations in which no arrangements can be made to ensure sustenance. Wolterstorff proposes that perhaps refusal to participate in "decent" work, when it is available, would forfeit a person's sustenance rights. Every other refusal to participate in sustenance rights' three correlative duties—to avoid depriving people of sustenance, to help protect the vulnerable from such deprivation, and to sustain the victims if deprivation does occur—is injustice. Thus all remediable poverty, except perhaps that caused by indolence, is necessarily due to unjust deprivation.

Though Wolterstorff's sustenance rights include access to a healthy environment and elementary healthcare, he clarifies his approach in terms of the right to food: "I want to say, as emphatically as I can, that our concern with poverty is not an issue of generosity but of rights. If a rich man knows of someone who is starving and has the power to help that person but chooses not to do so, then he violates the starving person's rights as surely and reprehensibly as if he had physically assaulted the sufferer."[33] Thus, whenever a reachable and therefore aidable person dies from starvation, all those, who had knowledge of her plight and possessed any means beyond those necessary for their own sustenance needs, commit murder by proxy. Wolterstorff's formulation appears to imply that anyone who wishes to remain free of gross injustice must give all of their non-sustenance resources away at the first familiarization with a famine or need crisis—so long as any sustenance needs remain outstanding. Wolterstorff does not address these implications in discussing his correlative duties. This is likely because he is anticipating the matter in terms of societal responsibility. He nevertheless articulates examples in global and yet individual terms: "The rich man who does not know how to prevent poverty and uses that as an excuse for not aiding the poor is nonetheless trampling on the rights of the poor man."[34] Corporate global responsibility is also affirmed in Wolterstorff's charac-

---

32. Ibid.
33. Ibid., 82.
34. Ibid., 85.

terization of the failure of the United States to budget greater amounts of economic aid as an enormous injustice.[35]

Wolterstorff's main contention is that all practicable aspects of helping the poor, providing perhaps that the poor are not indolent in the face of "decent" work, are matters of justice. And so our adopted methodology must assist us in evaluating whether Wolterstorff's three sustenance rights duties are genuinely issues of biblical justice.

Of the three recent ends-oriented theological approaches, Wolterstoff's conception is not only the most actual but also the most winsome. His evangelical approach to Scripture coupled with his personal concern for justice and compassion have made his influence among Evangelicals well deserved. It is out of the respect that they are due that Wolterstorff's influential ideas will receive the most evaluative attention during our interaction with the NT texts.

SEEING ANTHROPOLOGY AND PASSING BY ON THE OTHER SIDE

These three recent influences highlight the broad theological dissonance over social justice, a dissonance which parallels the philosophical options. The contentions between more socialist thinkers such as Moltmann, himself influenced by Ernst Bloch, and more libertarian scholars such as Wolfhart Pannenberg, being indebted to Emil Brunner's personalism, are certainly dependent on dissension over the proper jurisdiction of justice.[36] But justice issues in theological ethics have also sometimes been argued at the level of anthropology.[37] Nevertheless this level, with its additional complexities, can be bypassed (and perhaps even evaluated to some extent) via a focus on the content of the biblical mandates themselves. The complexity that the anthropological level brings arrives via its significantly increasing the size of the biblical data set. This potential increase in indeterminacy is methodologically avoid-

35. Ibid.

36. The ranks of means-oriented Christian thinkers also include the likes of Michael Novak and Ronald Nash. See Novak, *The Spirit of Democratic Capitalism*; Novak, *The Catholic Ethic and the Spirit of Capitalism*; Nash, *Social Justice and the Christian Church*; Nash, *Poverty and Wealth: The Christian Debate over Capitalism*; Nash, *Poverty and Wealth: Why Socialism Doesn't Work*; Nash, *Why the Left Is Not Right*. As implied, Emil Brunner's attention was also drawn to this issue. See Brunner, *Justice and the Social Order*.

37. See, for example, Pannenberg, *Anthropologie in theologischer Perspektive*.

able if anthropological systems are not permitted to censor and filter the biblical prescriptions concerning justice and mercy. Providing this, theological anthropology contentions do not ultimately alter the justice level data—they merely seek to support justice understandings on differing foundations. We will turn our attention more fully to the effects of data filtering in chapter 3.

SOCIAL GAMES

Our philosophical particularity is itself variously conditioned. Pragmatics will limit us to talking about this variety along two broad-reaching axes. Theologians, like everyone else, participate in both contextual and psychological particularity. Such particularity affects and motivates, to significant degrees, our preferences with respect to justice constructs. These common particularities help to account for the disparate appeal of various justice formulations among Christian ethicists. For they act to significantly mold the interpreter's plausibility structures which then, in turn, serve to filter the philosophical possibilities. The most common particularities that affect understandings of justice toward the poor result from participation in a particular social game and our subjective attraction to a particular psychology of helping, discipline, and change. Not to be completely passed by, anthropological preferences are naturally related to these common particularities—both as a stimulus to, and as a consequence of, being particular. Why not begin with a consideration of our social particularity?

The five social game categories germinated by Mary Douglas, in building on the work of Basil Bernstein, and later expanded by Michael Thompson, Richard Ellis, and Aaron Wildavsky, remain influential in contemporary analytical culture theory.[38] Although this grid-group model has been employed to better interpret the general "personality" of a culture, it is more properly confined to social games—as several social games may coexist within a given culture. Familiarity with, and a preference for, a particular social game almost invariably influences one's conception of justice—particularly social justice—as well as one's understanding of how justice should be sought. The terminology of

---

38. M. Thompson et al., *Cultural Theory*. The more recent GLOBE Study engagements continue to build upon the grid-group model. See R. House et al., eds., *Culture, Leadership, and Organizations*; Chhokar et al., eds., *Culture and Leadership Across the World*.

"cultural bias" aims to describe this significant manner in which one's submergence into a particular social game influences one's predispositions. This grid-group model has also appropriately found its way into research concerning poverty and developmental economics.[39] The four general social games that form a socially-situated person's cultural bias can be helpfully described as Authoritarian, Individualist, Hierarchist, and Egalitarian.[40] The fifth social game is that of the autonomous hermit, one who shuns social interaction, and thus is not relevant to addressing issues of social justice. This heuristically utile grid-group model of how our social games manage risk is depicted below.

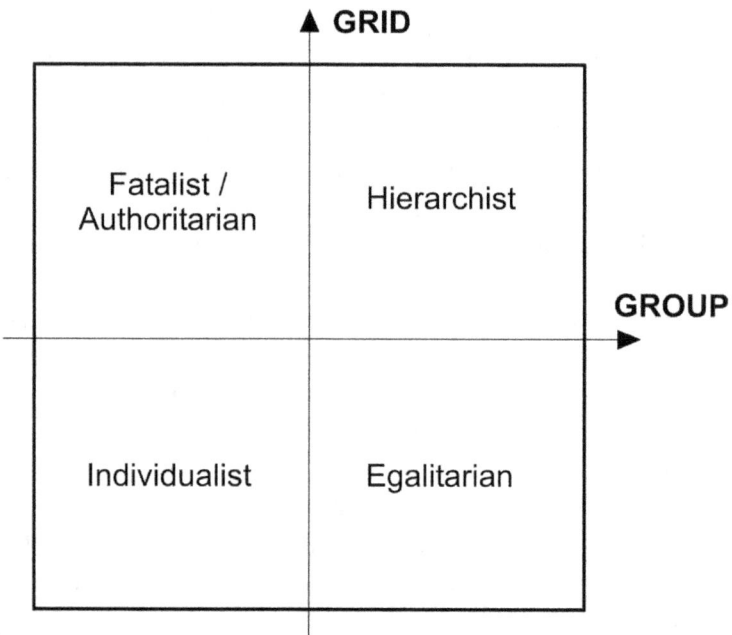

Figure 2: Social Games[41]

---

39. J. Lingenfelter, "The Impact of Cultural Bias on Ministry Strategies to Help the Poor"; J. Lingenfelter, "Why Do We Argue over How to Help the Poor?"; S. Lingenfelter, *Agents of Transformation*; S. Lingenfelter, *Transforming Culture*.

40. J. Lingenfelter, "Why Do We Argue over How to Help the Poor?" 156–57.

41. This figure is adapted from Judith Lingenfelter (ibid., 157).

In the grid-group model the proclivity toward collective decision making increases along the horizontal axis while the strictness of social roles increases along the vertical axis. Thus people in social games on the left (low-group) consider themselves in individualistic terms and make their decisions accordingly. The bottom two social games (low-grid) support levels of role elasticity often practically unimaginable elsewhere. Social games are intricately bound up with their social, economic, and political contexts. In most low Gross Domestic Product contexts an Individualist social game is not a survivable option and therefore garners little following. Political instability and settings with very high "start-over" barriers generally create an aversion to risk and, correspondingly, to the low-group social games that increase it. So people trapped in poor contexts which are nonetheless Authoritarian are generally in the most precarious position. The two-edged sword of fatalism is often the greatest comfort that such a social game can offer.

Differing social game contexts readily affect our perceptions pertaining to helping and justice. Judith Lingenfelter astutely harnesses the extant social game possibilities to identify why Christians enmeshed in different social contexts disagree amongst themselves regarding how to help the poor.[42] In terms of addressing poverty, the following general schema may be discerned: the Authoritarian social game adopts a stance of powerlessness, the Individualist social game focuses on personal "boot-straps" responsibility, the Hierarchist approach seeks to provide professional assistance, and the Egalitarian social game organizes against the oppressiveness of social stratification.

Prevalent social games are deeply intertwined with evaluations of the main causes of poverty in their domain and determine which practical solutions are contextually workable. The Authoritarian context blames poverty on fate or God's hidden will, the Individualist focuses on sloth and personal sin, the Hierarchist targets incompetence, ignorance, and calamity, while the Egalitarian challenges oppression and the system. Our contextual social game realities make certain understandings of justice unthinkable and others seemingly common sense. While each context, save the Authoritarian, is likely best engaged with poverty strategies that mimic the prevailing social game,[43] the domain of justice cannot automatically be defended or determined on the pragmatics of

42. Ibid., 157–65.
43. Ibid., 155, 165–66.

the situation alone. The Authoritarian social game proves this. It avoids focusing on human causes and so only germinates resignation. It has no solutions to offer in itself. The evaluative impetus, especially if it seeks to transcend the particularity of contextual perspectives and tendencies, must prove to be, in some manner, "external."

PSYCHOLOGY OF HELPING AND CHANGE

Interpreters' notions of mercy and justice are also colored by their personally subjective perceptions of the types of helping that are permissible. Psychologists advocate several different understandings of helping, discipline, and change—these dissonant understandings appear to appeal to people to differing degrees largely as a function of their personality and life experience. The Psychoanalyst, Behavioralist, Humanist, and Existentialist philosophies of helping and intervention constitute the common four model differentiation scheme.[44] Most people's understanding of helping and discipline, whether they are familiar with psychology or not, slots squarely into one of these camps. The four models are themselves founded on the four classic personality theories: Psychodynamic, Behavioral, Humanistic, and Existential.

Perhaps some names will help in placing the various approaches. The central theorists behind Psychoanalyst personality theory are Sigmund and Anna Freud, Carl Jung, Alfred Adler, and Karen Horney. John Watson, Burrhus F. Skinner, Joseph Wolpe, and Hans Eysenck championed the Behavioralist view. The Humanist model was shaped by Abraham Maslow, Carl Rogers, and Erich Fromm. Lastly, the Existentialist approach was forwarded by Viktor Frankl, Ludwig Binswanger, Rollo May, and Medard Boss. Each of the four understandings of helping anticipate justice differently and consequently what should be expected of people.

Each approach likewise develops its own preferred model of helping—a model which extends to helping the poor, particularly the indolent poor. The Psychoanalyst approach attempts to expose hidden hindrances through "transference." The Behavioralist aims to reinforce positive traits via notions of reward and punishment. The Humanist attempts to woo via acceptance and the Existentialist seeks to provide

---

44. A pragmatically focused introduction may be found in Miller and Jackson, *Practical Psychology for Pastors*, 77–78. The contemporary ascent of cognitivism in psychology has not reduced the utility of these four categories for the present purpose.

cognitive challenge unto personal responsibility. Of the categories mentioned, only the Behavioralist and Existentialist models are generally comfortable with enabling intended consequences to carry out a pedagogical purpose. Consequently, our individual preferences for a particular understanding of helping taint our assumptions concerning moral agency, justice applicability and utility, and the obligation level of mercy. Even some of our personal attraction to a particular social game is likely intertwined with our psychology of helping and change. For some social games are more readily compatible with a particular psychological preference.

Our preferred psychology of helping provides a composite, higher level summary of our interpersonal values. And these values become a diagnostically useful means of categorizing our prevailing assumptions—for mapping our particularity. As with social games, this subjectivity functions to make justice and mercy confoundingly difficult to make out on the grounds of personal reflection. The inherent potency of our contextual and subjective particularities affirms the necessity and desirability of pursuing a methodological approach which is not only text-based rather than extra-textual but one which, in addition, pursues its differentiation at the passage level. For pursuing a purely systematic level text-based approach—one which does not seek to differentiate its notion of justice at the passage level but rather at the level of theological constructs—is defenseless against the influence and alterations intrinsic to our variously conditioned particularities.

THE HERMENEUTICAL NEXUS

Biblical ethics, if it is anything, is prescriptive for it seeks to prescribe human behavior. Granting this, it becomes necessary to discern whether all the biblical prescriptions are "flat," or if they really do communicate some central differences in obligation. Can justice and mercy prescriptions really be untwined? In answering questions such as "what is biblical justice?" and "how can biblical justice be isolated?" it is not uncommon for theologians to turn to philosophical definitions of justice to differentiate the biblical prescriptions. This reliance is not always self-conscious or even conscious. Such definitions then serve to delineate which inter-human treatments are understood as issues of justice and, consequently, where the domain of justice ends so that justice no longer legitimately applies to the treatment or complaint at hand. Due to their beguiling influence, if anything deserves to be ruminated with a healthy helping of suspicion, it is our definitions.

With so many dissonant extents of justice being proposed as biblical, how are these various proposals to be textually evaluated? Left to themselves, justice preconceptions seem to entail justice indeterminacy. Perhaps the Christian ethicist is, after all, confined to the better categorizations of philosophy in isolating the proper domain of justice. Perhaps acceptable compatibility levels with biblical and systematic theology is as "better" as it gets.

Certainly it is fair to ask why the long-respected philosophical formulations are not sufficient. Why isn't a differentiation based on *suum cuique*, rendering to each what is due, sufficiently biblically compatible? The definition seems flexible enough to incorporate biblical content on what is deserved or owed. Perhaps justice can be defined as giving the offended party the "good" they deserve and the offending party the "bad" they deserve. Similarly, mercy may constitute giving someone "good" which they do not deserve. Even though the Bible seldom speaks in terms of what is deserved—save concerning remedial or retributive justice—this differentiation is immediately commendable to our moral intuition. Only one thing is lacking: how do we distinguish what is deserved from what is not? How do we discern what the Bible makes us unconditionally "responsible for" toward others?[45]

The philosophical and sociological indeterminism appears insurmountable. Thus Aristotle's formal principle of justice, "to treat equals equally and unequals unequally," leads immediately into the abyss of the material principle.[46] The material component's quest remains: how and what do equals and unequals merit besides inter-peer impartiality?[47] Our intuition that justice and mercy present different obligation levels

---

45. Wright, *Walking in the Ways of the Lord*, 253.

46. This ubiquitous paraphrase of the formal principle finds its source in the following claim of *Nicomachean Ethics* 5.3: "And the same equality will exist between the persons and between the things concerned; for as the latter the things concerned are related, so are the former; if they are not equal, they will not have what is equal, but this is the origin of quarrels and complaints—when either equals have and are awarded unequal shares, or unequals equal shares." Aristotle, *Nicomachean Ethics*, 76.

47. Even turning aside to fairness alone proves equally frustrating—for fairness is a highly enculturated notion. What constituent factors, what values, should be weighed? What constellation of equilibriums is fairness befittingly trying to achieve? Hierarchies of values vary—so what is fair by one is seen as gross injustice by another.

seems correct, but differentiating the two textually appears particularly difficult. What beyond the formal principle, in terms of the impartial application of a society's laws in judicial process (as affirmed by texts such as Lev 19:15; Deut 1:17; 16:19), can be biblically identified as an issue of justice? Can any light be shed beyond the reach of the few texts which explicitly label a particular moral prescription as an issue of justice or mercy?

Why are all our variously conditioned preconceptions—the hungry troll under the biblical bridge—such a fearsome obstacle? What is at the heart of the issue—why is it so difficult to escape our particularity textually? The existence of so many preconception possibilities invariably leads to significant hermeneutical indeterminism precisely because biblical mandates pertaining to our justice and mercy obligations come in the same general grammatical forms.[48] Jussives, future indicatives with imperative overtones, syntax, and speech acts provide no assistance to differentiation. No solace is to be found in pronouncing commands to be the bearers and delimiters of justice. The text quickly rebels in a crescendo of commands unto mercy, gracious benevolence, and forgiveness. As it is widely agreed that forgiveness is not required by justice, any appeal to a differentiation based on commands crumbles.

As the text appears to be a play of shadows, Sophia beckons at the cave's entrance. Unfortunately, courting philosophical differentiations concerning what is deserved and undeserved on the basis of a perceived "biblical compatibility" only backtracks us onto our own variously conditioned notions of justice and mercy. Too few are the passages which explicitly label a particular interhuman treatment as an instance of justice or mercy. Extrapolations from these few explicit cases inevitably lead into the extra-biblical *cul-de-sac* of what we subjectively pre-assume to be just. This is why we can take several revolutions on the hermeneutical spiral and still come out where we started. Indeed, it is the lack of a facile textual level differentiation that serves as the nexus for the present hermeneutical elusiveness. This indictment reveals, in significant part, why various theological contingents claim biblical support for radically

---

48. Mercy, like justice, is an obligation because it inhabits the moral space. Biblically, mercy is both a mandated issue and a morally evaluated issue. Thus mercy mandates possess moral weight and moral significance before God but not the quality of moral constraint. In this way, justice and mercy differ from morally neutral willings, treatments, and choices in that they receive divine evaluation and prescription. And so, in my usage, obligation and duty are not synonymous—for duty entails moral constraint.

different justice and mercy prescription sets. The prevailing calculus is cheerless: the text plus variously conditioned presuppositions minus a textual *discrimen* equals the entrenchment of significant theological disagreement.

One other textual level option exists—but it is very unfavorable. The pessimistic temptation to surrender the distinction in obligation between justice and mercy must be resisted. Too much is at stake. Soteriology would disintegrate like a falling star.[49] Furthermore, it is the appreciation of justice prescriptions as being fully and unconditionally binding upon everyone who is able to actualize them that drives appeals to human rights and all demands for justice. This common conviction is what gives appeals to justice their ethical power. Even postmodernists, such as Jacques Derrida, are loathe to speak against justice, but rather claim it as their undeconstructable goal.[50] By contrast, indignant demands for mercy upon everyone who is able to provide it possess no such ethical power. Mercy is simply not morally enforceable by its prospective recipient—though it may be demandable by God. In contradistinction to justice, mercy is only conditionally binding such that its obligation level may be reduced or even negated by other considerations including the contextually appropriate goals of love.[51] Erasing the obligating power of justice is repulsive, and making mercy prescriptions of equal obligation is a ready-made recipe for frustration.[52] Fortunately this frustration is merely an evanescent form of idealism which is quickly wrestled to the mat by a little praxis.

---

49. The differentiation between justice and merciful grace would be erased making verses such as Rom 4:4–5 incomprehensible and self-contradictory.

50. Derrida, "Force of Law," 945.

51. The purposive component of love may be summarily identified as seeking another's "good" via actualizing biblical prescriptions while aiming at biblically applicable goals. The means matter. Such a notion of love is significantly unlike Joseph Fletcher's malleable conception for it incorporates specific content. See Fletcher, *Situation Ethics*, 95–97, 115, 119.

52. While Wolterstorff postulates understanding the so-called "duties of charity" as third-party duties unto God alone, this possibility—as clarified in personal communication—is not intended to suggest that *even* forgiveness, clemency, and gracious charity may be subsumed under binding moral constraint. See Wolterstorff, *Justice*, 383–84. Wolterstorff concurs that such an amalgamation is deeply undesirable and, like the author, neither does he presently affirm the existence of such "duties" in the ethical sense of the word.

In sum, Miroslav Volf has aptly asked how we can arbitrate between competing justices.[53] While Volf's concern is largely for practical reconciliation and justice in situations of armed conflict, the same question applies to conceptual accounts of justice. Without a biblically generated isolation of justice there is no convincing way to arbitrate among the many variously conditioned preconception possibilities. The domain of justice remains untamed and self-consciously defiant. What is deserved, what is just, forever remains in the eye of the beholder. Approaches to poverty and justice both Marxist as well as capitalist, liberationist as well as libertarian, remain safely beyond evaluation. The biblical mandates will be "innocently" assumed to communicate justice or mercy obligation levels congruent with each preconception set. As a result, the challenge before all who care deeply about these matters is to isolate a way of differentiating justice and mercy prescriptions at the textual level and, by extension, the domains of both of these levels of obligation.

And, if we go down that way, we will meet social justice and charity as well.

BASELINE DEFINITIONS OF JUSTICE AND MERCY

While no sustained attempt has been made up to this point to significantly focus the reader's conception of justice and mercy, it is now pertinent, for the sake of clarity, to offer a minimalist baseline definition of each. While justice may be thought of both in terms of its goal as well as in terms of its ethical impetus, it is the latter conception which best distinguishes it from mercy. Said another way, while mercy and justice may seek the same goals in a particular circumstance, the ethical obligation that a matter of justice exerts upon those it obligates is comparatively supercedent.

Though often commingled, this distinction between justice as result and justice as an ethical motivation is important. Considering justice in terms of a state of affairs, a macro level goal, does not identify the moral obligations that function in bringing about this state of affairs. A focus on justice as a state of affairs obscures the question of who is ethically bound to bring about this state of affairs—it thus has sometimes been made to indiscriminately obligate everyone to remedy each injustice. All goals of justice, then, take on the appearance of entailing injustice if not

---

53. Volf, *Exclusion and Embrace*, 205.

pursued. Who is obligated and whether a mercy or justice impetus is at play is obscured.[54] Yet this differentiation in impetus is assumed in all calls for justice—for it is the recognition of justice obligation on the part of the addressed that is being sought. For it is in communicating obligation, rather than in communicating a description of some state of affairs, that justice possesses its ethical power.

May I say this more provocatively? Justice as a state of affairs is innocuous. Justice as a state of affairs to which one is bound by the moral obligation of duty is what all calls for justice assume. To claim that "that is unjust" does not mean "that is not in line with some state of affairs," what is meant rather is "that is not in line with a state of affairs which others are morally bound to preserve."[55]

While this distinction is sometimes, likely innocently, lost in contemporary missiological material, it has also at times been purposefully avoided for the sake of garnering apparent moral justification and force for certain causes. Seeking justice and doing justice is not the same thing. Achieving justice and acting justly may entail different obligation levels. The existence of mercy terminology in the Bible with respect to aiding the victimized certainly supports this contention.

When conceptually separated out from its concrete content and the state of affairs it seeks to bring about, justice is a level of obligation. Justice is the unconditional, providing no higher mandate intrudes, obligation level that makes the avoidance or accomplishment of a particular interhuman treatment ethically binding upon everyone (in the intended obligator category). By way of contradistinction, interhuman mercy entails only conditional obligation levels. Mercy obligations are contingent—a concept partially analogous to the philosophical notion of being ethically voluntary. Such mitigation or distribution of responsibility is simply not permitted with justice—and this is why appeals to justice possess an ethical force missing from appeals to mercy. The differentiation concerns itself with the level of moral impetus. And seems unobtrusive enough. Justice is obligatory while non-justice is only conditionally so. It is this comprehensive obligatoriness which makes justice

---

54. By way of example, in an instance of theft it is the guilty party that is justly obligated to provide recompense and the judiciary to secure this judicial justice. Not everyone is obligated by justice constraint to see the loss made up and this justice done—and unambiguously so in the case of the rich stealing from the rich.

55. So Oliver O'Donovan speaks of this state of affairs as being "morally requisite." See O'Donovan, *The Ways of Judgment*, 6.

expectable—even demandable.⁵⁶ Mercy composes the set of remaining interhuman moral obligations which are not justice obligations. Thus compassion (σπλαγχνίζομαι, *splanchnizomai*), due to its empathetic source, is likewise to be distinguished from justice itself which is obligatory independently of sympathetic considerations.

Baseline Definition of Justice

Justice—an interhuman moral impetus that extends an unconditionally binding, providing no higher mandate intrudes, obligation level upon its intended obligator set.

Baseline Definition of Mercy

Mercy—an interhuman moral impetus that does not extend an unconditionally binding obligation level upon its intended obligator set.

PARCELING JUSTICE: THE MAIN SUBCATEGORIES

Because justice is a multifaceted conception, some additional focus is required. For the sake of conceptual clarity, the main subcategories of justice, its *preceptive* and *remedial* components, need to be differentiated. I noted this demarcation earlier in terms of disassociating prescriptive justice—what Plato and Aristotle call "general justice"—and judicial justice. Wolterstorff labels the former primary justice and calls the latter rectifying justice.⁵⁷ For it has long been agreed that, at a foundational level, justice divides into precepts and remedies.⁵⁸ Justice precepts are binding, all things being equal, on everyone in their intended obligator category. Justice remedies are the sanctions that entail when the justice precepts are transgressed. Said another way, preceptive justice enfolds the biblical prescriptions that pertain to the non-remedial aspects of justice—components commonly referred to as commutative, distributive,

---

56. The demandable character of justice is widely affirmed. So Nicholas Wolterstorff, drawing upon Joel Feinberg, employs it to differentiate justice and rights from compassion and charity. See Wolterstorff, *Until Justice and Peace Embrace*, 83.

57. Wolterstorff, *Justice*, ix, 71, 75.

58. This distinction is mirrored, to a degree, in the general difference between צְדָקָה (*tsedaqah*) and מִשְׁפָּט (*mishpat*)—but with the former encompassing a much broader range of meaning. See Jer 22:3 as an internally symmetric text representative of this distinction. The standard lexical works, such as *HALOT*, provide further detail.

and human rights within the philosophical realm. Because, unlike biblical Israel, believers no longer constitute a national entity, the remedial component of justice is more open to adjustment via local convention.[59] In any case, it is the domain of preceptive justice that establishes whether a particular non-judicial interhuman treatment is a genuine occurrence of injustice or not.[60] It is this domain that justifies or refutes any claim of unjust treatment, and due to its inherent "conventionlessness," is the aspect of justice obligation that constitutes the present concern. Correspondingly, the term "justice," as used throughout the remainder of this book, will be employed as a synonym for what has been, in the above, identified as preceptive justice.

This focus is particularly appropriate as no mandated instances of remedial justice, with respect to the treatment of the poor, are to be found within the NT. While consequences are noted in this regard within the NT, they nevertheless do not possess the nature of interhuman judicial remedy.

Finally, whether justice is best thought of in terms of subjective rights—rights which attach to the subject—as Wolterstorff contends or rather in terms of right order and judgment, as Oliver O'Donovan argues, need not detain us.[61] For careful translations from rights to responsibilities and back do not, of themselves, alter the domain of biblical justice. Both conceptions are compatible with our baseline definition of justice as a moral impetus possessing a constraining level of obligation.

---

59. While adherents of the Theonomic Reformed view of Law and Gospel, such as Greg Bahnsen, may differ in this regard, the continued applicability of OT civil sanctions is certainly open to contention.

60. Technically, preceptive justice also extends its reach into regulating the judicial process of arriving at remedial justice.

61. A helpful discussion of these matters is available in O'Donovan, *The Desire of Nations*, 243–71; O'Donovan, *The Ways of Judgment*, 6–12, 31–32; and Wolterstorff, *Justice*, 68–75.

TWO

Seeing Eye to Eye on Poverty

WHAT CONSTITUTES POVERTY? OUR notions of social justice are necessarily bound up with who we perceive as belonging among its rightful recipients. Our preferred definitions of poverty not only affect what we perceive social justice to be but also recursively affect whether we think such justice is accomplishable or not. Broad definitions of poverty reduce the possibility of being able to carry out our possible justice obligations to the poor. Such definitions serve to alter, perhaps inadvertently, the conception of social justice toward some form of unattainable, Reinhold Niebuhr-like ideal.[1]

SURVEYING THE OPTIONS

While a variety of utilitarious definition permutations have been developed for isolating the domain of poverty, the various trajectories can be summarized in terms of four broad categories. We may label these four definition categories as the absolute, relative, alienation, and non-*shalom* conceptions.

Absolute definitions of poverty take as their delimiter some concrete dividing line. Various absolutes have been employed such as having less to live on per day than the equivalent—in terms of purchasing power parity—of the 1985 value of $1 USD.[2] Aside from setting some absolute income cutoff, consumption definitions—such as those defining a certain minimal daily calorie intake—have also been suggested. While calorie requirements differ based on various factors including climate, minimums such as 1,800 or 2,112 calories per day have been forwarded.[3] In agricultural contexts, owning less than half an acre of cul-

---

1. Niebuhr is widely known for considering Jesus' actual love ethic to be an "impossible ethical ideal" (Niebuhr, *An Interpretation of Christian Ethics*, 22, 32, 62, 263).

2. World Bank, *World Development Report 1990*, 27; Alter and Snodgrass, "An Assessment of the Impact of SEWA Bank in India," 25.

3. Todd, *Women at the Center*, 37–38; Khandker, *Fighting Poverty with Microcredit*, 55.

tivatable land has been suggested as a suitable poverty definition.[4] Other definition possibilities include considerations of the number of income earners in a family, illiteracy, female headedness, or having a disabled household head.[5] It is notable that absolute definitions, which tend to be readily employed in non-Western and non-safety-net state contexts, also surface in the Western context via "market basket measure" notions of the "poverty line." The "market basket measure" enumerates the yearly income necessary to cover the set of goods and services that are deemed minimal in one's locale. Such first world poverty lines are nevertheless drawn at comparatively much higher daily income levels and aim to provide for much more than the basics of survival. Accordingly, the "market basket measure" calculations generally also cover transportation, furniture, personal grooming, household supplies, and some recreational expenditures. And so Nicholas Wolterstorff's adaptation of Article 25 of the *Universal Declaration of Human Rights* is noteworthy because it seeks to span both the welfare state and non-welfare state contexts.[6] In enumerating the rights of the poor, Wolterstorff provides an implicit definition of poverty as being in the state of lacking the "food, clothing, and shelter that are adequate for sustaining health and making it possible to contribute to society."[7] Wolterstorff further includes a lack of access to "water and air that are not injurious to health; and . . . elementary medical care" as part of his implicit definition.[8] Still, his definition remains absolute because it does not define poverty as a condition relative to other members of a society or social group.

Definitions which are based on statistical comparisons to the economic standing of the other members of a social group or society are properly considered relative. Such definitions are very common and generally define poverty as constituting less than the income level of a certain percentile of the population—taking some nuances into account. The "low income measure" approach—which defines "low income" as

4. Pitt and Khandker, "Household and Intrahousehold Impact of the Grameen Bank," 17; Yunus, "The Grameen Bank," 114–19; Zaman, *Assessing the Poverty and Vulnerability Impact of Micro-Credit in Bangladesh*, 10.

5. Zaman, *Assessing the Poverty and Vulnerability Impact of Micro-Credit in Bangladesh*, 2.

6. United Nations, *Universal Declaration of Human Rights*, General Assembly resolution 217 A (III).

7. Wolterstorff, *Until Justice and Peace Embrace*, 85.

8. Ibid.

earning one-half of the median income of equivalently sized households in a given country—is often employed in international comparisons. In Canada, the "low income cut-off" calculation has traditionally been adopted by the majority of analysts as the poverty line.[9] This cut-off represents the income threshold at which a household will generally spend twenty percentage points more on shelter, clothing, and food than the average equivalently sized household.[10] In 2009, this line represented $19,950 USD (in rural areas) to $30,500 USD (in cities of more than half a million) of after-tax income for a four person household.[11] Taken from another angle, this definition classifies a household as poor when it spends sixty-three percent or more of its after-tax household income on shelter, clothing, and food.[12] Such relative wealth rankings are also employed in non-Western contexts.[13]

The approach of quantifying alienation and powerlessness as a means of defining poverty has also become widely adopted. Once largely in the domain of the liberation theologians, an understanding of poverty as alienation has in recent times been adapted within evangelical missiology and practical theology. David Claerbaut, as one representative of this stream of thought, suggests that poverty constitutes being alienated from the key institutions in one's city and thus experiencing powerlessness.[14] While Claerbaut's poverty definition is largely aimed at urban environments, it may be extrapolated as inhabiting a position of low access in any context.

While Wolterstorff would certainly be sympathetic to understanding poverty as a lack of *shalom*, the broader definitions included in this final category go beyond his conception. Non-*shalom* definitions of poverty often begin with the poor person's own definition of poverty. In this sense, such an approach is necessarily parasitic on prior poverty definitions and understandings—to identify who is to be heard. Poor people may define poverty in terms of, for example, self-respect, dignity,

---

9. Statistics Canada, *Low Income Cut-Offs for 2006 and Low Income Measures for 2005*, 7; Evangelical Fellowship of Canada, "Issue Summary: Poverty & Homelessness."

10. Statistics Canada, *Low Income Lines*, 7–9.

11. Ibid., 18.

12. Ibid., 7–8.

13. McNelly and Dunford, "Impact of Credit with Education on Mothers and Their Young Children's Nutrition," 14.

14. Claerbaut, *Urban Ministry in a New Millennium*, 85–114.

and the state of one's relations with one's neighbors.[15] But for all their furnished insight, such definitions tend to significantly inflate the understanding of poverty. One such example is the background paper on poverty produced by the Social Action Commission of the Evangelical Fellowship of Canada—a fellowship which functions as the primary national association for Evangelicals within Canada.[16] This background paper defines poverty in subjective terms—as being in a position of not being able to fulfill one's "calling." People, according to this definition, are called to, among other things, "nurture children, to work creatively, to care for neighbours, to play, and to steward the earth."[17] Consequently, hindrances to fulfilling these various callings become indicators of poverty—for "poverty exists when persons, associations or institutions lack the resources and space they need to fulfil their God-given responsibilities and callings."[18]

In ascertaining the biblical domain of social justice it is thus helpful and congruent to also ascertain the domain of biblical poverty. With so many extra-textual definitions of poverty being advocated, entertaining the biblical notion of poverty becomes acutely necessary. Which category of definition is most compatible? Is finding a constrained domain for poverty biblically permitted?

DEFINING POVERTY

The contemporary formulation of this demarcation issue arrives in the form of a practically significant question. Which "poor" are we supposed to help? The classification of someone as poor is often warmly contested against the background of our individual and sociocultural particularity. When we ask which poor we are supposed to help we are asking of the textual witness who it classifies as rightfully among the poor. Who are the poor such that the biblical mandates to help the poor extend unto them? Or at least that is what we want to be asking if we are seeking a biblical delineation of the proper recipients of social justice and charity. Consequently it becomes important for the present concern to discern the NT domain of the poor. While our pre-hermeneutical particularity

---

15. Ondari, "Poverty and Wealth," 347.

16. Social Action Commission of the Evangelical Fellowship of Canada, "Good News to the Poor."

17. Ibid.

18. Ibid.

concerning the legitimate domain of poverty is formidable, it is happily evaluable on the basis of Scripture nonetheless.

TEXTUAL USAGE

Some have argued that since certain sections of the NT do not articulate clear distinctions regarding the nature of the poor, it is therefore God's intent that such delineation be avoided.[19] Nonetheless the semantic and contextual identification of the poor in the NT provides a significant level of detail concerning the plight of those it identifies as among the poor. This detail deserves consideration.

The key terms for the poor in the NT are πτωχός (ptōchos), πένης (penēs), πενιχρός (penichros), and ἐνδεής (endeēs). The first of these is, by far, the most attested. The others occur but one time each. The last, ἐνδεής (endeēs), is generally translated as "needy" but communicates impoverishment in its solitary NT occurrence. The terms signifying poverty are πτωχεία (ptōcheia) and ὑστερέω (hystereō, impoverishment or need) along with additional cognates for need—such as χρεία (chreia).

The major lexical works affirm that the term πτωχός (ptōchos) refers, originally and in common Greek usage, to those who are completely dependent on others for their survival—those variously known as beggars, mendicants, or as the indigent.[20] Thus it was these destitute persons who were considered the natural recipients of alms.[21] Classical writers such as Aristophanes, sometimes honored as "the prince of ancient comedy," confirmed that "the life of a beggar [πτωχός, ptōchos] . . . means existence with nothing, but that of the poor [πένητος, penētos] means sparse living and sticking to the job."[22] His differentiation captures the common semantic usage quite well. Terminologically, πένης (penēs; or πένητος, penētos) commonly referred to those that were relatively poor and lived

---

19. Charlton, "Sharing Food: Charity or Justice?" 2.

20. Bammel, "πτωχός, πτωχεία, πτωχεύω," TDNT 6:885–86; Esser and C. Brown, "πτωχός," NIDNTT 2:821; "πτωχός, πτωχεία, πτωχεύω," BDAG 896; Merklein, "πτωχός, πτωχεία, πτωχεύω," EDNT 3:193; "πτωχεία, πτωχός," MM 558–59.

21. Lothar Coenen affirms this "recipienthood" in his contrasting of πτωχός (ptōchos) poverty with πένης (penēs) poverty. See Coenen, "πένης," NIDNTT 2:820.

22. Aristophanes, Plutus, 552–53. The present translation was taken from BDAG which, despite allowing for a broadened domain for πτωχός (ptōchos) in the NT, nonetheless affirms the force of the classical understanding of πτωχός (ptōchos) as beggarliness ("πένης," BDAG 795). A survey of additional confirming quotations from antiquity is available in Bammel, "πτωχός, πτωχεία, πτωχεύω," TDNT 6:885–86.

"from hand to mouth" while earning "a bare and scant livelihood."[23] And πτωχός (ptōchos) referred to those poor enough to be beggars.

Unfortunately this is where the lexical agreement begins to waiver. Having concurred on the original meaning and semantic focus of πτωχός (ptōchos), the lexical studies begin to quibble over the extent to which they are willing to broaden the term's meaning with respect to its NT usage. Kittel's *TDNT* is predisposed to tether πτωχός (ptōchos) to being as poor as a beggar.[24] Freedman's *ABD* concurs that it refers to the beggarly poor who are utterly destitute.[25] So do Moulton and Milligan.[26] In contrast, Danker's *BDAG* supports an extension of the original meaning to also include those who are "simply poor."[27] Balz and Schneider's *EDNT* affirms that πτωχός (ptōchos) refers to being as poor as a beggar while also emphasizing the metaphorical and spiritual usages made possible by the influence of the OT.[28] Colin Brown's *NIDNTT* likewise steers a middle road by emphasizing beggarly poverty while allowing for the broader meaning of poor as a translation possibility.[29] After all, almost all contemporary English translations render πτωχός (ptōchos) as poor rather than as beggarly.

But Philip Esler would argue that leaving this more general translation possibility open is pulling a Philo. For in seeking not to bring any offence to his Hellenized audience, Philo was willing to translate all references to poverty in the OT as referring to πένης (penēs) level poverty—though it even meant breaking with the LXX.[30] Esler makes his case by claiming that Luke–Acts was written to a Greco-Roman urban

---

23. W. Evans, "Poverty," *ISBE* 2427. Such relatively poor were composed of the handworkers and the peasants—those who did not own enough land to live off of its proceeds and subsequently possessed little and had to be frugal. See Coenen, "πένης," *NIDNTT* 2:820; Hanks, "Poor, Poverty: New Testament," *ABD* 5:415; "πένομαι," *DÉLG* 881. Friedrich Hauck notes that while these poor could sometimes earn enough so as to even own slaves, under hard circumstances their lot became meagerness and poverty (Hauck, "πένης," *TDNT* 6:37–38).

24. Bammel, "πτωχός, πτωχεία, πτωχεύω," *TDNT* 6:885.

25. Hanks, "Poor, Poverty: New Testament," *ABD* 5:415, 417–18, 421.

26. "πτωχεία, πτωχός," MM 558–59.

27. "πτωχός," *BDAG* 896. But this support is only partial as the entry for πένης (penēs) demurs at any such extension ("πένης," *BDAG* 795).

28. Merklein, "πτωχός, πτωχεία, πτωχεύω," *EDNT* 3:193–94.

29. Coenen, "πένης," *NIDNTT* 2:820; Esser and C. Brown, "πτωχός," *NIDNTT* 2:821–28.

30. See, for example, Philo, *De virtutibus*, 90.

audience, that it was written in a city within the Roman Empire—most likely in one of the Eastern provinces.[31] He claims that such an audience would understand the terminology as per their own common usage rather than via the ambiguities introduced in the Septuagint translation. Now, historical investigation confirms that a first century Greco-Roman urban audience would employ the terminology of πτωχός (*ptōchos*) and πένης (*penēs*) in the common sense. So, as the argument goes, we can be sure—at least within Luke–Acts—that πτωχός (*ptōchos*) does indeed refer to the indigent.[32]

The extension of meaning in BDAG appears to be guided by an interest in preserving the logic of referring to Jesus' disciples as πτωχοί (*ptōchoi*, plural of *ptōchos*, Luke 6:20) and of referring to the commended widow of Luke 21:2–3 as both πενιχρός (*penichros*) and πτωχός (*ptōchos*). Let us consider Jesus' commendation of the poor widow's offering first. Though both πενιχρός (*penichros*) and πένης (*penēs*) derive from πένομαι (*penomai*), they are not synonymous for while the latter normally "does not lack the necessities" the former denotes the very poor end of the working poor—those who are experiencing such need.[33] This distinction corresponds well with the widow's portrayal. For this singular NT occurrence of πενιχρός (*penichros*) is contextually related to the πτωχός (*ptōchos*) level of poverty by way of verse 3 and the parallel in Mark 12:42–43. The depth of the widow's poverty is also explicitly described within both passages for she put into the offering "all she owned, all she had to live on" (Mark 12:44 // Luke 21:4). This explicit description reveals that the overlap concerns indigence. So while πενιχρός (*penichros*) denotes the working indigent who are not begging, πτωχός (*ptōchos*) refers to the indigent who are perhaps begging. The widow may have had a place to stay but her offering sacrificed, at minimum, her grocery

---

31. Esler, *Community and Gospel in Luke–Acts*, 30, 169, 180.

32. Ibid., 164, 180.

33. Aristophanes, *Plutus*, 554 (author's translation of μὴ μέντοι μηδ' ἐπιλείπειν). Thus charging usury (interest) can spiral πένης (*penēs*) poverty into πενιχρός (*penichros*) poverty (πενιχρότερον ἀπεργαζόμενος τὸν πένητα)—see Philo, *De specialibus legibus* II, 75. So Friedrich Hauck affirms that πενιχρός (*penichros*) signifies the "very poor" while Thomas Hanks relates it to the beggarly poverty of πτωχός (*ptōchos*). See Hauck, "πενιχρός," *TDNT* 6:40; Hanks, "Poor, Poverty: New Testament," *ABD* 5:417. For indeed, unlike πένης (*penēs*), πενιχρός (*penichros*) highlights being in some need of the material possessions related to livelihood. See "πενιχρός," BDAG 795; "πένομαι," *DÉLG* 881; "πενιχρός," *EDNT* 3:69; *contra* Coenen, "πένης, πενιχρός," *NIDNTT* 2:820; W. Evans, "Poverty," *ISBE* 2427 (both of whom consider the two terms synonyms).

fund. Though she was now indigent she was nevertheless not necessarily a beggar—a probable reason for the occurrence of the clarifying term πενιχρός (*penichros*). She, like Jesus' immediate disciples, was poor enough to be a beggar—in terms of possessions—without resorting to begging. In this sense she joined the ranks of those who occasionally "hunger now" (Luke 6:21). These passages temper Esler's contention that πτωχός (*ptōchos*) should always be translated as referring to a beggar but they do not challenge the notion that a beggarly level of poverty is in view.

Are there any other possible counter-texts? The most likely candidate is to be found in 2 Cor 8:2. In their desire to aid the indigent poor in Jerusalem, the Macedonian believers gave even despite their own deep indigent poverty—their βάθους πτωχεία.[34] So even indigent people—those in a state poor enough to justify begging—are apparently able to sacrifice in order to help others in a similar predicament. They were the working poor who were nevertheless not able to provide for a stable livelihood. Their sharing likely meant that they would have to go hungry longer than was usually the case. This is what makes their participation in the collection for Jerusalem so exceptionally exemplary.

So, with no clear textually-driven reason for expanding the poverty domain of πτωχός (*ptōchos*) beyond experiencing indigence in terms of possessing immediate sustenance need, why all the lexical uncertainty? A significant portion of the ambiguity stems from scholarly disagreements over the degree of influence that the LXX exerted on terminological usage within the early church. Though the common differentiation between πτωχός (*ptōchos*) and πένης (*penēs*) has been somewhat obscured in the Septuagint translation of the OT terms for poor, it remains in effect within other contemporaneous Jewish material.[35] The NT is generally recognized to follow the OT conceptual usage—in contrast to the LXX—in affirming that πτωχός (*ptōchos*) represents the indigent poor who have "nothing to bring" either materially or spiritually (when employed in the metaphorical sense).[36]

---

34. The Greek text used throughout is NA[27] while the Hebrew text is *BHS*.

35. Coenen, "πένης," *NIDNTT* 2:821. It is precisely the awareness of this distinction that, as mentioned earlier, drives Philo to fastidiously avoid the term πτωχός (*ptōchos*).

36. Ibid. See also Nixon, "Poverty," *NBD*[2] 955–56; Spender, "Theology of Poor and Poverty," *EDBT* 617–18; Stambaugh and Balch, *The New Testament in Its Social Environment*, 64.

Even so, the LXX was certainly respected. In fact, the only NT occurrences of πένης (*penēs*) and ἐνδεής (*endeēs*) are, respectively, a quotation from and an allusion to the Septuagint. The former is found solely in 2 Cor 9:9 where it is embedded within a quotation from Ps 112:9 (Ps 111:9 LXX). Within this quotation, πένης (*penēs*) translates אֶבְיוֹן (*ebyon*)—a term which generally signifies the beggarly poor.[37] Nevertheless it is translated as πένης (*penēs*) in the LXX and quoted as an encouragement to the Corinthians to increase their righteousness by helping to alleviate the want (ὑστέρημα, *hysterēma*, 2 Cor 8:14) being experienced by the church in Jerusalem. The quotation fits well for Paul because he desires to assure the Corinthians that God will multiply their "seed for sowing" (2 Cor 9:10) so that they can generously scatter it abroad (v. 9) and so "increase the harvest" of their righteousness (v. 10).[38] But even here, this sowing, this scattering abroad, is intended to meet the needs of the indigent—"the poor [πτωχοί, *ptōchoi*] among the saints in Jerusalem" (Rom 15:26).[39] For this is the poverty descriptor Paul himself chooses when not quoting from the Septuagint.

The final term for poor, ἐνδεής (*endeēs*), signifies experiencing lack—even destitution—and occurs in Acts 4:34.[40] The first part of this verse is generally agreed to be an allusion to Deut 15:4 (LXX) which affirms that, as a result of the blessing of the LORD, "there shall be no poor [אֶבְיוֹן, *ebyon*] among you."[41] Luke desires to reveal that the nascent church was so blessed—that there was no unmet indigence among them.

---

37. Pleins, "Poor, Poverty: Old Testament," *ABD* 5:403–5.

38. The context, 2 Cor 9:8–11, maintains its flow of thought and OT fidelity best when the quotation is taken as encouragement for the Corinthians in their "good deed" (v. 8) for the Jerusalem church rather than as an assurance of God's concern for them (this is taken care of in v. 8). See M. Harris, *The Second Epistle to the Corinthians*, 639–41; Plummer, *A Critical and Exegetical Commentary on the Second Epistle of St. Paul to the Corinthians*, 257, 260–62.

39. Paul's intended hearers would likely have struggled to take the genitive as epexegetic here—as primarily signifying a self-designation of the Jerusalem saints (Dunn, *Romans*, 875). Such an interpretation is made the more unlikely upon the acceptance of the concretizing testimony concerning the recipients of the contribution in Second Corinthians 8–9.

40. "ἐνδεής," BDAG 331; "δέω," *DÉLG* 270; Hauck, "πένης," *TDNT* 6:37; "ἐνδεής," MM 211; *pace* Esler, *Community and Gospel in Luke–Acts*, 180.

41. Barrett, *Acts*, 254; Polhill, *Acts*, 152–53.

The driving significance of all this is that mandates in the NT—whenever their poor recipients are explicitly identified—are solely given with respect to alleviating πτωχός (*ptōchos*) level poverty.

But some are not so quickly convinced. Bruce Malina takes a broader anthropological perspective. He initially contends that NT passages which do not provide additional clarification of the state of the poor, beyond identifying them as πτωχοί (*ptōchoi*), are open to interpretation.[42] He nevertheless goes on to agree that the label of poor, when it receives contextual clarification, is connected to the blind, lame, crippled, diseased, leprous, deaf, hungry, thirsty, naked, shabbily clothed, widowed, and imprisoned.[43] Despite this correlation, Malina nevertheless asserts that the poor label "would most certainly not be an economic designation" but rather an indication of a loss of "inherited status."[44] Nonetheless, the conceded relation between being πτωχός (*ptōchos*) and not being able-bodied or experiencing hunger and thirst makes Malina's extra-textual contention unconvincing. He is surely correct that disability and calamity brought with them shame and loss of social status, but the focus of the text is on the need they generated.

In order to further address Malina's contention—and to verify the semantic content of πτωχός (*ptōchos*)—a brief biblical investigation of the NT textual indicators of poverty and need is required. As noted earlier, even Malina concedes that the term πτωχός (*ptōchos*) is textually related to being non-able-bodied or unable to provide for oneself due to circumstances such as imprisonment. Such predicaments entail dependence upon others to provide for one's sustenance—for, in the first century context, an inability to work entailed experiencing such need (for all but the few landed rich).[45] Such sickly and non-able-bodied are described as the physically "weak" that ought to be helped via giving in Acts 20:35.[46] Luke 14:12–14 similarly identifies the πτωχοί (*ptōchoi*) with the disabled as those who do not have the means to repay a dinner invitation. This clarification provides strong affirmation for the semantic

---

42. Malina, *The New Testament World*, 99.

43. Ibid.

44. Ibid., 100.

45. Esler, *Community and Gospel in Luke–Acts*, 174.

46. This connection is likewise affirmed extra-canonically by the early church father Clement in *1 Clement* 38:2.

identification of πτωχός (*ptōchos*) as indeed referring to the indigent—those that lack even the means whereby to return an invite to a meal.

Furthermore, the domain of poverty is also demarcated, via implication, by the content of the provision which is intended to be given to the poor. Revealingly, Luke 3:11 mandates the sharing of clothes or food with "him who has none"—someone who is indigent. Similarly, Jas 2:15 enjoins the provision of "what is necessary for their body" to "a brother or sister . . . without clothing and in need of daily food." Such poverty, which entails not even being able to provide for one's nakedness and daily sustenance, is a matter of immediate indigence. The parable of the sheep and the goats in Matt 25:31–46 likewise describes the needy as those that are dependent upon the provision of sustenance and sustaining assistance. Those who are to be helped are the hungry, the thirsty, the foreigner without shelter, the naked, those suffering from the weakness of sickness, and the imprisoned (who were dependent on outside provision). And so it is not surprising that Jesus consoles the disciples, in Matt 6:25–32, concerning God's promise to provide them with food and clothing. In this regard, 1 Tim 6:8 also asserts that "if we have food and covering, with these we shall be content." Correspondingly, meeting needs also involves providing food or drink to an enemy who is (at least momentarily) indigent and is experiencing hunger or thirst (Rom 12:20). The parable of the rich man and Lazarus brings our two investigated aspects—the semantic content of the terminology and the intended provision—together. For here in Luke 16:19–31 the poor man whom Jesus labels as πτωχός (*ptōchos*, vv. 20, 22) is revealed to be non-able-bodied and is even identified as experiencing hunger and as someone who should have been helped in terms of receiving sustenance. For even the rich man's table scraps would have met the poor man's dire sustenance want.

These considerations concerning the contextual hemming in of πτωχός (*ptōchos*) and the needs which are to be met affirm that poverty, whenever it is further specified in the NT, is consistently connected to its expected semantic meaning. The elaborating NT texts affirm that they are addressing indigent poverty with remarkable consistency. The onus therefore falls on those who, like Malina, would expand the poverty definition to prove why the contextually unspecified passages should be understood more broadly.

What I have briefly argued for in this chapter is the majority position among biblical theologians. Even Joel Green, a partial dissenter, agrees that a "near consensus" on this issue has developed in recent years.[47] But scholarly opinion has shifted before. What reasons do we have for considering the other extant suggestions as not really tempting or ultimately relevant for our present concern? For the sake of efficiency, let us confine our response to a consideration of Luke—the writer who has the most to share with respect to the πτωχοί (*ptōchoi*).

In considering Luke–Acts, Luke Johnson creatively suggests that the poverty that it mentions is but a literary motif and so "is not an economic designation, but a designation of spiritual status."[48] Furthermore, these "poor" who accept Jesus become outcasts while the "rich" rejecters enjoy their role as in-group leaders of Israel.[49] And so for Johnson the poor are the pious outcasts—the followers of Jesus. Johnson's approach is representative of understanding the πτωχοί (*ptōchoi*) as either the pious, the spiritually humble, or as those composing the believing remnant of Israel. But are we really to believe that the pious, irrespective of their economic position, are the proper recipients of alms (when comparing Luke 12:33 to Luke 18:22)? That well-off disciples of Jesus, like Joseph of Arimathea (Luke 23:50–51), were to receive such aid? Who does Zaccheus give half of his possessions to (Luke 19:8)? And so the metaphorical interpretation of pious stumbles over all of the Lukan mandates to aid the poor.[50]

Charting another tack, Joel Green suggests that Jesus, in His concern for the "poor" in Luke, "is concerned fundamentally with those defined as 'them,' as outsiders—a social state that may or may not have economic roots."[51] So he too contends that we should see the πτωχοί (*ptōchoi*) in Luke as outcasts—but not of the particularly pious sort. They are the unclean, the sinners, the Gentiles, and those of low "status honor." Green confines his investigation to the Gospel of Luke because his primary concern is to decipher "to whom Jesus proclaims good news."[52] To identify His mission. Green is right that Jesus does not just

47. Green, "Good News to Whom?" 63, 62.
48. Johnson, *The Literary Function of Possessions in Luke–Acts*, 139.
49. Ibid.
50. Thus even Johnson occasionally succumbs to acknowledging and employing the literal meaning of the terminology (ibid., 142).
51. Green, "Good News to Whom?" 60.
52. Ibid., 74.

spend time with the poor. Luke mentions His interaction with the rich too. And the crowds are not all indigent. But neither are they *all* anything else.[53] They are not likely to be all outsiders either.[54] Green assumes an exclusive view of Jesus' commission—that the good news is preached only to the poor. As opposed to this being just a willful, though not exclusive, focus for Jesus. His firm determination that the poor be not left out. Green's assumption proves fateful for his approach, for neither does Jesus just preach the good news to outsiders. The rich young ruler is told too (Luke 18:18–25). As is Joseph of Arimathea (Luke 23:50–51) who, as part of the Sanhedrin, is a person very much on the inside—a person of high status and honor. And among those who heard Jesus' itinerant preaching (Luke 8:1) are also "Joanna the wife of Chuza, Herod's steward . . . and many others who were contributing to their support out of their private means" (Luke 8:3). Jairus, a synagogue official, also receives Jesus' attention (Luke 8:40–42, 49–56). Furthermore, Jesus did not just dine with outsiders like Zaccheus but also dined with respected insiders like Simon the Pharisee (Luke 7:36). Nor was this an isolated instance (Luke 14:1). Moreover, the "Pharisees and teachers of the law . . . who had come from every village of Galilee and Judea and from Jerusalem" heard His teaching (Luke 5:17).[55] And so Green's claim that "Jesus repeatedly goes to those on the outside; this is his mission" is only a part of Luke's record.[56] Because Green affirms the Gospel of Luke's concern for the "economically destitute" and contends that "the material side of Luke's message . . . cannot be overlooked," he does not imply that rich tax collectors and sinners with expensive perfume (Luke 7:37–38) are the proper recipients of alms. For he constrains himself to but attempting to unravel Jesus' mission.

David Seccombe also carefully confines himself to considering Jesus' *mission* in Luke—as it is revealed in Mary's *Magnificat* (Luke 1:46–55) and Jesus' Nazareth sermon (Luke 4:16–27). He contends that the πτωχοί (*ptōchoi*) mentioned in these passages refer to the nation Israel

---

53. Except perhaps Israel in need of salvation (with the occasional exception).

54. Jesus' repeated "woe to you" in His Sermon on the Plain suggests that the rich may have been among the listening multitude (Luke 6:24–26). See Morris, *Luke*, 141.

55. Though not in Luke, Jesus' acceptance of believing scribes into the kingdom of heaven in Matt 13:52 is noteworthy.

56. Green, "Good News to Whom?" 74.

in its need of salvation.⁵⁷ But for other contexts Seccombe agrees that the poor are indeed the economically needy.⁵⁸ And so Seccombe's proposal, like Green's, is ultimately inconsequential for our present purpose. For we are concerned with the other contexts—with passages that contain biblical mandates concerning the interhuman treatment of the poor. Whatever we come to in terms of understanding Jesus' *mission* is not ultimately a relevant concern for it does not clearly contain an interhuman mandate.⁵⁹

Other suggestions for the rightful referents of the πτωχός (*ptōchos*) terminology are equally constrained to a possible fit with but a few passages. Whether the poor are those not belonging to the religious establishment or whether they are the persecuted and suffering (such as Jesus' disciples) are understandings that may only sometimes be superimposed atop the literal meaning. So it is not, in the end, difficult to agree with Schottroff and Stegemann that: "It is clear in all strata of the Jesus tradition that when the synoptic Gospels speak of the 'poor' [= *ptōchoi*] they are in fact thinking of extreme want and often even of destitution."⁶⁰ And that the same conclusion applies to the rest of the NT.

A DISTILLATION

The above considerations allow us to articulate the NT delineations of sustenance needs and poverty. Of the definition options considered earlier in the chapter, the below provided definitions are most analogous to those which are implicitly provided by Nicholas Wolterstorff—though somewhat more limited by the data of the NT.⁶¹

> *Sustenance Needs*—the bodily needs that a person in a particular location must have met so as to remain relatively physically healthy.
>
> *Immediately Poor*—a person who is unable to provide for all of his sustenance needs by his own legitimate industry.

---

57. Seccombe, *Possessions and the Poor in Luke-Acts*, 21–43, 95.

58. See particularly chapters 3 and 4 of Seccombe, *Possessions and the Poor in Luke-Acts*.

59. Further defense of this claim is provided in chapters 3 and 5 to come.

60. Schottroff and Stegemann, *Jesus and the Hope of the Poor*, 16. Robert Karris is among the throng who also agree (Karris, "Poor and Rich," 112–13).

61. Wolterstorff, *Until Justice and Peace Embrace*, 85.

Potentially Poor—a person that is in direct danger of becoming immediately poor if she encounters even commonly experienced, comparatively small-scale financial setbacks.

In this way the immediately poor definition subsumes the domains of πτωχός (*ptōchos*), πενιχρός (*penichros*), and ἐνδεής (*endeēs*) while the potentially poor definition mirrors πένης (*penēs*). This latter category of poverty receives greater attention, both semantically and in terms of conceptual occurrence, within the OT. When the NT addresses πτωχός (*ptōchos*) poverty it is concerned with both the non-able-bodied beggars and those who are not beggars but are nevertheless experiencing beggar level sustenance want. While beggars are the most obvious recipients, the concern is with indigence. With those who, as in πενιχρός (*penichros*) and ἐνδεής (*endeēs*) poverty, suffer some privation. For during the early centuries, it was not uncommon for famine or crop failure to reduce the potentially poor to the ranks of the immediately poor for a time.

While provided here in individualistic terms, the definitions are intended to readily adapt to appraising family or household sustenance needs and provision levels. With our poverty deliberations behind us, our arrived-at definitions will be employed within the remainder of the book—and particularly during the presentation of the textual data in chapter 5.

THREE

What's Hermeneutics Got to Do with It?

HERMENEUTICAL CONTENTIONS

APPROACHING THE BIBLE AS a source for adjudicating our dissonance over justice and mercy also entails deciphering whether any filter should be applied to the biblical data. Whereas our pre-hermeneutical particularity accounts for our variously conditioned presuppositions in coming to the text, the following theological and procedural variances condition the admissible data set itself. So what manner of biblical data is legitimately admissible in ascertaining the domain of justice? How should it be processed? Our hermeneutical contentions coalesce around five main flashpoints: disagreements over the continued applicability of OT obligations, the hermeneutical mode of appropriation that we employ, the managing of the human/divine disjunction, the cultural containment of certain obligations, and the data post-processing entailed in concept formation. While we will find some of these contentions to be, in the end, immaterial for the present investigation of the NT data, they are nevertheless surfaced here to make this conclusion explicit, and to chart a little of the way for any subsequent theological forays into the data of the OT. Our guiding aim in engaging these contentions is to increase awareness concerning our hermeneutical presuppositions and to articulate the need for the proposal of the "resolution principle."

LAW AND GOSPEL

When contemplating the whole Bible, considerations concerning the relationship between Law and Gospel are of primary importance in assessing the breadth of the appropriate data set. How much of the OT data is to be considered deprecated? While many evangelical demarcations have been put forward, noting five general views will suffice to paint the general picture.[1]

The Theonomic Reformed view maintains the broadest data set by affirming the authority of what is heuristically identified as the moral and civil portions of the OT—of its laws—while deprecating only the ceremonial component. The Holiness Code view considers the Decalogue, along with the moral portion of the Law and the Holiness Code (specifically Leviticus 18–19), undeprecated. Consequently, this second view maintains the applicability of *some* of the OT civil components—namely those present in the Holiness Code—though they are, on Walter Kaiser's approach, understood to apply only "indirectly." By this he intends that they apply to the present spiritual, no longer political, theocracy only in the form of principles.[2] The Westminster Reformed view maintains the applicability of only the moral sections from the Law of Moses. The Dispensational view argues that the Law of Moses is displaced by the Law of Christ so as to limit the Christian ethicist's data set to the NT. And Douglas Moo's formulation of the Modified Lutheran view, in arguing for a non-divisible and synecdochic understanding of νόμος (*nomos*, law) in the NT, rejects the Law in its synecdochic totality—as both the Law and the Prophets.[3] This approach, like the Dispensational one, also effectively truncates the biblical data set at the opening lines of Matthew.

While all positions agree that where the NT specifically amends an OT mandate the NT specification should be considered preeminent, choosing any additional data masking technique should be done with much self-conscious care. As a result of this project's focus on the NT data, contentions over the continued applicability of OT prescriptions—as important as they may be—become immaterial for the present concern. Other hermeneutical issues will not lay down as quietly.

---

1. Though the author's own approach does not completely coincide with any of these views, the general categories followed here are from Bahnsen et al., *Five Views on Law and Gospel*. Related positions not covered here for the sake of brevity include the covenantal and variegated nomism approaches inspired by E. P. Sanders and the New Perspective on Paul. See, for example, Sanders, *Paul and Palestinian Judaism*; Sanders, "On the Question of Fulfilling the Law in Paul and Rabbinic Judaism," 103–26. See also Dunn, *The New Perspective on Paul*; Carson et al., eds., *Justification and Variegated Nomism*.

2. Kaiser, "The Law as God's Gracious Guidance for the Promotion of Holiness," 154.

3. Moo, *The Epistle to the Romans*, 145–46, 151.

MODES OF APPROPRIATION

How does the text communicate moral obligation? What should the hermeneutical process emphasize and distill during the transformation of textual data into Christian obligation itself? Five general categories of contemporary textual engagement may be outlined: divine command, principle, paradigm, virtue, and "metaphor-making."[4] While there appears to be a developing concern among contemporary thinkers to attempt to arbitrate the issues involved at a meta-hermeneutical level—a level that is concerned with articulating the necessary prior conditions that are required for any legitimate pursuit of biblical hermeneutics—these attempts to defend a particular mode of biblical appropriation do not ultimately bypass the hermeneutical level appropriation concerns.[5] So it will be the hermeneutical level of concern that will receive our attention.

The divine command approach focuses on the concrete rule and principle prescriptions of Scripture. Obligation is transferred directly from non-deprecated prescriptions and moral evaluations to parallel contemporary contexts, principlizing extrapolation is reserved only for issues not addressed in the biblical text. Parallel contemporary contexts are expected on the basis of a commonality secured via the human condition and its common moral concerns.[6] As a result, mandate integration is sought at the textual data level. Karl Barth at one time employed a modified version of this approach which, building upon his bibliology, posited immediate access to the general and concrete moral demands of God.[7] Despite Barth's broad theological influence, evangelical divine command approaches generally maintain a place for careful interpretive practice and thus Barth's one-time bypass of the interpretation element within this mode of appropriation goes largely unheeded.[8]

Principle-driven appropriation modes prefer to extrapolate principles from prescriptions, norms from rules, the general from the concrete.

---

4. This is Richard Hays's own term. See R. Hays, *The Moral Vision of the New Testament*, 298–304.

5. Two of the latest such attempts include Brock, *Singing the Ethos of God*; and Burridge, *Imitating Jesus*.

6. An articulation of this conviction is found even among writers favoring other approaches. See Burridge, *Imitating Jesus*, 395.

7. Barth, *Church Dogmatics* 2/2, 663–65.

8. R. Hays, *The Moral Vision of the New Testament*, 228–29.

What's Hermeneutics Got to Do with It?

The task of integration is done at the level of principles. This common theological approach is utilized by many contemporary thinkers including Walter Kaiser and J. Daniel Hays.[9] Richard Burridge's appropriation focus on the words and actions of Jesus, which he defends on the basis of the mimetic purpose implied in the bibliographic genre of the Gospels, is also a species of this principle approach.[10] Authority and applicability is sought at the principlized level.

Paradigmatic appropriation approaches attempt to discern the goals and intents behind the textual prescriptions and make these the normative principles of obligation. Due to this narrowed focus, the paradigmatic approach is considerably more constrained in its desired distillation than the principle-driven approach. As a result, obligation integration is carried out at the goals and intents level. The most prominent evangelical proponent of this approach is Christopher Wright.[11] Analogous appropriation strategies include seeking to identify the rationale behind biblical prescriptions and having these rationales become a key component of ethical obligation.[12]

Virtue-based approaches have experienced a renewal of interest that is based, in no small part, on the recent and influential philosophical efforts of Alasdair MacIntyre.[13] Virtue modes of appropriation focus on the internal states which make obedience to biblical prescriptions possible and make this extrapolation the primary focus of obligation. This appropriation approach arrives at integration via the generally complimentary nature of virtues.

The metaphor-making approach of Richard Hays attempts to discern and isolate the biblical text's "focal images."[14] These focal images serve to facilitate a "Kelseyian" synoptic judgment regarding the main themes of biblical ethics.[15] This thematic or motif approach stretches

---

9. Kaiser, "A Comparison of a Paradigm Approach to Biblical Law with a Principled Approach"; D. Hays, "Applying the Old Testament Law Today," 21–35.

10. Burridge, *Imitating Jesus*, 4, 28–31, 73–79, 144–48, 179, 183–84, 222–24, 280–82, 343–45, 389–91.

11. Publications which argue for and explain this approach include Wright, *Walking in the Ways of the Lord*; Wright, *An Eye for an Eye*; Wright, *God's People in God's Land*; Wright, *Old Testament Ethics for the People of God*.

12. Radant, "Headcovering, Holy Kisses, Hierarchy, and Homosexuality."

13. MacIntyre, *After Virtue*.

14. R. Hays, *The Moral Vision of the New Testament*, 310.

15. As noted earlier, Richard Hays affirms (with slight modification) David Kelsey's

beyond the principle and paradigm trajectories in seeking a small set of themes to integrate the biblical data set. These motifs subsequently become the overarching lenses of moral obligation—conforming all of the textual data to their guiding image.

The reader will likely have noticed that the author's proposed differentiation of the hermeneutical modes of appropriation does not contain equivalents to Richard Hays's "paradigms" and "symbolic world" appeal modes.[16] In Hays's terminology, the paradigms mode focuses on the exemplary modeling of positive and negative conduct narrated within Scripture while the symbolic world mode appeals to the representations of the human condition and God's character. Fortunately, Hays's paradigms and symbolic world modes readily dissolve into our proposed mode categories upon further inspection. This occurs because we must still determine by which conduit exemplary modeling and God's character are to be appropriated into ethical obligation. Should these modes be given rule-like, principle-like, goal-like, virtue-forming, or metaphor-making authority? In other words, the extrapolations derived from Hays's paradigm and symbolic world textual data are still necessarily modulated by the options distinguished in the author's appropriation categories.

Can anything be said by way of evaluation? All of the above mentioned approaches, save divine command, needfully abstract the biblical data in hermeneutically deriving our justice and mercy obligations. Such abstractions serve to adjust, reform, or transpose the obligation data set—for this data restructuring is a part of the practical benefit they seek to offer. Consequently, disagreement over the best hermeneutical mode of appropriation leads to differing data sets.

By extracting the general from the specific, principle-based appropriation loses the concrete content of the specific mandates. In excerpting goals and intents, the paradigmatic approach loses the specific as well as the general mandates for the sake of their teleological intents. This information is likewise lost in the distilling inherent in the virtues-based

---

contention that such a synoptic judgment is indispensable to any systematic theology or ethics (ibid., 194; Kelsey, *Proving Doctrine*, 163, 166).

16. Richard Hays's influential rules, principles, paradigms, and symbolic world differentiation scheme is itself an adaptation of James Gustafson's seminal considerations (Gustafson, "The Place of Scripture in Christian Ethics," 430–55). Hays's work, in turn, continues to be adopted within contemporary ethical discussion. See, for example, Burridge, *Imitating Jesus*, 363.

appropriation process. By seeking a synthetic motif set, the metaphor-making approach produces an interpretive grid which systemically discriminates against the non-motif mandates. Only the divine command approach maintains both the specific and the general mandates.

Though data loss makes integration easier by reducing overall complexity, it does this by reducing the detail—the resolution of the data. Such early and systemic data discrimination makes indeterminism in contested matters hard to avoid. Climbing the ladder of abstraction with a reduced data set necessarily increases the interpretive potency and sway of an interpreter's variously conditioned preconceptions—the loss of a part of the textual constraint means there is more room to maneuver. Any such construal can, and likely will, be challenged on the basis of the lost data. Justifying this data loss requires a justification of the accuracy and fidelity of the extrapolation process. But on what basis, save an investigation of the unfiltered data itself, can this justification be provided? Such considerations reaffirm the necessity of avoiding any mode of appropriation filtering within our hermeneutical methodology. Abstraction and extrapolation is best left to the very last mile.

In the Introduction I assumed that methodological indeterminism is a bed of nails. Why is it so pointedly undesirable? Why is methodological determinism preferable to methodological indeterminism? Because it is useful in critiquing our methods. Granting such determinism entails that—as far as method is concerned—approaches which lead toward conceptual containment are preferable to those which entrance greater ambiguity, indefiniteness, and indeterminacy. Preferring methodological determinism is another way of affirming that, methodologically, an answer is being sought—rather than merely a cacophonous presentation of variously arrayed possibilities. Affirming methodological determinism means that we are seeking to uncover something more than a perpetual play of unconstrained hypotheticals. For methodological indeterminism cannot bring us closer to any target.[17]

---

17. Methodological determinism is to be distinguished from "textual forcing," which mutates and balloons this assumption into a "will to a system," which filters and manipulates the *data itself* for the sake of conceptual "fit." What we are concerned with here is rather the "will to a process of elimination" regarding method.

HUMAN/DIVINE DISJUNCTION

To what extent are God's unmandated actions and treatments applicable for interhuman obligation? Are they really exemplary in such a way as to generate some level of human obligation? Is God ever merely "indirect"—in the sense of leading by example only—in His expectations of people? Due to the biblical discontinuity between God's role and the role of humans in the created order, extrapolations from the former to the latter are non-trivial. Some texts reveal that divine justice and interhuman obligation are at times diametrically distinct. One such example is Rom 12:19: "Never take your own revenge, beloved, but leave room for the wrath of God, for it is written, 'VENGEANCE IS MINE, I WILL REPAY,' says the Lord."[18] Certainly some recursiveness exists in mandates such as "love one another, even as I have loved you" (John 13:34; 15:12), but it exists on the basis of the interhuman prescription. Explicit and recursive poverty-related examples include Deut 10:18–19 which states, "He [God] executes justice for the orphan and the widow, and shows His love for the alien by giving him food and clothing. So show your love for the alien, for you were aliens in the land of Egypt." Nonetheless, a broad-based God-human parallel is contested. It is possible that God's unmandated treatments of people are something that only God should or could accomplish. Among such examples is Ps 113:7–8, which reveals that "He [God] raises the poor from the dust And lifts the needy from the ash heap, To make them sit with princes, With the princes of His people." Only God, from our "commoner" standpoint, is able to make the poor sit among princes and nobles (1 Sam 2:8) or have large families (Ps 107:41). While God can open the eyes of the blind (Ps 146:8) and provide a barren woman with children (Ps 113:9), such intervention remains largely unaccomplishable from a human standpoint.

The example of Jesus, while significantly illuminatory and nuancing for many biblical mandates, is similarly constrained. Few feel bound by Jesus' unmandated, beyond His immediate apostles and disciples, example of living in humble conditions and general homelessness. Similarly, not all believers are itinerant teachers as He was and few feel that Jesus' example constrains believers to confront Jewish leaders and theologians in the same manner and authoritative vehemence. An unambiguously ethics-related disjunction can be identified in Jesus' failure to offer any

---

18. Such considerations also needfully extend beyond theological ethics into spheres such as soteriology (G. Williams, "Penal Substitution," 73).

defense when brought before unjust accusers during His judicial process.[19] In sum, the ethical applicability of Jesus' example is mediated to us through the nexus of parallel biblical mandates. Even Richard Burridge's recent and plenteous argument for the *mimesis*-assuming bibliographic genre of the Gospel narratives does not sufficiently address the question of the extent of the precedent—despite offering significant engagement with the issue.[20] As with God's actions, Jesus' treatments of the poor are sometimes out of the range of human possibility. Luke 7:12–16 recounts the restoration of an only son to his widowed mother. It is very likely that the death of the widow's son meant that her main source of provision had been taken away. Nonetheless such compassion (v. 13) is beyond the range of human intervention—it cannot be mimicked. Similarly, emphasis on Jesus' miraculous intervention on behalf of the poor also establishes less than is sometimes maintained—for the Messiah provides such treatment for the poor and non-poor alike (as for the centurion who could afford to build a synagogue in Matt 8:5–13 // Luke 7:1–10, for a non-poor synagogue official in Mark 5:22–43 // Matt 9:18–26 // Luke 8:41–56, and for the royal official in John 4:46–54).[21] Jesus' preaching and teaching, like John the Baptist's, likewise extended to the non-poor—such as tax collectors.

The author's contention, which is derived on the basis of analyzing all of the NT texts concerning divine treatments of the poor, is that filtering purely divine treatments and examples does not result in data loss with respect to humanly accomplishable treatment. No humanly accomplishable treatments of the poor are merely exemplified in divine action. While some theologians may contend that removing the consideration of how God personally treats something may reduce the frequency with which certain treatments appear for analysis, this need not be worrisome unless theological significance is attached to the frequency with

---

19. Though slaves are instructed to follow Jesus' example in innocently suffering without reviling or threatening (1 Pet 2:18–23), all believers—when brought before the authorities—are consoled not to "become anxious about how or what you should speak in your defense, or what you should say; for the Holy Spirit will teach you in that very hour what you ought to say" (Luke 12:11–12).

20. Burridge, *Imitating Jesus*, 4, 28–31, 73–79, 144–48, 179, 183–84, 222–24, 280–82, 343–45, 389–91.

21. The presence of the "flute-players" (plural of αὐλητής, *aulētēs*) indicates that these professional musicians thought the synagogue official would be able to pay for their services (Hagner, *Matthew*, 249).

which an ethical issue surfaces in the text.[22] In this sense I am disputing the independent helpfulness of Richard Hays's "symbolic world" "representations of the human condition . . . and the character of God" for the issue at hand.[23] Similarly, Hays's "paradigmatic" appeal mode, which encompasses positive and negative character narratives, is necessarily parasitic on the divine evaluations and prescriptions present in the context (or elsewhere).[24] The gist of the argument is that all non-mandate texts are ideationally parasitic on mandate texts for their ethical significance. Passages which do not evaluate the interhuman treatment described are necessarily dependent upon the evaluations that we read into them on the basis of texts which contain such evaluations. This "intertextuality" is the best case scenario—at the worst we are merely reading in our variously conditioned presuppositions.

It is worth acknowledging that believers have always tended to be concerned with following the example of Jesus—and the Mennonite tradition perhaps more so than most. So it is perhaps helpful to mention John Howard Yoder at this point. In his influential work, *The Politics of Jesus*, Yoder rises to the challenge and develops an argument for what believers are, and are not, to emulate about Jesus.[25] Yoder's goal is to identify and defend a criterion that is capable of sustaining this important distinction. His desire is to thwart Franciscan-like conceptions: that we are to emulate everything about Jesus.[26] He does this by surveying NT texts that clarify what the early church—as visible from the NT documents—considered mimic-worthy about Jesus. These texts subsequently fall into one of two categories. They either convey statements of fact concerning a Christian's existential reality as similar to Christ's existential reality or they are mandate texts. Things such as persecution (John 15:20: "'A slave is not greater than his master.' If they persecuted Me, they will also persecute you") and being loved by the Father fit into the

---

22. Such theological weighing, though relatively common, is at minimum nontrivial. Few Evangelicals would argue, for example, that usury is more weighty than bestiality—even for OT believers.

23. R. Hays, *The Moral Vision of the New Testament*, 209.

24. Richard Hays grants theological primacy to this paradigmatic mode in the NT (ibid., 209, 310).

25. Yoder begins this argument in chapter 6, "Trial Balance," but the heart of the matter arrives in chapter 7—which he entitles "The Disciple of Christ and the Way of Jesus."

26. Yoder, *The Politics of Jesus*, 132.

former category. Yoder employs these former texts to affirm a continuity between Christ and the believer—so as to broadly justify mimicking. And he uses the latter to show *what* believers are to normatively emulate about Christ. There is no emulation necessary for the former—one has no need to somehow emulate an already existent reality. Consequently, Yoder's *argument* turns out to be identical to our position.[27] Only what is mandated is to be emulated. This is how Yoder is able to say that celibacy, carpentry, long retreats, etc. are not to be emulated: because these aspects of Jesus' life do not find affirmative articulation in the NT and hence the nascent church.

Yoder proceeds to summarize this textual data: "Servanthood replaces dominion, forgiveness absorbs hostility. Thus—and only thus—are we bound by New Testament thought to 'be like Jesus.'"[28] To the extent that Yoder confines this synthesis to the mandate texts that are crucial for his argument, it is easy to agree. Unfortunately, Yoder goes on to subsume other aspects under the umbrella of his synthetic extrapolation: ends such as affecting societal structures to do justice, the forming of an Anabaptist-like counterculture, etc.—aspects for which he will have a harder time finding mandates. To the degree to which Yoder appears to do this, he moves beyond what his own argument allows him to pursue.

There is, in this matter, at least one more thing that keeps systematic theologians up at night. How then are we to understand the incarnation? Yoder builds upon his teacher, Karl Barth, in affirming that Jesus discloses the proper nature and vocation of "man." Yoder argues that either Christ is normative man in all the ways he perceives Him to be normative or we are in heresy.[29] Perhaps we can agree that Jesus lived the perfect and exemplary life but that it is nevertheless not normative in all its respects because Jesus fulfilled two roles: perfect man and unique promised Messiah. And these two roles do not fully overlap. We are to mimic Jesus in His example of perfect man but not in His role of Messiah. This, as previously argued, means emulating Him in what we are mandated to mimic—and not otherwise.

---

27. Ibid., 130–31.
28. Ibid., 131.
29. Specifically in ebionitic and gnostic heresy (ibid., 10, 98–99).

CULTURAL CONTAINMENT

The extent of the cultural tainting or contingency of the biblical data, with the possibility of making some aspects of it presently inapplicable, is also contested. Such dissonance logically manifests itself in the hermeneutical stances taken toward the biblical text. Many positions have been taken along the continuum between accepting everything as morally applicable and deeming everything to be culturally contingent and vestigial. Richard Hays, to return to a prominent example, argues that everything in the text is culturally tainted but nevertheless metaphorically applicable via a motif-guided extraction of the analogous aspects of the ethical data.[30] Unfortunately, the contours of Hays's analogousness remain a largely ineffable component of the imaginative leap he prescribes.

A favorable development in this area is the expanding nature of the contemporary theological concern for helping the poor. Amidst the current theological tenor of engagement, it is somewhat less needful to argue strenuously that helping the poor is something more than a no-longer-applicable cultural taint. And furthermore, in taking a longer term view, the predominant trend in the history of church thinking correlates well with the contention that helping the poor is a transcultural biblical concern—legitimately applicable beyond the initial recipients.

This does not mean however that the text's applicability regarding our obligations toward the poor goes completely unchallenged even now. More sociologically inclined thinkers often find that their reconstructions might come to constrain the text's applicability, to greater or lesser extents, to some bygone particularities of the original context. We will turn to these contentions shortly. But it is helpful to first lay out our cultural containment options in a little more detail, for there are a good many ways of categorizing the breadth of the suggested possibilities.[31] Still a *functional* categorization will prove most efficient to describe—particularly when it is just an expanded adaptation of the modes

---

30. R. Hays, *The Moral Vision of the New Testament*, 299–300.

31. Evangelical engagements with this issue include Marshall, *Beyond the Bible*; Webb, *Slaves, Women & Homosexuals*; Grudem, "Should We Move Beyond the New Testament to a Better Ethic?" 299–346; Swartley, *Slavery, Sabbath, War, and Women*; Veerman, *How to Apply the Bible*; McQuilkin, *Understanding and Applying the Bible*; Larkin, *Culture and Biblical Hermeneutics*; Doriani, *Getting the Message*; Duvall and D. Hays, *Grasping God's Word*; Fee and Stuart, "The Problem of Cultural Relativity," 80–86.

of appropriation categories we have already encountered. For there is a natural causal connection between our notions of cultural tainting and our modes of appropriation. The more levels we consider to be tainted, the higher up the ladder of abstraction we will climb before we are willing to appropriate. Our options? In encountering a differing aspect in terms of culture we may, in spite of our own particular enculturation, accept the rules and principles of Scripture as untainted in a divine command manner. Or we may consider the textual prescriptions tainted at the rules level and siphon only the principle. Or perhaps we might consider the matter tainted at even the principles level so as to only retain the paradigmatic goals. Or we may piggyback the tainting even further into the goals and intents level whereby leaving only virtue applications. And if the level of virtue has been tainted besides, then perhaps only creatively expounded motifs should survive—along with the largely uninhibited metaphorical leaps that are their offspring. In each of these steps the textual "how" is increasingly rescinded until only the general "what"—some kind of concern for the poor—remains. And following up on all this as the additional option is complete deprecation—the view that particular biblical prescriptions are inextricably attached to and wholly dependent upon their cultural circumstance. That they have no business swimming in other waters.

Two matters need immediate clarification. Firstly, the issue of the continued applicability of the OT and the issue of cultural tainting need to be kept separate. While the NT clearly deprecates certain OT prescriptions, it is the remaining undeprecated ones in both testaments that cultural tainting seeks to contain. Secondly, the lowest rung divine command approach to cultural differences welcomes some immediate extrapolation (even before engaging in systematic considerations to address uniquely post-biblical issues)—but of such a slight distance as to almost not warrant the name. This extrapolation can be thought of as coming in two flavors. The first of these burgeons the specific detail in a passage—but only along the axis of each detail's contextual contribution. Only along the spectrum of what the detail justifiably signifies in terms of its passage "function." We can think of this burgeoning as akin to adding error bars or plausible uncertainty to the contribution of each detail. It is a "near field" expansion along but the *immediate* spectrum. Though most interpreters do this relatively naturally, it is nevertheless very difficult to articulate for its many nuances—especially without examples. Two well-known parables, the one about the good Samaritan and the parable of the rich man and Lazarus, will serve our purpose. Within the former, the detail of the inn readily conveys the provision of shelter while the bandaging of the victim's wounds readily implies furnishing needed medical attention. The engaging of the innkeeper is plausibly expanded to affirm the employing of a third party to provide care on one's behalf—and not solely a third party of but one profession. In the parable of the rich man and Lazarus the detail about Lazarus being at the rich man's gate implies that he was immediately present and accessible to the rich man. In Lazarus' longing for that which fell from the rich man's table, it is readily implied that he desired to benefit from the rich man's scraps and castoffs. So in all of this, all we are doing is de-confining an exemplifying detail. But in a conscientiously myopic rather than broadly imaginative way. To the extent that Hays intends to showcase this de-confining, no disagreement is necessary. It is his much more open-ended license that is precariously tricky theologically.

The second flavor entails broadening the cause of the textually detailed need to enfold those in a closely parallel predicament. The highlighted need remains unchanged—only its cause acquires some error bars. We add but a small causal uncertainty for *that* particular kind of need. We induce a broader causal category from the exemplifying subcategory. So we perceive in the bandits mentioned in the parable of the good Samaritan a wider means of ushering an innocent victim into physical incapacitation. The peasant bandits of the first century may in this one way become not so completely different from a contemporary drug gang. Perhaps even a single well-armed assailant may do such damage. Similarly, the detail of the road functions merely as a setting for the exemplifying cause, and the biblical prescription applies equally if the attack had occurred in an open field. In the parable of the rich man and Lazarus, the sore-covered Lazarus is "laid" (Luke 16:20) at the rich man's gate thus conveying that he is diseased and immobile. But wider manifestations of being non-able-bodied—predicaments such as blindness or being handicapped of limb—would have also resulted in someone needing to beg to eat in Lazarus' day. And so Lazarus' condition readily implies being non-able-bodied.

Such rule level detail broadening is a necessary and acknowledged part of the divine command approach because it is understood that we do not get out of these parables on a technicality. It did not happen on a road. There was no inn nearby. The immobile beggar was at my fence rather than at my gate. It surely does not apply to me, for I do not even have a gate. And so the immediate extrapolation pursued within divine command appropriation remains but the process of de-confining a well-depicted example. And in some ways this de-confining is like taking just the first few steps of what the parable of the good Samaritan itself enjoins in its elaborating role for the second greatest commandment. In this sense this particular parable anticipates broader appropriation from the start. For it is but an exemplification for its accompanying principle. This does not mean however that as an example it adds nothing. For it broadens who all and what all is subsumed in loving your neighbor as yourself (particularly when compared to the contextual emphasis in Lev 19:17–18). In providing a further radius point, it draws a broader circle. It reduces some of the uncertainty otherwise inherent in the expression of the principle by itself. And so we are ultimately called to help even if it was a lion or a runaway zamboni that attacked our neighbor. And all this is not at all the same as considering the textual prescriptions to be culturally contained to their initial context.

Can anything be said by way of conceptual evaluation before we engage some representative proposals? The extent to which we move away from the prescribed *how* toward the abstracted and "how-less" *what*, we experience a contraction of available data. Our possibilities may see expansion but our working data set atrophies. The further we demote the textual *how* the less guidance is available to us for the fulfilling of our obligations. We will naturally prefer our variously conditioned subjectivity for regulating the levels that we consider culturally confined. And with this we consign ourselves to less, if any, practical agreement. We fill up the glass of options, and toast the dissonance.

But there is a snag on the way to this merriment. For it is indeed very hard to prove cultural tainting. Particularly from the position of our own various enculturations. But it is much less difficult to assume it. However, this will be challenged. How shall we justify the data loss and data discrimination? Even tougher, how do you prove what all rightfully disappears—how high up the ladder the tidewaters of culture have risen? On what basis do we remand something as a matter of cultural accommodation rather than divine intent? On the basis of our own enculturated disagreement with it? The tainted leading the tainted?[32] How

---

32. Several routes have nevertheless been attempted. The most common involves

will we ever defend this—especially before those who stand to benefit if we kept to an untainted approach? "Oh, we do not like those textual details in our culture."

It is never too late in life to begin dabbling in a little deconstruction. When we ponder the nature of our attempts at justification we quickly notice a recurring system. We come to Scripture and observe some differences in sentiment. These differences become the reason for wanting cultural containment. But we know that this alone is not enough to justify what we long for. And so we look for differences in circumstances—between theirs and ours—to justify the change in our sensibilities. And fortunately there will always be some difference to pick up on. But if we become wise and a little cynical to this process, our readymade justifications become as hard to prove as they should be.

Perhaps we can return to our earlier example of the parable of the good Samaritan to illustrate our predicament. Let us just for the moment, for the sake of simplicity, consider our parable as shorn free of its accompanying principle. The path of least resistance regarding the parable's first century elements is to cut what is different and keep the rest. Though rough and dirty, this is the road most traveled. But say we are not particularly fond of the parable's mandate. We could just as easily argue that the parable's call is predicated on their having no hospitals and well-trained emergency personnel back in the first century like we do now. That this is the instigating element. That their peculiar circumstances necessitated the first century concern. But our culture is no longer tainted with that particular lack and moreover we now have cars and—at least in the Western world—roadside banditry is no longer a familiar part of our socioeconomic context. Our situation is altogether different, the parable was meant to lose its voice. The only question that remains is how much? May its abstracted principles, its paradigmatic goals, its virtues, or perhaps its motif contribution still sing? Or perhaps we do not need to do anything for a beaten-up stranger after all because the difference in circumstances heralds complete deprecation.

---

noting differences in textual angle or emphasis and treating them in a "divide and conquer" rather than integrative manner. See Fee and Stuart, "The Problem of Cultural Relativity," 82–83. Thus wherever we can evoke some apparent non-uniformity we may assume cultural tainting—and pick the side of our preference. But adopting this fashion of theological systematization is not proof sufficient. Are we saved by grace through faith or by works?

So what may we conclude from our brief conceptual foray? That data discrimination in terms of our obligations toward the poor is not readily defendable. That we should, in good conscience, demand proof—not just of cultural differences—but that these differences are meant to be tainting. Furthermore, are not the first century and ours sufficiently parallel in terms of the causes of poverty—at least in a fair portion of them—so why should our moral response and priorities be different? But this assessment will have to be defended in more detail presently.

As noted, the intent of this section is not to address all of the nuances raised by the hermeneutics of cultural containment. Our concern is only with the *prescriptive* passages, and then only with those which pertain to our obligations toward the poor. Here the mollifying difference that is commonly sought out is the difference in structural economic realities. But disagreement and uncertainty invades even this arena.[33] Primitivist reconstructions contend that the majority of people in the Roman Empire of the first century were peasants—and that these were largely tied to agriculture and that the substantial taxation and rents that were extracted from their meager living were used to support the cities. The wealthy who controlled the all-encompassing centralized system of goods distribution (in a given region) kept these potentially poor under their thumb with a system of patronage, debts, and coercion. Trading and market commerce were not an appreciable part of this majority's experience due to central planning, extraction, and redistribution.[34] And moreover, these peasants are thought to have held a zero sum view of economics—that goods are limited and thus the betterment of one necessarily entails detriment to another.[35] In contrast, moderniz-

---

33. Philip Harland provides a helpful summary of the key areas of ongoing debate: "(1) the agrarian nature of the economy, (2) the relative significance of trade, (3) the distribution or ownership of land, and (4) the social-economic conditions of the peasantry, including the impact of taxation" (Harland, "The Economy of First-Century Palestine," 514).

34. Consequently, in building on the work of Lenski and Kautsky, Hanson and Oakman prefer to refer to this arrangement as a "political economy" (Hanson and Oakman, *Palestine in the Time of Jesus*, 95–96, 113, 117; Lenski, *Power and Privilege*; Kautsky, *The Politics of Aristocratic Empires*).

35. While Moses Finley is probably the most influential proponent of the primitivist model, he is supported by many including Hanson and Oakman (Finley, *The Ancient Economy*; Hanson and Oakman, *Palestine in the Time of Jesus*, 93–120). Bruce Malina joins them in endorsing a zero sum worldview reconstruction (Malina, *The New Testament World*, 97–98, 105).

ing reconstructions claim that the historical circumstance was not quite as dire and that it approximates—though on a smaller scale—the later medieval and early modern economies. On this view, zero sum thinking was *passé* and trade and commerce was much more pervasive—so much so that one may even speak of their economy in capitalistic terms.[36] The mediating position—what we could call a "progressive primitivist" reconstruction—affirms much of what the primitivist contends concerning the subsistence livelihoods of the peasants while making more space for an ongoing transition toward greater trade and declining zero sum perceptions (if they existed at all). This "qualified primitivist" position has been spurred on, in part, by archeological finds that suggest greater degrees of international and local trade.[37] While still not as commonly held as the primitivist model, it is a position that is experiencing an uptick in assent.[38]

So to what extent does Michael Novak's earlier appraisal of Latin America as "not open to the poor but protective of the rich" apply to Jesus' Palestinian context and to the Roman Empire of the first century?[39] Thoroughgoing answers are hard to nail down. Not only because of our disagreements but also because a large helping of uncertainty is the ever-present side dish to our reconstructions. Philip Harland warns all parties to remember well that our archeological evidence and literary sources are presently fragmentary.[40] Furthermore, many of our assumptions about conditions in Galilee (in particular) are largely extrapolative from

---

36. The leading proponent of this modernizing approach is Mikhail Rostovtzeff, who pursues it in a number of his works, including *A History of the Ancient World*, 10–11.

37. Harland, "The Economy of First-Century Palestine," 518, 523.

38. Supporters of progressive primitivism include D'Arms, *Commerce and Social Standing in Ancient Rome*; Engels, *Roman Corinth*; Pleket, "Urban Elites and the Economy in the Greek Cities of the Roman Empire"; Nijf, *The Civic World of Professional Associations in the Roman East*; Harland, "The Economy of First-Century Palestine," 520, 523–25; Noell, "A 'Marketless World?'" 106–7. Gildas Hamel, in his own mixing of the models of George Foster and James Scott, is also in agreement in preferring a very flexible understanding of "limited good" (Hamel, "Limited Good," 5–6; Foster, *Tzintzuntzan*, 153; J. C. Scott, *The Moral Economy of the Peasant*). For such flexibility—where one person's betterment need not be gained solely at the cost of someone else's deprivation—dovetails much better with a biblical cosmology of plenty (whereas zero sum understandings assume scarcity).

39. Novak, *Will It Liberate?* 5.

40. Harland, "The Economy of First-Century Palestine," 522–25.

data about circumstances elsewhere in the Empire—an extrapolation that is contested.⁴¹

Keeping these uncertainties in mind, we can now delve into the cultural containment possibilities of two—for our purposes—representative proposals. K. C. Hanson and Douglas Oakman will shoulder our primitivist reconstruction, while Edd Noell will forward some implications of a progressive primitivist proposal.⁴² Because modernizing reconstructions discern less discontinuity between our socioeconomic circumstances and the first century—whereby leaving less space for tainting—they subsequently are not as interesting for our present investigation.

Hanson and Oakman contend that a small set of rich families controlled both production and redistribution within the thoroughly centralized Palestine economy.⁴³ The economy is envisioned as highly extractive and comprehensively dominated. As it was the *system* that made the livelihood of the poor majority precarious, the wealthy were just as handily considered "bandits" as they were potential patrons.⁴⁴ And, for Hanson and Oakman, if that is how it was—if this was the economic circumstance—then Jesus *must* have been trying to do something about it. He *must* have given Himself to attacking this political economy. His emphasis on the reign of God sought the "reorganization of society through fictive kinship patterns" whereby the peasants receive what they need as the *gifts* of "general reciprocity."⁴⁵ A general reciprocity wherein repayment is not expected immediately but "whenever."⁴⁶ And so Jesus' attempted dismantling of the centralized redistribution economy was

---

41. Sean Freyne and Eric Meyers are among those formulating this challenge. See Freyne, *Galilee from Alexander to Hadrian*; Meyers, "Galilean Regionalism as a Factor in Historical Reconstruction"; Meyers, "Galilean Regionalism"; Meyers, "The Cultural Setting of Galilee."

42. Hanson and Oakman, *Palestine in the Time of Jesus*, 93–148; Noell, "A 'Marketless World?'" 85–114.

43. Hanson and Oakman, *Palestine in the Time of Jesus*, 104.

44. Ibid., 103.

45. Ibid., 119, 117–18. The fictive kinship patterns refer to the "brotherhood" espoused within the "Jesus faction."

46. Ibid., 105. Correspondingly, "It is more blessed to give than to receive" (Acts 20:35) is identified as Jesus' general *economic* principle (ibid., 119–20, 118).

meant to leave the peasants better off by minimizing taxable commerce.[47] This was the way to "beat the system."

So what are the possible implications of such a reconstruction for cultural containment? That Jesus' mandates regarding our obligations toward the poor, like those found throughout the NT, were all an enculturated response to the primitivist political economies of the first century. That they are now, like the overarching reorganization plan they buttressed, wholly irrelevant everywhere that economic system is not retained—or perhaps just irrelevant up to some higher rung on the ladder of abstraction. But the main challenge facing this containment possibility is that Jesus did not confine His poverty mandates to aiding only the victims of structural parasitism—a cause subset that is, for its part, conspicuously lacking in explicit textual mention. The non-able-bodied such as the crippled, lame, and blind (Luke 14:13) as well as the physically weak and diseased (Matt 25:36, 39, 43–44; Acts 20:35) were also to be aided—even though their sustenance needs did not arise from the system itself but from personal calamity. And these causes did not evaporate away with the aristocratic agrarian societies of antiquity. Said another way, Jesus' concern for aiding the poor was demonstrably wider than His possible concern for dismantling the system, and thus the passing away of this system does not obsolete His mandates and concern. And so the primitivist reconstruction does not elicit a convincing enough argument for cultural tainting.

But perhaps the more interesting possibility here is the untainted one. That affecting poverty causes with the aim of moving to a broadly egalitarian economic system is what Jesus actually intended. Unfortunately the proof offered up for this take is not sufficiently convincing. Hanson and Oakman confess that, from their vantage point, this important aim of Jesus has been obscured in the text.[48] Confidently looking below the scriptural record is required. We may need to prefer distant or partial analogies to the forbidden fruit of the immediate context. But the same thing is always present below the text: a reflection of our own sensibilities.

The approach that Hanson and Oakman take perceives enculturated social comment most "everywhere" in the text. Briefly considering two central proofs will concretize what that looks like. The master in

47. Ibid., 118–19.
48. Ibid., 117, 98.

the parable of the talents and its conceptual parallel concerning minas affirms that "to everyone who has, *more* shall be given . . . but from the one who does not have, even what he does have shall be taken away" (Matt 25:29 // Luke 19:26). For Hanson and Oakman, this affirmation is Jesus' attempt to expose the parasitism of the political economy, to dress down the system before His hearers, and thus to show them how they as the "have-not" majority have become the losers.[49] The rich have been reaping where they "did not sow" (Matt 25:24 // Luke 19:21).[50] And Luke 19:23—there in the midst—is about using "debt manipulations" to make money—a veritable "text of terror" to the peasants.[51] But this reading faces some textual resistance. The parables are contextually about Jesus' coming absence and ultimate return to settle accounts with His estate-managing slaves (Luke 19:11).[52] It is He, as the master, that approves of His stewards putting His money to work (likely by trading, Matt 25:16) and doing business (Luke 19:13).[53] Gain is praised within these parables. And even procuring interest is better than merely storing the allotment for later (Matt 25:27 // Luke 19:23). While this gain speaks to properly serving the kingdom of God during Jesus' absence, it is Jesus who is the rich nobleman that "takes away" and reaps where He "did not sow."[54] Granting the primitivist reconstruction, we could just as easily read in that Jesus' intent was to defend the current system from all detractors—as made in His image. Jesus' readiness to frequently describe God as a rich landowner or ruler—to identify Him with the system's parasites—also does not play well with the subversive agenda. Similarly, in the parable

49. Ibid., 118.

50. Ibid., 98, 118.

51. Ibid., 116.

52. In Matthew the context is set up earlier by Matt 24:3—under the heading of "Tell us, when will these things happen, and what *will* be the sign of Your coming, and of the end of the age?" And it is the disciples who asked the question that are to be the faithful and sensible slaves of Matt 24:45–51 and the prudent virgins of Matt 25:1–13 during Jesus' absence.

53. In light of Hanson's and Oakman's take, it is fittingly ironic that for Noell these same parables—by way of the concrete analogy employed therein—are proof that Jesus acknowledged the transition away from zero sum thinking and approved of risk-taking, market exchange, trade, and commerce (Noell, "A 'Marketless World?'" 106–7).

54. Incidentally, this "taking away" is common practice for God (Matt 13:10–15 // Mark 4:10–12, 24–25). And the intended gain is indeed the inverse of contenting ourselves with apathy and nominalism (Davies and Allison, *Matthew*, 3:411; Nolland, *Luke*, 918–19).

of the good Samaritan just as in Jesus' clearing of the temple, bandits are taken as harmful rather than being sympathetically held up as economic victims (as they tend to be for Hanson and Oakman). And so for the parables of the talents and minas, Jesus' self-referentially ironic intent remains but an acontextual presumption.[55]

Hanson and Oakman perceive another key indicator of Jesus' socioeconomic intent in His clearing of the temple (Matt 21:12–13 // Mark 11:15–17 // Luke 19:45–46 // John 2:13–16). These parallels probably constitute as good an argument against trade and market commerce as one is going to find in Scripture, but even Hanson and Oakman do not take it quite that far.[56] Jesus is read as recognizing that the burden of the temple tribute was primarily upon the peasants. And so He agrees with their alleged appraisal of the temple system as institutionalized banditry. Rejecting it for its parasitic redistribution that benefited but the elite few. Thus the "Jesus faction" sought to control and become the beneficiary group of the "temple institution."[57] Reorganizing it on "the model of Passover" in terms of communal sacrifices and a solidarity that would meet "the needs of the many."[58] The temple's redistribution was to take a sharp egalitarian turn. This take is more plausible than that regarding the parables of the talents and minas because it rests upon the OT antecedent of assistive sharing during the Feast of Unleavened Bread (as joined to the Passover), the Feast of Weeks, and the Feast of Booths (Deut 16:1–17). Perhaps Jesus intended this same sharing to spread beyond the three feasts to the year-round operation of the temple. But Jesus' words and actions here could just as easily be directed against the actual temple commerce conducted in the outer court of the Gentiles—the only portion of the "temple area" (ἱερόν, *hieron*, in all parallels) open to uncircumcised proselytes and adherents.[59] And, in fact, this is the most textually suggested option.[60] For Jesus desires the

---

55. Note especially the broader context of the surrounding parables of Matthew.
56. Hanson and Oakman, *Palestine in the Time of Jesus*, 144.
57. Ibid.
58. Ibid., 144, 145.
59. Köstenberger, *John*, 102–3, 105–6. For additional discussion, see Barrett, "The House of Prayer and the Den of Thieves," 13–20. Note that Jesus drove out not only the sellers but also the buyers (Matt 21:12 // Mark 11:15).
60. John Nolland provides a helpful listing of the various proposed interpretive options in *Luke*, 935–36.

temple complex to be what it was fully intended to be—"A HOUSE OF PRAYER FOR ALL THE NATIONS [πᾶσιν τοῖς ἔθνεσιν]" (Mark 11:17 from Isa 56:6–7). And this entailed clearing out the disruptive and inconsiderate commercial distraction occurring in the Gentiles' sole place of worship. The synoptic reference to the "ROBBERS' DEN" (Matt 21:13 // Mark 11:17 // Luke 19:46 from Jer 7:11) likely condemned profiting (John 2:16) on sacred observance—perhaps even assailing it as banditry against travelers when a more hospitable (ministry conscious) approach was called for.[61] And so the assumption of Jesus' transformative plan remains unsubstantiated.

And the other examples fair no better. Jesus' mention of the sparrows (in Matt 10:29–31 // Luke 12:6–7) is not inevitably a commentary on the "deplorable state of affairs when something as insignificant as sparrows are up for sale."[62] His mention of giving stones and snakes and scorpions (in Matt 7:7–11 // Luke 11:9–13) is not demonstrably a disguised "commentary on the prevailing political economy."[63] And His affirmation that "the sons are exempt" of the temple tax (in v. 26 of Matt 17:24–27) also does not convincingly convey a repudiation of the "parasitic burden" of the temple tribute.[64] And so neither Jesus' broadly

---

61. This accompanying condemnation was not likely a direct attack on the high priest and Sanhedrin as it is the sellers, money traders, *and* buyers that are cast out and these are not likely to be helpfully classed as "insurrectionists" (a possible meaning of the term λῃστής, *lēstēs*, bandits).

62. Hanson and Oakman, *Palestine in the Time of Jesus*, 118. The contextual intent here is to argue, from the lesser to the greater, that if God does not forget the sparrows then He surely will not forget the disciples. And in order to make the point as strong as possible Jesus needfully chooses a comparative example of truly insignificant value before men.

63. Ibid., 119. It is important not to miss the "if *you*" and "*your* children" focus (Matt 7:11 // Luke 11:13, italics added, note also Matt 7:9 // Luke 11:11) upon Jesus' hearers—by context primarily the disciples in both passages. Such a focus is dissuasive of taking Jesus' words as referring to the parasitic elite.

64. Ibid., 144. Many Western commentators miss that it is "the kings" (plural) who do not collect taxes from "their sons" (plural) in Matt 17:25, and thus misjudge the plural in verse 26. Jesus, the subject of the matter (v. 24), is exempt from the temple tax because He is the son of the king to whom that house belongs. Others might rightly build and maintain God's house but Jesus—as *the* Son of God—is exempt of this responsibility (as a member of the set of regal sons). And since a shekel pays the half shekel temple tax for two, Peter's fishing is rewarded as well—so correctly L. Williams, *St. Matthew*, 2:180; Calvin, *Commentary on a Harmony of the Evangelists*, 2:370–71 (affirms that Jesus alone is the referent); *pace* Blomberg, *Matthew*, 270; Davies and Allison, *Matthew*, 2:745; Hagner, *Matthew*, 512. The subsequent miracle serves to confirm that Jesus is indeed the Son of God.

egalitarian economic aims nor His supposed engagement in addressing the causes of poverty find ready support.

Taking it one step further still, even if we accept the primitivist socioeconomic reconstruction as what *was*—though shorn of Jesus' supposed response—it still does not add anything to our textual obligations. The extractive system may represent a key specific cause of immediate and potential poverty in those days, but it takes its place among other coconspiring causes of economic weakness and depression. We are still to address the results—whether coming from one economic specific or another.

Noell, as a progressive primitivist, naturally affirms a more trade and commerce affirming reconstruction. So Jesus is noted, largely on the basis of the parables of the talents and minas, as "recognizing a growing role for market exchange and a legitimate pursuit of economic gain through risk-taking" while still leaving some space for Hanson's and Oakman's "general reciprocity."[65] Zero sum views were fading away as market activity and the pursuit of economic gain grew within the first century.[66] But the rich elite, benefiting from the extractive political economy, were still perceivably parasitic and seen as collaborators with the Romans.[67] The wealthy, in Noell's reconstruction, were looked upon with suspicion and invariably branded as avaricious and greedy.[68]

And for Noell, this circumstance entails some tainting. It was the institutional features of the system that made wealth and the wealthy look bad. Because of this the cultural view of market exchange suffered. And so the warnings of Jesus directed to the rich and against riches are culturally tainted.[69] And besides, "Jesus' severe teachings" about the renunciation of possessions are directed at "those who have gained wealth through some form of exploitative redistribution."[70] Only remedial justice was in play. And so Noell's cultural containment downplays the applicability, for us, of Jesus' teaching on wealth. It must be toned down,

---

65. Noell, "A 'Marketless World?'" 85, 106–7, 89.

66. Ibid., 87, 107.

67. Ibid., 85, 87, 101–2.

68. Ibid., 92, 100. Noell here accepts as helpful the position of Bruce Malina (Malina, "Wealth and Poverty in the New Testament and Its World," 355).

69. Noell, "A 'Marketless World?'" 85–87, 90, 100–102.

70. Ibid., 104.

and the textually communicated onus upon the rich constrained and reduced.

But there are counter-indications to account for. The most significant of which is that the Gospels do not present a consistent picture of the wealthy as unanimously under God's condemnation, as needfully evil, and as all being wickedly avaricious. Perhaps the most conspicuous example of this is to be found in the disciples' and Jesus' interaction regarding the rich young ruler. The disciples, called largely from among the poorer majority, are "amazed" (Mark 10:24) that it is hard for the "wealthy to enter the kingdom of God" (v. 23), and then are "even more astonished" (v. 26) to learn that it is humanly impossible (vv. 25, 27). They do not exclaim: "It figures!" But rather: "Then who can be saved?" (Matt 19:25 // Mark 10:26 // Luke 18:26). For they, despite the suggested reconstruction, retained an OT view of wealth as something that God generally orchestrates as a manifestation of His favor. The disciples, like Jesus who "felt a love for him" (Mark 10:21), had a good view of the rich young ruler—the parasitic estate owner! And Jesus' readiness to describe Himself and the Father as very rich elites, as rulers, and as wealthy estate owners is just as troubling for Noell's reconstruction as it is for that of Hanson and Oakman. For surely God is not avaricious and wholly contemptible. Furthermore, it is not at all easy to confine Jesus' call unto renunciation to the unjustly enriched for, as we shall see, He required this of all His immediate disciples.[71] As the rich are not revealed to be widely despised and culturally construed as parasitic and avaricious by Jesus and His audience, the toning down of His warnings and mandates should be foregone. The impetus is not deemphasized or deprecated. The onus is not contained.

So what can we make of all this? That the various possible cultural containment implications arising out of our socioeconomic reconstructions are not well defendable. That it is indeed one thing to notice cultural or socioeconomic differences, and quite another to *know* that they taint the divine mandates. Cultural placement does not entail cultural syncretism. And so with little reason to consider our obligations to the poor deprecated or inapplicably tainted we can gainfully work with the lowest rung of hermeneutical appropriation. Thus cultural tainting, by

---

71. There is also the associated issue, noted earlier, of Jesus' call—even upon the rich (as in the parable of Lazarus)—to aid those who are not poor due to the system but as a matter of disability.

and large, shuffles into the background within the present hermeneutical challenge.

DATA POST-PROCESSING

Once the hermeneutical methodology has been applied to locate and spotlight all of the biblical data concerning our ethical obligations to the poor, another form of filtering may be applied. This filtering option is present within the concept formation process. The proper manner of data integration is significantly contested, with many thinkers pursuing their own uniquely individualized approach. Due to the assumptional nature of this interpretive step, the approaches employed are not always consciously self-reflexive. Thus the continuum between data overriding integration and non-overriding integration contains an innumerable contingent of data post-processing strategies. Despite this tremendous diversity, two general aims may be discerned. Approaches that aim to produce a "non-destructive" integration can be differentiated from those which are prepared to adopt a "divide and conquer" approach. Adopting a guiding motif, or set of motifs, to integrate the data is one such overriding and data filtering approach. Indeed, at the heart of the issue in the process of data structuring is the possibility of data suppression.

What are we to make of this gantlet? Allowing for data suppression invariably leads to greater indeterminism. Richard Hays formulates his guiding themes (community, cross, new creation) to provide controls to the unbounded nature of his metaphor-making mode of appropriation—a mode which allows for a metaphorical leap while never clarifying which aspects of the data can successfully make the jump.[72] Hays further admits that other theme sets are also possible and that there exists, on his view, no real way to arbitrate between them. His focal images are "not derived in some strictly scientific or objective manner."[73] Consequently, it is difficult to see how his data post-processing approach escapes its indeterministic tendencies. In this way Hays's approach is like other concept formation strategies that construct a discriminating data hierarchy—whether it be on the basis of the frequency of textual occurrence, a biblical author's overarching themes, or some suchlike pattern.

---

72. R. Hays, *The Moral Vision of the New Testament*, 298–304.
73. Ibid., 198.

For our project, in concert with a purposed desire to avoid data loss, a "non-destructive" integration will be sought. One aspect of avoiding overriding within the process of integration is to allow specific mandates to funnel their content to the general mandates—and not the other way around. Perhaps an example may prove helpful. The general biblical mandate to love, when kept nebulous and not informed by the content of specific love mandates, becomes malleable and prone to situationalism.[74] If this conception is then allowed to migrate its presumed content down to the specific mandate level it can override the meaning of any concrete prescription. Any concrete biblical mandate involving consequences, such as "if anyone is not willing to work, then he is not to eat, either" (2 Thess 3:10), can be overridden by a top-down concept of love or mercy. Only a bottom-up—the specific informing the general—approach to concept formation avoids such overriding. With deep apologies to Kierkegaard: specific informing general is the way to heaven, general overriding specific is the way to hell.[75] Maintaining this concrete to broad direction within concept formation may be referred to as applying the "resolution principle."

> *The Resolution Principle*—the higher resolution (in the detail sense) mandate informs the lower resolution mandate provided the two mandates are parallel in the sense that integrating the high resolution data does not contradict aspects already present within the lower resolution mandate.

As with the seeking of a textual level *discrimen*, the resolution principle is bound to ruffle some feathers. Some biblical theologians may protest about basic trans-human author irreconcilability. Some may wish to contain the resolution principle to the bounds of biblical books or authors. They may want to integrate at this level before moving beyond it (to the whole NT). But we are ultimately interested in the grand composite—whether it is drawn by broader (aggregated) book strokes or by the smaller (non-aggregated) ones. Since the proposed integration is non-destructive, whether initially pursued at the book level or beyond, the final composite should not vary. We are simply skipping the

---

74. It may even become as utilitarian as Joseph Fletcher's conception (Fletcher, *Situation Ethics*, 95–97, 115, 119).

75. In this sense, it is not very hermeneutically felicitous to contend that "Rules serve principles, not the other way around" (Stassen and Gushee, *Kingdom Ethics*, 103).

presentation of the intermediate step. Applying the resolution principle to the whole NT entails that we will lose the aggregate stroke summary.[76] That we will not slow down to fully take in some of the unique emphases and their nuanced fit within a particular author's presentation. Scholarly commentaries fill this important need. To avoid overriding, all mandates are deemed important, not just those which receive significant cumulative focus from a particular author. All we are assuming is that the Bible does not contradict itself in the progressive sense (thus allowing for some deprecation) and that God intends to communicate a cohesive worldview and way of life as opposed to disparate, contradictory versions of the same. That systematic theology is possible. That a NT theology is not out of bounds. While this cannot be proven without recourse to assumptions, the counterargument cannot be well proven either. The impossibility of integration is a procedural and methodologically-dependent claim. Textual resistance is, to some extent, a methodological function. Both stances are ultimately assumptions about divine communication. Still, all this does not mean that individual passages should not be heard with all the force of their authorial context.

RESOLUTION PRINCIPLE CONSIDERATIONS

The resolution principle allots content priority to higher resolution mandate data—data which is more specific and detailed. Nevertheless, this finer grained data is only integrateable with lower resolution data if such integration does not entail data contradictions. In other words, legitimate integration requires that the lower resolution data conceptually overlap the higher resolution data. This insures that no data is lost and that differing concepts are kept separate.

The aspects that must be kept from contradicting in pursuing concept integration via the resolution principle are such things as the obligation level of the mandate, the main cause of the poverty, the obligator set, and the recipient set.[77] Non-contradicting overlaps are welcome and expected.

---

76. For those seeking the intermediate step, the Appendix lists all of the relevant NT texts by book—and so should provide some aid to those who wish to reconstruct the aggregate step.

77. These latter aspects, the main cause of the poverty, the obligator set, and the recipient set, will be discussed at the beginning of chapter 5.

The resolution principle is compatible with the recommended approach of pursuing parallel mandate *clarification* first at the textual immediacy level, then the biblical book level, then possibly at the author level, and finally at the NT level. This procedure allows for authorially related material to maintain its elucidating priority within the mandate clarification process.

MAIN RESOLUTION LEVELS

The degree of specificity or resolution that is provided by the biblical data varies from text to text. Sometimes quite significantly. The main levels of resolution, as they pertain to the interhuman treatment of the poor, may be helpfully labeled as either entailing "moral impetus," "general," "principle," "concrete," or "specific" resolution levels. These resolution levels are differentiated by their degree of specificity and by their degree of focus. By specificity, these levels are divided into those which entail broad ethical impetuses (such as "be merciful" in Luke 6:36), principles (such as "be on your guard against every form of greed" in Luke 12:15), and specifics (such as "sell all you possess and give to the poor" in Mark 10:21). By focus, these levels are divided into those which address interhuman treatment generally and those which address interhuman treatment as it pertains to the poor in particular. Figure 3 presents these main resolution levels along with their respective abbreviations (which will be employed in chapter 5).

		Focus	
		Universal Treatments	Treatments of the Poor
Specificity	Impetus	I = Moral Impetus	–
	Principle	G = General	P = Principle
	Specific	C = Concrete	S = Specific

FIGURE 3: Main Resolution Levels

So the "general" resolution level encompasses prescriptions possessing a principle level of specificity though they are aimed universally at humankind in general. Similarly, the "concrete" resolution level encompasses prescriptions possessing a specific level of specificity while being aimed, in a non-focused manner, at humankind in general. Moral impetuses possess no poor focused equivalent for, by their very nature, they are needfully broadly reaching. Abbreviations further down the alphabet are reserved for mandates which expressly focus on regulating interhuman treatments of the poor.

In concert with the resolution principle, the ordering of these resolution levels in terms of decreasing resolution, is as follows: "specific," "concrete," "principle," "general," and finally, "moral impetus."

NECESSARY CHARACTERISTICS OF A TEXTUAL RESOLUTION

As part 1 comes to a close, our considerations of our variously conditioned particularities permit us to be more specific about the kind of solution that we require. If greater agreement is dependent upon the identification of a textual level *discrimen*, the necessary characteristics of any successful set of differentiation criteria deserve to be identified. On the basis of our considerations, the following five characteristics constitute the minimum requirements for a textual level resolution.

Firstly, the textual *discrimen* should be heuristic in the sense that it utilizes a general formulation derived from, and dependent upon, an observed set of textual patterns—analogously to how current antivirus software finds yet unknown viruses by the suggestive characteristics that betray their identity. This requirement aims to insure that the differentiation possesses a textual level foundation.

Secondly, the *discrimen* must adequately function within all biblical genres and speech act categories such as Finegan and Besnier's directives (imperatives and spurrings), verdictives (assessments), representatives (descriptions), commissives (promises and threats), declarations (blessings and curses), and expressives (attitude expressions).[78] This condition allows for the possibility of ultimately discerning a "whole-Bible theology" and aims to avoid a methodological filtering of the biblical data.[79]

---

78. Finegan and Besnier, *Language*, 329.

79. Elmer Martens is among the biblical theologians who advocate the supercession of exclusively NT or OT theologies with an approach akin to the "unitary canonical

Thirdly, the heuristic needs to incorporate a text-level filter for identifying what may be called "discriminate" mandates—those that are not intended to apply widely beyond their immediate recipient set. This aspect allows for the isolation of localized prescriptions which are textually revealed to not pertain to others within the same obligator category. This constraint identifies contextual, rather than cultural, containment.

Fourthly, the results of the differentiation must synchronize with the semantic labeling present within the explicit data texts and remain consistent across the data so as not to generate contradictions. Logically, fidelity to the explicit passages is indispensable for any methodology which intends to further their conceptual reach. And consistency is a requirement for any proposal which aims to decrease indeterminism.

The fifth and final requirement is that the *discrimen* be identifiable in a large amount of mandate texts. While identifiability in anything beyond the explicit data is a step in the right direction, the broader the textual reach of the hermeneutical proposal, the better.

A SUMMARY

The aim of part 1 was to outline the pre-hermeneutical and hermeneutical disagreements that make seeking and approximating the domain of biblical justice and mercy difficult and contentious—even when sought from within a hermeneutic of trust. Our pre-hermeneutical particularity, save our conception of poverty, fashions the required *discrimen*. Some of our hermeneutical divergences, such as our variance over the continued applicability of OT mandates, prove to be moot for the present concern. The hermeneutical navigation of the human/divine disjunction was also deemed to be inconsequential, but not in a logically *a priori* manner. This hermeneutical contention is ultimately immaterial only because adding a consideration of divine action and modeling does not expand the content of the data set presented in the NT. In the case of divergences over the proper modes of appropriation and data post-processing, the author has argued that avoiding greater indeterminism requires adopting the approach that leads to the least data loss and, consequently, best maintains the breadth of the biblical voice. Our possible divergences over cultural containment are of a similar feather—though a lack of

---

biblical theology" of Paul House (Martens, "Old Testament Theology since Walter C. Kaiser, Jr.," 688–90; P. House, "Biblical Theology and the Wholeness of Scripture," 267–79). See also Hafemann and House, *Central Themes in Biblical Theology*.

textual evidence relegates the suggested taintings to the hermeneutical back burner.

Thus, in sum, the intent of part 1 was to briefly concretize the necessity of the methodology to be proposed and to begin to establish its hermeneutical parameters.

PART TWO

Lowering the White Flag
A Hermeneutical Methodology

FOUR

The Hermeneutics of Demarcating Biblical Justice

WITH OUR PARTICULARITIES UNCOMFORTABLY visible, we have reached the hermeneutical moment on which everything hangs. We are reaching for the fulcrum of Justitia's scales—the interpretive pinnacle from which we are ever tempted to fall. Blindfolded and confident of her conception, she has averted her gaze from such things—but we must do all we can to keep our eyes wide open. For we are seeking an experience out of the body of our particularity.

Our focused hermeneutical approach will incorporate two aspects: the delimitation of the relevant data set and the proposal of a textual level *discrimen*. So our first aim will be to delineate which texts are relevant for ascertaining our obligations unto the poor. Relevant texts will be identified as those which contain interhuman mandates concerning the treatment of the poor.[1]

Our second goal is to present the proposed textual *discrimen*. The latter half of this chapter will delineate this alternative, heuristic approach to identifying the differing obligation structures of biblical justice and mercy at the textual level. The procedure is heuristic in the sense that it utilizes a general formulation derived from and dependent upon a set of textual patterns. The proposed hermeneutical approach uses the communicated sinfulness of transgressing certain biblical prescriptions as the textual differentiation criteria. The ultimate aim of this hermeneutical approach is to identify a methodology which would allow those utilizing a hermeneutic of trust to asymptotically approximate the domain of biblical justice with greater consistency.

The proposed *discrimen* meets the set of necessary criteria identified earlier. Correspondingly, the *discrimen* is derived and articulated in

---

1. We will also let some "clarifier passages" tag along leechlike, but only to the extent that they clarify our true focus—the content of the mandates themselves.

such a way as to apply to the whole of Scripture—for it is designed to be broad enough to be applicable to the OT data as well.

MANDATES

Pursuing the domains of biblical justice and biblical mercy necessarily begets some initial considerations regarding the delimitation of the relevant biblical data set—where all should we be looking? This set consists of divinely evaluated interhuman treatments. Such biblical prescriptions come in the form of "mandates." Mandates are textual expressions of God's ethical evaluation: what He deems culpable and what He commends. As such, mandates subsume both justice and mercy. But they also subsume more than justice and mercy as each relates to human treatment one of another. Biblical mandates also address the "internal" willing and desiring of sin or righteousness. These prescriptions for the heart spill over into the classical, and contemporary, discussion of virtues.[2] As important as these internal mandates are, at the ethical claims level, it is those that address "external" interhuman treatment that are relevant for justice and mercy *between* people. And it is the content of this justice and mercy which is in question.

Speaking of the biblical text: how do external interhuman mandates give themselves away? The scanning criteria for mandates involves locating all divine "commands," "instructions," "valuations," and "implied valuations." When wedded to an exclusive focus upon treatments which affect the poor, these categories serve to delineate the biblical data set that is relevant for our pursuit of social justice and charity.

COMMANDS

Commands are grammatically revealed imperatives and appear in two forms within English translation. Expressions which inform the addressee that she "shall," "will," or "must" do or not do something are commands.[3] Deuteronomy 15:11 illustrates this command relation to

---

2. Some mandates may exist outside of the categories pursued here. Nonetheless, a thorough conceptualization is beyond the scope of the present concern. The categories mentioned are sufficient for our considerations concerning the moral treatment of the poor.

3. This categorization applies unless the "shall" or "will" refers to a consequence or an outcome rather than a command, such as in Exod 22:24: " . . . your wives shall become widows and your children fatherless." Said another way, future indicatives are pertinent only if they possess imperative overtones.

translated "shall" terminology: "For the poor will never cease to be in the land; therefore I command you, saying, 'You shall freely open your hand to your brother, to your needy and poor in your land.'" Translated imperative mood expressions, which do not possess the above "shall" terminology but merely assert what must or must not be done, are also commands. An example is Isa 1:17 which mandates: "Learn to do good; Seek justice, Reprove the ruthless, Defend the orphan, Plead for the widow." Thus imperative mood commands are recognizable to the interpreter as abbreviated forms of the "shall"-type translations.[4] Correspondingly, mentally appending the "you shall" onto a translated imperative mood command does not, in any way, vary its intent or meaning. If God commands that something be done it is logical to presume that He likewise approves of it being done and that God's command is therefore also His endorsement.[5]

Commands can also be helpfully divided into three general categories by their textual form. Like the apodictic laws they subsume, apodictic commands can be defined as those without an if/then case structure. Casuistic commands, like their casuistic law subset, include an if/then structuring and appear in two distinguishable forms. Casuistic commands subdivide into the sanctional ones which prescribe sanctions and the non-sanctional ones which do not. Leviticus 25:25 is an example of the latter: "If a fellow countryman of yours becomes so poor he has to sell part of his property, then his nearest kinsman is to come and buy back what his relative has sold."[6]

---

4. While much of this methodology is accessible to those without original language competency, when ambiguous wordings (which could reference a mandate) are perceived in the translation, the original language texts must be pursued for the purpose of additional clarification. Accordingly, clearer grammatical constructions such as jussives need to be identified in tandem with the more ambiguous constructions—such as future indicatives with possible imperative overtones.

5. Worthy of note is the evangelical affirmation that the entire Bible is a profitable revelation concerning the mind of God. Consequently, hermeneutical disassociations of God's direct "speech acts" from His indirect communication via the biblical writers need not complicate the heuristic, as all of God's bequeathed mandates will be regarded as relevant.

6. Admittedly this categorization scheme differs somewhat from the common appraisal, but it has the advantage of being more heuristically consistent—*pace* Klein et al., *Introduction to Biblical Interpretation*, 275–77 (where capital casuistic laws are considered apodictic).

INSTRUCTIONS

Instructions are information or guidelines concerning how to do something—such as how to concretely fulfill a command. Biblical probing reveals that instructions are often entwined with commands. One example is 1 Tim 5:3–16 where instructions are provided concerning how local churches are to take care of widows. Here the instructions themselves are commanded. Since this intertwining is quite common, the instruction category is revealed to be closely related to the command category.

VALUATIONS

Valuations are approvals or disapprovals of an action or a volitional inclination.[7] Valuations can be subdivided into those which express God's description or categorization of something, His affective response to something, and His treatment of something. This subdivision is heuristically helpful even though different valuation subcategories do sometimes overlap and intertwine within a given passage.

Descriptive Valuations

God's descriptive valuations are concerned with His moral descriptions and categorizations. What matters here is God's description or categorization of an interhuman treatment as either a sin or an act of righteousness. This requires detecting God's identification of something as sinful, evil, wicked, a transgression, requiring repentance, a deed of the flesh, worldly, not good (in the Prov 24:23 and 28:21 sense), an abomination, or a disobedience. By extension, detecting an act of righteousness, obedience, or good is also relevant. Texts which claim that sinners, the unrighteous, the wicked, and those who practice iniquity "do this," as well as passages which communicate a notion tantamount to "a righteous person does this," are also of relevance. An example is Prov 29:7 which reads: "The righteous is concerned for the rights [דִּין, *din*] of the poor, The wicked does not understand such concern."[8] The wisdom literature deserves special attention here. God's description of something as an

---

7. Nevertheless, only actions are relevant for interhuman ethics—in the sense that they alone are readily visible, possibly claimable, and sometimes even judicially remediable.

8. Arguably "judicial justice" is a better translation of דִּין (*din*) than "rights" in this passage. See, for example, Murphy, *Proverbs*, 221.

act of righteousness or sin is connected to the notions of wisdom and folly in the wisdom literature—particularly in the book of Proverbs.[9] Detecting acts of wisdom and what a wise person—in the non-worldly sense—"does," is highly applicable. Equally relevant are passages concerning acts of folly and what a fool—in the non-*naïve* sense—"does." The Hebrew terminology and context are helpful in distinguishing *naïveté* and sinful folly in the OT wisdom literature.[10] The term פֶּתִי (*pethi*) identifies a *naïve* fool, נָבָל (*nabal*) the unrighteous fool, while כְּסִיל (*kesil*), סָכָל (*sakal*), and אֱוִיל (*evil*) must be contextually distinguished.[11] Correspondingly, פֶּתִי (*pethi*) also signifies *naïve* folly, נְבָלָה (*nebalah*) unrighteousness folly, while the import of כֶּסֶל (*kesel*) or כְּסִילוּת (*kesiluth*), סֶכֶל (*sekel*) or שִׂכְלוּת/סִכְלוּת (*sikluth*), and אִוֶּלֶת (*ivveleth*) must needfully be determined by their context.[12] The moral weight of the NT terms for fool and foolish—ἄφρων (*aphrōn*), μωρός (*mōros*), and ἀνόητος (*anoētos*)—along with their folly derivatives, must be determined from their context.

Affective Valuations

God's affective response to interhuman treatments reveals what God loves and hates. If God discloses that He loves, desires, is pleased by, or delights in something then such treatments possess His approval. Conversely, when God reveals that He hates, loathes, or is displeased by something then these very treatments possess His affective disapproval. An example of an affective valuation is "God loves a cheerful giver"—which, in its 2 Cor 9:7 context, is combined with the command to give only as one has "purposed in his heart" and "not grudgingly."

---

9. Schultz, "Fool, Foolishness, Folly," *EDBT* 264–65; Lasor et al., *Old Testament Survey*, 461–62; Plantinga, "The Sinner and the Fool," 24–29.

10. A helpful resource, in this regard, is Donald, "Semantic Field of 'Folly' in Proverbs, Job, Psalms, and Ecclesiastes," 285–92.

11. For additional information regarding נָבָל (*nabal*), see Kraus, "The Sin of Folly," 289–300. See also Schultz, "Fool, Foolishness, Folly," *EDBT* 264–65; Donald, "Semantic Field of 'Folly' in Proverbs, Job, Psalms, and Ecclesiastes," 289–92.

12. Additional lexical background on these terms is also efficiently accessible via "Folly, Fool, Madness, Shameless," *NIDOTTE* 5:83–84.

Treatment Valuations

God's treatment of interhuman actions ties into His role as Creator, Sustainer, and Judge. Thus passages which identify what God will judge or punish, as well as what He repays positively, are relevant. Actions which God considers worthy of curse or blessing as well as those which He warns consequences over are likewise pertinent. Consequences come in two forms: "direct" ones that God applies personally and "indirect" ones that God has built into His moral order. The book of Proverbs is full of warnings concerning "indirect" consequences. Exodus 22:22–24 is an example of a command coupled with a treatment valuation: "You shall not afflict any widow or orphan. If you afflict him at all, and if he does cry out to Me, I will surely hear his cry; and My anger will be kindled, and I will kill you with the sword, and your wives shall become widows and your children fatherless." God's promises of reward for various interhuman treatments likewise constitute a part of His treatment valuations.

IMPLIED VALUATIONS

Implied valuations are implied approvals or disapprovals of an action or a volitional inclination.[13] Some passages presume God's disapproval or approval of something in such a way as to imply that this presumption is indeed accurate and not simply human wish-fulfillment. Implied valuations are present whenever legitimate accusations of others or legitimate personal defense is laid out before God. In these cases God is also often requested to take action as His concurrence on the issue is assumed. An example is Job's statement of defense in Job 29:11–12 where he claims that "... when the ear heard, it called me blessed, And when the eye saw, it gave witness of me, Because I delivered the poor who cried for help, And the orphan who had no helper." An expectation of fault or blessing for something before God similarly indicates God's implied valuation in texts that reveal that this expectation is indeed divinely affirmed (such as in, for example, Job 31:16–22). Implied valuations require very careful heuristic investigation as many of the indictments and defenses recorded in the Scriptures do not clearly bear God's affirmation. By way of additional clarification, this requirement entails that the generalizing

---

13. Here again, as opposed to unactualized inclinations, it is actions alone that are relevant for interhuman ethical claims.

implications of genre or the implied approval of positive narrative (as instanced in Acts 2:43–47) does not constitute an implied valuation—as it is here defined.[14]

Summarized another way, biblical mandates are present throughout the range of speech act theory categories advocated by Finegan and Besnier.[15] Not only are directives (imperatives and spurrings) and verdictives (assessments) capable of containing mandate speech acts, but likewise representatives (descriptions), commissives (promises and threats), declarations (blessings and curses), and expressives (attitude expressions).

HAMARTIOLOGICAL DISCRIMEN

Detecting mandates is not enough. What are the heuristic indicators of the sinfulness of a mandate's transgression? The domain of sin is broad. Sin also incorporates an inherent condition, an inner force, a controlling resonance, and a noetic blindness.[16] External interhuman justice is more concerned with "sins" than "sin."

Perhaps some brief thoughts on the generation of a biblical relation between justice and sin are relevant here. The term "justice" is often used to reference judicial justice in the Bible. Judicial justice is concerned with rectifying transgressions to mandates the non-transgression of which is, by implication, just. Similarly, "overlapping" apodictic laws are related to their parallel sanctional casuistic laws in that they proscribe actions that the sanctional casuistic laws identify rectifying sanctions for. In this way the apodictic laws participate in the justice status of their mirrored sanctional casuistic laws. Some apodictic and casuistic laws (for example Deut 24:14–15 and Deut 19:11–15 respectively) explicitly identify the justice mandate transgression as sin. By contrast, passages referencing "mercy" and its synonyms never denote transgressing the described mercies as sin.[17] Neither are any of sin's textual indicators, as further

---

14. *Contra* Richard Burridge who argues that the bibliographic genre of the Gospels entails that every act of Jesus is a mandate via implied valuation (*Imitating Jesus*, 23–31).

15. Finegan and Besnier, *Language*, 329.

16. For additional discussion concerning these common Reformation emphases, see, for example, Erickson, *Christian Theology*, 582.

17. Mercy's synonyms include, at minimum, treatments labeled as sympathy, compassion, a gift, or kind favor (χάρις, *charis*—excluding its alternate usages such as the reward sense in Luke 6:32–34 and 1 Pet 2:19–20).

developed in the following pages, present in such passages. Extensive biblical investigation allows for extrapolation based upon a consistent pattern. The unwavering pattern of explicit mercy mandates never being related to sin and explicit justice mandates being so related permits sin to become the distinguishing trait between justice and mercy.

As a result, contexts which identify the transgression of a particular mandate as wickedness, evil, iniquity, wrongdoing, an abomination, being counted amongst the transgressors, fleshly, or sin disclose the justice obligation level of the mandate. If a particular treatment justifies its recipient to cry out unto God against the perpetrating party then such treatment is likewise a transgression of justice (such as in Deut 15:9 and 24:15). Treatments entailing a textually legitimatized expectation of guilt before God are similarly matters of justice.[18]

Interestingly, this relation between justice and sin is correctly sensed in liberation theology and the social gospel. There is also a logical relation. Believers are obligated to always refrain from sin—or, in the case of a possible moral conflict, from the greater sin. Our obligation in this regard is an unwavering and comprehensively binding constraint. It functions just like justice does.

Pursuing another angle, Nicholas Wolterstorff proposes that forgiveness, when it is deemed an appropriate response to a particular transgression, helps us to perceive that people possess subjective rights—rights which attach to their subject.[19] Wolterstorff's appraisal of biblical forgiveness language is ripe for hermeneutical extrapolation. Interhuman forgiveness, when it is a biblically appropriate response, reveals that interhuman sin has occurred. And so treatments which are textually related to biblically sanctioned forgiveness—as inciters—are thus also revealed to be matters of justice rather than mercy.

DISCRIMINATE AND INDISCRIMINATE MANDATES

Biblical mandates address people discriminately and as they participate in three general obligator categories: individuals, the church, and rul-

---

18. It may be helpful at this point to briefly affirm that not all instances of injustice possess equal weight. Some transgression instances, while nevertheless unjust, are not claim-worthy because they entail very limited effects and so possess limited significance in this world.

19. Wolterstorff, *Justice*, 93–94, 105–7, 129–30; Wolterstorff, "How Social Justice Got to Me and Why It Never Left," 672.

ers.[20] Discriminately applied mandates subsume God's "personal" directives to particular persons. Personal mandates do not apply to everyone and therefore are not part of interhuman justice. Thus, failing to lead the Israelites out of their slavery in Egypt would not be a sin for Jethro since God did not call him to do it. But Moses, unlike everyone else, is constrained by God's personal mandate to obey or sin. All mandates that appear solely in the discriminate and lack explicit role dependence have no claim on indiscriminateness—indeed, the reader makes this distinction quite naturally in most instances.[21]

These qualifications permit us to heuristically identify a justice mandate as one whose transgression is semantically or contextually identified as sinful for everyone within the intended obligator category. Such mandates are universal and indiscriminate in their application within their obligator category. Reciprocally, any omissions which are semantically identified as not entailing sin for those in the intended obligator category betray mercy mandates.

A few more considerations regarding discriminate mandates are in order. When a mandate is given in such a way that it is not applied to peers in the same obligator category, it is given as a discriminate mandate (even though it may be broader than a "personal" mandate). Similarly, if a mandate's aim is to accomplish a specific time-bound, localized purpose such a mandate is likewise discriminate because of its "localized" nature. These localized discriminates are identified by being intentionally aimed at an obligator subset while entailing an intent which expires when the mandate is fulfilled. Nevertheless, some of the mandates that are given to an obligator subset are not ultimately discriminate because an indiscriminate mandate overlaps with their localized intent at the same resolution level. This latter requirement of the same content resolution level is crucial because only such overlap—rather than a gen-

---

20. Rulers would include political, government, and judicial leaders as well as others in positions of societal responsibility. In contemporary democratic societies, citizens can affect, to some degree, the leadership of the societal rulers. As a result, this obligator category is closest to modern notions of societal responsibility.

21. The troublesome instances involve discriminate mandates that conceptually overlap with indiscriminate ones and hence appear to imply obligation via their parasitical importing of the indiscriminate mandate's obligation status. Were they solitary, such discriminate mandates would have nothing to import. Conversely, mandates possessing explicit role dependence, such as those given to Timothy on the basis of his ministry, apply indiscriminately to those possessing the same role by virtue of the explicit association.

eral moral impetus overlap—assures that the mandate is indiscriminate. Thus Jesus' command in Matt 17:27 regarding how to pay for the annual Jerusalem temple upkeep tax does not entail that when believers need to pay some tax—something mandated for us at lower resolution in Rom 13:7—that they ought to go fishing.[22] Yet all the while we readily recognize in Paul's urging of Euodia and Syntyche "to live in harmony" (τὸ αὐτὸ φρονεῖν, Phil 4:2) the indiscriminate imperative for all believers to be "of the same mind" (τὸ αὐτὸ φρονῆτε, Phil 2:2). And it is precisely this parasitic overlap with an indiscriminate mandate (at the same level of resolution) that endows such apparently discriminate mandates with broader pertinence. As such, these discriminate mandates do not extend the domain of indiscriminate obligation though they sometimes, by way of parasitic overlap, participate in it.

Some localized mandates are very straightforward to identify as their range of applicability is completely exhausted—they cannot be presently applied. The Bible incorporates many such mandates as given by the apostles, the prophets, Jesus, and even the Father. Such mandates are often reflexive and so constrained to the presence of their mandator. They may also be tied to something which no longer exists. Thus, Jesus' command, "Bring Me a denarius to look at" in Mark 12:15 cannot be obeyed because Jesus is no longer physically present. Similar examples include Paul's command regarding the cloak and books (2 Tim 4:13), Elijah's mandate to the widow of Zarephath to "give me your son" (1 Kgs 17:19), and God's instructions concerning the capturing of Jericho (Joshua 6).

HAMARTIOLOGICAL COROLLARIES

Two important corollaries increase the differentiation range of the sin heuristic—these concern divine punishment and divine reward. Sin incites a particular response from God. God cannot reward, in the positive-connotation sense, sin. Rather, He judges and punishes it (as seen in texts such as Rom 2:6–8). Consequently, any interhuman treatment which God punishes or prescribes human punishment for is an instance

---

22. Jesus' mandates concerning the forsaking of one's possessions for the benefit of the poor, as we shall see in the next chapter, are another example of prescriptions which extend to but an obligator subset and are never more broadly exserted at equivalent resolution—despite ample NT calls to give alms to the poor and to heed the moral impetus of showing mercy.

of justice. This first corollary envelops sanctional casuistic commands as well as transgressions which receive warnings of curses, punishment, or direct negative consequences (which are intended as punishment). Correspondingly, texts which explicitly reveal that a particular transgression does not receive punishment are promulgating mercy mandates.

By way of clarification, a few passages, such as Matt 25:31–46, require careful contextual and perhaps even systematic evaluation. Upon first glance, eternal punishment in this parable of the sheep and the goats appears to be connected to transgressing mandates which are elsewhere referred to as instances of mercy. The parable of the good Samaritan reveals that providing food, drink, clothing, and shelter in order to care for a sick stranger (as implied in Luke 10:30, 34, 35) are mercy treatments (Luke 10:37). While not much biblical data is extant on the obligation level of visiting prisoners so as to assist them, Heb 10:34 connects it to "sympathy" and Phil 4:17–18 refers to such assistance as a "gift" to Paul during his imprisonment.[23] Such terminology intimates that a mercy obligation is in view.

But commentators are divided. Donald Hagner affirms that Matt 25:31–46 is concerned—for both the righteous and the unrighteous—solely with charitable deeds of mercy.[24] Rudolf Schnackenburg, the well respected German Catholic scholar, maintains the same exclusive emphasis on the "call of mercy" unto "merciful love."[25] Whether carried out or omitted, the treatments described are matters of mercy.[26] Such interpretations understand the treatments concerned to be external indicators (and counter-indicators) of one's participation in the kingdom.

John Calvin straddles the fence. For most of his commentary on Matt 25:31–46 he refers to the treatments as kindness, good works of mercy, and exercises of charity for which reward is promised.[27] Yet near the end of his comments he speaks of the "wicked indifference" with which the reprobate despise the poor.[28] Calvin does contend that this is

---

23. Paul's imprisonment is generally acknowledged. See, for example, Silva, *Philippians*, 1.
24. Hagner, *Matthew*, 744–47.
25. Schnackenburg, *The Gospel of Matthew*, 258, 259.
26. Ibid., 257–58.
27. Calvin, *Commentary on a Harmony of the Evangelists*, 3:176, 178–80.
28. Ibid., 3:182, 183.

principally an issue of their "pride towards the poor."²⁹ The temptation to consider this extrapolation concerning punishable despising as pastoral or homiletical license on Calvin's part is great but, for many, resistible.

D. A. Carson, Leon Morris, David Turner, and Michael Wilkins are among those who assert that not accomplishing such treatments constitutes committing sins of omission.³⁰ Turner nonetheless refers to these treatments as "merciful ministry."³¹ Wilkins, for his part, agrees that these treatments are also "external behavioral evidences" of "association with the kingdom of God" but nevertheless sees their omission as sin.³² Craig Blomberg is more difficult to place. For while arguing that the goats are "condemned for sins of omission as well as commission," he nevertheless appears to constrain the sins of omission to an "improper response to Christian witnesses."³³

How are we to evaluate such a wide range of disagreement? The first thing to note is that, beyond the employed contrast of the blessed ones (v. 34) with the accursed ones (from καταράομαι, *kataraomai*, v. 41), no sin terminology is present. Few Protestants would argue that the sheep are blessed on account of their works, and thus the accursed need not necessarily be so on account of their lack of good works. All of the foregoing evangelical commentators agree that these works do not earn the inheritance (v. 34). So any categorization of the omission of these treatments as a matter of sin is a matter of assumption. The purposeful parallelism of the passage tips the scales in favor of claiming that, in Matt 25:31–46, salvation or damnation is not a function of the good

---

29. Ibid., 3:183.

30. Carson, *Matthew*, 521–22; Morris, *The Gospel According to Matthew*, 641; Turner, *Matthew*, 329; Wilkins, *Matthew*, 812.

31. Turner, *Matthew*, 329, 330. William Davies and Dale Allison are of the same mind in referring to abstaining from such treatments as committing sins of omission while nevertheless identifying them as "works of mercy" (Davies and Allison, *Matthew*, 3:431).

32. Wilkins, *Matthew*, 810, 812.

33. Blomberg, *Matthew*, 379. This same constraint appears in Blomberg's summary where he asserts that "ultimately there will only be two kinds of people in the world. These will be distinguished on the basis of their response to the gospel and its emissaries" (ibid.). Blomberg is among those who adopt a "receiving messengers" interpretation of this parable as opposed to the "believers serving believers" reading. And so the sin may be tied up to the lack of a positive response rather than to the concrete manifestations of this missing response. The sources and implications of this interpretation will be addressed in chapter 5.

deeds described. Rather, this passage should be understood as Jesus' annunciation of yet another distinguishing feature between the righteous and the unrighteous—functioning akin to preparedness for His coming and the faithful use of talents in the previous parables of Matthew 25. Thus, via the parallelism, the condemned are considered damned on the basis of both a lack of faith and its accompanying works—entailing that the works are not necessarily matters of justice. The fit of this interpretation with other parallel treatment texts—which identify the considered treatments as matters of mercy—also speaks in its favor. As does the occurrence of the term διακονέω (*diakoneō*, v. 44), which indicates service and ministry, as a semantic descriptor of these treatments.[34]

Some mercy mandates also require special attention in that they are recursive. Their transgression results in a corresponding loss of a significant mercy benefit. If believers fail to forgive or refuse a particular mercy while expecting a similar forgiveness or mercy from God, they act hypocritically and God opts not to show them a transposed degree of mercy (Luke 6:37; Jas 2:13) or to forgive them (Matt 6:15; 18:35). Nonetheless, these special recursive mandates remain instances of mercy—for they are labeled as such—but with a particularly elevated obligation level. The transgression of such mercy mandates, though it entails very significant consequences, is not referred to as a sin—for such transgression only functions to hinder or prevent the application of divine forgiveness and mercy to the transgressor's *bona fide* sins.[35]

The second corollary which increases the precision of the hamartiological *discrimen* concerns the textual intimation of rewards. A scriptural pattern emerges with respect to God not specifically rewarding the avoidance of sin. Thus failing to murder, steal, or bear false witness

---

34. These issues will receive some further attention as the passage resurfaces in the following chapter.

35. The consequences of blocking ourselves from receiving God's merciful forgiveness may indeed be dire. The parable of the unforgiving servant in Matt 18:25–35, in echoing Matt 6:15, confirms that refusing to show mercy (ἐλεέω, *eleeō*, v. 33), so as to forgive, has apparent eschatological consequences (Hagner, *Matthew*, 540; Turner, *The Gospel of Matthew*, 243; L. Williams, *St. Matthew*, 2:216). The unforgiving slave is now called πονηρός (*ponēros*, wicked, evil, toilsome) and his accumulated debt is reinstated. This terminology of wickedness would normally imply a justice level of obligation, but in this passage, which is an exception, it is explicitly allotted on the basis of failing to show recursive merciful forgiveness (which is generally agreed to be a matter of mercy obligation). Jesus is affirming that forgiving the sins of a "brother" done against us (v. 21) is a form of clemency which is nevertheless required of the forgiven.

does not entail specific divine reward. Consequently, any interhuman treatment which God specifically rewards is apparently an instance of mercy. This differentiation does not include rewards, such as those of Deuteronomy 28, which are generated by a broad or general set of obediences.[36] In other words, the general eudaemonistic consequences of walking in obedience before God are extraneous here.[37] The relevant rewards are produced by a specific obedience, the transgression of which entails no corresponding curses. Thus as far as reward goes, in Kantian terms, biblical ethics is heteronomous while biblical justice, beyond general eudaemonia, is not.

AN OBJECTION CONSIDERED

One objection remains. Several biblical texts appear to blur the boundary line between sin and non-sin. Whereas some biblical mandates are semantically branded as mercy concerns within Scripture, the following two passages would initially seem to reclaim even this domain for justice (as per the proposed heuristic). James 4:17 asserts, "Therefore, to one who knows the right thing to do and does not do it, to him it is sin." The "right thing" or "good" (καλός, *kalos*) referred to within this verse likely pertains to the avoidance of committing the particular arrogance that is decried within the immediately preceding verses (Jas 4:13–16). The "right thing" may also extend to not speaking against "one another" among the brethren (Jas 4:11) or even further to not submitting to worldliness (Jas 4:4). Arrogance, speaking against one's brother, and worldliness are themselves branded as sins in other passages.

A focalized and contextual interpretation would perceive James to be saying, "Now that I've taught you what is right, not doing what you now know to be right would be a sin." Corroboratively, the "therefore" at the beginning of Jas 4:17 appears to connect this verse to the previously

---

36. The general eudaemonism of Deuteronomy 28 is attributed to the broad obedience of God's commands: "Now it shall be, if you diligently obey the LORD your God, being careful to do all His commandments which I command you today . . . All these blessings will come upon you and overtake you if you obey the LORD your God" (Deut 28:1–2). The curses for disobedience entail similar breadth: "But it shall come about, if you do not obey the LORD your God, to observe to do all His commandments and His statutes with which I charge you today, that all these curses will come upon you and overtake you" (Deut 28:15).

37. For additional discussion see Kaiser, *Toward Old Testament Ethics*, 301–4.

outlined sins of James 4 and, in particular, to arrogance concerning future endeavors.

A more individually "principlizing" and subjective interpretation would endeavor to perceive a general principle within this verse. James would be understood to be saying, "If you realize that something is good, choosing not to do it is a sin." If the "something" within the previous paraphrase were a treatment extraneous to the biblical justice mandates, then this text would concern "personal" sins—something which is not sinful for everyone. Consequently, such discriminate, "personal" sin realizations remain outside the domain of interhuman justice—as do all similarly indiscriminate discriminates.

The second passage is Rom 14:23: "But he who doubts is condemned if he eats, because his eating is not from faith; and whatever is not from faith is sin." Here the question revolves around how broadly the term "whatever" or "everything" ($\pi\tilde{\alpha}\nu \ldots \delta$) extends. The same contextual and subjective interpretive options are extant here as in Jas 4:17. If $\pi\tilde{\alpha}\nu \ldots \delta$ is limited to the issues Paul is discussing, such as the eating of meat or the drinking of wine, then the verse states that the weaker believer should do what she believes God wants her to do in these instances.[38] Failing to obey what one is "fully convinced" of (Rom 14:5) with respect to these issues would be sinful for one obeys it "for the Lord" (Rom 14:6).[39]

The subjective interpretation would go beyond the context in emphasizing the general principle that the "violation of the dictates of conscience, even when the conscience does not conform perfectly to God's will, is sinful."[40] Even providing that this broader interpretation somehow proves preferable, its particular applications would once more prove non-universal, "personal," and discriminately perceived. As a result, Rom 14:23, like Jas 4:17, would be placed outside of our concern: the realm of interhuman justice.

---

38. Whereas the one who does not doubt must be careful not to "tear down the work of God for the sake of food"—for even though "all things indeed are clean" such tearing down is unjust (Rom 14:20).

39. Such an interpretation correlates well with Rom 14:14 where Paul clarifies that he knows and is "convinced in the Lord Jesus that nothing is unclean in itself; but to him who thinks anything to be unclean, to him it is unclean."

40. Moo, *The Epistle to the Romans*, 863–64.

METHODOLOGICAL SUMMARY

The hermeneutical methodology proposed in this chapter, and employed in the next, will be summarized below for the sake of methodological clarity. The textual *discrimen* serves to augment the semantic identification of justice and mercy at the textual level.[41]

JUSTICE MANDATES

The justice level obligation of a mandate is disclosed upon the occurrence of any of the following three textual indicators: the mandate's transgression is revealed to be a matter of sin, or as a matter which entails divine or divinely sanctioned punishment, or the mandate possesses the semantic labeling of justice.

Sin

A mandate's transgression is revealed to be a matter of sin in instances where it is textually labeled as sin (ἁμαρτία, *hamartia* and cognates), sinful, wicked, evil (κακός, *kakos*, πονηρός, *poneros*, and cognates), iniquity, wrongdoing, an abomination, wickedness, being counted amongst the transgressors, fleshly, and as what defiles. The mandate is likewise concerned with sin if its transgression is something which God hates or loathes. Similarly, any mandate which reveals that "sinners" or its synonyms—such as the wicked, the unrighteous, and those who practice iniquity—"do this," reveals the sin nature of its transgression. If some treatment justifies its recipient to cry out to God, such treatment is a sin. A textually legitimatized expectation of guilt before God is also a matter of sin. Transgressions which are causally connected to biblical forgiveness language likewise betray their sinfulness.

Punishment

Interhuman mandates which, when disobeyed, entail divine or divinely sanctioned punishment are also instances of justice. This subsumes all of the sanctional casuistic commands—the transgressions which remedial justice seeks to remedy. It also includes interhuman treatments which God curses or punishes and those treatments for which God pro-

---

41. For the sake of brevity and present utility, only NT semantical labeling will be noted.

vides warnings of direct negative consequences (which are intended as punishment).

Semantic Label

Mandates that are semantically labeled as being associated with the δίκη (dikē) word group come in two terminological shades—some terms need to be contextually disclosed as matters of justice while others are always so.[42] This semantic connection overlaps with the hamartiological because δίκη (dikē) itself is concerned with punishment and legal penalty. Justice or righteousness, δικαιοσύνη (dikaiosynē), takes its place among the heap of derivatives that must be contextually distinguished.[43] Whereas injustice, ἀδικία (adikia), a cognate of sin, though translated variously throughout the NT, acts as an exception and consistently refers, along with its immediate semantic relatives (ἀδικέω, adikeō, ἀδίκημα, adikēma, ἄδικος, adikos, ἀδίκως, adikōs), to the justice level of obligation.[44] As does κρίσις (krisis)—another common NT term for justice or judgment.

In the Introduction I mentioned that even the semantic identifications are contested. Nicholas Wolterstorff astutely observes that, in almost all English translations of the NT, δικαιοσύνη (dikaiosynē) is translated as "righteousness" much more frequently than as "justice."[45] While acknowledging that δικαιοσύνη (dikaiosynē) tends to be semantically flexible, Wolterstorff argues that this translation tendency has made it easier to miss the concern for justice in the NT.[46] Languages such as German and Slavic tongues such as Czech are like NT Greek in that they have only one practicable term available with which to translate δικαιοσύνη (dikaiosynē).[47] Consequently, "justice" receives more stage time. Such languages nonetheless possess an ability to discern the nu-

---

42. For additional information, see Falkenroth, "δίκη," NIDNTT 3:92; "δίκη," BDAG 250.
43. C. Brown and Seebass, "δικαιοσύνη," NIDNTT 3:352–71.
44. Ibid.; Günther, "ἀδικία," NIDNTT 3:573–76.
45. Wolterstorff, Justice, 110–13.
46. Ibid., 112.
47. Czech, for example, experiences this to a greater degree than does German. For while German has both Gerechtigkeit and Rechtschaffenheit available, only the former is able to subsume both justice and righteousness and so it has been almost exclusively employed in translation. English has lost this dual sense for the word justice.

ances and connotative meaning of their single term so as to perceive when it is being used in the righteousness sense.

Perhaps some additional background may be helpful. For the sake of argument, let us confine ourselves to German lexical aids (which in English translation also tend to prefer righteousness terminology within their discussions). In common Hellenistic usage, δίκαιος (*dikaios*, one who is just or righteous) "hovers between the two senses of 'faithful to the law' and 'virtuous.'"[48] The latter component includes fulfilling one's obligations toward the gods.[49] So in the LXX, the δίκαιος (*dikaios*) "fulfils his duties towards God and the theocratic society, meeting God's claim in this relationship."[50] This concept of right relationship distinguishes even the NT usage of δικαιοσύνη (*dikaiosynē*) "from Greek and Hellenistic ethics and links it firmly with the OT."[51] The ethical uprightness that is also in view falls under this relational obligation. So δικαιοσύνη (*dikaiosynē*) refers to the "right conduct of man which follows the will of God and is pleasing to Him," to "rectitude of life before God," and to "uprightness before His judgment."[52] Even here right relationship subsumes mere notions of interhuman justice—or even mere personal moral rectitude. Paul's distinctive usage of δικαιοσύνη (*dikaiosynē*), and particularly of δικαιοσύνη θεοῦ (the righteousness of God), has lately received a significant resurgence of interest. Though perhaps somewhat overstated, it is helpful to summarize that "the concept of righteousness belongs more to the subject of *soteriology* for Paul than to the subject of ethics."[53]

Why does all this background matter? Because it is sometimes tempting to assume that if we can find δίκη-stem (*dikē*-stem) terminology in a passage then our text must be referring to justice level obligation. The sheep in Jesus' parable of the sheep and the goats are referred to as the δίκαιοι (*dikaioi*, plural of *dikaios*) and this leads some to believe that their assistance to the "least of these" (Matt 25:45) is a matter of justice.[54] The same thing transpires in Jesus' mandate to, "when you give a

---

48. Schrenk, "δίκαιος," *TDNT* 2:183.

49. Ibid., 2:182. Incidentally, non-German theological dictionaries are in agreement (or indebted)—see, for example, C. Brown, "δικαιοσύνη," *NIDNTT* 3:353.

50. Schrenk, "δίκαιος," *TDNT* 2:185.

51. Schrenk, "δικαιοσύνη," *TDNT* 2:198. See also Kertelge, "δικαιοσύνη," *EDNT* 1:326.

52. Schrenk, "δικαιοσύνη," *TDNT* 2:198.

53. Kertelge, "δικαιοσύνη," *EDNT* 1:327, emphasis original.

54. Wolterstorff, *Justice*, 118.

The Hermeneutics of Demarcating Biblical Justice

reception, invite *the* poor, *the* crippled, *the* lame, *the* blind" (Luke 14:13) for "you will be blessed . . . for you will be repaid at the resurrection of the righteous" (δίκαιοι, *dikaioi*, Luke 14:14).[55] The assumption is that the δίκη (*dikē*) word group always, or at least here, denotes ethical uprightness in terms of justice rather than the rightness of proper relational fidelity to God. And this is far from certain.

It is not hard to find passages which will affirm the lexical contention that interhuman justice cannot be assumed to be the referent of all the δίκη-stem (*dikē-stem*) terminology. A quick sample will suffice. When John the Baptist tried to prevent Jesus from being baptized in Matt 3:15, Jesus replied, "Permit it at this time; for in this way it is fitting for us to fulfill all righteousness [δικαιοσύνη, *dikaiosynē*]." It is not possible to see this as a matter of interhuman justice. Similarly, when Joseph, "being a righteous man [δίκαιος, *dikaios*]," wanted to save Mary disgrace and desired "to send her away secretly," he was acting righteously in a manner that was beyond biblical justice (Matt 1:19)—for he was acting in accordance with mercy. The commendation of Zacharias and Elizabeth as "righteous [δίκαιοι, *dikaioi*] in the sight of God, walking blamelessly in all the commandments and requirements of the Lord" (Luke 1:6) reveals that the terminology is concerned with more than just keeping interhuman justice.[56] As noted earlier, Paul's use of δικαιοσύνη (*dikaiosynē*) seldom fits—for his emphasis is that it is reckoned on account of faith (Rom 1:17, 4:3–22, 9:30–32, 10:3). For Paul has a habit of making interhuman justice jealous. What then can we conclude? That we can only be sure that δικαιοσύνη (*dikaiosynē*)—and its heap—refers to interhuman justice when the context confirms it.

With this in mind we can now reopen another issue that we had previously noted. When used in the sense of relational righteousness, צְדָקָה (*tsedaqah*) can be accurately translated as ἐλεημοσύνη (*eleēmosynē*) in the Septuagint—for it extends to mercy. No mixing of justice and mercy obligation levels occurs. Righteousness is merely acting as an umbrella concept which subsumes both. The same thing occurs in Matt 6:1–4 where almsgiving (ἐλεημοσύνη, *eleēmosynē*, vv. 2–4) is referred to as practicing righteousness (δικαιοσύνη, *dikaiosynē*, v. 1). As צְדָקָה (*tsedaqah*) incorporated a sense of righteousness in terms

---

55. Ibid., 125.

56. Note the participle—accordingly, Bock, *Luke*, 77; Marshall, *The Gospel of Luke*, 52; Nolland, *Luke*, 26.

of benevolent activity and not merely in terms of moral rectitude, the Semitic expression עָשָׂה צְדָקָה, "doing righteousness (by giving alms)," became ποιεῖν δικαιοσύνην or ποιεῖν ἐλεημοσύνην.[57] In each case charity, rather than interhuman justice, is being enjoined (as we shall see). And it is to mercy that we now turn.

MERCY MANDATES

The mercy level obligation of a mandate is revealed upon the occurrence of any of the following four textual indicators: the mandate's transgression is explicitly revealed as not a matter of sin, or is explicitly identified as not entailing divine punishment, or is disclosed to specifically entail divine reward, or the mandate possesses the semantic labeling of mercy.

Explicit Non-Sin

When a mandate's omission is explicitly described, at the textual level, as not entailing sin or its synonyms (as outlined earlier in this chapter) it is a mercy mandate.

Explicit Non-Punishment

Similarly, texts which explicitly reveal that the transgression of their enclosed mandate does not receive divine punishment are promulgating mercy mandates.

Specifically Entailed Reward

Any interhuman treatment which God specifically rewards—rather than eudaemonistically as part of a broader set of obediences—is an instance of mercy. Such rewards are produced by a specific obedience, the transgression of which possesses no corresponding sin indicators.

Semantic Label

Mandates that are semantically labeled as being associated with showing pity are mercy mandates. It seems to me that being motivated by pity is opposite to being motivated by the comprehensive constraint of justice. The main NT cognates of pity include: ἔλεος (*eleos*, mercy), οἰκτιρμός (*oiktirmos*, compassion), σπλαγχνίζομαι (*splanchnizomai*, compassion),

---

57. Bultmann, "ἐλεημοσύνη," *TDNT* 2:486; Esser, "ἔλεος," *NIDNTT* 2:597.

and συμπαθέω (*sympatheō*, sympathy).⁵⁸ These cognates, and their semantic relatives, entail a mercy obligation level analogous to the graciousness and kindness communicated by χάρις (*charis*). The Jerusalem collection, for example, is explicitly described as a mercy endeavor in 2 Cor 9:7 (as corroborated by 2 Cor 8:8) and is likewise connected to mercy terminology elsewhere (χάρις, *charis*, in 1 Cor 16:3 and 2 Cor 8:6–7 and ἐλεημοσύνη, *eleēmosynē*, in Acts 24:17). This same collection also corroborates that the διακονία (*diakonia*, service, ministry) word group is similarly related to mercy (2 Cor 9:1).⁵⁹

But not everyone is so quick to agree. Some of those who are keenly familiar with the classical Greek philosophers will remind us that in classical and common Greek, ἔλεος (*eleos*) is a πάθος (*pathos*)—an emotion aroused in the presence of undeserved affliction. For John Caputo, all of ethics is reduced to this mere feeling of "obligation"—a feeling which is the manifestation of "the power of powerlessness"—and subsequently, ethics is not philosophically safe but merely existentially groped.⁶⁰ So perhaps ἔλεος (*eleos*) and its cognates only disclose an emotion—a mere emotional motivation to pursue either charity or justice. Perhaps the textual presence of this terminology simply cannot tell us anything about the obligation level of its referent. That it is purely motivational such that an act of mercy is not enjoined as its outflow.⁶¹

In chapter 1 I argued that, in terms of understanding justice and mercy, we are interested in discerning our obligations and not merely in describing a certain state of affairs. That moral constraint is what grounds rights and makes justice demandable. When justice is conceived as merely a "social condition"—where "persons are related to each other in a certain way"—it ceases to be a motivator of action.⁶² So mercy and sympathy are rounded up to fulfill this role, to become the motivators of interhuman treatment—and particularly to be the stron-

---

58. Esser, "ἔλεος, οἰκτιρμός, σπλάγχνα, σπλάγχνον," *NIDNTT* 2:594–600; "συμπαθέω, συμπαθής," BDAG 958.

59. Such service, διακονία (*diakonia*), unto others is also revealed as being divinely rewarded in a multitude of passages and this hamartiological correlation affirms its mercy status.

60. Caputo, *Against Ethics*, 5.

61. This possibility was helpfully raised by Nicholas Wolterstorff in personal communication and so much of the challenge engaged here is but a restatement of his interpretive proposal.

62. Wolterstorff, *Justice*, 112, 111.

gest motivators unto justice. Nevertheless, justice, if it is a moral duty, cannot but generate motivation. Which believer wants to be immoral? And so the issue has coalesced. Does the NT employ mercy terminology as a motivation unto justice or, as the author claims, as a signpost for identifying charity level treatments? Or is the terminology, after all, morally non-determinative?

As classical Greek usage saw ἔλεος (eleos) as "an emotion rather than a moral relationship to others," the Stoics went so far as to consider it a "sickness of the soul."[63] For, in this sense, it was a thwarter of justice in that it produced partiality. For them, and Plato's Socrates, ἔλεος (eleos) did not motivate toward justice.[64] But the usage found in the Septuagint is significantly more relevant. Here it predominantly translates חֶסֶד (khesed) and sometimes רַחֲמִים (rakhamim, only six times).[65] חֶסֶד (khesed) refers to faithfulness and lovingkindness, and sometimes to a composite of the two. As faithfulness, it refers primarily not to an attitude or disposition, but to a helpful act.[66] It is not primarily a motivation. As lovingkindness, חֶסֶד (khesed) encapsulates the kindness and grace of a superior—and most often this superior is God. God's חֶסֶד (khesed) describes His "faithful and merciful help"—an act of favor.[67] And so חֶסֶד (khesed) and ἔλεος (eleos) naturally spill over into clemency—pardoning grace. Here too Bultmann affirms that חֶסֶד (khesed), even as gracious lovingkindness, is primarily concerned with acts rather than motivations.[68]

What about רַחֲמִים (rakhamim)? Good stories are worth hearing again. While originally connected to emotion and sympathy, רַחֲמִים (rakhamim) is better translated as love. It too denotes "the act or expression of love rather than the emotion."[69] It is love expressed in acts of grace and so too in clemency—for it allays the wrath of judgment.

---

63. Bultmann, "ἔλεος, ἐλεέω," *TDNT* 2:478.
64. Plato, *Apologia*, 34c, 35b.
65. Bultmann, "ἔλεος, ἐλεέω," *TDNT* 2:479.
66. Ibid. Due to this relational faithfulness sense, חֶסֶד (khesed) is occasionally translated as δικαιοσύνη (dikaiosyne). Even so, the lovingkindness sense, and its ἔλεος (eleos) translation, predominates.
67. Ibid., 2:480.
68. Ibid.
69. Ibid., 2:480–81.

So in the LXX ἔλεος (*eleos*) represents helpful acts, clemency, and grace. The focus is not on motivations. Furthermore the concern is with mercy treatments rather than justice ones—with grace and clemency. And Bultmann argues that the observed focus of the OT upon showing kindness and gracious faithfulness continues on in the NT usage of ἔλεος (*eleos*).[70] He has good reason to do so.

Whenever ἔλεος (*eleos*) and its cognates are embedded in soteriological texts they necessarily refer to grace—to mercy. The grace and mercy of God, as expressed in His provision of salvation, simply cannot mean that God is experiencing motivation to give us justice. He is providing clemency—the opposite of our just deserts. Did you hear that? It is the sound of Stoics rolling over. Many texts confirm this usage. Paul, though "formerly a blasphemer and a persecutor and a violent aggressor," was shown ἔλεος (*eleos*) because he "acted ignorantly in unbelief" (1 Tim 1:13). He did not receive the justice he deserved but rather "the grace [χάρις, *charis*] of our Lord was more than abundant" (1 Tim 1:14). Jesus Christ treated Paul's injustice with patience in order to demonstrate His clemency (ἔλεος, *eleos*, 1 Tim 1:16). It is the firm hope of believers that on the day of judgment we will receive gracious clemency (ἔλεος, *eleos*) rather than justice (Rom 9:22–23; 2 Tim 1:18; Jude 1:21).

So Matt 5:7 teaches us that "Blessed are the merciful [ἐλεήμων, *eleēmōn*], for they shall receive mercy [ἐλεέω, *eleeō*]."[71] The context suggests that receiving clemency is in view for the blessed "shall see God" (Matt 5:8).[72] The mercy we receive is not God's motivation to do justice toward us. Throughout the OT, as in Luke 18:7–8, God commits Himself to bringing about justice—He does not need to be merciful to be inclined to do so. Nor is His commitment to justice conditioned by our mercifulness. The parallelism found in Matt 5:7 mandates that believers be similarly gracious and willing to give mercy. Other texts, such as 2 Cor 4:1; Heb 4:16; and 1 Pet 2:10, also address *receiving* mercy, and in each case it refers to receiving grace rather than justice. The issue here is that in order for such passages to make sense, mercy has to be some-

---

70. Ibid., 2:482–85.

71. For discussion of the preceding verse, Matt 5:6, see the Possessions Mandates During Jesus' Ministry section of the following chapter.

72. The author contends that the makarisms of Matthew 5 are best understood as a unit describing what Jesus' followers are to be like and the multitude of benefits such blessed ones will enjoy.

thing—such as unmerited favor or clemency—rather than a motivation unto some such thing—and especially not a motivation unto justice.

Such passages are not at all rare. James 2:13 warns that "judgment [κρίσις, krisis, judicial justice] will be merciless [ἀνέλεος, aneleos] to one who has shown no mercy [ἔλεος, eleos]; mercy [ἔλεος, eleos] triumphs over judgment [κρίσις, krisis]." This verse reveals that not *doing* mercy, μὴ ποιήσαντι ἔλεος—which indicates that motivation cannot be the referent—means that God will not extend His clemency. Clemency is also the issue in Eph 2:4–5 and 1 Pet 1:3. One more example should suffice. In Rom 11:30–32, Paul explains that the Gentiles have benefited from the disobedience of the Jews: "For just as you once were disobedient to God, but now have been shown mercy [ἐλεέω, eleeō] because of their disobedience, so these also now have been disobedient, in order that because of the mercy [ἔλεος, eleos] shown to you they also may now be shown mercy [ἐλεέω, eleeō]. For God has shut up all in disobedience that He might show mercy [ἐλεέω, eleeō] to all." In His impartiality, God provides clemency—and not justice—to all the repentant. A few verses later in Rom 12:8 this same terminology is used of believers showing gracious mercy.

In terms of clemency, ἔλεος (*eleos*) can never be understood as a motivation unto justice. The same is true of its usage in contexts of grace. When the rich man of Luke 16:24 "cried out and said, 'Father Abraham, have mercy [ἐλεέω, eleeō] on me, and send Lazarus, that he may dip the tip of his finger in water and cool off my tongue; for I am in agony in this flame,'" he was not asking for justice. That he had already received. It is logically unthinkable that the mercy spoken of here is a call to a motivation for Abraham to do justice—rather it is a call requesting something undeserved. Such undeserved mercy is also in view in Luke 1:58; 2 Tim 1:16 (where it is given, δίδωμι, didōmi); Heb 4:16; and Jude 1:23—where showing grace to others is to be done while fearfully hating sin (and thereby still maintaining a knowledge of what is right).

Building upon these notions of clemency and grace, ἔλεος (*eleos*) and its cognates are often textually juxtaposed with justice. In Paul's defense of God's justice in the face of rampant Jewish unbelief in Rom 9:14–16 he argues "What shall we say then? There is no injustice [ἀδικία, adikia] with God, is there? May it never be! For He says to Moses, 'I will have mercy [ἐλεέω, eleeō] on whom I have mercy [ἐλεέω, eleeō], and I will have compassion [οἰκτείρω, oikteirō] on whom I have compassion [οἰκτείρω, *oikteirō*].' So then it *does* not *depend* on the man who wills or the man who runs, but on God who has mercy [ἐλεέω, *eleeō*]." And so the defense of God's justice (v. 14) requires that God's mercy (vv. 15, 16) and compassion (v. 15) be, at least to some degree, voluntary—and certainly not constrained by a justice level of obligation (v. 18). Erasing the semantic divide between justice and mercy would make passages such as this altogether self-contradictory. The biblical texts demonstrate significant resistance to such an amalgamation—for they often contrast mercy terminology with just deserts (as seen, for example, in Matt 18:23–34; Rom 4:4–5; Eph 2:8–9; and Titus 3:5). For such merciful grace is a favor (Rom 4:4), a "gift [δῶρον, *dōron*] of God" (Eph 2:8).

Passages which speak to doing or giving mercy, as noted earlier, also rebel against understanding ἔλεος (*eleos*) as merely a motivation or emotion. In Luke 1:72 God's doing of mercy describes His faithfulness to act graciously on behalf of His covenant people—to save them from their enemies (vv. 71, 74) and sins (v. 77). After giving His parable of the good Samaritan, Jesus asked His interlocutor who had loved their neighbor as themselves, "And he said, 'The one who showed mercy [ποιήσας τὸ ἔλεος] toward him.' And Jesus said to him, 'Go and do [ποιέω, *poieō*] the same'" (Luke 10:37). It is indeed very hard to understand "did the mercy" (ποιήσας τὸ ἔλεος) as meaning "did the motivation."[73] The same constraint is evident, and reinforced, in Jas 2:13 and 2 Tim 1:16—passages noted earlier.

The epistolary greetings bear the same witness. The writers are not praying for and wishing their audience God's motivation to do justice to them (1 Tim 1:2; 2 Tim 1:2; 2 John 1:3; and Jude 1:2). This would make for a most unusual greeting. One which is internally at odds with the other well-wishes of grace and peace.

Furthermore, even when people asked Jesus to "have mercy" on them they were not asking Him to be motivated to do justice unto them (Matt 9:27; 15:22; 17:15; Mark 10:47–48; Luke 17:13). They were begging for a gracious act of kindness. Even if we are somehow initially tempted

---

73. Particularly as the phrase has all the markings of a Hebraism for "doing a kindness" (compare Gen 24:12; 40:14; Judg 1:24; 8:35; 2 Sam 3:8 in the MT and LXX). See Bultmann, "ἔλεος, ἐλεέω," *TDNT* 2:482–83; Plummer, *A Critical and Exegetical Commentary on the Gospel according to St. Luke*, 287, 289; Marshall, *The Gospel of Luke*, 450. And so the Samaritan's feeling of compassion (Luke 10:33) grew into acts of kindness (vv. 34–35). See Calvin, *Commentary on a Harmony of the Evangelists*, 3:61–62; Lightfoot, *Horæ Hebraicæ et Talmudicæ*, 3:109.

to consider Jesus' healings and exorcisms as matters of justice, we have to agree that Jesus is not unjust. And yet, Jesus does not always heal. In Nazareth, He does not do many miracles because of their unbelief (Matt 13:54–58 // Luke 4:23–27). If responding to cries for mercy is a matter of being motivated to do justice, Jesus would be, at least on such occasions, committing injustice. But Jesus defends His right to withhold mercy on the basis of God's own right to do so. For Elijah was sent by God to none of the "many widows in Israel" (Luke 4:25) but only to one widow in Zarephath (v. 26); and "there were many lepers in Israel in the time of Elisha the prophet; and none of them was cleansed, but only Naaman the Syrian" (v. 27). So healing lepers and aiding indigent widows—even in a time of famine (v. 25)—is a matter of mercy.[74] As is providing exorcism (Mark 5:19).[75] And to round things off, Jesus' compassion (σπλαγχνίζομαι, *splanchnizomai*) does not always feed (John 6:26–27). It too is a matter of mercy.[76]

---

74. This effect does not detract from Jesus' primary focus of declaring that "no prophet is welcome in his hometown" (Luke 4:24 // Matt 13:57) and hence God is bound to send Him to do miracles elsewhere. And so, preferring an interpretive link based on Jesus' "prophetic identity" ends up entailing the same conclusion (though it misses the reason for the initial statement)—that prophets act outside of their home turf where they are more welcome and thus no healing will happen here (Nolland, *Luke*, 200, 201).

75. Healing believers falls under gracious mercy as well (Phil 2:27).

76. To be moved in the inward parts, σπλαγχνίζομαι (*splanchnizomai*), does mean to *feel* compassion. In this sense, along with συμπαθέω (*sympatheō*, sympathy) and occasionally οἰκτιρμός (*oiktirmos*, compassion), σπλαγχνίζομαι (*splanchnizomai*) is most compatible with being viewed as an emotion and a motivation. Yet where it appears most within the NT, in Jesus' healings (including exorcism and raising from the dead) and feedings, the non-binding nature of these treatments reveals that σπλαγχνίζομαι (*splanchnizomai*) motivates unto mercy. This same motivation unto mercy is affirmed in the parable of the good Samaritan (Luke 10:33), in the parable of the unforgiving servant (concerning forgiveness of debt and ultimately forgiveness itself, Matt 18:27), and in the parable of the prodigal son—where the compassion of the father on the undeserving son cannot be perceived as a matter of justice (Luke 15:20). In Matt 9:36, Jesus has compassion on the multitude "because they were distressed and dispirited like sheep without a shepherd" and enjoins prayer for more workers. The remaining instance, the partial parallel in Mark 6:34, leads to teaching and a feeding. Even if we were tempted to consider missionary and pastoral ministry a matter of justice obligation, Jesus considers His own teaching ministry as a matter of mercy for He teaches, in part, so that "while seeing they do not see, and while hearing they do not hear, nor do they understand" (Matt 13:13–15 // Mark 4:11–12). The remaining terms, συμπαθέω (*sympatheō*) and οἰκτιρμός (*oiktirmos*), are very seldom distinctly employed with respect to the poor in the NT (with the concern for prisoners in Heb 10:34 being one of the likely implicit exceptions).

While צְדָקָה (*tsedaqah*)—in its relational righteousness sense—can be accurately translated as ἐλεημοσύνη (*eleēmosynē*), in the NT ἐλεημοσύνη (*eleēmosynē*) always refers to almsgiving. This sense is also found in the Septuagint where the act of showing favor (חָנַן, *khanan*) to the poor is translated as ἐλεημοσύνη (*eleēmosynē*, Dan 4:27, 4:24 in BHS).

While the argument here has revolved around the ἔλεος (*eleos*) terminological family, the earlier noted overlaps—such as with the Jerusalem collection—affirm that the same meaning extends to its cognates. The applicable semantic meaning of χάρις (*charis*, gracious favor, gift), for example, is hardly contested. Grace is the opposite of justice.[77] And justice is not a kindness.

So what are we to conclude? All of the contextually elucidated and hence observable instances connect the semantic label of mercy to acts of a mercy level of obligation. Mercy terminology was not found to refer merely to an emotion or psychological motivation—and especially not to a motivation unto justice. This result is completely unlike our investigation of δικαιοσύνη (*dikaiosynē*)—where clear textual instances showed it did not always mean justice. So the burden of proof rests on those who would see the mercy terminology otherwise within the remaining unspecified passages (and there are not many) to prove that it sometimes carries merely a motivational meaning. Or better still, that it sometimes motivates unto justice. Nevertheless, to show why these few uncertain passages are to be taken in a way contrary to the certain will be most challenging. In any case, the most important semantically labeled passages for our concern are already categorized by the above considerations.

MANDATES OF UNCERTAIN OBLIGATION

Under certain conditions the justice or mercy status of a mandate remains uncertain. This occurs when the following conditions converge: it is unclear whether the transgression of the mandate is a sin or not, thus it does not entail punishment for its transgression (nor explicit non-punishment for its transgression), it does not specifically entail reward, and it is not semantically labeled as denoting "mercy" or "justice" (or their synonyms).

---

77. It even functions to forgive transgressions (Eph 1:6–7).

So this is the proposed hermeneutical methodology. This methodology will be employed in part 3 to analyze the NT data concerning the moral treatment of the poor—to help us identify justice and mercy at the textual level.

PART THREE

New Testament Contours
An Analysis of the Data

FIVE

Everything the NT Says about Helping the Poor

As part of a group of three seminary friends, I once visited a poor widow's home in the Carpathian Ruthenia region of the Ukraine. The house was an old wooden structure that consisted mostly of a bedroom and a tiny foyer fulfilling the dual role of a kitchen. She had no electricity though the new millennium was impatiently waiting on her doorstep. A hole in the roof, half a meter in diameter, provided light and meant that the dear lady was rained on when the wind was wrong, for she was bedridden on her small bed. No longer able to move, and unable to afford any care, the neighbor from across the street would come by twice a day to roll her over, fix a meal, and help her eliminate. On one side she had already sagged and her flesh was infected and green. The smell was hard to forget. All the sudden, the few foodstuffs we had brought seemed painfully inadequate. Hauntingly, she was joyful, despite her pain. In her exuberance she asked us to pray with her and sing for her some Slavic hymns. Most of the men in the surrounding villages had worked for the last half a year at a vinegar production plant, the only work available, on promises of being paid after the first big shipment. The plant had just closed and their only recompense for half a year of work was two cartonfuls of bottled vinegar each. Help for this believing widow was scarce. It was hard not to wonder whether justice rather than just mercy was at stake.

So what does the NT reveal? Is its message concerning the moral treatment of the poor congruent after all? Whose justice, which mercy? In all this we are rightfully at the mercy of the passage data.

First, some organizational considerations. In terms of a tally, this data concerning helping the poor represents 114 mandate passages and an additional 52 clarifier passages. But these numbers represent verse groupings which are, to some extent, malleable. Accordingly, our methodology and analysis does not depend, in any way, upon this pragmatic enumeration. Some additional passages also appear, upon first glance, to be of possible relevance. Only a selection of these—specifically those which commonly receive treatment in scholarly literature concerning Christian obligations to the poor—will be noted and addressed.[1]

The mandate passages enclose biblical mandates while the clarifier passages subsume clarifiers which serve to elucidate the components and contours of these mandates (but are not mandates themselves). The content of the textual mandates will be, in turn, collocated into 23 pragmatically chosen obligation "aspects." These aspects serve to group the biblical data by the common goal or specific issue that the mandates aim to address. These aspects function solely to enable an orderly presentation of the biblical data. Some of the passages address several aspects and thus will necessarily recur within the data presentation.

These data aspects will be presented in the order of their scriptural resolution, from highest to lowest (primary sorting), coupled with the order of their attestation, also from high to low (secondary sorting). Lower resolution aspects, save the moral impetus level, will be integrated into this order at the first instance of their overlap with a higher resolution aspect. Consequently, the first aspect of helping the poor to be addressed will be almsgiving as this aspect, from among the specific resolution level mandates, possesses the widest attestation within the NT biblical data. The Jerusalem collection, in being identified as an instance of almsgiving, overlaps with it at the same resolution level and will be addressed next. The Jerusalem collection's overlap with the lower resolution aspect of sharing means that it receives treatment after that. And the share mandates' own overlap with the even lower resolution aspect of working brings this aspect up next. And so on. The lowest resolution mandates, those at the moral impetus level, will receive only concise summary after all the other (higher resolution) aspects have been considered. Thus the data will be presented in an ordering consonant with the resolution principle.

The following figure functions as a legend for the main passage differentiation indicators. These indicators will be appended to the biblical

---

1. The Appendix itemizes the references of the minimal set of biblical mandate, clarifier, and possibly relevant passages (including those not addressed in this chapter) which are pertinent to any NT study of the moral treatment of the poor.

Everything the NT Says about Helping the Poor

texts as they are presented in order to summarize their characteristics.[2] Figure 4 also outlines the abbreviations that will be employed (and the order in which they will be presented).

RESOLUTION LEVEL	OBLIGATION LEVEL	OBLIGATION DISCLOSURE	POVERTY FOCUS
S = Specific (Poor) C = Concrete P = Principle (Poor) G = General I = Moral Impetus / = uncertain	J = Justice M = Mercy *blank* = uncertain	H = Hamartiologically S = Semantically *blank* = undisclosed	I = Immediately Poor P = Potentially Poor *blank* = beyond Poor / = uncertain

FIGURE 4: Differentiation Indicators Legend

The clarifier passages will only have the resolution level and poverty focus appended to them as the mandate related columns are, to a large degree, extraneous for clarifiers. Clarifiers often provide more detail concerning particular mandates but are not themselves mandated. As such, clarifiers may only contain a semantic disclosure of the mercy level of obligation (which will be noted when it occurs). This is because the other three categories of disclosure, the semantic disclosure of justice, the hamartiological disclosure of mercy (in terms of specific reward), and the hamartiological disclosure of justice, all entail that the texts concerned are mandates.[3] The hamartiological disclosure of mercy, in terms other than specific reward (such as in explicitly entailing non-

---

2. A cautious approach will be adopted toward these indicators and only what is assured will be thus appended. Beyond these safe summations, what is likely in addition will be developed within the explanations that follow the texts themselves.

3. The distinction is very fine, if it exists at all. In Tabitha's garment-making (Acts 9:36, 39–41) for example, we readily perceive a concretization, a clarifying description, of mercy—but less readily a mandate. Why? Though what she does is described as good works and almsgiving, this description does not communicate moral impetus as unambiguously as a passage that labels its treatments as justice. While both such passages clarify what mercy and justice look like respectively, and it takes other passages to mandate the actual doing of mercy and justice, it is the uniquely constraining obligation level of justice that connects its description to the mandate to do justice with greater immediacy (for many interpreters). This distinction is maintained here as a procedural concession for the sake of those who, like Nicholas Wolterstorff, would perceive but only an emotional motivation behind the mercy terminology. As clarifiers will be permitted to clarify the mandates, no harm is done. Either route works. We have merely erred on the side of caution in identifying our mandates.

punishment or non-sin), does not occur with respect to the poor within the NT.

Three more delineations provide for a secondary differentiation of the textual data: the main cause of the poverty, the recipient breadth, and the main obligator. These differentiations are also important for the process of conceptual integration as they identify possible discontinuities of focus within the data. Accepting this role, these differentiations facilitate the desired end of seeking a non-contradictory conceptual integration. They assist us in thinking through the biblical data in more manageable chunks while at the same time preserving more of its detail.

MAIN CAUSE OF POVERTY

The main causes of poverty may be utilitariously divided into three categories: injustice, calamity, and personal sin. The category of injustice subsumes injustice generally as well as oppression—which is the use of entrusted or financial power to perpetrate injustice with significant immunity upon those with less influence. The category of calamity subsumes both personal calamity, such as disability or disease, and general calamity such as famine or the destructiveness of war. The personal sin category subsumes both sin and personal weakness on the part of the poor.

RECIPIENT BREADTH

Two broad categories of recipients are identified within the NT data set concerning the treatment of the materially poor: believers and people in general. The former recipient category may be further subdivided into local believers (such as the widows within one's local assembly), remote believers (such as those to whom the Jerusalem collection was sent), and believers generally (in an unspecified manner).

MAIN OBLIGATOR

Biblical mandates can also be differentiated in terms of whom they aim to obligate: whether rulers, the church corporate, individuals generally, or the immediate disciples of Jesus during His earthly ministry. The ruler category subsumes political, government, and judicial leaders as well as others fulfilling positions of societal responsibility. Because contemporary democratic societies enable citizens to affect, to some degree, the leadership of the societal rulers, this obligator category becomes the closest analogue to modern notions of societal responsibility. The church category subsumes the mandates that are to be accomplished by local assemblies of believers. The individual category pertains to mandates which obligate the believer on a unary level.

DATA ASPECTS

By way of overview, the main pragmatically chosen aspect categories concern: almsgiving, the Jerusalem collection, sharing, working, good works, possessions, wealth, covetousness, generosity, giving and lending, being first or last, receiving the least, widows, satiation, partiality, and oppression. The passages in each aspect will be ordered canonically with the exception of parallels, which will be grouped together with their first representative. The biblical text will be presented in the NASB translation but without its original italics—as italics will be employed to highlight sections of particular importance. The communicated level of obligation, whether justice or mercy, will receive primary interest in our discussion. Important but contentious texts will require us to consider a larger number of commentators and to present greater exegetical detail. Both via semantic and conceptual linkage, the provision of alms receives, by far, the greatest NT textual attestation.

ALMS

Providing alms, ἐλεημοσύνη (*eleēmosynē*), is semantically related to acting out of mercy, ἔλεος (*eleos*). This connection in obligation level is affirmed in Acts 24:17, where Paul is recorded as referring to the collection for the poor in Jerusalem as ἐλεημοσύνας ποιήσων (bringing alms). Paul asserts that this same collection is fully voluntary in 2 Cor 9:7: "Each one *must do* just as he has purposed in his heart, not grudgingly or under compulsion, for God loves a cheerful giver." The additional mercy terminology attached to this collection, such as διακονία (*diakonia*, service) and χάρις (*charis*, gracious favor, gift), further confirms the linguistic contention that almsgiving is an act of mercy obligation.[4] This

---

4. While Rudolf Bultmann notes, on the basis of Tobit 2:14; 12:9; 14:11; and Baruch 5:9, that Hellenistic Jews could use δικαιοσύνη (*dikaiosynē*, righteousness) to subsume almsgiving, such references are always combined with ἐλεημοσύνη (*eleēmosynē*) akin to Matt 6:1–4 (Bultmann, "ἐλεημοσύνη," *TDNT* 2:485–86). As such, this observation merely restates that the δίκη (*dikē*) derivatives are not always related to justice

contention, that the semantic overlap between alms and mercy parallels an equivalent obligation level overlap, is also, as shall be seen, affirmed by the *discrimen*. This affirmation occurs within the broader range of almsgiving mandates—thus revealing that the collection for Jerusalem is not an isolated mercy subset.

Alms Mandates

> Matt 6:1-4 Beware of practicing your righteousness before men to be noticed by them; otherwise you have no reward with your Father who is in heaven. 2 So when you *give to the poor* [ἐλεημοσύνη, *eleēmosynē*], do not sound a trumpet before you, as the hypocrites do in the synagogues and in the streets, so that they may be honored by men. Truly I say to you, they have their reward in full. 3 But when you *give to the poor* [ἐλεημοσύνη, *eleēmosynē*], do not let your left hand know what your right hand is doing, 4 so that your *giving* [ἐλεημοσύνη, *eleēmosynē*] will be in secret; and your Father who sees what is done in secret will reward you. (S | M | HS | I/P)

In Matt 6:1-4 Jesus provides instructions concerning the "how" of almsgiving—that alms should be given without fanfare (vv. 2-3). Commands to give alms, the "do" rather than the "when," appear in later passages. The fact that one's left hand should not know what the right hand is doing is most likely a reference to how secretive this almsgiving should be rather than an indication of the extent of its generosity (v. 4).[5] The mercy obligation level of this mandate is affirmed by the offer of reward (μισθός, *misthos*, vv. 1-2) and divine recompense (ἀποδίδωμι, *apodidōmi*, v. 4).[6]

---

but sometimes envelop the broader notion of righteousness. See "δίκαιος, δικαιοσύνη," BDAG 246-49. See also Esser, "Mercy, Compassion," *NIDNTT* 2:594, 598.

5. Hagner, *Matthew*, 140. In their concise summary of the concern for the poor in Luke, Paul Achtemeier, Joel Green, and Marianne Thompson propose that in Jesus' context almsgiving would have been understood as extending a kinship type friendship to the poor (Achtemeier et al., *Introducing the New Testament*, 172-73). But this socioeconomic reconstruction is not certain. It is badgered by the fact that even kin apparently expected a non-able-bodied kinsman to beg for alms in order to "spread the load." So it was, for example, with the blind beggar of John 9:1-23 who begged alms even though he likely lived with his parents (Köstenberger, *John*, 287).

6. The doing of righteousness (δικαιοσύνην . . . ποιεῖν) in verse 1 could be a synonym for alms-doing—the doing of mercy in verse 2 (ποιῇς ἐλεημοσύνην) and verse 3 (ποιοῦντος ἐλεημοσύνην). So the majority of the late manuscripts have no trouble substituting ἐλεημοσύνην for δικαιοσύνην in verse 1. But it is nonetheless more likely to refer

Bultmann contends that, in the NT, ἐλεημοσύνη (*eleēmosynē*) is "always to the poor," and this affirmation accounts for the English translation above.⁷ This observation likewise accounts for the poverty focus levels assigned to Luke 12:22–34 and Acts 10:2, 4, 31. Because ἐλεημοσύνη (*eleēmosynē*) is semantically revealed to be pity-driven, in its empathetic sense, it makes sense that alms would be given to objects of sympathy— the needy poor.⁸

> Matt 19:21–22 Jesus said to him, "If you wish to be complete, go and *sell your possessions* and *give* [δίδωμι, *didōmi*] *to the poor*, and you will have *treasure in heaven*; and come, *follow Me*." 22 But when the young man heard this statement, he went away grieving; for he was one who owned much property. (S | M | H | I)
>
> // Mark 10:21–22 Looking at him, Jesus felt a love for him and said to him, "One thing you lack: go and *sell all you possess and give* [δίδωμι, *didōmi*] *to the poor*, and you will have *treasure in heaven*; and come, *follow Me*." 22 But at these words he was saddened, and he went away grieving, for he was one who owned much property. (S | M | H | I)
>
> // Luke 18:22–23 When Jesus heard this, He said to him, "One thing you still lack; *sell all that you possess and distribute* [διαδίδωμι, *diadidōmi*] *it to the poor*, and you shall have *treasure in heaven*; and come, *follow Me*." 23 But when he had heard these things, he became very sad, for he was extremely rich. (S | M | H | I)

In these parallels, Jesus tells the rich young ruler to sell all of his possessions and give the proceeds to the immediately poor (πτωχοί, *ptōchoi*, plural of *ptōchos*). Jesus' mandate offers a reward for its accomplishment—"treasure in heaven" (θησαυρὸν ἐν οὐρανοῖς)—as likewise promised, particularly to His disciples, in Matt 6:20. The mandate to

---

to the doing of righteousness more generally so as to introduce almsgiving (vv. 2–4), praying (vv. 5–6), and fasting (vv. 16–18). For in terms of form, the consistent parallelism of the subsections, in moving from unrewarded "hypocrisy" to reward, supports the introductory statement, general righteousness interpretation (Hagner, *Matthew*, 137–38; Blomberg, *Matthew*, 116).

7. Bultmann, "ἐλεημοσύνη," *TDNT* 2:486.

8. Comparing Luke 12:33 with Luke 18:22 (// Matt 19:21 // Mark 10:21) corroborates that it is the immediately poor who are the natural beneficiaries of almsgiving. And so Matt 6:1–4, like other mandates unto ἐλεημοσύνη (*eleēmosynē*), is much more likely to address immediate poverty (despite the above-indicated theoretical possibility of aiding the potentially poor).

give up one's possessions will receive attention in the Possessions section to come, important at present is that the giving of alms is revealed, by the hamartiological *discrimen*, to be an issue of mercy.

> Luke 12:22-34 And *He said to His disciples, "For this reason I say to you*, do not worry about your life, as to what you will eat; nor for your body, as to what you will put on. 23 For life is more than food, and the body more than clothing. 24 Consider the ravens, for they neither sow nor reap; they have no storeroom nor barn, and yet God feeds them; how much more valuable you are than the birds! 25 And which of you by worrying can add a single hour to his life's span? 26 If then you cannot do even a very little thing, why do you worry about other matters? 27 Consider the lilies, how they grow: they neither toil nor spin; but I tell you, not even Solomon in all his glory clothed himself like one of these. 28 But if God so clothes the grass in the field, which is alive today and tomorrow is thrown into the furnace, how much more will He clothe you? You men of little faith! 29 And do not seek what you will eat and what you will drink, and do not keep worrying. 30 For all these things the nations of the world eagerly seek; but your Father knows that you need these things. 31 But seek His kingdom, and these things will be added to you. 32 Do not be afraid, little flock, for your Father has chosen gladly to give you the kingdom. 33 *Sell your possessions* and *give to charity* [ἐλεημοσύνη, *eleēmosynē*]; make yourselves money belts which do not wear out, an unfailing *treasure in heaven*, where no thief comes near nor moth destroys. 34 For where your treasure is, there your heart will be also." (S | M | HS | I/P)

Luke 12:22-34 merges the semantic and hamartiological indicators together in explicitly clarifying that Jesus' call to His disciples (v. 22)—to sell their possessions for the purpose of giving the proceeds away—is an act of almsgiving that shall be divinely rewarded.[9] Thus almsgiving, a giving to the poor out of pity for their needy condition, is affirmed to be an act of mercy obligation.

> Acts 10:2, 4, 31 [Cornelius] a devout man and one who feared God with all his household, and gave many *alms* [ἐλεημοσύνη, *eleēmosynē*] to the Jewish people and prayed to God continually. . . . 4 And fixing his gaze on him and being much alarmed, he said, "What is it, Lord?" And he said to him, "Your prayers and *alms*

---

9. The disciples mentioned here, the little flock of verse 32, enfold a larger group of immediate followers than just the twelve. See Bock, *Luke*, 1159.

[ἐλεημοσύνη, eleēmosynē] have ascended as a *memorial* before God." . . . 31 and he said, "Cornelius, your prayer has been heard and your *alms* [ἐλεημοσύνη, eleēmosynē] have been remembered before God." (S | M | S | I/P)

God's approval of Cornelius' almsgiving in Acts 10:2, 4, 31 is described as a "memorial" (v. 4) that has attracted God's favor. As with Tabitha in Acts 9:36, 39–41, a commitment to almsgiving receives divine favor—even miracles. Such approval serves to encourage emulation.

Alms Clarifiers

Matt 26:6–13 Now when Jesus was in Bethany, at the home of Simon the leper, 7 a woman came to Him with an alabaster vial of very costly perfume, and she poured it on His head as He reclined at the table. 8 But the disciples were indignant when they saw this, and said, "Why this waste? 9 For this perfume might have been sold for a high price and the *money given to the poor*." 10 But Jesus, aware of this, said to them, "Why do you bother the woman? For she has done a *good deed* to Me. 11 For you always have the poor with you; but you do not always have Me. 12 For when she poured this perfume on My body, she did it to prepare Me for burial. 13 Truly I say to you, wherever this gospel is preached in the whole world, what this woman has done will also be spoken of in memory of her." (S | I)

// Mark 14:3–9 While He was in Bethany at the home of Simon the leper, and reclining at the table, there came a woman with an alabaster vial of very costly perfume of pure nard; and she broke the vial and poured it over His head. 4 But some were indignantly remarking to one another, "Why has this perfume been wasted? 5 For this perfume might have been sold for over three hundred denarii, and the *money given to the poor*." And they were scolding her. 6 But Jesus said, "Let her alone; why do you bother her? She has done a *good deed* to Me. 7 For you always have the *poor* with you, and whenever you *wish* you can *do good* to them; but you do not always have Me. 8 She has done what she could; she has anointed My body beforehand for the burial. 9 Truly I say to you, wherever the gospel is preached in the whole world, what this woman has done will also be spoken of in memory of her." (S | I)

// John 12:3–8 Mary then took a pound of very costly perfume of pure nard, and anointed the feet of Jesus and wiped His feet with her hair; and the house was filled with the fragrance of the

> perfume. 4 But Judas Iscariot, one of His disciples, who was intending to betray Him, said, 5 "Why was this perfume not sold for three hundred denarii and *given to poor people*?" 6 Now he said this, not because he was concerned about the poor, but because he was a thief, and as he had the money box, he used to pilfer what was put into it. 7 Therefore Jesus said, "Let her alone, so that she may keep it for the day of My burial. 8 For you always have the *poor* with you, but you do not always have Me." (S | I)

Matthew 26:6–13; Mark 14:3–9; and John 12:3–8 reveal that the disciples were sensitive to the need to give alms, though Judas is said to have mixed this concern with selfish motives. This fits well with Jesus' call to His disciples to give the proceeds of their possessions to the poor. Jesus' acceptance of this costly "good deed" (καλὸν ἠργάσατο, Matt 26:10) confirms that He counted almsgiving as a mercy level obligation. Only at such a level is His acceptance of the perfume morally acceptable rather than a condoning of sinful injustice. If the very poor were to possess Wolterstorff's sustenance rights, Jesus' acceptance would prove unjust—a trampling of their rights.[10] The disciples' reaction affirms that there were immediately poor people within reach. These could have been assisted with the perfume's proceeds. Jesus' defense of this action as a "good deed" ascribes to almsgiving, even in the face of immediate poverty, a mercy status.[11]

> John 13:29 For some were supposing, because Judas had the money box, that Jesus was saying to him, "Buy the things we have need of for the feast"; or else, that he should *give something to the poor*. (S | I)

---

10. The only way out is to consider this good deed to be an "even higher priority" of justice itself (Wolterstorff, *Justice*, 118). On this proposal, preparing Jesus for burial is one of the highest obligations of interhuman justice—at minimum for all those with nard or the means to buy it. All those who gave alms instead of anointing Jesus during this time would have committed injustice by failing to heed the higher obligation. This, at minimum, does not appear congruent with Jesus' own response to the disciples in Mark 14:7.

11. Some are troubled by Jesus' statement that the immediately poor will remain (Matt 26:11 // Mark 14:7 // John 12:8). This was certainly the case in the apostles' day—to whom the saying was addressed—and remains true, when taken globally, even now. Nevertheless the disciples, in being encouraged to "do good" (Mark 14:7), were still called to give to these immediately poor. Jesus' enunciation that they could do this whenever they desired (θέλω, *thelō*, Mark 14:7) also implies that this is a matter of mercy—as it certainly does not sound like comprehensive constraint.

John 13:29 affirms that Jesus and the disciples often gave alms from out of their support (Luke 8:1–3). For this reason Judas' suspicious exit did not garner the attention that it would have otherwise.

> Acts 9:36, 39–41 Now in Joppa there was a disciple named Tabitha (which translated in Greek is called Dorcas); this woman was abounding with *deeds of kindness and charity* [ἔργων ἀγαθῶν καὶ ἐλεημοσυνῶν] which she continually did. . . . 39 So Peter arose and went with them. When he arrived, they brought him into the upper room; and all the widows stood beside him, weeping and showing all the *tunics and garments* that Dorcas used to make while she was with them. 40 But Peter sent them all out and knelt down and prayed, and turning to the body, he said, "Tabitha, arise." And she opened her eyes, and when she saw Peter, she sat up. 41 And he gave her his hand and raised her up; and calling the saints and widows, he presented her alive. (S | I/P)

Tabitha's "deeds of kindness and charity" (ἔργων ἀγαθῶν καὶ ἐλεημοσυνῶν, Acts 9:36) reveal that good works and alms are related. Tabitha's example reveals that the giving of clothing, and not just the donation of funds, is a legitimate component of almsgiving (v. 39). Tabitha's alms appear to have been focused on widows—women who find themselves in immediate or potential poverty by way of the calamity of losing their husbands (the main provider).

In summary, the almsgiving mandates are all directed at individuals and possess a broad recipient range that extends beyond needy believers to the poor generally. Almsgiving, which is the giving of sustenance aid to the poor, is semantically and hamartiologically identified as an act of mercy in the text.

JERUSALEM COLLECTION

As noted earlier, the collection for the believing poor in Jerusalem is also identified as a form of almsgiving in Acts 24:17. This provision of alms is unique in the NT because its purpose is to alleviate the poverty of believers who are remote from the donors. While most alms were given locally, this collection was taken for remote believers who were, for the most part, of a different nationality and descent. This latter aspect also plays a role in this collection because "the Gentiles have shared in their [Jewish believers'] spiritual things" and thus "they are indebted to minister to them also in material things" (Rom 15:27). Paul's concern that the "service for Jerusalem may prove acceptable to the saints" (Rom

15:31) reveals that the goals of the collection encompass a desire for unity among Jewish and Gentile Christians. Paul's desire is that, as a result of the "proof given by this ministry, they [Jewish believers] will glorify God for your obedience to your confession of the gospel of Christ" (2 Cor 9:13).[12]

Jerusalem Collection Mandates

> 1 Cor 16:1–3 Now concerning the collection for the saints, as I directed the churches of Galatia, so do you also. 2 On the first day of every week each one of you is to put aside and save, *as he may prosper*, so that no collections be made when I come. 3 When I arrive, whomever you may approve, I will send them with letters to carry your *gift [χάρις, charis]* to Jerusalem. (S | M | S |)

In 1 Cor 16:1–3, Paul mandates that the collection be carried out on a weekly basis and that all believers, likely as believing households, are to participate. The donation is to be given in accordance to the "prosperity" (εὐοδόω, *euodoō*) which each one experiences. In accordance to the "whatever extra you earn" (NRSV).[13] Such prospering, here as in 3 John 1:2, is seen as a positive occurrence which enables this contribution to the needs of the Jerusalem saints. The collection is described as a gift, χάρις (*charis*)—a grace or compassionate kindness. This description identifies the collection as an instance of mercy. This passage also indicates that in Corinth, as well as in Galatia, believers did not pool their resources—and were not instructed to do so.

> 2 Cor 8:6–8 So we urged Titus that as he had previously made a beginning, so he would also complete in you this *gracious work* as well. 7 But just as you abound in everything, in faith and utterance and knowledge and in all earnestness and in the love we inspired in you, see that you abound in this *gracious work* also. 8 *I am not speaking this as a command*, but as proving through the earnestness of others the sincerity of your love also. (S | M | S |)

This collection for Jerusalem receives the most attention in Paul's second letter to the Corinthians—particularly in chapters 8 and 9. Paul

---

12. Dunn, *Romans*, 879.

13. Those living at subsistence are not obligated and a first world notion of prosperity is not intended. See Garland, *1 Corinthians*, 754; Robertson and Plummer, *A Critical and Exegetical Commentary on the First Epistle of St. Paul to the Corinthians*, 385; and Thiselton, *The First Epistle to the Corinthians*, 1323.

affirms that the collection is a χάρις (*charis*) in 2 Cor 8:6–7. He further clarifies that this collection is not something commanded and, consequently, is driven by love in a voluntary fashion (v. 8). The earnestness of the churches of Macedonia is to prove an inspiration to them (2 Cor 8:1–5).[14]

> 2 Cor 8:11–12 But now finish doing it also, so that just as there was the readiness to desire it, so there may be also the completion of it *by your ability*. 12 For if the readiness is present, it is acceptable *according to what a person has*, not according to what he does not have. (S | | |)

Second Corinthians 8:11–12 reaffirms that the collection is to be done in accordance with each one's ability and not so as to drive one to poverty—for "it is acceptable according to what a person has" (v. 12).

> 2 Cor 8:13–15 For this is not for the ease of others and for your affliction [θλῖψις, *thlipsis*], but by way of equality— 14 at this present time your abundance [περίσσευμα, *perisseuma*] being a supply for *their need* [ὑστέρημα, *hysterēma*], so that their abundance also may become a supply for your need, that there may be equality; 15 as it is written, "HE WHO gathered MUCH DID NOT HAVE TOO MUCH, AND HE WHO gathered LITTLE HAD NO LACK." (S | | |)

In the following verses, 2 Cor 8:13–15, Paul clarifies that the example of the Macedonians, in giving "beyond their ability" (2 Cor 8:3), is not normative. The collection is not intended to result in the distress (θλῖψις, *thlipsis*) of poverty for them (v. 13). The commended equality is not communist in the commonly perceived sense of aiming toward an equal distribution of goods—and it is certainly, as noted earlier, voluntary. The Corinthians are told not to distribute so as to themselves become afflicted with poverty. Similarly, the collection is intended to meet the need (ὑστέρημα, *hysterēma*) among the Jerusalem saints rather than establish an economic equilibrium or parity. This is reasserted by Paul's quotation of Exod 16:18 which reaffirms the gathering of as much manna as each household needed (Exod 16:16). In 2 Cor 8:15, this proportional-to-need gathering of manna becomes a model for those with abundance to "not have too much" and for those with need to have "no lack." The sharing of the collection is thus intended to voluntarily "shave

---

14. Martin, *2 Corinthians*, 262.

off" the Corinthians' surplus for the sake of alleviating the immediate poverty among some of the Jerusalem saints (the πτωχοί, *ptōchoi*, in Rom 15:26).[15] Paul explains that a reverse flow of abundance (v. 14) may come, as a reciprocity, at some future time.[16] These considerations help to clarify the extent and assistance goals of this almsgiving collection. The sharing is need-based.

> 2 Cor 8:24 Therefore openly before the churches, show them the proof of your love and of our reason for boasting about you. (S | | |)

Here Paul connects participation in the collection with love. Thus love explicitly provides the overarching moral impetus behind the Jerusalem collection.

> 2 Cor 9:5–6 So I thought it necessary to urge the brethren that they would go on ahead to you and arrange beforehand your previously promised bountiful *gift*, so that the same would be ready as a bountiful *gift* and not affected by *covetousness*. 6 Now this I say, he who sows sparingly will also reap sparingly, and he who sows bountifully will also reap bountifully. (S | M | S |)

The collection is also referred to as a gift in 2 Cor 9:5. The term employed, εὐλογία (*eulogia*), refers to a blessing or thank offering and is thus analogous to the "acceptable sacrifice" of meeting Paul's own needs in Phil 4:18.[17] Paul's desire that covetousness, πλεονεξία (*pleonexia*), not

---

15. M. Harris, *The Second Epistle to the Corinthians*, 590–94; Garland, *2 Corinthians*, 384; Plummer, *A Critical and Exegetical Commentary on the Second Epistle of St. Paul to the Corinthians*, 245; Theissen, *The Social Setting of Pauline Christianity*, 99–110. This understanding is *contra* Ralph Martin who guardedly sees the abundance as spiritual rather than material (in both directions). See Martin, *2 Corinthians*, 266–68. But this eschatological reading—where Israel's future blessedness will enrich the engrafted Gentiles—assumes a break in the flow of argument, an abstracting diversion from the topic at hand, and so is the less likely.

16. The future view of this reciprocity makes it more difficult to conceive of it in spiritual terms akin to the past spiritual sharing of Rom 15:27—a sharing which occurred for these Gentiles when they were grafted into the faith. See also Bernard, *The Second Epistle to the Corinthians*, 88; M. Harris, *The Second Epistle to the Corinthians*, 591–92. In this sense, Paul may be challenging them to consider this collection along the lines of K. C. Hanson's and Douglas Oakman's "general reciprocity"—as the reciprocal giving entailed by their adoptive kinship (*Palestine in the Time of Jesus*, 118–19). This possibility makes it that much more intriguing that the collection is identified as a matter of mercy.

17. Martin, *2 Corinthians*, 285.

affect the contribution identifies avarice, which is the desire for wealth and the love of money, as something which would make for an unbountiful gift.[18] In this manner covetousness is related to almsgiving as its nemesis. The notion of reward in 2 Cor 9:6 may not be strong enough to provide a hamartiological differentiation but proves suggestive.

> 2 Cor 9:7 Each one must do just as he has *purposed in his heart, not grudgingly or under compulsion,* for God loves a cheerful giver. (S | M | |)

The next verse, 2 Cor 9:7, explicitly clarifies that the contribution, even though it is for poor believers to whom the Corinthians are spiritually indebted (Rom 15:27), is a matter of mercy obligation. Each person must decide how to give so that the giving is cheerful and ungrudging. The provision of the gift is without compulsion (ἀνάγκη, *anankē*) and thus the opposite of fulfilling a sustenance right.

Jerusalem Collection Clarifiers

> Acts 11:28–30 One of them named Agabus stood up and began to indicate by the Spirit that there would certainly be a great famine all over the world. And this took place in the reign of Claudius. 29 And *in the proportion that any of the disciples had means,* each of them determined to send a contribution for the *relief* [διακονία, *diakonia*] of the brethren living in Judea. 30 And this they did, sending it in charge of Barnabas and Saul to the elders. (S |)

This first passage is widely agreed to refer to an Antiochene collection prior to the main Jerusalem collection itself.[19] The recipients of this "proto-collection" were Christian believers living in Judea. The givers gave in proportion to their individual financial means or "prosperity" (εὐπορέω, *euporeō*). So the community in Antioch also did not pool its resources.[20] Their contribution is referred to as a service or ministry (διακονία, *diakonia*) and hence identifies this collection as an act of mercy. An act of mercy that was not confined to those who are nearby nor

---

18. The possibility that πλεονεξία (*pleonexia*) refers to extortion in 2 Cor 9:5 is unlikely (ibid., 286; M. Harris, *The Second Epistle to the Corinthians*, 629–30).

19. Barrett, *Acts*, 559; Witherington, *The Acts of the Apostles*, 79, 440–43; F. Bruce, *The Book of the Acts*, 230–31; Bock, *Acts*, 417–19; Knox, *Chapters in a Life of Paul*, 38.

20. Barrett, *Acts*, 565.

to those of the same ethnicity or land. This famine occurred somewhere between AD 46 and 48 and appears to have resulted from a destructively high flooding of the Nile in 45–46 or 46–47.[21] Egypt was at this time the breadbasket of the Roman world and, in Judea, the famine was likely further aggravated by the Sabbatical Year of 47–48.[22] Famines among the poorer classes, though usually more localized, were a common occurrence in the ancient world.[23] Regional crop failure, and the associated spike in food prices, meant enduring hunger and possibly facing death for even those who were usually just potentially poor. So while the main Jerusalem collection is not explicitly revealed to be instigated by famine, it may have been a regional factor.

> Acts 24:17 Now after several years I came to bring alms [ἐλεημοσύνη, *eleēmosynē*] to my nation and to present offerings. (S | I/P)

As previously mentioned, Acts 24:17 is important because it relates the main Jerusalem collection to almsgiving.[24]

> Rom 15:25–27 but now, I am going to Jerusalem *serving* [διακονέω, *diakoneō*] the saints. 26 For Macedonia and Achaia have been pleased to make a *contribution* [κοινωνία, *koinōnia*] for the *poor* [πτωχοί, *ptōchoi*] among the saints in Jerusalem. 27 Yes, they were pleased to do so, and they are indebted to them. For if the Gentiles have shared in their spiritual things, they are indebted to minister to them also in material things. (S | I)

Paul also identifies the collection as serving (διακονέω, *diakoneō*) the Judean saints in Rom 15:25–27. This service is recognized as an expression of fellowship—a participatory sharing (κοινωνία, *koinōnia*)—with the immediately poor in Jerusalem. Consequently, such almsgiving to needy believers, even when remote, is an expression of the fellowship and unity of the body of Christ. Paul also affirms that this expression of fellowship is particularly fitting because as "the Gentiles have shared in

---

21. Gapp, "The Universal Famine under Claudius," 258–65; Witherington, *The Acts of the Apostles*, 79–80.

22. Barrett, *Acts*, 563; Witherington, *The Acts of the Apostles*, 80.

23. Esler, *Community and Gospel in Luke–Acts*, 177–78, 188.

24. This almsgiving, as we have witnessed from Second Corinthians 8–9, was intended for the materially poor in the Jerusalem church (Barrett, *Acts*, 1108; Bock, *Acts*, 693; Witherington, *The Acts of the Apostles*, 712).

their [Jewish believers'] spiritual things, they are indebted to minister to them also in material things" (v. 27).

> 2 Cor 8:2–5 that in a great ordeal of *affliction* [θλῖψις, *thlipsis*] their abundance of joy and their *deep* [βάθος, *bathos*] poverty [πτωχεία, *ptōcheia*] overflowed in the wealth of their *liberality* [ἁπλότης, *haplotēs*]. 3 For I testify that according to their ability, and beyond their ability, they gave *of their own accord* [αὐθαίρετος, *authairetos*], 4 begging us with much urging for the favor of participation in the *support* [διακονία, *diakonia*] of the saints, 5 and this, not as we had expected, but they first gave themselves to the Lord and to us by the will of God. (S | I)

The Macedonian believers referred to in 2 Cor 8:2–5 were exemplary, though not normative, because they contributed out of their financial distress (θλῖψις, *thlipsis*) and their deep poverty (βάθους πτωχεία). Their contribution was generous (ἁπλότης, *haplotēs*) and it appears they may have had to convince Paul to accept their merciful διακονία (*diakonia*) to the saints (on account of their poverty). Paul explains that the Macedonians "first gave themselves to the Lord" (v. 5) and this trusting entrusting appears analogous to the trust required to not worry in a fashion akin to the Sermon on the Mount (Matt 6:25–34). Trusting God's provision and acknowledging His lordship appears to have been an important part of their contribution. The poor in Jerusalem appear to have been, by implication of Paul's desire to not alleviate the needs of one group at the expense of the distress of another (2 Cor 8:13–15), very poor.

> 2 Cor 8:9 For you know the *grace* [χάρις, *charis*] of our Lord Jesus Christ, that though He was rich, yet for your sake He became poor, so that you through His poverty might become rich. (S | I)

Jesus' merciful and gracious (χάρις, *charis*) example, of becoming poorer in order to make others richer, is held up as a model in 2 Cor 8:9. As already noted, this mimetic application to the collection is mandated in other passages. The extent of the mimesis is narrowed in the verses that follow (2 Cor 8:13–15).

> 2 Cor 8:19–20 and not only this, but he has also been appointed by the churches to travel with us in this *gracious work* [χάρις, *charis*], which is being administered by us for the glory of the Lord Himself, and to show our readiness, 20 taking precaution so that no one will discredit us in our administration of this generous gift. (S |)

Second Corinthians 8:19–20 likewise reaffirms that the contribution is an instance of χάρις (*charis*) and hence mercy obligation.

> 2 Cor 9:1 For it is superfluous for me to write to you about this *ministry* [διακονία, *diakonia*] to the saints. (S |)

Similarly, the collection is also referred to as a service (διακονία, *diakonia*) in 2 Cor 9:1.

> 2 Cor 9:8–11 And God is able to make all grace abound to you, so that always having *all sufficiency* in everything, you may have an abundance for every *good deed*; 9 as it is written, "HE SCATTERED ABROAD, HE GAVE TO THE POOR, HIS RIGHTEOUSNESS ENDURES FOREVER." 10 Now He who supplies seed to the sower and bread for food will supply and multiply your seed for sowing and increase the harvest of your righteousness; 11 you will be enriched in everything *for all liberality* [ἁπλότης, *haplotēs*], which through us is producing thanksgiving to God. (S |)

In 2 Cor 9:8–11, Paul asserts that God is able to provide the Corinthians with self-sufficiency (αὐτάρκεια, *autarkeia*, v. 8) so that they do not need to fear becoming immediately poor and beggarly themselves as a result of donating their current excess. God is also able to give them an abundance for enabling every good work: πᾶν ἔργον ἀγαθόν (v. 8). As a result, self-sufficiency is affirmed as a legitimate value, along with the close relationship of almsgiving to good works.

The use of πένης (*penēs*) for poor in 2 Cor 9:9 follows the Septuagint translation of Ps 112:9. But even here, in the only occurrence of this term in the NT, it functions as a "placeholder" for πτωχός (*ptōchos*) level poverty. For the Corinthians' scattering is intended to meet the needs of the immediately poor—"the poor [πτωχοί, *ptōchoi*] among the saints in Jerusalem" (Rom 15:26). This integration is indeed difficult to avoid for πτωχός (*ptōchos*) is the terminology Paul himself employs when he is not quoting from the Septuagint.[25]

Paul further consoles the Corinthians in verse 11 that God's supply will enrich (πλουτίζω, *ploutizō*) them and thus enable all their engage-

---

25. As noted in chapter 2, Rom 15:26 is unlikely to employ this language of poverty to signify a self-designation of the Jerusalem saints (Dunn, *Romans*, 875). Particularly in light of the clarifying concretization of the recipients that is found in Second Corinthians 8–9.

ments in generosity (ἁπλότης, *haplotēs*).²⁶ Such enrichment is subsequently not bad in itself—at least as long as it is used as God intends (v. 11). This passage also serves to highlight the connection between good works, almsgiving, and "all" generosity (πᾶσαν ἁπλότητα, v. 11)—which is here suggestively connected to helping the poor.²⁷

> 2 Cor 9:12-13 For the *ministry* [διακονία, *diakonia*] *of this service* is not only fully supplying the *needs* of the saints, but is also overflowing through many thanksgivings to God. 13 Because of the proof given by this *ministry* [διακονία, *diakonia*], they will glorify God for your obedience to your confession of the gospel of Christ and for the *liberality* [ἁπλότης, *haplotēs*] of your *contribution* [κοινωνία] to them and to all. (S |)

The immediately following verses, 2 Cor 9:12-13, reinforce the mercy character of the collection, which is referred to as a ministry of sacred service (διακονία τῆς λειτουργίας) in verse 12 and again as a service (διακονία, *diakonia*) in verse 13.²⁸ The participatory sharing of fellowship (κοινωνία, *koinōnia*) is connected to alleviating the needs (ὑστέρημα, *hysterēma*, lack) of the Judean believers.²⁹

Perhaps Gal 6:2, which mandates that Christians "Bear one another's burdens, and thereby fulfill the law of Christ," also deserves a brief

---

26. Ralph Martin's translation of 2 Cor 9:11, that "you will be made rich in every way so that you can always be generous" captures the thought well (Martin, *2 Corinthians*, 292).

27. The occurrence of צְדָקָה (*tsedaqah*) in the here quoted Ps 112:9—which sometimes refers to preceptive justice rather than broader righteousness—does not override Paul's explicit categorization of the main Jerusalem collection as a matter of voluntary mercy (2 Cor 9:7). Even so, the context of Psalm 112 itself suggests the broader righteousness usage. For additional discussion of δικαιοσύνη (*dikaiosynē*), the translation, as it is used here, see M. Harris, *The Second Epistle to the Corinthians*, 640-41.

28. "λειτουργός," BDAG 591-92.

29. The broadening extension to "all" (v. 13) appears to reaffirm that the sharing fellowship which the Corinthians experience is not just with their Judean brethren but with all believers—that it is a fellowship that would help even elsewhere if need be (Martin, *2 Corinthians*, 294). Another possibility is that Paul intends the Corinthians to understand that helping the Jerusalem church helps all believers—all those bonded together with the Judean saints—by way of benefiting an integral part of the universal body and strengthening Christian unity (Plummer, *A Critical and Exegetical Commentary on the Second Epistle of St. Paul to the Corinthians*, 267). It is the occurrence of the term κοινωνία (*koinōnia*) that makes an extension to all people, believing and unbelieving, unlikely (even to other Judeans also suffering hardship)—*pace* M. Harris, *The Second Epistle to the Corinthians*, 655.

note. Some, such as John Strelan, have argued that the burden-bearing mentioned here is a reference to the financial support of the Jerusalem church.[30] It is nevertheless more likely that the burdens of Gal 6:2 relate to the temptations of Gal 6:1 and, by extension, to other heavy burdens that a believer may face.[31]

The collection for Jerusalem obligated believers, who gave as members of their local churches (2 Cor 8:1), to provide alms to their remote brethren in Judea. For the Antiochene "proto-collection," the cause of the Judean poverty is revealed to be calamity, the "great famine" during "the *reign* of Claudius" (Acts 11:28).[32] The main Jerusalem collection is also need-focused, just like the almsgiving of which it is a subset, and its recipients are identified as the immediately poor. This contribution, despite the extra additive of its obligators' spiritual indebtedness, is both semantically and explicitly identified as possessing a mercy level of obligation. The maintaining of this mercy status, particularly in the face of a famine (as with the proto-collection), contradicts the claimed justice status of Wolterstorff's third duty—to sustain the victims of sustenance deprivation.

SHARE

The giving of alms is conceptually related to beneficent sharing and to providing for sustenance needs. Jesus mandates such sharing in the parable of the sheep and the goats.

Share Mandates

> Matt 25:31–46 But when the Son of Man comes in His glory, and all the angels with Him, then He will sit on His glorious throne. 32 All the nations will be gathered before Him; and He will separate them from one another, as the shepherd separates the sheep from the goats; 33 and He will put the sheep on His right, and the goats on the left. 34 Then the King will say to those on His right, "Come, you who are blessed of My Father, inherit the kingdom prepared for you from the foundation of the world. 35 *For I was hungry, and you gave Me something to eat; I was thirsty, and you gave Me something to drink; I was a stranger, and you invited*

---

30. Strelan, "Burden-Bearing and the Law of Christ," 266–76.
31. E. M. Young, "Fulfill the Law of Christ," 31–42; Longenecker, *Galatians*, 274.
32. Knowling, *The Acts of the Apostles*, 270.

Me in; 36 *naked, and you clothed Me; I was sick, and you visited* [ἐπισκέπτομαι, *episkeptomai*] *Me; I was in prison, and you came to Me.*" 37 Then the righteous will answer Him, "Lord, when did we see You hungry, and feed You, or thirsty, and give You something to drink? 38 And when did we see You a stranger, and invite You in, or naked, and clothe You? 39 When did we see You sick, or in prison, and come to You?" 40 The King will answer and say to them, "*Truly I say to you, to the extent that you did it to one of these brothers of Mine, even the least of them, you did it to Me.*" 41 Then He will also say to those on His left, "Depart from Me, *accursed ones* [καταράομαι, *kataraomai*], into the eternal fire which has been prepared for the devil and his angels; 42 for I was hungry, and you gave Me nothing to eat; I was thirsty, and you gave Me nothing to drink; 43 I was a stranger, and you did not invite Me in; naked, and you did not clothe Me; sick, and in prison, and you did not *visit* [ἐπισκέπτομαι, *episkeptomai*] *Me.*" 44 Then they themselves also will answer, "Lord, when did we see You hungry, or thirsty, or a stranger, or naked, or sick, or in prison, and did not *take care of* [διακονέω, *diakoneō*] You?" 45 Then He will answer them, "*Truly I say to you, to the extent that you did not do it to one of the least of these, you did not do it to Me.*" 46 These will go away into eternal punishment, but the righteous into eternal life. (S | M | S | I)

The parable of the sheep and the goats is perhaps the most famous mandate passage concerning helping the poor. When we first encountered this passage in the previous chapter I argued that, despite initially appearing to assume a justice obligation status for its mandates, this passage entailed mercy treatments. For just as the general reward of eternal life is not specific enough to classify these mandates as issues of mercy, the warning of eternal punishment is best understood to extend to lacking the broader righteousness of being a genuinely believing follower of the Messiah. In this way, this passage's obedience is seen as analogous to possessing the living faith of Jas 2:14–17 and having the love of God abide in the believer in a 1 John 3:16–18 manner. The fact that most of the components of verse 35 are explicitly labeled as matters of mercy in the parable of the good Samaritan (Luke 10:30–37) prepares the reader for the labeling of all of these instances of care as διακονέω (*diakoneō*) in verse 44. This service terminology intimates that these specific mandates are issues of mercy. As a result, in terms of needy believers (v. 40), feeding the hungry, providing drink to the thirsty, showing hospitality to strangers, clothing the naked, and caring for the sick and imprisoned are acts of mercy.³³ Such needs are characteristic of those in immediate poverty. The imprisoned were often dependent on those outside to provide for their sustenance needs and the ἀσθενέω (*astheneō*, vv. 36, 39, ἀσθενής, *asthenēs*, vv. 43, 44), whether sick, disabled, or physically feeble, were similarly in need of external assistance.

But this interpretation needs some defending. We are faced with two plausible interpretive options. Is this passage really about believers aiding and serving the least among themselves or rather about unbelievers receiving Jesus' messengers and their message? What if it really is all about the message?³⁴

The matter is complex. Still, adjudicating the disparity hinges on identifying who "the least" (vv. 40, 45) are and on isolating the likelier passage prequel via subject matter similarity and conceptual fit. The difficulty with the term for "the least," ἐλάχιστος (*elachistos*), is that it is the superlative of μικρός (*mikros*)—the term Jesus employs when speaking of the "little ones" (Matt 10:42; 18:6, 10, 14; Mark 9:42; Luke 17:2). And, so the argument goes, if the "little ones" are Jesus' disciples, then "the least" likewise refers to His followers. This approach takes the genitive, τῶν ἐλαχίστων, as a synonym for "these brothers of Mine" rather than as a subcategory of them—"the least of these who are members of my family" (NRSV). So who are the intended referents—all believers or the socially least among the brethren? Even a deference to Jesus' "little ones" terminology is not conclusive. For even in Matthew it may well refer to believing children rather than to believers generally. How may we go about reconstructing Jesus' intent? Matthew 18 provides the most context in this respect for the term recurs here the most. The "one such child" of Matt 18:5 refers most naturally to other believing children like the exemplar Jesus had just set before His disciples in verses 2–4.³⁵

---

33. Within the remainder of Matthew, all of the referents to Jesus' "my brothers" statements are His followers (Matt 12:48–49; 28:10). It is therefore unlikely that humankind generally is intended here. This consistent pattern, when not referring to biological kin, is maintained even outside of Matthew (John 20:17; Rom 8:29; Heb 2:11–12). Craig Blomberg rightly identifies this as the "majority perspective" throughout church history (Blomberg, *Neither Poverty nor Riches*, 126). For additional argumentation see Hagner, *Matthew*, 744; Blomberg, *Matthew*, 377.

34. So Sherman Gray contends that "the main point of the parable is the acceptance or the rejection of the Christian faith" (Gray, *The Least of My Brothers*, 353). The "receiving messengers" option has drawn many contemporary supporters, including Hagner, *Matthew*, 746–47; Blomberg, *Matthew*, 379–80.

35. *Pace* Blomberg, *Matthew*, 273; Hagner, *Matthew*, 521. The logic of verses 3–4

The parallel passages, Mark 9:34–37 and Luke 9:46–48, concur that the disciples' humbling is to be manifest precisely in receiving and serving "one child like this" (Matt 18:5 // Mark 9:37). That in so doing, in putting themselves in the position of the least so as to be logically required to wait upon a child, is how they can become the greatest. So Luke 9:48 has "this child" to remove all possible ambiguity. And so, even in Matthew, "one child like this" is not likely to metaphorically refer to the disciple who has humbled himself—but rather to believing children like the one shown. Furthermore, just like in Mark and Luke, Jesus says these things to the disciples in Matthew ("the twelve" in Mark 9:35) without indicating any change in the intended obligators. Jesus' already believing disciples are to receive such children.

So what are we to make of Matt 18:6? If we had just this passage, the continuity between "whoever receives one such child in My name" (v. 5) and "but whoever causes one of these little ones who believe in Me to stumble" (v. 6) would suggest the same referent.[36] That these "little ones" are believing children. That the "little ones" *are* little ones. But just like with Matt 25:40, the genitive, τῶν πιστευόντων (of the believing), may be taken as a synonym which clarifies who the "little ones" are rather than as demarcating the subcategory of little ones—the believing among them. Jesus does occasionally call His followers "babes" or "infants" when contrasting them to the "wise and intelligent" (Matt 11:25; Luke 10:21), but the present context does not, in itself, demand or expect a sweeping change of referents.[37] Furthermore, Matthew 18 makes it difficult to consistently adhere to this proposed change. Particularly if Richard France is correct that the "despising" of verse 10 is the opposite of the "welcoming" of verse 5—for it is believing children that are welcomed there.[38] Perhaps even stronger is the implication present in verse 10 that a subset of believers is in view. For its punch line is highly

---

implies that the child was converted. Furthermore, Richard France suggests that the "in My name" of verse 5 also "implies that the child represents Jesus" (France, *The Gospel of Matthew*, 679). In agreement are Davies and Allison, *Matthew*, 2:760.

36. The Gospel writers wrote with hearers in mind. And such an auditory audience relates things backwards rather than forwards—for it cannot "scan" ahead of the public reader.

37. Outside of Matthew, Jesus also addresses the disciples as "children" (plural of τέκνον, teknon) in Mark 10:24 and "generically" as "children" (plural of παιδίον, paidion)—in a social way before they recognize Him—in John 21:5.

38. France, *The Gospel of Matthew*, 686.

diminished on the view that the "little ones" are actually *all* believers. For its mandate is given to Jesus' followers.[39] So "their angels in heaven continually see the face" of the Father—yeah, big deal, so do mine.[40] This verse just does not sound like a "one another" command. So even Craig Blomberg, an advocate of the "receiving messengers" interpretation, allows the "little ones" to perhaps focus particularly on the least.[41] The final reference to the "little ones" in this passage (v. 14), a call to help the straying rather than causing them to stumble, is compatible with both referent definitions. God is attentive to "the little ones"—whether children or the spiritually weak among the brethren. And so this verse cannot dissuade from the general proclivity of Matthew 18 toward depicting believing children as the primary referent for μικρός (*mikros*). So why the change in terminology from "child" (παιδίον, *paidion*, vv. 2–5) to "little ones" (μικροί, *mikroi*, plural of *mikros*, vv. 6, 10, 14)? Perhaps to allow for a slight broadening to those that are like the children in social status—the particular aspect that made the child exemplary (in vv. 3–4). Indeed, it is not the serving humble that are naturally "despised" but those who, like children, were the socially least. Still this extrapolation of the child's exemplary function to the "little ones" remains but tentative.

What about the remaining passages which refer to the μικροί (*mikroi*) but one time each? The only other occurrence within Matthew does, by way of its context (Matt 10:5–6, 14), pertain to unbelievers receiving Jesus' messengers and their message (Matt 10:40–42). The symmetry within the Greek text of Matt 10:41–42 (brought out well in the NRSV translation) requires that the "little ones" be disciples—or some subset of the disciples. So even here the "little ones" need not refer to believers generally. For indeed, Jesus' point is made the more poignant by not only downsizing the receiving to its least significant manifestation but by also downsizing its recipients to the socially least among the disciples. This approach fits very amiably with Jesus' intended buildup and contrast here.[42] For receiving the least of the disciples with the least token

---

39. This observation is important. The "whoever" of verses 4–6 and the "yours" and "you" of verses 8–13 confirm that believers—and the disciples in particular (v. 1)—remain the intended audience.

40. Or "so does mine"—the passage allows for both understandings.

41. Blomberg, *Matthew*, 274. And others concur, including Davies and Allison, *Matthew*, 2:753, 777; Meier, "Matthew, Gospel of," *ABD* 4:633.

42. *Pace* France, *The Gospel of Matthew*, 412–13; Davies and Allison, *Matthew*, 2:227; Hagner, *Matthew*, 295.

of welcome nonetheless surprisingly still earns the highest reward—the one which shall never perish (οὐ μὴ ἀπολέσῃ τὸν μισθὸν αὐτοῦ, v. 42). A reward which dwarfs the ones given by the prophet or the righteous man.[43] And so the NLT has: "And if you give even a cup of cold water to one of the least of my followers, you will surely be rewarded" (v. 42). Thus the twelve (v. 5) have nothing to worry about or to be ashamed of. If welcoming even the least follower of Jesus brings such blessing, they may now go with expectant confidence. For all of Jesus' followers are worthy of welcome—if even the lesser, than how much more the greater.

And so "these little ones" of Matt 10:42 may have referred (as an object lesson) to some believing children who happened to be nearby or may have well been understood by the disciples as referring to the socially least among Jesus' followers.[44] A referral to believers generally is not required—or even, as I have argued, to be preferred. So even Blomberg, though arriving via different interpretive considerations, allows for this possibility.[45]

Of the remaining two passages, Mark 9:42 is given in a context which allows for both meanings while Luke 17:2, for its part, appears relatively contextless. Though the immediately preceding verse to Mark 9:42 concerns receiving Jesus' emissaries, receiving the exemplary child as part of being the "last of all and servant of all" (v. 35 of vv. 34–37) is close by. And so some scholars support a referral back to the literal children.[46] Luke 17:2 can also go either way, though the immediately following verse is parallel to Matt 18:15—the verse which follows right after

---

43. While the genitive might be taken as receiving a reward like the one the prophet or righteous man receives, receiving the disciples is receiving Jesus (Matt 10:40)—thus it best concerns what the disciples can bless the receiver with. Richard France provides further argumentation for taking the genitives as genitives of origin while others allow for the possibility (France, *The Gospel of Matthew*, 414; Davies and Allison, *Matthew*, 2:227).

44. Interestingly, the adjectival form of μικρός (*mikros*) occurs in Luke 9:48, a parallel verse for Matt 18:4, to describe the least *among* the disciples (rather than all the disciples). To describe the one who takes on the social position of the least. This same form also occurs on Jesus' lips in Matt 11:11 (// Luke 7:28) to speak of the least among those "in the kingdom of heaven"—to refer to those of the least objective status among Jesus' followers.

45. Blomberg, *Matthew*, 182.

46. See, for example, C. A. Evans, *Mark 8:27—16:20*, 70.

the "little ones" section in Matthew 18. This too would hint at the least, though, as mentioned, the context here is not particularly forthcoming.[47]

So what may we conclude about the "little ones"? That the precedent in Matthew, if anything, favors a referral to believing children or the socially least among the brethren—those that the children represent. At the very minimum we may agree that "believers generally" are not the clear shoo-ins. The remaining instances are uncertain. And so, of the three options—that μικρός (mikros) refers to believing children as the least, to Jesus' followers, or to both depending on the context—the first option appears most tempting while the last remains a viable possibility.[48] So we will have to cope with some uncertainty here. Still, the least we can say is that the usage of μικρός (mikros) is not determinative for identifying its superlative as referring to all the disciples (or messengers or believers). And this is a significant result.

Furthermore, beyond the precedent found in the use of μικρός (mikros) in Matthew, the term for "the least" (ἐλάχιστος, elachistos) is never employed to signify Jesus' followers generally in the Gospel—or anywhere else. But rather, when Jesus employs it in Matt 5:19, it refers to the least *among* those "in the kingdom of heaven." To the least in terms of objective status—just like with the commandments of the lowest rank and standing. So Paul uses ἐλάχιστος (elachistos) to refer to himself as the least *among* the apostles due to his persecution of the church (1 Cor 15:9). And as the least *among* the saints in Eph 3:8.[49] And so the precedent within Matthew, like elsewhere, is to understand the superlative ἐλάχιστος (elachistos) of Matt 25:40, 45 as referring to a subset among the believers—to those of the lowest status. And this precedent is indeed more semantically immediate than the possible precedent to be found within the use of μικρός (mikros).

---

47. So the possibility of literal children or the low status poor is acknowledged. See Marshall, *The Gospel of Luke*, 641.

48. A number of scholars recognize that a reference to literal children is a possibility for Jesus' intent—even when they prefer another interpretation. See, for example, Davies and Allison, *Matthew*, 2:763. Thomas Manson is perhaps the most acknowledged advocate of the children view (Manson, *The Sayings of Jesus*, 138–39). Referring back to Zech 13:7 does not accomplish much to strengthen the "believers generally" view for Jesus only quotes the sheep component—rather than the "little ones" portion—as referring to the disciples (Matt 26:31 // Mark 14:7).

49. The use of ἐλάχιστος (elachistos) as a comparative is consistent throughout the NT. In Luke 12:26; 16:10; 19:17; and 1 Cor 4:3 it comparatively signifies the least thing. And in 1 Cor 6:2 and Jas 3:4 it refers to the least thing in terms of form or size. It nowhere hints of a metaphorical meaning.

But even when we agree that "the least" actually refers to the least in status among the brethren, the parable of the sheep and the goats may still be about unbelievers receiving such messengers and their message rather than about believers serving the least among themselves. For both mandates find conceptual prequels in Matthew. If Matt 10:40–42 is taken as the appropriate precedent then the parable's call concerns unbelievers receiving Jesus' emissaries—even the least among them. Yet if Matt 18:5 is the more probable prequel then the mandate rather compels believers to aid and serve the least among the brethren. That Matt 18:5 mandates such interbeliever receiving is, as we have seen, strongly affirmed by its parallels and furthermore demanded by the passage itself where the disciples themselves, rather than unbelievers, are the addressed—the ones who are to receive one such low status child. Still, both prequel passages harbor the same "receives Me" language that suggests a similarity of subject matter with the "did it to Me," ἐμοὶ ἐποιήσατε, of Matt 25:40, 45.

So where does the precedent fall? Which passage prequel is the better conceptual fit? The verdict appropriately comes down to assessing the indicators present within the disputed parable itself. What kind of receiving is the more likely in Matt 25:31–46? *That* of believers aiding the least among themselves. For it is very unlikely that unbelievers would *come to*, ἤλθατε πρός, messengers who were sick and shut in, non-able-bodied, or in prison (Matt 25:36, 39). That the unbelieving would "go to see" (ἐπισκέπτομαι, *episkeptomai*) Jesus' emissaries while they were enfeebled and locked away (Matt 25:43). For that is not how the missionary calling works. It is the emissaries that do the coming to unbelievers—it is they that are sent out. How would unbelievers go about seeking out and visiting messengers who are imprisoned or at home sick? So this is not the welcoming of Matt 10:42. It is the serving of the least like in Matt 18:5. So the parable of the sheep and the goats can, in the end, say what it initially appears to say when taken in itself.[50] And believers are mandated to aid and serve the least among themselves—whether they be missionaries or not.[51]

Forsaking the "receiving messengers" interpretation does not entail that this passage is urging salvation by works. Providing this kind of aid to needy brethren is what believers do out of brotherly love. It is part of

---

50. There is no intimation of messengers or their message within the parable itself. Such suppositions must be imported from outside.

51. So John Calvin identifies "poor and distressed" believers as the rightful beneficiaries of this mandate (*Commentary on a Harmony of the Evangelists*, 3:181).

how we show that we love one another to the world. There is no soteriological difference in considering this serving to be the works of a proper response to Jesus' messengers and their message as opposed to the works of faith. There is no soteriological problem.[52]

So having shored up this parable as indeed intending to benefit the least among the brethren as they experience sustenance needs, we may return to considering its implications. While not the objects of this mandate, it is not an unfounded extrapolation to presume that doing such service to unbelievers would also constitute mercy. Because believers have a higher obligation to "do good" to "those who are of the household of the faith" (Gal 6:10), it is indeed hard to conceive that providing such assistance to unbelievers would be an issue of justice.[53] Jesus' mention of "the least of these" (Matt 25:40, 45) appears to the author as a vehicle for affirming that providing such care even—nay, especially (v. 45)—to the least socially or spiritually significant believer is nevertheless rendering it unto the lofty King (vv. 31, 34). From a sociological point of view, such "least significant" were, in Jesus' day, the young, the literal servants, and the low class poor. Nevertheless, Jesus may have had spiritual "worthiness" in view as in Matt 5:19—which, as noted, constitutes the only other use of ἐλάχιστος (*elachistos*), as it refers to people, in Matthew. A similar referral to spiritual status occurs with the adjectival form of μικρός (*mikros*) in Matt 11:11—while Matthew 18 seems to go in the social status direction with this terminology. The present context leans, if anywhere, toward social and physical neediness rather than spiritual

---

52. That is, unless the interpreter assumes that the totality of salvation is being addressed here in an exclusive manner. That this is all there is to being a brother of Jesus rather than just one aspect of being a believer. Dispelling this notion requires but observing that the earlier parable of Matt 24:45–51 speaks of proper and improper leadership as that which leads to reward or eternal punishment. And so taking either parable as a totality subverts the other—is salvation a function of serving the least or sensibly providing for those one leads? Matthew 24:45–51 is addressed to the disciples (v. 3)—specifically so (v. 44)—because it pertains to the manner of their leading of the other servants that they are given charge over—*contra* Blomberg, *Matthew*, 367–69 (who, while acknowledging that leaders "must serve more than rule," generalizes to everyone); Bock, *The Gospel of Mark*, 320–21; Hagner, *Matthew*, 725. This is affirmed all the more clearly in Luke 12:40–48—the parallel (Marshall, *The Gospel of Luke*, 540–41, 544; Nolland, *Luke*, 704–5). And so such parables nuance and mandate what believers are to be like rather than individually articulating everything that pertains to being saved.

53. This same concern for prioritizing the serving of believers is also found, as we have seen, within the Synoptics (Matt 18:1–5; Mark 9:34–37; and Luke 9:46–48).

neediness. While going (ἔρχομαι, *erchomai*, vv. 36, 39) to the sick and imprisoned is somewhat nonspecific in itself, the clarification that this going constitutes visiting (ἐπισκέπτομαι, *episkeptomai*, vv. 36, 43) these recipients confirms that the provision of aid is intended.[54]

> Luke 3:11 And he would answer and say to them, "The man who has *two tunics is to share with him who has none; and he who has food is to do likewise.*" (S | | | I)

In Luke 3:11, John the Baptist mandates that anyone possessing two or more sets of clothes ought to share with the immediately poor person who has none. Similarly if one has sufficient food he is to share with the immediately poor person who has none. The obligation status of such sharing is not clarified in this passage nor in the analogous Jas 2:14–17 and 1 John 3:16–18 passages (though it is hinted at in the latter).

> Luke 10:27-37 And he answered, "YOU SHALL LOVE THE LORD YOUR GOD WITH ALL YOUR HEART, AND WITH ALL YOUR SOUL, AND WITH ALL YOUR STRENGTH, AND WITH ALL YOUR MIND; AND YOUR NEIGHBOR AS YOURSELF." 28 And He said to him, "You have answered correctly; DO THIS AND YOU WILL LIVE." 29 But wishing to justify himself, he said to Jesus, "And who is my *neighbor*?" 30 Jesus replied and said, "A man was going down from Jerusalem to Jericho, and fell among robbers, and they stripped him and beat him, and went away leaving him half dead. 31 And by chance a priest was going down on that road, and when he saw him, he passed by on the other side. 32 Likewise a Levite also, when he came to the place and saw him, passed by on the other side. 33 But a Samaritan, who was on a journey, came upon him; and when he saw him, he felt *compassion*, 34 and came to him and bandaged up his wounds, pouring oil and wine on them; and he put him on his own beast, and brought him to an inn and took care of him. 35 On the next day he took out two denarii and gave them to the innkeeper and said, 'Take care of him; and whatever more you spend, when I return I will repay you.' 36 Which of these three do you think proved to be a neighbor to the man who fell into the robbers' hands?" 37 And he said, "The one who *showed mercy* [ποιήσας τὸ ἔλεος] toward him." Then Jesus said to him, "Go and do [ποιέω, *poieō*] *the same.*" (SPI | M | S | I)

---

54. This "looking after," communicated through the language of "visiting," is also mandated in Jas 1:27. See Hagner, *Matthew*, 745; Beyer, "ἐπισκέπτομαι, ἐπισκοπέω," *TDNT* 2:604.

Luke 10:27, 33, 36–37 clarifies that part of the content of the command to love one's neighbor is to have mercy on the immediately poor person who has come to this state as a result of injustice. Providing shelter, care, and medical care to a half dead (ἡμιθανής, *hēmithanēs*) crime victim is nevertheless related to taking pity on such a victim. This passage affirms that acting out of compassion (σπλαγχνίζομαι, *splanchnizomai*, v. 33) and showing mercy (ποιήσας τὸ ἔλεος, v. 37) is indeed congruent. The Samaritan provided his aid to someone who would have looked down upon him and extended his aid to allow for the victim's recovery. Jesus' command to go and do likewise (v. 37) extends the specific nature of this mandate to the principle resolution level and as far as the impetus resolution level of love (v. 27). Jesus' parable of the good Samaritan likewise controverts Wolterstorff's third duty.

> Luke 14:12–14 And He also went on to say to the one who had invited Him, "When you give a luncheon or a dinner, do not invite your friends or your brothers or your relatives or rich neighbors, otherwise they may also invite you in return and that will be your repayment. 13 But when you give a reception, *invite the poor, the crippled, the lame, the blind,* 14 and you will be *blessed*, since *they do not have the means to repay you*; for you will be *repaid at the resurrection of the righteous.*" (S | M | H | I)

In this passage, Jesus commands His hearers to invite the immediately poor to their receptions and feasts. His intent is not that they never invite their relatives but that such generosity is likely to be repaid (v. 12) and is therefore not meritorious before God. The recipients are revealed to be immediately poor (πτωχοί, *ptōchoi*) both semantically and by the fact that they cannot repay the invite (v. 14). It is both revealing and logical that this category of poor would readily enfold the disabled—"the crippled, the lame, the blind" (v. 13). The disabled of Jesus' day would have had virtually insurmountable difficulties in finding employment and were commonly among the beggarly poor due to this personal calamity. Jesus' offer of reward identifies this hospitable sharing as an issue of mercy even when extended to those who could not provide for themselves because they were not able-bodied.

> Rom 12:13 *contributing* [κοινωνέω, *koinōneō*] to the *needs* of the saints, practicing *hospitality* [φιλοξενία, *philoxenia*]. (S | | | I/P)

Here Paul enjoins κοινωνέω (koinōneō)—the participatory fellowship of meeting the needs of the needy among the saints.[55] Paul later uses κοινωνία (koinōnia) in speaking of the collection for the immediately poor in Jerusalem in Rom 15:26 (and in 2 Cor 9:13). Practicing a love of strangers or foreigners, φιλοξενία (philoxenia), is also mandated. Such hospitality was necessary to supply the needs of traveling or itinerant brethren. Jesus extols it in the parable of the sheep and the goats (Matt 25:35, 38, 43, 44).

> Rom 12:20-21 "BUT IF YOUR ENEMY IS HUNGRY, FEED HIM, AND IF HE IS THIRSTY, GIVE HIM A DRINK; FOR IN SO DOING YOU WILL HEAP BURNING COALS ON HIS HEAD." 21 Do not be overcome by evil, but overcome evil with good. (S | | | I)

Paul's command in Rom 12:20-21, to provide for the sustenance needs of one's enemy if given the opportunity, reveals that doing good (v. 21) is accomplished even in such "basic" immediate poverty alleviation. This command is quoted from Prov 25:21-22, which reveals that God explicitly rewards such treatment (v. 22).

> Heb 13:16 And do not neglect *doing good* and *sharing* [κοινωνία, koinōnia], for with such sacrifices God is pleased. (SP | | | I/P)

This principle level command relates doing good to sharing, κοινωνία (koinōnia), in the intended sense of assisting in the support of other believers.[56] The recipients of this sharing are immediately or potentially poor believers, for which other believers would need to be shared with as a matter of doing good?[57]

> Jas 2:14-17 What use is it, my brethren, if someone says he has faith but he has no works? Can that faith save him? 15 If a brother or sister is *without clothing and in need of daily food*, 16 and one of you says to them, "Go in peace, be warmed and be filled," and yet you do not give them *what is necessary for their body*, what

---

55. Dunn, *Romans*, 743; Schreiner, *Romans*, 666; R. Mounce, *Romans*, 238.

56. Campbell, "ΚΟΙΝΩΝΙΑ and Its Cognates in the New Testament," 21-22; Thurén, *Das Lobopfer der Hebräer*, 177; Lane, *Hebrews*, 552.

57. This sharing is nevertheless most likely to be aimed toward the immediately poor as the hearers were themselves, on balance, likely in a situation of potential poverty. This is intimated in Heb 13:5-6, which asserts that their contentment with what they have will require of them a reliance on God's faithful help (formerly they had already experienced having their possessions seized, Heb 10:34). See Lane, *Hebrews*, 518.

> use is that? 17 Even so faith, if it has no works, is dead, being by itself. (S | | | I)

The remaining two mandate passages are analogous to the parable of the sheep and the goats. James 2:14–17 affirms that saving faith entails works.[58] The works specified are those that also drew a mandate from John the Baptist (Luke 3:11)—namely the provision of clothing and food. The recipients are revealed to be immediately poor because they are in need of "clothing" and "daily food" (v. 15). Providing "what is necessary for their body" (v. 16) likewise intimates meeting immediate sustenance needs. Such specific sharing possesses the significant obligation of manifesting a useful and living faith. Nevertheless, its exact status is uncertain here.[59]

> 1 John 3:16–18 We know love by this, that He laid down His life for us; and we ought to lay down our lives for the brethren. 17 But whoever has the *world's goods*, and sees his brother in *need* [χρεία, *chreia*] and closes his heart [σπλάγχνον, *splanchnon*] against him, how does the love of God abide in him? 18 Little children, let us not love with word or with tongue, but in *deed* and truth. (SGI | | | I)

First John 3:16–18 continues in this train of thought by asserting that having "the love of God abide" in a believer entails that she, provided she has the "world's goods" (v. 17), use this means to help believers who are in need (χρεία, *chreia*).[60] Such assistance is a deed of love (v. 18). And the reference to closing one's inward parts (σπλάγχνον, *splanchnon*) may imply that this mandate is related to being moved by mercy.[61]

---

58. A negative answer, in terms of salvation, is explicitly expected in verse 14: μὴ δύναται ἡ πίστις σῶσαι αὐτόν. And so Craig Blomberg rightly wonders why "we hear few applications of our much-vaunted plain-meaning hermeneutic" to this passage (Blomberg, "The Globalization of Hermeneutics," 585).

59. Though Jas 2:13, the transitionary verse, is perhaps suggestive of mercy.

60. Whether ἡ ἀγάπη τοῦ θεοῦ is taken as a subjective genitive, objective genitive, or descriptive genitive is ultimately of little prescriptive consequence—for possessing God's love, or a love for God, or a divine love is all a part of being truly His (Akin, *1, 2, 3 John*, 161; Marshall, *The Epistles of John*, 194–95; Smalley, *1, 2, 3 John*, 197).

61. "σπλάγχνον," BDAG 938.

Share Clarifiers

> Acts 2:44–46 And all those who had believed were together and had all things in common; 45 and they began selling their property and possessions and were *sharing* [διαμερίζω, *diamerizō*] them with all, as anyone might have *need* [χρεία, *chreia*]. 46 Day by day continuing with one mind in the temple, and breaking bread from house to house, they were taking their meals together with gladness and *sincerity* [ἀφελότης, *aphelotēs*] of heart. (S | I)

The sharing of Acts 2:44–46 involved the perspective that a believer's possessions were intended to meet the needs of other believers. The distribution (διαμερίζω, *diamerizō*) of the proceeds was done to those in need.[62] The believers' practice of "taking their meals together" (v. 46) also involved sharing for they "shared their meals with great joy and generosity" (NLT). The generosity mentioned here is ἀφελότης (*aphelotēs*), a NT *hapax legomenon* which likewise does not occur in the LXX, but is nevertheless considered to be equivalent to ἁπλότης (*haplotēs*, generosity).[63] These meals are "regular meals" but carried out in a "generous" manner.[64] The generous sharing that occurred when they ate together is thus similar to the love feast mentioned in Jude 1:12 and would have benefited "those who have nothing" (1 Cor 11:22).

> Acts 6:1 Now at this time while the disciples were increasing in number, a complaint arose on the part of the Hellenistic Jews against the native Hebrews, because their *widows* were being overlooked in the *daily serving of food*. (S | I/P)

A concern for providing "daily food" to immediately poor widows is revealed in Acts 6:1. The overlooking of the Hellenistic widows prompted the selection of apparently Hellenistic deacons (Acts 6:5) who were to make sure that this merciful service (διακονία, *diakonia*, v. 1) was provided to all the believing widows.[65]

---

62. The believers' attitude of having all things in common will be engaged in the upcoming section concerning Possessions Clarifiers Following Jesus' Ministry.

63. This equivalence is generally affirmed—even when the terminology is taken in its simplicity sense—as by Barrett, *Acts*, 171; Knowling, *The Acts of the Apostles*, 97.

64. Bock, *Acts*, 154.

65. All the deacons' names are suggestively Greek (Volf, *Exclusion and Embrace*, 230).

> 1 Cor 11:21–22, 33–34 for in your eating each one *takes his own supper first*; and one is *hungry* and another is drunk. 22 What! Do you not have houses in which to eat and drink? Or do you despise the church of God and shame *those who have nothing*? What shall I say to you? Shall I praise you? In this I will not praise you. . . . 33 So then, my brethren, *when you come together to eat, wait for one another*. 34 If anyone is hungry, let him eat at home, so that you will not come together for judgment. The remaining matters I will arrange when I come. (S | I)

Paul's instructions concerning the common meal connected with the taking of communion appear in 1 Cor 11:21–22, 33–34. Sharing with the hungry is an aspect of not shaming "those who have nothing" (v. 22).[66] Thus the immediately poor are to benefit from this common meal. This instance of sharing is likewise confined to believers (1 Cor 11:26–27, 29)—the brethren of the church (vv. 22, 33).

> Gal 2:10 They only asked us to *remember the poor*—the very thing I also was eager to do. (SP | I)

The concern to remember the poor (πτωχοί, *ptōchoi*) in Gal 2:10 refers to possessing an active concern for the plight of the Jewish brethren. It is quite likely that "the poor" here is shorthand for "the poor among the saints in Jerusalem" of Rom 15:26. With Rom 15:27 and Second Corinthians 8–9 clarifying that this longer expression is not merely epexegetical, the referents are the immediately poor members of the Jerusalem church.[67] For from its early days "the Jerusalem church faced a condition of grinding poverty."[68] Paul's main collection for Jerusalem flows out of this concern to provide alms for the believing Judean poor.

> Jude 1:12 These are the men who are hidden reefs in your *love feasts* [ταῖς ἀγάπαις] when they feast with you without fear, caring for themselves; clouds without water, carried along by winds; autumn trees without fruit, doubly dead, uprooted. (S |)

---

66. Schrage, *Der erste Brief an die Korinther*, 3:24–26; Garland, *1 Corinthians*, 533, 539–42.

67. *Contra* Merklein, "πτωχός," *EDNT* 3:195.

68. George, *Galatians*, 165; F. Bruce, *The Epistle to the Galatians*, 126. Richard Longenecker argues that general ministry support and sensitivity to the delicate circumstances of the Judean mission might be intended but nevertheless subsumes the Jerusalem collection under this broader understanding (Longenecker, *Galatians*, 60).

This verse contains the only explicit NT mention of the believers' love feasts, ταῖς ἀγάπαις, but provides support for seeing echoes of these common meals in Acts 2:44–46 and 1 Cor 11:21–22, 33–34.

In summary, sharing in the NT is consistently concerned with alleviating the sustenance needs of the immediately poor. Whenever the obligation level is communicated, this sharing is semantically or hamartiologically identified as an act of mercy. Even when the cause of the immediate poverty is the calamity of disability or the injustice of violent robbery, the provision of food, clothing, shelter, and medical assistance is a mercy. The specific forms of sharing addressed in Matt 25:31–46; Jas 2:14–17; and 1 John 3:16–18 are, with the exception of caring for the imprisoned, explicitly identified as issues of mercy in the parable of the good Samaritan (which extends the mercy mandates of Matt 25:31–46 to strangers). Caring for the imprisoned is identified as a mercy in Heb 10:34.

Sharing naturally connects to generosity—a forthcoming aspect. Many additional instances of sharing occur in the NT including the κοινωνέω (*koinōneō*) and συγκοινωνέω (*synkoinōneō*) of providing for Paul during his distress (θλῖψις, *thlipsis*) as described in Phil 4:14–17. A sharing that is both semantically ("gift," v. 17) and hamartiologically (as entailing reward, v. 17) identified as a matter of mercy.[69] Similarly, the generosity and readiness to share (being κοινωνικός, *koinōnikos*) of 1 Tim 6:17–19 is an example of a principle level mandate to share. Acts 20:35 and Eph 4:28, in turn, affirm that the ability to engage in such sharing is one of the moral impetuses to work.

WORK

Mandates concerning helping the poor expectedly enfold mandates concerning the securing of the provision necessary to enable such helping. These mandates also clarify who is to be helped and what limits, if any, are to be placed upon this helping.

---

69. On first blush this mercy categorization makes for an uncomfortable fit as Paul is surely a pastoral and missionary worker. Why is supporting *him* not a matter of justice—particularly during his imprisonment? This issue will be addressed in the Pastoral section to come.

Work Mandates

> John 6:27 Do not work for the food which perishes, but for the food which endures to eternal life, which the Son of Man will give to you, for on Him the Father, God, has set His seal. (C | | |)

Jesus' command in John 6:27 to "not work for the food which perishes" is intended to stimulate those seeking Him to do so for more than the feeding He had miraculously supplied (John 6:26). Consequently, this mandate is not intended to forbid work but to invite those seeking Him to believe that He is the Messiah (John 6:28–29). As such, this mandate proves irrelevant to the present concern.

> Acts 20:33–35 I have *coveted* no one's silver or gold or clothes. 34 You yourselves know that these hands ministered to *my own needs and to the men* who were with me. 35 In everything I showed you that by *working hard* in this manner you must *help the weak* [ἀσθενέω, *astheneō*] and remember the words of the Lord Jesus, that He Himself said, "It is more blessed to *give* than to receive." (S | | | I/P)

Acts 20:33–35 records how Paul, in speaking to the elders at Miletus, reminds them of his own conduct and mandates that they work hard (κοπιάω, *kopiaō*) in order to help the weak. Paul connects his own hard work for the purpose of meeting his own as well as his companions' needs (v. 34) to not coveting (ἐπιθυμέω, *epithymeō*) other people's "silver or gold or clothes" (v. 33).[70] Paul thus implies that not working entails inappropriately desiring the belongings of others. Paul's example of working hard is to be mimicked for the purpose of helping those who are ἀσθενέω (*astheneō*)—those who are not able-bodied so as to be able to work to provide for themselves (and others).[71] Paul's example, the one

---

70. Darrell Bock and David Williams suggest that coveting "silver or gold or clothes" (v. 33) has to do with "seeking personal status" (Bock, *Acts*, 632; D. Williams, *Acts*, 356–57). While having an abundance of these things certainly increases a person's status, making this Paul's point disrupts the flow of thought. For Paul could certainly have worked tirelessly for the purpose of increasing his status. Similarly, gold, silver, and clothes need not refer to wealthiness—as the passage itself suggests that the others possessed these things (v. 33). This is confirmed in Matt 10:9–10 and Acts 3:2–6, where silver and gold refers to coins (Barrett, *Acts*, 182). Augustus had issued such coinage and it was in wide circulation (Matt 26:15; 27:3–10; Luke 15:8; Acts 8:20; 19:19; 1 Pet 1:18).

71. Bodily weakness, the feeble lack of strength, disease, and sickness are the natural referent of ἀσθενέω (*astheneō*) and thus Paul's occasioned spiritual use is dependent

to be mimicked, concerns meeting his physical needs (χρεία, *chreia*) and those of his missionary coworkers. For how could working hard serve to meet the needs of the spiritually weak? Any notion of understanding ἀσθενέω (*astheneō*) as referring to spiritual weakness is further ruled out by the presented reminder of Jesus' mandate to give (v. 35). While Gustav Stählin suggests that ἀσθένεια (*astheneia*) can mean "economic weakness" or "poverty," it is more probable that this inference is merely the logically implied result of being physically powerless and feeble.[72] Consequently, the logic of Acts 20:33–35 is preserved and those able to work are to help the non-able-bodied who are impotent to do so. Thus the proceeds of a believer's diligent work are to be shared with the feeble, handicapped, and diseased. Such sharing is blessed (μακάριος, *makarios*)—implying, even in this text, that it may be an instance of mercy.[73]

> Rom 12:11 not *lagging behind* [ὀκνηρός, *oknēros*] in *diligence*, fervent in spirit, serving the Lord. (G | | |)

---

upon this literal meaning (Link, "ἀσθενέω," *NIDNTT* 3:993–94; Barrett, *Acts*, 983). Ben Witherington suggests that perhaps the weak are "those of low social status" whom the "higher social status" leaders should serve—so as to avoid the common temptation of having the lowly serve the leadership (Witherington, *The Acts of the Apostles*, 625, 626). But this possibility is unconvincing because the call to help the weak in verse 35 is connected to working hard *in the manner* of verse 34 which itself is also for the purpose of meeting one's needs so as not to require aid from others (v. 33). The idea that verse 35 refers to "servant leadership" in the church is starkly counter-contextual.

72. Stählin, "ἀσθενής, ἀσθένεια, ἀσθενέω, ἀσθένημα," *TDNT* 1:493. The apposition of the physically strong and healthy (ἰσχυρός, *ischyros*) with the physically weak, feeble, or sickly (ἀσθενής, *asthenēs*) in *1 Clement* 38:2 both affirms this literal usage and differentiates it from the resulting poverty itself: "The strong must take care of the weak; the weak must look up to the strong. The rich must provide for the poor; the poor must thank God for giving him someone to meet his needs" (C. Richardson, *Early Christian Fathers*, 61).

73. This saying of Jesus is not found in the Gospels and thus Paul's admonishment to remember it (Acts 20:35) attests to it being a familiar and influential tradition (Knowling, *The Acts of the Apostles*, 440). Jesus made this mandate memorable by playing it off of cultural assumptions—for it was the wealthy patrons who quipped that it was more honorable to give than to receive (Theissen, *The Religion of the Earliest Churches*, 90–91). But Jesus adapted these patron values by stretching them out to subsume even the non-wealthy among the addressed. So Aristides the apologist, composing *circa* AD 124, commends believers as having taken this to heart: "If among them there is some poor and needy person and they have no surplus, they fast for [two or three] days so that they can satisfy the need of the needy for food" (*Apologia* 15:9, preserved in Syriac). See ibid., 91 (corrected translation); and compare Pouderon et al., *Aristide*, 406; Geffcken, *Zwei Griechische Apologeten*, 25; R. Harris, *The Apology of Aristides on Behalf of the Christians*, 49; *The Apology of Aristides* (ANF 9:277).

Paul's mandate in Rom 12:11 to not be indolent (ὀκνηρός, *oknēros*) in diligence may have the wisdom literature in mind and therefore imply diligence in "secular" endeavors in addition to spiritual endeavors.[74]

> Eph 4:28 He who steals must steal no longer; but rather *he must labor*, performing with his own hands what is good, *so that he will have something to share with one who has need.* (SC | | | I)

The mandate in Eph 4:28, that those who used to be thieves must now labor so that they "will have something to share with one who has need," echoes the concerns of Acts 20:33–35. The injustice of stealing is forbidden and hard work (κοπιάω, *kopiaō*) mandated.[75] The proceeds of the hard work are to be shared (μεταδίδωμι, *metadidōmi*) with those who experience need (χρεία, *chreia*).[76] The emphasis on working with one's own hands reinforces the need to provide for oneself by means of legitimate work.

> 1 Thess 4:11–12 and to make it your ambition to lead a quiet life and attend to *your own business and work with your hands*, just as we *commanded* you, 12 so that you will *behave properly toward outsiders and not be in any need.* (C | | |)

In 1 Thess 4:11–12, believers are also commanded to engage in legitimate, self-supporting labor. Behaving "properly toward outsiders" entails not being "in any need" (v. 12) as a result of the provision of one's own industry.[77]

> 1 Thess 5:14 We urge you, brethren, admonish the unruly [ἄτακτος, *ataktos*], encourage the fainthearted, *help the weak* [ἀσθενής, *asthenēs*], be patient with everyone. (S/P | | | I/P)

First Thessalonians 5:14 parallels Acts 20:33–35 in mandating believers to help the weak: ἀντέχεσθε τῶν ἀσθενῶν. Due to the terminological similarities it is highly probable that this mandate enjoins the support of the non-able-bodied.[78] Furthermore, the immediately preceding

---

74. Dunn, *Romans*, 741; Schreiner, *Romans*, 665.

75. Lincoln, *Ephesians*, 303. Peter O'Brien even contends that this text suggests "labor to the point of weariness" (O'Brien, *The Letter to the Ephesians*, 343).

76. The term μεταδίδωμι (*metadidōmi*) refers to a partial giving (rather than to giving all) and so makes *sharing* the explicit intent wherever it occurs.

77. For additional discussion of this warning against indolent dependence see F. Bruce, *1 and 2 Thessalonians*, 91.

78. Knowling, *The Acts of the Apostles*, 440.

mandate, to "encourage the fainthearted," would become redundantly superfluous if ἀσθενής (*asthenēs*) was to denote spiritual weakness. The admonition of the disorderly (ἄτακτος, *ataktos*) is likely aimed at the indolent—those who F. F. Bruce, following James Moffatt, identifies as "loafers."[79] This identification correlates well with the subsequent command to help those who are not able-bodied.

> 2 Thess 3:6–13 Now we *command* you, brethren, in the name of our Lord Jesus Christ, that you keep away from every brother who leads an unruly [ἀτάκτως, *ataktōs*] life and not according to the tradition which you received from us. 7 For you yourselves know how you ought to *follow our example*, because we did not act in an undisciplined [ἀτακτέω, *atakteō*] manner among you, 8 *nor did we eat anyone's bread without paying for it*, but with labor and hardship we kept working night and day so that we would not be a *burden* to any of you; 9 not because we do not have the right to this, but in order to offer ourselves as a *model* for you, so that you would *follow our example*. 10 For even when we were with you, we used to give you this *order: if anyone is not willing to work, then he is not to eat, either*. 11 For we hear that some among you are leading an *undisciplined life* [ἀτάκτως, *ataktōs*], doing no work at all, but acting like busybodies. 12 Now such persons we *command and exhort* in the Lord Jesus Christ to work in quiet fashion and *eat their own bread*. 13 But as for you, brethren, do not grow weary of doing good. (S | | |)

Greater resolution is provided in 2 Thess 3:6–13. Those who are indolent (ἀτάκτως, *ataktōs*) are to be shunned by believers (v. 6). Paul mandates that his example of not living in indolence (ἀτακτέω, *atakteō*) is to be mimicked (v. 7). This example included not living off of others, so as to receive their bread (v. 8), but rather successfully avoiding being a burden (ἐπιβαρέω, *epibareō*) to anyone by means of working hard—even in hardship. This model was provided even though pastors and missionaries have a right to be sustained in their ministry (v. 9). Consequently, "if anyone is not willing to work, then he is not to eat, either" (v. 10). This mandate, when coupled with the mandates to not associate with any indolent believer (2 Thess 3:6, 14), meant that such a brother would not receive any sustenance aid to enable his indolence.[80] Those living an

---

79. F. Bruce, *1 and 2 Thessalonians*, 122–23.

80. John Calvin asserts that this exactly was the writer's purpose: "He forbids the Thessalonians to enable—by their generosity or dissimulation—the indolence of these

indolent (ἀτάκτως, *ataktōs*) life, "doing no work at all," are commanded and exhorted "in the Lord Jesus Christ" to work (vv. 11–12). Their utilitarious industry, rather than their "busybody-ness" (περιεργάζομαι, *periergazomai*), is to provide for their needs so that they may "eat their own bread" (v. 12). Thus the able-bodied (vv. 10, 12) but indolent believer, even when experiencing the immediate poverty of being without food, is to receive no sustenance support from other believers. The mandated consequence of not associating with such a brother may imply that such indolence, particularly when it desires to be sustained from the alms and sharing of other believers, is sinful (akin to the sins of 1 Cor 5:9–11). This passage ends with an additional mandate to reaffirm the non-indolent brethren in their desire to do good and share with those in need not brought on by indolence.[81] This additional resolution clarifies that giving one's "bread" to those needing sustenance, specifically other Christians, is something believers are not to grow weary of doing. Consequently, this text encompasses mandates to help the poor and mandates concerning how this help is to be limited.

> Titus 1:12–13 One of themselves, a prophet of their own, said, "Cretans are always liars, evil beasts, *lazy* gluttons." 13 This testimony is true. For this reason *reprove them severely* so that they may be sound in the faith. (C | | |)

Titus 1:12–13 contains a mandate, via a severe (ἀποτόμως, *apotomōs*) reproval, against idle laziness (ἀργός, *argos*) among believers.[82] This cross-cultural mandate is intended to produce soundness of faith in its final recipients. The inclusion of laziness amongst the sins of lying, evil viciousness, and gluttony suggests that it is also likely a sin.

The mandates unto work reveal that the indigent who are to receive aid are the non-able-bodied poor. This requirement prevents the work mandates from undermining themselves in their aim to aid those with

---

people" (author's translation of "Il defend aux Thessaloniciens d'entretenir par leur liberalite ou dissimulation l'oisiuete de telles gens"). See Calvin, *Commentaries on the Epistle of Paul to the Philippians, Colossians, and Thessalonians*, 352. The forbidden dissimulation refers either to protective concealment or perhaps to maintaining a hypocritical pretense that everything is okay—that no steps need to be taken with respect to the indolent brother.

81. Ibid., 356, 358.

82. Believers rather than false teachers are here in view for the latter are unlikely to become sound in the faith (Knight, *The Pastoral Epistles*, 298–300).

sustenance needs. Sustenance needs that arise from indolence, even when they occur among the brethren, are not to be alleviated. If even the participatory fellowship that is mandated among the brethren does not extend to an indolent brother (who is to be shunned), it is logical that aiding the poor who are outside the church, and to whom believers possess less responsibility, will not be more lenient. These mandates, like the mandates to share, also reveal that meeting the needs of other believers is of repeated and primary concern.

GOOD WORKS

Mandates to engage in good works are found throughout the NT. Believers are saved unto good works (Eph 2:10), are to be careful to engage in them (Titus 3:8), and are to be a people zealous to do them (Titus 2:14). While mandates to "do good" and participate in "good works" may be widely encompassing (as in Rom 2:7, 10), they are also often focused and connected to helping the poor.

Some of these mandates and clarifiers have already been encountered. Tabitha's ἔργων ἀγαθῶν καὶ ἐλεημοσυνῶν (Acts 9:36), works of goodness and almsgiving, were manifested in the making of clothes for poor widows (Acts 9:39). The collection for Jerusalem is subsumed under God's promised provision of sufficiency and abundance for every good work, πᾶν ἔργον ἀγαθόν (v. 8 of 2 Cor 9:8–11). The provision of food to the indigent poor is related to doing good, καλοποιέω (kalopoieō, v. 13), in 2 Thess 3:6–13. Similarly, doing good and sharing with needy believers, εὐποιΐας καὶ κοινωνίας, are sacrifices which please God (Heb 13:16).

Mandates not yet encountered include the requirements for widows who are to be placed on the local church's support list (1 Tim 5:3–16). These requirements include having often participated in good works, ἔργοις καλοῖς, such as having "shown hospitality to strangers," having served the church by having "washed the saints' feet," and by herself having "assisted those in distress [θλίβω, thlibō]" (v. 10). These specifics are all part of having been devoted to every good work, παντὶ ἔργῳ ἀγαθῷ (v. 10). The instructions, in 1 Tim 6:17–19, to the "rich in this present world" (v. 17) relate being rich in good works, ἔργοις καλοῖς, to being generous (εὐμετάδοτος, eumetadotos) and being ready to share (κοινωνικός, koinōnikos) with the needy (v. 18). Such good works are matters of mercy for they store up future reward (v. 19). Titus 3:13–14 mandates providing hospitality and travel assistance to Christian missionaries such as Zenas and Apollos in order to meet their needs (v. 13). Such assistance is related to engaging in good deeds, καλῶν ἔργων, that are intended to meet pressing needs, ἀναγκαίας χρείας (v.14). The description of "the wisdom from above" in Jas 3:17 relates, in this case, good fruits with mercy (ἔλεος, eleos).[83]

The general mandate of Gal 6:9–10 has received previous mention. This mandate promises reward for doing good, καλὸν ποιοῦντες (v. 9), and instructs believers, as they have opportunity, to work good, ἐργαζώμεθα τὸ ἀγαθόν, to "all people, and especially to those who are of the household of the faith" (v. 10). This prioritization of good works toward believers is consonant with the expressed concern for the mutual participation of fellowship and the many mandates that explicitly name co-believers as their recipients.

POSSESSIONS

The possessions mandates can be helpfully subdivided into those which were given as a part of Jesus' earthly ministry and those which were asserted after this ministry was completed. Jesus' mandate to His disciples to sell their possessions gains relevance because the proceeds of this sale are to be given as alms to the poor.

Possessions Mandates During Jesus' Ministry

> Matt 6:19–21, 24–34 *Do not store up for yourselves treasures on earth*, where moth and rust destroy, and where thieves break in and steal. 20 *But store up for yourselves treasures in heaven*, where neither moth nor rust destroys, and where thieves do not break in or steal; 21 for where your treasure is, there your heart will be also. . . . 24 No one can serve two masters; for either he will hate the one and love the other, or he will be devoted to one and despise the other. *You cannot serve God and wealth. 25 For this reason I say to you*, do not be worried about your life, as to what you will eat or what you will drink; nor for your body, as to what you will put on. Is not life more than food, and the body more than clothing? 26 Look at the birds of the air, that they *do not sow, nor reap nor gather into barns*, and yet your heavenly Father

---

83. Ralph Martin asserts that this mercy mandate refers to helping the poor (Martin, *James*, 134).

feeds them. Are you not worth much more than they? 27 And who of you by being worried can add a single hour to his life? 28 And why are you worried about clothing? Observe how the lilies of the field grow; they do not toil nor do they spin, 29 yet I say to you that not even Solomon in all his glory clothed himself like one of these. 30 But if God so clothes the grass of the field, which is alive today and tomorrow is thrown into the furnace, will He not much more clothe you? You of little faith! 31 *Do not worry then, saying, "What will we eat?" or "What will we drink?" or "What will we wear for clothing?"* 32 For the Gentiles eagerly seek all these things; for your heavenly Father knows that you need all these things. 33 But seek first His kingdom and His righteousness, and all these things will be added to you. 34 So do not worry about tomorrow; for tomorrow will care for itself. Each day has enough trouble of its own. (CG | M | H |)

// Luke 12:22–34 And *He said to His disciples, "For this reason I say to you*, do not worry about your *life*, as to what you will *eat*; nor for your *body*, as to what you will *put on*. 23 For life is more than food, and the body more than clothing. 24 Consider the ravens, for they *neither sow nor reap; they have no storeroom nor barn*, and yet God feeds them; how much more valuable you are than the birds! 25 And which of you by worrying can add a single hour to his life's span? 26 If then you cannot do even a very little thing, why do you worry about other matters? 27 Consider the lilies, how they grow: they neither toil nor spin; but I tell you, not even Solomon in all his glory clothed himself like one of these. 28 But if God so clothes the grass in the field, which is alive today and tomorrow is thrown into the furnace, how much more will He clothe you? You men of little faith! 29 And do not seek what you will eat and what you will drink, and do not keep worrying. 30 For all these things the nations of the world eagerly seek; but your Father knows that you need these things. 31 But seek His kingdom, and these things will be added to you. 32 Do not be afraid, *little flock*, for your Father has chosen gladly to give you the kingdom. 33 *Sell your possessions* and *give to charity* [ἐλεημοσύνη, *eleēmosynē*]; make yourselves money belts which do not wear out, an unfailing *treasure in heaven*, where no thief comes near nor moth destroys. 34 For where your treasure is, there your heart will be also." (S | M | HS | I/P)

Both the Sermon on the Mount and its counterpart, the Sermon on the Plain, were primarily addressed to Jesus' disciples (Matt 5:1; Luke

6:20).[84] In Luke, this group is identified as being larger than the twelve apostles for both the Sermon on the Plain (Luke 6:17) and for the mandates concerning worry (Luke 12:32).[85] Both sermons are also given in the presence of a larger crowd (Matt 7:28–29; Luke 6:17; 7:1).[86]

The mandate to not store up treasure on earth but rather in heaven entails not worrying about one's sustenance needs (Matt 6:19–21, 24–34 // Luke 12:22–34). Because the disciple cannot serve both "God and wealth" (Matt 6:24 // Luke 16:13), this failure to store up treasures on earth necessarily entails trusting in God for his food and clothing. Jesus highlights that these mandates concerning sustenance trust are "for this reason"—that the disciples cannot serve wealth in being rich toward God (Matt 6:25; Luke 12:21). Luke 12:33 makes explicit that which is implied in Matt 6:19–34, that the disciples are to sell their possessions and give the proceeds as alms (ἐλεημοσύνη, *eleēmosynē*). Following Jesus during His earthly ministry as an immediate disciple entailed immediate poverty.[87] This poverty was not acutely immediate because the ministry and its workers were supported by others (Luke 8:1–3; Matt 10:9–10). Jesus affirms that maintaining neither a "storeroom nor barn" in addition to not being "secularly" employed in "sowing" and "reaping" (Luke 12:24 // Matt 6:26) was a part of participating in the kingdom work. Thus Jesus' disciples are commanded to not "seek" (ζητέω, *zēteō*) what they "will eat and . . . drink" in addition to not worrying (Luke 12:29). This selling of one's possessions as a means for the provision of alms to the poor is an act of mercy that is divinely rewarded (Luke 12:33–34).

> Matt 10:9–10 Do not acquire gold, or silver, or copper for your money belts, 10 or a bag for your journey, or even two coats, or sandals, or a staff; for the *worker is worthy of his support*. (C | | |)
>
> // Mark 6:8–9 and He instructed them that they should take nothing for their journey, except a mere staff—no bread, no bag,

---

84. Hagner, *Matthew*, 85; Nolland, *Luke*, 281; Bock, *Luke*, 570.

85. Bock, *Luke*, 1159.

86. Hagner, *Matthew*, 85; Nolland, *Luke*, 690.

87. This is why gaining the kingdom is like seeking "a treasure hidden in the field" and a "pearl of great value" in Matt 13:44–46—it required the immediate disciple to *sell* "all that he has." For hinting affirmation see Hagner, *Matthew*, 397; Davies and Allison, *Matthew*, 2:435–37. Though certainly not a credible data point, the gnostic *Gospel of Thomas* 76, for its part, connects seeking the pearl (at the cost of all else one has) to finding treasure that does not perish—as it endures where no moth comes near.

no money in their belt— 9 but to wear sandals; and He added, "Do not put on two tunics." (C | | |)

// Luke 9:3 And He said to them, "Take nothing for your journey, neither a staff, nor a bag, nor bread, nor money; and do not even have two tunics apiece." (C | | |)

Luke 10:4 Carry no money belt, no bag, no shoes; and greet no one on the way. (C | | |)

When the apostles and disciples are sent out as missionaries in Matt 10:9–10; Mark 6:8–9; Luke 9:3; and Luke 10:4 (the partial parallel concerning the broader seventy or seventy-two others), they are sent out as immediately poor pastoral workers who are to be sustained by those to whom they minister (Matt 10:10).[88] This requires that those who favorably receive them have the possessions (Matt 10:12–14 // Mark 6:10 // Luke 9:4; Luke 10:5) necessary to provide for these missionaries.

Matt 19:21–25 Jesus said to him, "If you wish to be complete, go and *sell your possessions and give* [δίδωμι, *didōmi*] *to the poor*, and you will have *treasure in heaven*; and come, *follow Me.*" 22 But when the young man heard this statement, he went away grieving; for he was one who owned much property. 23 And Jesus said to His disciples, "Truly I say to you, *it is hard for a rich man to enter the kingdom of heaven.* 24 Again I say to you, it is easier for a camel to go through the eye of a needle, than for a rich man to enter the kingdom of God." 25 When the disciples heard this, they were very astonished and said, "Then who can be saved?" (S | M | H | I)

// Mark 10:21–26 Looking at him, Jesus felt a love for him and said to him, "One thing you lack: go and *sell all you possess and give* [δίδωμι, *didōmi*] *to the poor*, and you will have *treasure in heaven*; and come, *follow Me.*" 22 But at these words he was saddened, and he went away grieving, for he was one who owned much property. 23 And Jesus, looking around, said to His disciples, *"How hard it will be for those who are wealthy to enter the kingdom of God!"* 24 The disciples were amazed at His words. But Jesus answered again and said to them, "Children, how hard it is to enter the kingdom of God! 25 It is easier for a camel to go through the eye of a needle than for a rich man to enter the

---

88. The seventy or seventy-two others are additional to rather than inclusive of the twelve (Bock, *Luke*, 994; Marshall, *The Gospel of Luke*, 415).

kingdom of God." 26 They were even more astonished and said to Him, "Then who can be saved?" (S | M | H | I)

// Luke 18:22–26 When Jesus heard this, He said to him, "One thing you still lack; *sell all that you possess and distribute* [διαδίδωμι, *diadidōmi*] *it to the poor, and you shall have treasure in heaven; and come, follow Me."* 23 But when he had heard these things, he became very sad, for he was extremely rich. 24 And Jesus looked at him and said, *"How hard it is for those who are wealthy to enter the kingdom of God!* 25 For it is easier for a camel to go through the eye of a needle than for a rich man to enter the kingdom of God." 26 They who heard it said, "Then who can be saved?" (S | M | H | I)

Jesus' interaction with the rich young ruler in Matt 19:21–25; Mark 10:21–26; and Luke 18:22–26 confirms His requirements for His immediate disciples during His ministry. All three Gospels record that Jesus attaches this mandate to an invitation to become His disciple. The present call to "follow Me" echoes Jesus' call to the apostles in Matt 4:19; 9:9; Mark 1:19; Luke 5:27; John 1:43, and elsewhere. The mandate to sell one's possessions for the sake of distributing the proceeds as alms to the poor is attached to the promise of divine reward—to "treasure in heaven" (Matt 19:21 // Mark 10:21 // Luke 18:22; compare Luke 12:33). This mandate is subsequently a mercy mandate. Jesus relates the rich young ruler's refusal to failing to enter the kingdom of heaven.[89] Because the rich were considered to be blessed of God, the disciples wonder who then can be saved.[90] Entering the kingdom required of this young ruler the complete disposal of his possessions and the direct following of Jesus. Other passages such as Luke 8:1–3; 19:2, 8–9; and John 19:38 clarify that not all those that are saved (Zaccheus) nor those that are broadly referred to as Jesus' disciples (Joseph of Arimathea) nor those who are among the many who support Jesus' ministry are similarly commanded to sell all their possessions. Similarly, while Martha, Mary, and Lazarus were beloved friends of Jesus (John 11:5, 11) they were not required to

---

89. Bruce Malina prefers to call him the "the greedy young man" (Malina, *The New Testament World*, 96).

90. Bock, *Luke*, 1486–87. Jesus' abbreviated repetition in Mark 10:24 leads fluidly into the following verse and so is not intended to extend the nigh impossibility to everyone—so, astutely, France, *The Gospel of Mark*, 398, 404; *contra* C. A. Evans, *Mark 8:27—16:20*, 101; Brooks, *Mark*, 164.

dispose of their home (Luke 10:38; John 11:31). The demoniac of the country of the Gerasenes was similarly sent back to his house (οἶκος, *oikos*), despite having pled to be allowed to become Jesus' immediate disciple (Mark 5:18–19 // Luke 8:38–39).[91] Such considerations suggest that extrapolating Jesus' mandate to the rich young ruler into a prerequisite for anyone's salvation is not correlative to Jesus' intent. The form of kingdom participation that Jesus required of the rich young ruler was that which He required of all His immediate disciples. Nevertheless the domain of those who could be saved was wider.

> Matt 19:27–30 Then Peter said to Him, "Behold, we have left everything and followed You; what then will there be for us?" 28 And Jesus said to them, "Truly I say to you, that you who have followed Me, in the regeneration when the Son of Man will sit on His glorious throne, you also shall sit upon twelve thrones, judging the twelve tribes of Israel. 29 And everyone who has left houses or brothers or sisters or father or mother or children or farms for My name's sake, *will receive many times as much*, and will inherit eternal life. 30 But many who are *first will be last*; and the *last, first*." (S | M | H |)

> // Mark 10:28–31 Peter began to say to Him, "Behold, we have left everything and followed You." 29 Jesus said, "Truly I say to you, there is no one who has left house or brothers or sisters or mother or father or children or farms, for My sake and for the gospel's sake, 30 but that he will receive a *hundred times as much now in the present age, houses and brothers and sisters and mothers and children and farms*, along with persecutions; and in the age to come, eternal life. 31 But many who are *first will be last*, and the *last, first*." (S | M | H |)

> // Luke 18:28–30 Peter said, "Behold, we have left our own homes and followed You." 29 And He said to them, "Truly I say to you, there is no one who has left house or wife or brothers or parents or children, for the sake of the kingdom of God, 30 who will not *receive many times as much* at this time and in the age to come, eternal life." (S | M | H |)

---

91. While the demoniac's house might possibly refer to his people—to his broad extended family or even generally to his countrymen—it is commonly taken as referring to his dwelling rather than functioning as a repetitive restatement in Mark ("οἶκος," BDAG 698–99). In any case, he is not called to forsake his normal residence.

Our contention is confirmed in Matt 19:27–30; Mark 10:28–31; and Luke 18:28–30 which record the disciples' response to Jesus' interaction with the rich young ruler. Jesus approves of their having forsaken everything, ἀφήκαμεν πάντα (Matt 19:27 // Mark 10:28), and promises to reward the apostles (Matt 19:28) and the broader group of disciples ("everyone" in Matt 19:29 // Mark 10:29 // Luke 18:29) for their following of Him.[92] Their forsaking of their houses and relations will be rewarded not only in the life to come but also in this life where they will gain many times as many "houses and brothers and sisters and mothers and children and farms" (Mark 10:30).[93] Gaining so many brothers and mothers along with the hospitality of their houses and farms requires that some of those who "do the will of My [Jesus'] Father" (Matt 12:50 // Mark 3:35 // Luke 8:21) do not sell and give away all of their possessions (Matt 12:46–50 // Mark 3:31–35 // Luke 8:19–21). Thus the disciples that have become immediately poor in order to physically follow Jesus during His earthly ministry, though they be last in the eyes of the world, become the first "in the regeneration" (Matt 19:28). Consequently such renunciation is an issue of mercy.

> Matt 5:3 Blessed are the poor in spirit, for theirs is the kingdom of heaven. (G | | |)
>
> // Luke 6:20 And turning His gaze toward His disciples, He began to say, "Blessed are you who are *poor*, for yours is the kingdom of God." (P | | | I)

The disciples' blessing in Matt 5:3 and Luke 6:20 is for their immediate poverty and their spiritual humility, for Jesus' immediate disciples

---

92. Some have taken the calling of Matthew Levi as a counter-indication (Matt 9:9–10 // Mark 2:14–15 // Luke 5:27–29). See Calvin, *Commentary on a Harmony of the Evangelists*, 1:399–400; Plummer, *A Critical and Exegetical Commentary on the Gospel according to St. Luke*, 159–60. For the house in which the subsequent reception banquet is given is Levi's—unambiguously so in Luke 5:29. But this need not be problematic for at this point, just after receiving the call, Levi would have still been in the process of forsaking his possessions—and the feast itself might have been part of this divestment. And so Peter's claim in these present passages, and Jesus' demand in Luke 14:33, stands.

93. Some provision for wives and families may have been made in the process of giving up all in order to follow Jesus as an immediate disciple. Still, we are not provided with any data in this regard. Relatives may have fulfilled this role. Along these same lines, it is also perhaps possible that the referral to the "eunuchs who made themselves eunuchs for the sake of the kingdom of heaven" in Matt 19:12 commended the immediate disciples for leaving their wives during the earthly ministry (Luke 18:29).

were indeed immediately poor and needfully poor in spirit.[94] They experienced hunger (Luke 6:21) and persecution (Matt 5:10–12 // Luke 6:22–23) in the present, but reward was coming in the *eschaton* (Matt 5:12 // Luke 6:23).[95]

> Luke 6:24 But woe to you who are *rich*, for you are receiving your comfort in full. (P | | |)

The warning and pronunciation of woe unto the rich in Luke 6:24 echoes the parabolic story of Lazarus (Luke 16:19–31) whereby the uncaring rich enjoy their good things and comfort in this life only to find they are to suffer (ὀδυνάω, *odynaō*, Luke 16:25) in the next.[96]

> Luke 12:13–21 Someone in the crowd said to Him, "Teacher, tell my brother to divide the family inheritance with me." 14 But He said to him, "Man, who appointed Me a judge or arbitrator over you?" 15 Then He said to them, "*Beware, and be on your guard against every form of greed* [πλεονεξία, *pleonexia*]; *for not even when one has an abundance does his life consist of his posses-*

---

94. This non-destructive integration is not only consistent with the situation of Jesus' disciples but is hermeneutically preferable to defeating Luke with Matthew or vice versa.

95. It is best, on the author's view, to perceive the Beatitudes as a unit which describes those who are the blessed and what their blessing entails. It is also noteworthy that some commentators have perceived interhuman oppression as Jesus' target in Matt 5:3, 5–6. The "poor in spirit" (of v. 3) are taken as those who are politically and socioeconomically afflicted by men (Hagner, *Matthew*, 87, 91; Keener, *A Commentary on the Gospel of Matthew*, 167–69). Yet the context (Matt 5:1–2 // Luke 6:20) indicates that the primary intended audience here is Jesus' immediate disciples who *voluntarily* renounce their possessions—those who are more so persecuted for *His* sake (Matt 5:11). The "gentle" (of v. 5) are similarly seen as the oppressed by way of Jesus' allusion to Ps 37:11 where the Hebrew references the poor or humble (Hagner, *Matthew*, 92). Still, as in verse 3, the humbled (materially or otherwise)—like those called to humble themselves—may fittingly describe Jesus' disciples. See Davies and Allison, *Matthew*, 1:450–51 (who prefer a call to humility). Whether δικαιοσύνη (*dikaiosynē*) refers to justice for the generally oppressed or personal righteousness in verse 6 is likewise ultimately uncertain—despite all arguments for the former (Hagner, *Matthew*, 93; Keener, *A Commentary on the Gospel of Matthew*, 169–70). For Matt 5:20 and 6:33 make the interpretive decision particularly difficult (Davies and Allison, *Matthew*, 1:452–53). And so political and socioeconomic oppression is not unambiguously the concern of these verses.

96. Bock, *Luke*, 583. And perhaps there is a sense in which Jesus' woes (Luke 6:24–26) are a rejoinder to those too enmeshed with their possessions, security, and public status to become His immediate disciples. Such that Luke 6:20–26 becomes a call—an invitation—to discipleship as well as a confirmation of those already there.

sions." 16 And He told them a parable, saying, "The land of a rich man was very productive. 17 And he began reasoning to himself, saying, 'What shall I do, since I have no place to store my crops?' 18 Then he said, 'This is what I will do: I will tear down my barns and build larger ones, and there I will store all my grain and my goods. 19 And I will say to my soul, "Soul, you have many goods laid up for many years to come; take your ease, eat, drink and be merry."' 20 But God said to him, '*You fool*! This very night your soul is required of you; and now who will own what you have prepared?' 21 So is the man who *stores up treasure for himself*, and is not *rich toward God*." (G | | |)

Luke 12:13–21 contains Jesus' mandate to "beware, and be on your guard against every form of greed" (v. 15). The rich man who stored up only for himself is morally evaluated as a "fool" (v. 20).[97] His greed is a sin before God. He greedily stored up treasure for himself on earth and had no further concern for storing up treasure in heaven (v. 21).[98] This passage leads into and informs the "do not worry" and "give alms" mandates of Luke 12:22–34. Luke 12:13–21 also intimates that the disciples are a separate group as far as Jesus' mandates are concerned, for those from the crowd (Luke 12:13) are only warned against churlish greed while the disciples are commanded to sell their possessions (Luke 12:22, 33).[99]

Luke 14:33 So then, none of you can be My disciple who does not *give up all his own possessions*. (S | | |)

---

97. Moral descriptions within parables (such as *being a fool* or *requiring repentance*) are generally evaluative—they function as descriptive valuations—rather than adding a new externally-sourced dimension. While Craig Blomberg assumes the latter in reading the parable of the rich man and Lazarus as well as the parable of the rich fool, this tendency is hermeneutically fragile (Blomberg, *Neither Poverty nor Riches*, 119, 123). For it is not the contextualized reading. Such descriptive references are not additive, they are internally evaluative. They do not import, they export.

98. Greed or covetousness, πλεονεξία (*pleonexia*), is a desire to have more (or keep more)—it is a love of money. It is the opposite of contentment (1 Tim 6:5–11; Heb 13:5–6). And so, greed is morally wrong, contentment is morally right, and generosity, as we have already seen in part, is morally supererogatory.

99. With the crowd immediately present (v. 13) it is unlikely that Jesus intended His response to pertain to the two brothers in singular isolation (vv. 15–16). See Nolland, *Luke*, 685; Marshall, *The Gospel of Luke*, 522. It is apparent, from His transition to addressing the disciples in verse 22, that Jesus intended those gathered to be listening in even though His warning may have been primarily addressed to the two brothers themselves. The particulars of the greed which Jesus proscribes here will be probed further when this passage resurfaces in the Covetousness section.

Luke 14:33 makes explicit what has been previously noted and deduced, that no one can be Jesus' immediate disciple unless he forsakes (ἀποτάσσω, *apotassō*) "all his own possessions."

> Luke 21:34 Be on guard, so that your hearts will not be weighted down with dissipation and drunkenness and the *worries of life*, and that day will not come on you suddenly like a trap. (G | | |)

In this verse, Jesus reaffirms His mandate against being weighed down with "the worries of life."

Possessions Clarifiers During Jesus' Ministry

> Matt 8:20 Jesus said to him, "The foxes have holes and the birds of the air have nests, but the Son of Man has *nowhere to lay His head*." (S |)

> // Luke 9:58 And Jesus said to him, "The foxes have holes and the birds of the air have nests, but the Son of Man has *nowhere to lay His head*." (S |)

In Matt 8:20 and Luke 9:58 Jesus confirms that He and, by extension, His disciples live a semi-homeless existence which involves a renunciation of possessions.[100] It is possible that this phrasing alludes to Ps 8:5–8 (LXX) so as to contrast, by way of irony, the position of the ruler and the ruled—to highlight that following the Son of Man is not as one might expect.

> Matt 27:57 When it was evening, there came a *rich man* from Arimathea, named Joseph, who himself had also become a *disciple of Jesus*. (G |)

> // Mark 15:43 Joseph of Arimathea came, a prominent member of the Council, *who himself was waiting for the kingdom of God*; and he gathered up courage and went in before Pilate, and asked for the body of Jesus. (G |)

---

100. This is not to say that Jesus and His immediate disciples slept under the stars every night—for they were often shown hospitality. To consider but the testimony of Mark—which does not cover the hospitality of Martha—Jesus stayed at the house of Simon and Andrew just after calling them (Mark 1:29–30, 33, 35) and likely returned to the same place when in Capernaum (Mark 9:33). Additionally, Jesus and His disciples were often hospitably welcomed wherever they were ministering (Mark 7:24; 9:28; 10:10; 14:14).

> // Luke 23:50–51 And a man named Joseph, who was a member of the Council, *a good and righteous man* 51 (he had not consented to their plan and action), a man from Arimathea, a city of the Jews, *who was waiting for the kingdom of God.* (G |)
>
> // John 19:38 After these things Joseph of Arimathea, being a *disciple* of Jesus, but a secret one for fear of the Jews, asked Pilate that he might take away the body of Jesus; and Pilate granted permission. So he came and took away His body. (G |)

As noted earlier, Mark 15:43; Luke 23:50–51; and John 19:38 confirm that Joseph of Arimathea was "a good and righteous man" (Luke 23:50) who was a "disciple of Jesus" but was nevertheless rich (Matt 27:57).[101]

> Mark 12:41–44 And He sat down opposite the treasury, and began observing how the people were putting money into the treasury; and many *rich* people were putting in large sums. 42 A poor widow came and put in two small copper coins, *which amount to a cent.* 43 Calling His disciples to Him, He said to them, "Truly I say to you, this *poor widow* put in more than all the contributors to the treasury; 44 for they all put in out of their *surplus, but she, out of her poverty, put in all she owned, all she had to live on."* (G | I)
>
> // Luke 21:1–4 And He looked up and saw the *rich* putting their gifts into the treasury. 2 And He saw a poor widow putting in two small copper coins. 3 And He said, "Truly I say to you, this *poor widow* put in more than all of them; 4 for they all out of their *surplus put into the offering; but she out of her poverty put in all that she had to live on."* (G | I)

Mark 12:41–44 and Luke 21:1–4 relate Jesus' approval of the poor widow who out of her immediate poverty gave "all she owned, all she had to live on" (Mark 12:44 // Luke 21:4). While this approval appears too "weak" to be considered a mandate, Jesus' commendation affirms the widow's trust in God for her sustenance needs.

> Luke 8:1–3 Soon afterwards, He began going around from one city and village to another, proclaiming and preaching the kingdom of God. The twelve were with Him, 2 and also some women who had been healed of evil spirits and sicknesses: Mary who was called Magdalene, from whom seven demons had gone out,

---

101. Nicodemus also assists in Jesus' burial (John 19:39–40).

> 3 and Joanna the wife of Chuza, Herod's steward, and Susanna, and *many others* who were *contributing to their support out of their private means.* (S |)

The source of Jesus' and the disciples' ministry support is revealed in Luke 8:1–3. This passage reveals that many women (αἵτινες is a feminine relative pronoun) were "contributing to their support out of their [αὐταῖς, also feminine] private means" (v. 3). Joanna, being the wife of Herod's steward, would have been "well to do." Nevertheless, she and the other contributors mentioned here were not disciples in the immediate sense as they were not called to give up all of their "private means" (v. 3).

> Luke 19:2, 8–9 And there was a man called by the name of Zaccheus; he was a chief tax collector and he was *rich.* . . . 8 Zaccheus stopped and said to the Lord, "Behold, Lord, *half of my possessions I will give to the poor, and if I have defrauded anyone of anything, I will give back four times as much."* 9 And Jesus said to him, "Today *salvation* has come to this house, because he, too, is a son of Abraham." (S | I)

The salvation of Zaccheus, who was rich, involved his own conviction to donate half of his possessions to the immediately poor in addition to providing remedial compensation to those whom he had defrauded (Luke 19:2, 8–9). Jesus confirms his salvation (v. 9) even though, unlike the rich young ruler, he had not been called to be His immediate disciple or to give up all of his possessions.

> Luke 22:35–36 And He said to them, "When I sent you out without money belt and bag and sandals, you did not lack anything, did you?" They said, "No, nothing." 36 And He said to them, "But now, whoever has a money belt is to take it along, likewise also a bag, and whoever has no sword is to sell his coat and buy one." (C |)

Here Jesus recalls the missionary trip that He had sent His apostles upon, apparently as co-laborers with the seventy others, and contrasts it with the present circumstance. The present reality demanded that the immediate poverty of the missionary journeys be eschewed and the disciples were to prepare to provide for and defend themselves. This transition is very suggestive and implies that the possession-free character of the earthly ministry was coming to a close—at the direct command of Jesus.[102]

---

102. It is indeed highly significant that this passage (Luke 22:35–38)—this transi-

To sum, Jesus' mandate to His immediate disciples to sell their possessions and give the resulting proceeds as alms to the poor did not extend to all believers—even during His ministry. Nevertheless, these mercy mandates served to benefit the immediately poor. On a final note, the disciples' prayer in Matt 6:9–13 and Luke 11:1–4 includes the petition to "give us this day our daily bread" (Matt 6:11 // Luke 11:3)—a petition which, by emphasizing daily sustenance (compare Jas 2:15), correlates well with the immediate poverty in which they followed Jesus.

Possessions Mandates Following Jesus' Ministry

> 1 Cor 7:29–31 But this I say, brethren, the time has been shortened, so that from now on those who have wives should be as though they had none; 30 and those who weep, as though they did not weep; and those who rejoice, as though they did not rejoice; and *those who buy, as though they did not possess*; 31 and *those who use the world, as though they did not make full use of it*; for the form of this world is passing away. (G | | |)

The general mandate found in 1 Cor 7:29–31 is the sole distinctly possessions-related mandate given after Jesus' earthly ministry. It affirms that in this present "between the times" context, "those who buy" should act "as though they did not possess" (v. 30).[103] This mandate affirms that believers may buy and own goods but that their possession of these goods should not be grasped.[104] This practical sense of detachment is reaffirmed in the mandate to use the things of the world but not as one making "full use of" them (v. 31).[105]

---

tion—is to be found within Luke–Acts. For Luke endeavors to provide the most detail concerning the immediate disciples' calling to forsake all their possessions in his Gospel and yet records that this calling did not extend to the nascent church of Acts. We may find this change less disconcerting if we allot this passage the attention it deserves. This mandate finds itself among the clarifiers simply because it is not a mandate that benefits the poor. Rather it clarifies that the disciples' poverty—a poverty that in its inception benefited the poor—was coming to an end.

103. Garland, *1 Corinthians*, 328.
104. Ibid., 330.
105. Ibid., 330–31.

Possessions Clarifiers Following Jesus' Ministry

> Acts 2:44–46 And all those who had believed were together and had *all things in common*; 45 and they began *selling their property and possessions and were sharing* [διαμερίζω, *diamerizō*] *them with all, as anyone might have need*. 46 Day by day continuing with one mind in the temple, and breaking bread from house to house, they were *taking their meals together with gladness and sincerity of heart*. (S | I)

Acts 2:44–46, a passage noted earlier, describes how the wealthier members of the nascent church sold their properties and possessions in order to alleviate the needs of other believers. Unlike Jesus' immediate disciples during His ministry, the believers owned houses—houses in which they generously shared their meals.

> Acts 4:32–37 And the congregation of those who believed were of one heart and soul; and *not one of them claimed that anything belonging to him was his own, but all things were common property to them*. 33 And with great power the apostles were giving testimony to the resurrection of the Lord Jesus, and abundant grace was upon them all. 34 For there was *not a needy person among them*, for all who were owners of land or houses would sell them and bring the proceeds of the sales 35 and lay them at the apostles' feet, and they would be distributed [διαδίδωμι, *diadidōmi*] to each as any *had need*. 36 Now Joseph, a Levite of Cyprian birth, who was also called Barnabas by the apostles (which translated means Son of Encouragement), 37 and who owned a tract of land, sold it and brought the money and laid it at the apostles' feet. (S | I)

This same attitude of not considering one's possessions as meant purely for one's own benefit is described in Acts 4:32–37. Though it was not mandated, the wealthy, who were owners of "land or houses" (v. 34), would sell them and give the proceeds to the apostles to distribute to believers who had need (v. 35). Thus, there was "not a needy person [ἐνδεής, *endeēs*] among them" (v. 34)—an allusion to the blessing described in Deut 15:4 (via the LXX). Joseph, called Barnabas, was one of those who owned "a tract of land" and sold it for the purpose of providing alms to the believing needy. As in Acts 2:44–46, this passage describes a partial selling of one's possessions for the benefit of immediately poor brethren.[106]

---

106. Though only the selling of houses and land is mentioned as opposed to all of one's possessions, C. K. Barrett agrees that even Acts 4:34 allows for a partial selling

> Acts 5:1-11 But a man named Ananias, with his wife Sapphira, sold a piece of property, 2 and kept back some of the price for himself, with his wife's full knowledge, and bringing a portion of it, he laid it at the apostles' feet. 3 But Peter said, "Ananias, why has Satan filled your heart to lie to the Holy Spirit and to keep back some of the price of the land? 4 *While it remained unsold, did it not remain your own? And after it was sold, was it not under your control* [ἐξουσία, *exousia*]? Why is it that you have conceived this deed in your heart? You have not lied to men but to God." 5 And as he heard these words, Ananias fell down and breathed his last; and great fear came over all who heard of it. 6 The young men got up and covered him up, and after carrying him out, they buried him. 7 Now there elapsed an interval of about three hours, and his wife came in, not knowing what had happened. 8 And Peter responded to her, "Tell me whether you sold the land for such and such a price?" And she said, "Yes, that was the price." 9 Then Peter said to her, "Why is it that you have agreed together to put the Spirit of the Lord to the test? Behold, the feet of those who have buried your husband are at the door, and they will carry you out as well." 10 And immediately she fell at his feet and breathed her last, and the young men came in and found her dead, and they carried her out and buried her beside her husband. 11 And great fear came over the whole church, and over all who heard of these things. (S |)

The attempted deception of Ananias and Sapphira is recorded in Acts 5:1-11. This passage clarifies that the partial selling of one's possessions, as described in the early chapters of Acts, was voluntary and a matter of mercy obligation. A believer's property remained his own—just as the proceeds of any such property were the believer's to control (v. 4). Ananias' and Sapphira's sin was that they lied about the total proceeds of the sale (v. 4) in order to gain for themselves the esteem rightfully deemed to believers such as Joseph who was called Barnabas. The believers' concern for seeing their possessions as common property, as opposed to exclusively for their own use, was a general attitude rather than a mandated institution. Their possessions remained under their control as long as they so desired.

> Acts 16:14-15 A woman named Lydia, from the city of Thyatira, a *seller of purple fabrics*, a worshiper of God, was listening; and

---

understanding for *even this* "land or houses" (Barrett, *Acts*, 255). Such a selling of *extra* land and houses would allow the house fellowship of Acts 2:46 to continue.

> the Lord opened her heart to respond to the things spoken by Paul. 15 And when she and her household had been baptized, she urged us, saying, "*If you have judged me to be faithful to the Lord,* come into *my house* and stay." And she prevailed upon us. (C |)

Acts 16:14–15 adds Lydia, "a seller of purple fabrics," to the list of wealthy believers who owned houses and could thus practice hospitality to the saints—including missionary saints such as Paul and his companions (v. 15).

> 1 Cor 13:3 And if *I give all my possessions to feed the poor,* and if I surrender my body to be burned, but do not have love, it profits me nothing. (S | I/P)

In 1 Cor 13:3 Paul clarifies that donating all of one's "possessions to feed the poor" is still considered commendable, even profitable, if it is done in love.[107] Paul's argument style in 1 Cor 13:1–3 is to appose the heights of gifting, faith, and selflessness with the necessity of love. This affirms that donating all of one's possessions to the poor is now no longer a normative component of "discipleship"—though it remains deeply commendable.

> 2 Cor 12:14 Here for this third time I am ready to come to you, and I will not be a *burden* to you; for I do not seek *what is yours*, but you; for children are not responsible to save up for their parents, but parents for their children. (G |)

Paul's concern in 2 Cor 12:14 to not "be a burden" to the Corinthians is consonant with his choice to not seek what is theirs. This affirmation of ownership also leads Paul to affirm the general principle that "children are not responsible to save up for their parents, but parents for their children." This affirmation, though its primary referent here is spiritual parenting, entails that the saving up of possessions is not forbidden to believers—for this is precisely what Paul intends to preserve for the Corinthians by not seeking what is theirs.

> Phil 4:11–13 Not that I speak from want, for I have learned to be content in whatever circumstances I am. 12 *I know how to get along with humble means, and I also know how to live in prosperity* [περισσεύω, *perisseuō*]; in any and every circumstance I have

---

107. The term ψωμίζω (*psōmizō*) refers to giving away in small portions and thus implies almsgiving to the poor—though feeding, the term's other use, is not clearly communicated here.

> learned the secret of *being filled and going hungry*, both of *having abundance* [περισσεύω, *perisseuō*] *and suffering need* [ὑστερέω, *hystereō*]. 13 I can do all things through Him who strengthens me. (G |)

In Phil 4:11–13 Paul clarifies that, as a believer strengthened by God (v. 13), he can get along in both immediate poverty and prosperity, hunger and satiation, abundance and need. This clarifier affirms that experiencing abundance is not forbidden to the believer.

> 3 John 1:2 Beloved, I pray that in all respects you may *prosper* and be in good health, just as your soul prospers. (G |)

Along these same lines, 3 John 1:2 contains the record of a prayer for another believer's wellbeing "in all respects"—a wellbeing which subsumes material prosperity (though it does not, like with Paul, have to imply great wealth but rather having some extra). Furthermore, it was out of such prospering (εὐοδόω, *euodoō*) that the Corinthian believers were to contribute to the Jerusalem collection (1 Cor 16:1–3; compare also 2 Cor 8:11–15).[108]

In summary, no mandates to sell all of one's possessions occur after the completing of Jesus' earthly ministry. The partial selling of one's possessions for the sake of alleviating the plight of needy brethren is manifested in Acts, but never mandated. The commendation in 1 Cor 13:3 is presented as superlative rather than normative. In fact, as previously noted, 2 Cor 8:11–13 mandates that the Jerusalem collection is to be carried out in such a way that the donors are not themselves ushered into poverty.

WEALTH

The NT witness concerning wealth is inextricably connected to its mandates toward the rich. These possessions-related mandates also include consideration of the believer's relation to "the world."

---

108. Still contentment (like that which Paul describes in Phil 4:11–13) rather than covetousness is to characterize our approach to possessions. We are mandated, in Heb 13:5, to be "free from the love of money" in "being content" with what we have. This related theme will receive further attention under the Covetousness aspect. For now it is sufficient to note that Heb 13:5 also intimates a post-Jesus'-ministry change from forsaking all toward contentment "with what you have"—in a manner reminiscent of John the Baptist's command to the soldiers, concerning their wages, in Luke 3:14.

Wealth Mandates

Matt 16:24–27 Then Jesus said to His disciples, "If anyone wishes to come after Me, he must deny himself, and take up his cross and follow Me. 25 For whoever wishes to save his life will lose it; but whoever loses his life for My sake will find it. 26 For what will it profit a man if he *gains the whole world* and forfeits his soul? Or what will a man give in exchange for his soul? 27 For the Son of Man is going to come in the glory of His Father with His angels, and WILL THEN REPAY EVERY MAN ACCORDING TO HIS DEEDS." (G | | |)

// Mark 8:34–37 And He summoned *the crowd with His disciples*, and said to them, "If anyone wishes to come after Me, he must deny himself, and take up his cross and follow Me. 35 For whoever wishes to save his life will lose it, but whoever loses his life for My sake and the gospel's will save it. 36 For what does it profit a man to *gain the whole world*, and forfeit his soul? 37 For what will a man give in exchange for his soul?" (G | | |)

// Luke 9:23–25 And He was saying to them *all*, "If anyone wishes to come after Me, he must deny himself, and take up his cross daily and follow Me. 24 For whoever wishes to save his life will lose it, but whoever loses his life for My sake, he is the one who will save it. 25 For what is a man profited if he *gains the whole world*, and loses or forfeits himself?" (G | | |)

These three passages follow, in all three Gospels, Jesus' warning that He will be rejected and killed. Matthew and Mark also precede this mandate with the counter-rebuke of Peter (Matt 16:23 // Mark 8:33). Mark and Luke connect this mandate, to be careful not to forfeit one's own soul, to being ashamed of the Son of Man (Mark 8:38 // Luke 9:26)—a mandate which, especially in this context, refers to the denial of Jesus in order to escape persecution (even if the persecution be lethal). Jesus asserts here, to a broad audience, that gaining the whole world at the cost of one's soul is a bad exchange. Whether gaining the whole world is a superlative for the life kept in safety, or a reference to the protection and power of wealth and authority, is uncertain. In any case, "it is hard to imagine a more powerful polemic against wealth"—at least choosing wealth over obedience, be it ever so costly, to the Messiah.[109]

---

109. Hagner, *Matthew*, 484. John 12:25–26 also entails not loving the world but provides less detail. See Carson, *The Gospel According to John*, 438–39; Keener, *The Gospel of John*, 873–75.

Luke 16:1–13 Now He *was also saying to the disciples*, "There was a rich man who had a manager, and this manager was reported to him as squandering his possessions. 2 And he called him and said to him, 'What is this I hear about you? Give an accounting of your management, for you can no longer be manager.' 3 The manager said to himself, 'What shall I do, since my master is taking the management away from me? I am not strong enough to dig; I am ashamed to beg. 4 I know what I shall do, so that when I am removed from the management people will welcome me into their homes.' 5 And he summoned each one of his master's debtors, and he began saying to the first, 'How much do you owe my master?' 6 And he said, 'A hundred measures of oil.' And he said to him, 'Take your bill, and sit down quickly and write fifty.' 7 Then he said to another, 'And how much do you owe?' And he said, 'A hundred measures of wheat.' He said to him, 'Take your bill, and write eighty.' 8 And his master praised the unrighteous manager because he had acted shrewdly; for the sons of this age are more shrewd in relation to their own kind than the sons of light. 9 And I say to you, *make friends for yourselves by means of the wealth of unrighteousness, so that when it fails, they will receive you into the eternal dwellings.* 10 He who is faithful in a very little thing is faithful also in much; and he who is unrighteous in a very little thing is unrighteous also in much. 11 Therefore if you have not been *faithful in the use of unrighteous wealth*, who will entrust the true riches to you? 12 And if you have not been faithful in the use of that which is another's, who will give you that which is your own? 13 No servant can serve two masters; for either he will hate the one and love the other, or else he will be devoted to one and despise the other. *You cannot serve God and wealth.*" (G/S | M | H |)

The parable of the unjust steward in Luke 16:1–13 is difficult to place. While directed to "the disciples" (v. 1), this mandate does not include an explicit command to sell all one's possessions. It does however mandate that they make friends for themselves "by means of the wealth of unrighteousness" (v. 9)—by way of being faithful in its use (v. 11).[110]

---

110. The "unjust" wealth Jesus mentions, τοῦ μαμωνᾶ τῆς ἀδικίας (v. 9) and τῷ ἀδίκῳ μαμωνᾷ (v. 11), does not refer to how it was gained—for then it would need returning rather than proper managing (vv. 11–12)—but rather highlights the seducing and tainting nature of money. See Plummer, *A Critical and Exegetical Commentary on the Gospel according to St. Luke*, 386; Nolland, *Luke*, 806, 808; Reiling and Swellengrebel, *A Handbook on the Gospel of Luke*, 563 (though both possibilities are offered). It is likely due to their deceitfulness (Matt 13:22 // Mark 4:19 // Luke 8:14) that Jesus refers to

Everything the NT Says about Helping the Poor   181

The promise of reward suggests that a mercy mandate is in view (vv. 9, 11–12).[111] The broader and more general principle, that one "cannot serve God and wealth" (v. 13), parallels Matthew's discussion of generosity (Matt 6:22–24). Because the context of this parallel within Matthew suggests that Matthew is guided to express the Lukan mandate to the disciples—that they should sell their possessions and give alms (Luke 12:22–34)—in broader terms, it appears appropriate to understand Luke 16:1–13 within the broader context of a general wealth mandate. That is certainly how the Pharisees extrapolate it. Being lovers of money, they scoff at Jesus (Luke 16:14). The Lord rejoins that their greed, "which is highly esteemed among men" is an abomination (βδέλυγμα, *bdelygma*) "in the sight of God" (Luke 16:15).[112] Thus, while this text may have originally been a call to Jesus' immediate disciples to sell all their possessions in order to give alms, the broader mandate, which extends beyond the confines of Jesus' ministry, is to be generous with God's money in such a way as to benefit others. Whether the forgiving of loans is the specific in view (unlikely due to the disciples' situation), or the generous giving of alms or even generally being generous with money, is ultimately similar and subsumed under the broader mandate to do God's will with His money.[113]

---

riches as accordingly "dirty"—a referral that cannot help but cause some discomfort for readers in the developed world.

111. The counter-indication suggested by the injustice terminology (ἄδικος, *adikos*) of verse 10 is ameliorated in probing the nature of the injustice which Jesus describes as diametric to being faithful with mammon—even when overlooking the interjective proverbial character of the phrase (Nolland, *Luke*, 806; Marshall, *The Gospel of Luke*, 623). What is the moral unrighteousness Jesus condemns? Luke 16:1–13 addresses an integrated theme as indicated by the "And I say to you" (of v. 9) and the reiteration concerning being *truly* faithful in managing "that which is another's" (v. 12)—*pace* Nolland, *Luke*, 805–6; Marshall, *The Gospel of Luke*, 622–23. As such, not being faithful (vv. 11–12) means having made no friends with God's mammon (v. 9)—for this is what makes for the reward (vv. 9, 11–12). And so the injustice of verse 10 most readily concerns greed—the love of money agitated in verse 14; the untrustworthy squandering of God's possessions upon but self. The greedy are unworthy of true riches while the disciples, in contrast, are to be more than content and prove themselves generously faithful with God's money. Making no friends is unjust greed, making many is the rewarded faithfulness of mercy.

112. It is much preferable to understand Luke 16:15 via its immediate context as a condemnation of covetousness and its worldly fruits rather than of making a show of almsgiving. See Nolland, *Luke*, 810; Klostermann, *Das Lukasevangelium*, 166; *contra* Bock, *Luke*, 1350; Marshall, *The Gospel of Luke*, 626.

113. The latter view, being generous generally, is advocated by Darrell Bock (*Luke*,

Luke 16:19–31 Now there was a rich man, and he habitually dressed in purple and fine linen, joyously living [εὐφραίνω, *euphrainō*] in splendor every day. 20 And a poor man named Lazarus was laid at his gate, covered with sores, 21 and longing to be fed with the crumbs which were falling from the rich man's table; besides, even the dogs were coming and licking his sores. 22 Now the poor man died and was carried away by the angels to Abraham's bosom; and the rich man also died and was buried. 23 In Hades he lifted up his eyes, being in torment, and saw Abraham far away and Lazarus in his bosom. 24 And he cried out and said, "Father Abraham, have mercy on me, and send Lazarus so that he may dip the tip of his finger in water and cool off my tongue, for I am in agony in this flame." 25 But Abraham said, "Child, remember that during your life you received your good things, and likewise Lazarus bad things; but now he is being comforted here, and you are in agony. 26 And besides all this, between us and you there is a great chasm fixed, so that those who wish to come over from here to you will not be able, and that none may cross over from there to us." 27 And he said, "Then I beg you, father, that you send him to my father's house— 28 for I have five brothers—in order that he may warn them, so that they will not also come to this place of torment." 29 But Abraham said, "They have Moses and the Prophets; let them hear them." 30 But he said, "No, father Abraham, but if someone goes to them from the dead, they will repent!" 31 But he said to him, "If they do not listen to Moses and the Prophets, they will not be persuaded even if someone rises from the dead." (S | J | H | I)

Luke 16:19–31 describes the unfavorable fate of a rich man who "habitually dressed in purple and fine linen, joyously living in splendor every day" (v. 19) while ignoring the immediately poor (πτωχός, *ptōchos*, v. 20) and sickly man at his gate who longed "to be fed with the crumbs which were falling from the rich man's table" (v. 21). The contrast is purposeful. And most Western commentators play it up. The rich man's everyday clothes were "extremely expensive" down to his "underwear."[114] His "striking luxury" would have been hard to miss for wearing "white garments under a purple robe—this is the sign of highest opulence."[115] Or, more modestly, a sign of being quite prosperous

---

1337). While Jesus quite likely refers to peasant farmer indebtedness within the parable, ascertaining this detail's extra-parabolic analogue is the challenging part.

114. Ibid., 1365; Marshall, *The Gospel of Luke*, 635.

115. Green, *The Gospel of Luke*, 605; Hamel, *Poverty and Charity in Roman Palestine*,

and socially esteemed.¹¹⁶ Some suggest he "lived like a king," feasting (εὐφραίνω, *euphrainō*) in a manner spoken of concerning King Agrippa II.¹¹⁷ Even his mansion's "high ornate gate," πυλών (*pylōn*, v. 20), might resemble "entrances to cities, temples, or palaces."¹¹⁸ As such, he lived the life of "enormous wealth" amidst "delicacies, and superfluity, and pomp."¹¹⁹ Though these comparisons are a little overdone, emphasizing the very high end of the rich man's possible wealth, his table certainly had more than enough scraps to spare.¹²⁰

---

81. Nevertheless Gildas Hamel is generally more cautious and affirms that the rich man's robe would have possessed purple markings rather than being solid purple—for such a display was reserved for kings (Hamel, "Poverty in Clothing," 77, 79). So it is this way in Esth 8:15 and done mockingly to Jesus in Mark 15:17, 20 // John 19:2, 5 (Luke 23:11 has "gorgeous robe" while Matt 27:28 employs "scarlet" for the violet mantle that is reminiscent of the depiction of King David's consecration found at Dura Europos). See ibid., 79; Blomberg, *Matthew*, 414. Still, red or purple markings denoted social distinction—whether economic or military—and so showcased wealth and importance (Hamel, "Poverty in Clothing," 80–81). Though the linen also need not have come from Egypt but rather from nearby Beth-Shean (Scythopolis), it was, even so, reserved for the wealthy (ibid., 77; *contra* Jeremias, *Rediscovering the Parables*, 145). And so the rich man's attire need not have signaled kingly wealth but rather denoted "an honorable person" of substantive means (Hamel, "Poverty in Clothing," 63).

116. So it is in Prov 31:21–23 where the excellent wife is dressed in "fine linen and purple" (v. 22) though not a queen and her husband is honored though not a king. See Garrett, *Proverbs, Ecclesiastes, Song of Songs*, 251; Murphy, *Proverbs*, 247; *contra* Pao and Schnabel, "Luke," 345; Marshall, *The Gospel of Luke*, 635. Interestingly, in the Syriac *Didascalia* the valiant wife of Prov 31:22 makes such attire of linen and purple for her husband (Vööbus, *The Didascalia Apostolorum in Syriac*, 1:22).

117. Fitzmyer, *The Gospel According to Luke*, 1130; Green, *The Gospel of Luke*, 605; Hamel, *Poverty and Charity in Roman Palestine*, 31 (describes the king's feasts). Still, the mention of this splendid feasting is not necessarily that extremely intended, the rich man need not have been as well off as Agrippa II, but rather wealthy enough to regularly enjoy feasts like the one given for the prodigal son (εὐφραίνω, *euphrainō*, Luke 15:23–24, 29, 32) or prosperous enough to build larger barns (εὐφραίνω, *euphrainō*, Luke 12:19). So Gildas Hamel does not, for his part, connect the legendary feasting of King Agrippa II with the rich man (Hamel, "Daily Bread," 23; Hamel, "Poverty in Clothing," 54–55).

118. Bock, *Luke*, 1366. But it might just as well resemble a common tanner's gate (Acts 10:17) or Mary's—"the mother of John who was also called Mark" (Acts 12:12, 13–14).

119. Calvin, *Commentary on a Harmony of the Evangelists*, 2:185, 184.

120. Who exactly is obligated by Jesus' parable of the rich man and Lazarus will be probed further and with greater specificity in the following chapters. For now it is sufficient to but ask ourselves why first world commentators generally desire to perceive the rich man as "obscenely" rich—with but relatively few exceptions. Among these few

The mentioning of the dogs is difficult to render. Perhaps even the dogs showed more compassion than this rich man (v. 21).[121] It is more likely however that the attention of these unclean animals was unwelcome, insulting, and embarrassing rather than positive. Some perceive these dogs to have been of the wild scavenger kind that usually lived at the edges of town.[122] Were this the case, the rich man did not even care enough to have the poor man brought in behind the gate in order to spare him this degradation. Contrariwise it is possible that the rich man owned these dogs, for domesticated dogs were kept as household pets (Matt 15:26–27 // Mark 7:27–28), and that he even allowed them to further humiliate Lazarus in his defenseless state.[123]

After his death the rich man finds himself in torment, agony, and flame (vv. 23–25, 28). Such rich are to repent (v. 30) and "listen to Moses and the Prophets" (v. 31). Whether this listening is to result in their acceptance of the Messiah and His mandates to have "mercy" on the poor or merely involves listening to the concern for the poor expressed in the OT, is on the onset contestable. Nevertheless, the content of the immediately preceding verses, Luke 16:16–18, suggests the latter. If this mandate is intended, as it appears, to address the Pharisees of Luke 16:14, then it serves as a graphic illustration of the love of money (Luke 16:14) which is an abomination in the sight of God (Luke 16:15).[124] Such callousness is, in this passage, identified as leading into torment and therefore unjust.

This hamartiologically communicated obligation level, which is at variance with the general proclivity of the NT (as it has been observed), might possibly be considered as conceptually analogous to the parable

---

are Blomberg, *Neither Poverty nor Riches*, 123 (makes no mention of great wealth); Nolland, *Luke*, 827, 832 (identifies him only as part of Israel's upper class).

121. John Calvin and Theodor von Zahn support this interpretation (Calvin, *Commentary on a Harmony of the Evangelists*, 2:185; Zahn, *Das Evangelium des Lukas*, 585).

122. Green, *The Gospel of Luke*, 606; Fitzmyer, *The Gospel According to Luke*, 1132; Bock, *Luke*, 1367.

123. John Nolland supports this latter interpretation on the basis of "syntax and flow" and argues that the rich man's dogs not only received the scraps from his table but were also subsequently permitted to lick Lazarus as well (Nolland, *Luke*, 828–29). I. Howard Marshall agrees and contends that the "dogs aggravated the sores by licking them" (Marshall, *The Gospel of Luke*, 635).

124. This connection to the Pharisees of Luke 16:14 is commonly affirmed. See Bock, *Luke*, 1377; Fitzmyer, *The Gospel According to Luke*, 1125; Green, *The Gospel of Luke*, 599; Marshall, *The Gospel of Luke*, 632; Nolland, *Luke*, 831.

of the sheep and the goats—a passage which also warns of punishment in the life to come as related to failing to help the immediately poor. Perhaps it may be that *faith* in Christ produces *works* which would help the immediately poor in such a situation, and that the rich man is here condemned on the basis of a lack of both (being analogous to the Pharisees which likewise lacked both). Nevertheless, such possibilities are suppositional, highly tenuous, and textually unsubstantiated. By comparison, the parable of the sheep and the goats does not, unlike the present passage, assert that failure to provide for the sustenance needs of the immediately poor is a matter of sin for its obligators. Luke 16:30, however, maintains that the present treatment deserves repentance, μετανοέω (*metanoeō*), and is therefore indicated as entailing sin.[125] Luke 16:19–31, for its part, certainly asserts that being rich and using one's surplus solely for the purpose of self-indulgence in the face of immediate, calamity-caused, non-able-bodied poverty is gravely precarious before God.[126] Despite the possible aforementioned integration of faith and works, a careful textual weighing affirms that this descriptive valuation and treatment valuation mandate possesses a justice obligation level.[127] The special character of this mandate insures that it will receive additional attention and analysis in the next chapter—the forthcoming integration stage.

> 1 Tim 6:17–19 Instruct [παραγγέλλω, *parangellō*, command] those who are rich in this present world not to be conceited or to *fix their hope on the uncertainty of riches*, but on God, who richly supplies us with *all things to enjoy*. 18 Instruct [command] them to do good [ἀγαθοεργέω, *agathoergeō*], to be rich in *good works* [ἔργοις καλοῖς], to be *generous* and ready to *share* [κοινωνικός, *koinōnikos*], 19 *storing up for themselves the treasure* of a good foundation for the future, so that they may take hold of that which is life indeed. (P/G | M | H | I/P)

---

125. Luke's use of μετανοέω (*metanoeō*)—which is itself consonant with the remainder of NT usage—reveals that, whenever it is further specified, repentance entails turning away from sin (Luke 5:32; 13:2–5; 15:7, 10; 17:3–4; 24:47; Acts 2:38; 3:19; 5:31; 8:22).

126. Luke 16:20 reveals that the poor man had to be "laid," ἐβέβλητο, (by others) at the rich man's gate. Such terminology pertains to the crippled or those diseased enough to be bedridden. See Fitzmyer, *The Gospel According to Luke*, 1132; Nolland, *Luke*, 828.

127. A broader and more detailed defense of this interpretive conclusion will be provided in the Defending Social Justice section of chapter 7.

The instructions in 1 Tim 6:17–19 command the rich to not "fix their hope on the uncertainty of riches, but on God" who supplies people with "things to enjoy" (v. 17). They are thus permitted to own and enjoy possessions provided that they do good (ἀγαθοεργέω, *agathoergeō*), richly abound in good works (πλουτεῖν ἐν ἔργοις καλοῖς), and are "generous and ready to share [κοινωνικός, *koinōnikos*]" (v. 18).[128] Such commitments to the "good works" of partial sharing, which are consonant with the generosity exhibited within the nascent church of Acts, are mercy commitments for they store up treasure in a manner that echoes the Sermon on the Mount. This echo reaffirms that, post Jesus' earthly ministry, His followers are not called to forsake all (as in Luke 12:33) but rather to maintain the same attitude of being generous in almsgiving.

> Jas 1:9–11 But the brother of humble circumstances is to glory in his high position; 10 and the rich man is to glory in his humiliation, because like flowering grass he will pass away. 11 For the sun rises with a scorching wind and withers the grass; and its flower falls off and the beauty of its appearance is destroyed; so too the rich man in the midst of his pursuits will fade away. (G | | |)

James burns with the passion of an OT prophet. In Jas 1:9–11, he commands the rich believer "to glory in his humiliation" by being well cognizant of the transience of riches (v. 11).[129] This mandate thus serves to prepare the way for the partiality mandates of Jas 2:1–12 (discussion to come).

> Jas 5:1–6 Come now, you rich, *weep and howl* for your *miseries which are coming upon you.* 2 Your riches have rotted and your

---

128. Incidentally, Paul does not intend to provide any sort of *carte blanche* here—for his emphasis is on the good works that wealth allows. And so he is not reticent to discourage—by way of direct command—the spending of wealth on "costly" adornments and hairstyles (1 Tim 2:9–10; compare 1 Pet 3:3). See Blomberg, *Neither Poverty nor Riches*, 207. Perhaps good works rather than such jewelry and garments are to receive a woman's financial attention (1 Tim 2:10).

129. While scholars are divided over the identity of the rich person in Jas 1:10, an immediately contextual reading favors the rich person's identification as a believer: Καυχάσθω δὲ ὁ ἀδελφὸς ὁ ταπεινὸς ἐν τῷ ὕψει αὐτοῦ, ὁ δὲ πλούσιος ἐν τῇ ταπεινώσει αὐτοῦ, ὅτι ὡς ἄνθος χόρτου παρελεύσεται (Jas 1:9–10, italics added). In addition, Jas 2:4 and Jas 4:13–17 confirm that rich believers were among the recipients of this letter. These rich believers have business pursuits (ἐμπορεύομαι, *emporeuomai*, Jas 4:13) which resemble the pursuits (πορεία, *poreia*) described in Jas 1:11. For further discussion from the alternate perspective see Martin, *James*, 25–26; Davids, *The Epistle of James*, 76–77.

> garments have become moth-eaten. 3 *Your gold and your silver have rusted*; and their rust will be a witness against you and will *consume your flesh like fire*. It is in the last days that you have stored up your treasure! 4 Behold, the *pay of the laborers who mowed your fields, and which has been withheld by you*, cries out against you; and the outcry of those who did the harvesting has reached the ears of the *Lord of Sabaoth*. 5 You have lived luxuriously on the earth and led a life of wanton pleasure; you have fattened your hearts in a *day of slaughter*. 6 You have *condemned and put to death the righteous man* [δίκαιος, *dikaios*]; he does not resist you. (C | J | H |)

In Jas 5:1–6 the unjust rich are treated to woes reminiscent of the mourning and weeping of Luke 6:24–25. These rich have pursued storing up their treasure on earth in diametrical opposition to Jesus' treasure mandates in the Sermon on the Mount and thus, in God's estimation, their "garments have become moth-eaten" (v. 2) and their "gold and . . . silver have rusted" (v. 3). Their sin, which will consume their "flesh like fire" (v. 3), involves the injustice of defrauding the "pay of the laborers" who harvested (ἀμάω, *amaō*) their fields and the condemnation unto death of those, who unlike them, are just and likely righteous too (δίκαιος, *dikaios*, v. 6). James is thus attacking the rich which are unjust in storing up their treasure at the immoral expense of the laborers who have worked for them and who are very likely to be potentially poor.[130] Their murders are equally heinous. These rich act in a way that is diametrically opposed to the mandates of 1 Tim 6:17–19.

Wealth Clarifiers

> Matt 13:22 And the one on whom seed was sown among the thorns, this is the man who hears the word, and the *worry of the world and the deceitfulness of wealth* choke the word, and it becomes unfruitful. (G |)

> // Mark 4:18–19 And others are the ones on whom seed was sown among the thorns; these are the ones who have heard the word, 19 but the *worries of the world, and the deceitfulness of riches, and the desires for other things* enter in and choke the word, and it becomes unfruitful. (G |)

---

130. Martin, *James*, 179.

// Luke 8:14 The seed which fell among the thorns, these are the ones who have heard, and as they go on their way they are choked with *worries and riches and pleasures* [ἡδονή, *hēdonē*] *of this life*, and bring no fruit to maturity. (G |)

Matthew 13:22; Mark 4:18–19; and Luke 8:14, because they are addressed to the crowd (though the disciples receive the explanation), appear to provide a general warning against the deceitfulness of riches. Such people "bring no fruit to maturity" (Luke 8:14). The "worry of the world and the deceitfulness of wealth" (Matt 13:22) causes them to pursue other desires (Mark 4:19) such as the "pleasures [ἡδονή, *hēdonē*] of this life" (Luke 8:14).[131]

Rev 3:17–18 Because you say, "I am *rich*, and have become *wealthy*, and have need of nothing," and you do not know that you are wretched and miserable and poor [πτωχός, *ptōchos*] and blind and naked, 18 I advise you to buy from Me gold refined by fire so that you may become rich, and white garments so that you may clothe yourself, and that the shame of your nakedness will not be revealed; and eye salve to anoint your eyes so that you may see. (G |)

The blinding of wealth also receives attention in the clarifier of Rev 3:17–18—for it has the ability to make even believers truly poor and pitiably pathetic before the Son and the Spirit.[132]

---

131. This worry of the world may be analogous to the worries that accompany seeking the "things the nations of the world eagerly seek" (Luke 12:30 // Matt 6:32) but apparently in a broader, extra-immediate-disciple sense. Analogous language is also found in Luke 21:34. This warning against friendship with the world and its pleasures is also reiterated in Jas 4:1–5 (which will receive subsequent attention).

132. Both verses refer to the wealth of Laodicea and its well-known economic pursuits in banking and commerce, pharmaceuticals, and the clothing industry. The material wealth of the Laodiceans blindered their eyes from true riches, honor, and clear self-perception. Having succumbed to an affluent lifestyle they assumed, in their self-sufficiency, that they were spiritually well-off too. See Osborne, *Revelation*, 206–10; Blount, *Revelation*, 82; Morris, *The Book of Revelation*, 82. Their material prosperity was taken as indicative of their spiritual wellbeing—but this, via the deceptiveness of riches, turned out to be mere illusion. See Beale, *The Book of Revelation*, 304; Plummer et al., *Revelation*, 116. Nursing a more conciliatory tack, some believe that Jesus judges the Laodicean believers miserable and poor on account of both their approach to wealth *and* their misplaced spiritual pride. See Charles, *A Critical and Exegetical Commentary on the Revelation of St. John*, 1:93, 96; R. Mounce, *The Book of Revelation*, 110–11. Ranging farther still, some contend that the Laodiceans were seduced by their spiritual "riches" *alone*—that their wealth was figurative only. See Aune, *Revelation*, 259; Moffatt,

In summary, Luke 16:19–31, the parable of the rich man and Lazarus, attributes a justice level of obligation to helping the calamity-caused, non-able-bodied immediately poor when one possesses a surplus of wealth and opportunity. This conceptual *hapax* will receive further attention during our concept integration stage.

The rich person's difficult entry into the kingdom (Matt 19:21–25 // Mark 10:21–26 // Luke 18:22–26) is related to this section's mandates but has received prior attention. Mary's *Magnificat* affirms that God has "FILLED THE HUNGRY WITH GOOD THINGS; And sent away the rich empty-handed" (Luke 1:53), but this general clarifier does not provide any needed detail.

The wealth mandates and clarifiers warn that riches are deceitful and that the wealthy must be careful to share with those in need—particularly with needy believers.

COVETOUSNESS

Covetousness is a sin which impinges on helping the poor because it acts in the opposite direction of generosity. The NT term πλεονεξία (*pleonexia*) refers to a desire for more (or for keeping more than one ought). It denotes—with terminological indivisibility—greed, insatiableness, avarice, and covetousness.[133] Elders and deacons, in particular, must be free of the love of money for they were responsible for the church's corporate sharing and almsgiving (1 Tim 3:2–3, 8; Titus 1:7). Because these coveting mandates and clarifiers impinge on helping the poor only via implication or not without some ambiguity, they will, save for the first exemplar, be discussed only briefly.

The Revelation of St. John the Divine, 371. Both David Aune and James Moffatt make their case on the basis of their dating of Revelation in proximity to the earthquake that befell Laodicea in AD 60—for Aune the date is too close while for Moffatt it is, ironically, too distant. But this final interpretation stumbles over the plenteous references to material wealth within the passage itself, its probable allusion to Hosea 12:8–11 (9–12 BHS, LXX) where literal wealth is also in play, and the likely contrasting of Laodicea with Smyrna (Rev 2:9). Interestingly, the letter to the Laodicean church identifies its relationship to its wealth as a matter of sin needing repentance (Rev 3:19). So what is its sin? Pride and trust in riches (like in 1 Tim 6:17) or a willingness to syncretize with Laodicea's idolatrous trade guilds and economic institutions in order to gain and maintain its wealth? Still, in either case, its sin was brought on by the deceitfulness of riches.

133. Selter, "πλεονεξία," *NIDNTT* 1:137–38.

Covetousness Mandates

> Luke 12:13–21 Someone in the crowd said to Him, "Teacher, tell my brother to divide the family inheritance with me." 14 But He said to him, "Man, who appointed Me a judge or arbitrator over you?" 15 Then He said to them, *"Beware, and be on your guard against every form of greed* [πλεονεξία, *pleonexia*]; for not even when one has an abundance does his life consist of his possessions." 16 And He told them a parable, saying, "The land of a rich man was very productive. 17 And he began reasoning to himself, saying, 'What shall I do, since I have no place to store my crops?' 18 Then he said, 'This is what I will do: I will tear down my barns and build larger ones, and there I will store all my grain and my goods. 19 And I will say to my soul, "Soul, you have many goods laid up for many years to come; take your ease, eat, drink and be merry."' 20 But God said to him, '*You fool!* This very night your soul is required of you; and now who will own what you have prepared?' 21 So is the man who *stores up treasure for himself,* and is not *rich toward God.*" (G | | |)

This text, as noted earlier, outs covetousness as moral folly before God. But what precisely is the greed of the rich man? What does its antidote taste like? Jesus commands His hearers to guard against such greed because a person's life does not "consist of his possessions" (v. 15). Jesus' response appears to make use of a chiastic conceptual arrangement. The first part of verse 15 warns against greed while the latter portion asserts that possessions do not sustain our lives; verse 20 subsequently confirms this claim concerning the impotence of possessions while verse 21 returns its gaze to the greed in question. Consequently, to be "superabundantly" blessed (vv. 16–18) and to give nothing of it away is exposed as greed. Being "rich toward God"—which in verse 21 functions as the contrast to treasuring up for oneself alone—is best taken in its straightforward meaning.[134] As denoting that some forms of giving are as unto God and hence store up "treasure in heaven" (v. 33)—for God always repays. So it is in Prov 19:17 when it asserts that "One who is gracious to a poor man lends to the LORD, And He will repay him for his good

---

134. *Pace* Bock, *Luke*, 1154; Calvin, *Commentary on a Harmony of the Evangelists*, 2:150; Marshall, *The Gospel of Luke*, 524; Nolland, *Luke*, 687; Plummer, *A Critical and Exegetical Commentary on the Gospel according to St. Luke*, 325; Reiling and Swellengrebel, *A Handbook on the Gospel of Luke*, 474; Stein, *Luke*, 352. Practically speaking, laying up for but oneself would have transparently subsumed the notion of storing up for one's household in a communal culture.

deed." This is how we can be liberal toward Him who owns the "cattle on a thousand hills" (Ps 50:10).

This reading is supported by the present text's explicit connection to what comes next (v. 22). While the notion of storing up in barns (vv. 18, 24), the matter of treasuring up (vv. 21, 33), and the assertion that life is more than the possessions which sustain it (vv. 15, 23) all resurface, it is the latter issue of pursuing security through possessions that provides the explicit connection (vv. 22–30). And prepares the way for the poor-benefiting call to relinquish possessions as part of immediately following Jesus (vv. 31–34). Jesus' disciples were not to worry about their sustenance needs (v. 22) and thus could sell their possessions and give the proceeds to the poor (v. 33). The rich man, in contradistinction, was so enmeshed with his sustenance needs and wellbeing (v. 19) that he gave away nothing (v. 21). This indeed was the rich man's greed: to be blessed with "abundance" (v. 15) and yet give nothing (v. 21). Living so is sinful and unjust. The other end of the spectrum is occupied by the mercy of being rich toward God—something that He rewards with treasures in heaven. And the "excluded middle" of justice requires those in the rich man's shoes to give something—for that is what contentment looks like under such "superabundant" circumstances.[135]

The passage, unfortunately, does not tell us how much to give—beyond condemning giving nothing at all.[136] And while the poor are certainly the recipients of the disciples' giving in verse 33 and are likely subsumed—as contended—even here, this is not unambiguously certain.[137] For Jesus gives this parable in response to a fraternal conflict over a family inheritance (v. 13).[138] Which brother does Jesus side with? Both were present for the one wanted Jesus to tell the other what

135. In this sense the present passage mirrors the contextually interrelated and similarly middle-excluding discussion of greed and generosity in Matt 6:22–23 (a passage which will receive attention in the upcoming Generosity section).

136. In this sense it is like Luke 16:1–13 (the parable of the unjust steward and its context).

137. Though, happily, John Nolland concurs (Nolland, *Luke*, 687). Within the framework of the parable itself—that is, prior to considering its intended extra-parabolic analogue—the rich man, upon obtaining his surplus, could have lent out to the poor or given some of it away as a patron or as alms (rather than committing it to newer barns).

138. While Jesus refuses to directly adjudicate the dispute in an official manner, the common "Western" assumption that He does not address the matter further is atomistic (*pace* Blomberg, *Neither Poverty nor Riches*, 119; Bock, *Luke*, 1149–50).

was right (v. 13, note also the plural "you," ὑμᾶς, in v. 14). Jesus' parable most directly upbraids the brother with the possessions—the one with the abundance all stored up for himself alone. So while everyone is warned against greed, it is the withholding brother who would have felt the most poignantly directed sting. And so being "rich toward God" (v. 21) entailed, in its nighest context, appropriately sharing the inheritance with the likely younger brother—who was not necessarily immediately poor.[139] This consideration means that despite the explicit tie-in to Luke 12:22–34 and the parable's reach to "every form of greed," we cannot be unambiguously certain that the poor are the immediately intended recipients of the present mandate to give, at minimum, something. Consequently it is most judicious to consider the parable of the rich fool, though it be highly suggestive, as not as clear as the parable of the rich man and Lazarus.

> 1 Cor 5:9–11 I wrote you in my letter not to associate with immoral people; 10 I did not at all mean with the immoral people of this world, or with the *covetous* and *swindlers*, or with idolaters, for then you would have to go out of the world. 11 But actually, I wrote to you *not to associate* with any so-called brother if he is an immoral person, or *covetous*, or an idolater, or a reviler, or a drunkard, or a *swindler—not even to eat with such a one.* (G | J | H |)

First Corinthians 5:9–11 identifies coveting (being πλεονέκτης, *pleonektēs*) and rapacious swindling (being ἅρπαξ, *harpax*) as grounds for shunning another believer. Coveting, or greed, is here connected to its manifestation in predatory defrauding and both assume their place in the present sin list.[140] Rapacious deceitfulness, an interhuman manifestation of coveting, is thus identified as an injustice.

> 1 Cor 6:7–10 Actually, then, it is already a defeat for you, that you have *lawsuits* with one another. Why not rather be *wronged*? Why not rather be *defrauded*? 8 On the contrary, you yourselves *wrong and defraud.* You do this even to your brethren. 9 Or do you not know that the *unrighteous* [ἄδικος, *adikos*] *will not inherit the kingdom of God*? Do not be deceived; neither fornicators, nor idolaters, nor adulterers, nor effeminate, nor homosexuals, 10

---

139. The auditory audience's predisposition to connect backwards rather than ahead (to the as yet unheard) commends this interpretive focus.

140. Garland, *1 Corinthians*, 185–86.

nor *thieves*, nor the *covetous*, nor drunkards, nor revilers, nor *swindlers*, will *inherit the kingdom of God*. (G | J | HS |)

Here Paul mandates that believers should rather be defrauded than pursue lawsuits with other believers. Yet the defrauding is part of being unjust (ἄδικος, *adikos*, v. 9) and those who practice it, theft, greed, or swindling will not "inherit the kingdom of God" (vv. 9–10).

> Col 3:5–6 Therefore consider the members of your earthly body as dead to immorality, impurity, passion, evil desire, and *greed, which amounts to idolatry*. 6 For it is because of these things that the *wrath of God* will come upon the sons of disobedience. (G | J | H |)

Because greed (πλεονεξία, *pleonexia*) "amounts to idolatry" (v. 5), the "wrath of God" (v. 6) is upon this significant sin.

> 1 Tim 6:5–11 and constant friction between men of depraved mind and deprived of the truth, who suppose that *godliness is a means of gain*. 6 But godliness actually is a means of great gain when accompanied by *contentment*. 7 For we have brought nothing into the world, so we cannot take anything out of it either. 8 If we have *food and covering, with these we shall be content*. 9 But those who *want to get rich fall into temptation and a snare and many foolish and harmful desires which plunge men into ruin and destruction*. 10 For the *love of money is a root of all sorts of evil*, and some *by longing for it have wandered away from the faith* and pierced themselves with many *griefs*. 11 But flee from these things, you man of God, and pursue righteousness, godliness, faith, love, perseverance and gentleness. (G | J | H |)

This passage mandates that believers are to be content if they "have food and covering" (v. 7). Because the "love of money is a root of all sorts of evil" (v. 10), those who "want to get rich fall into temptation and a snare and many foolish and harmful desires which plunge men into ruin and destruction" (v. 9). Thus greed is again affirmed to be unjust and a source of apostasy (v. 10).[141]

> Heb 13:5–6 Make sure that your character is free from the *love of money*, being content with what you have; for He Himself has said, "I WILL NEVER DESERT YOU, NOR WILL I EVER

---

141. W. Mounce, *Pastoral Epistles*, 347–48. Accordingly, true pastoral and missionary workers are free of greed (1 Thess 2:5) while "false teachers" (2 Pet 2:1) swim in it (2 Pet 2:3, 14).

> FORSAKE YOU," 6 so that we confidently say, "THE LORD IS MY HELPER, I WILL NOT BE AFRAID. WHAT WILL MAN DO TO ME?" (G | | |)

The mandate to be content rather than money-loving is reaffirmed in Heb 13:5–6. Believers can heed this admonition to "simplicity and detachment from material possessions" because God will never forsake us (v. 5) but rather help us (v. 6) when need arises.[142]

> Jas 4:1–5 What is the source of quarrels and conflicts among you? Is not the source your *pleasures* [ἡδονή, *hēdonē*] that wage war in your members? 2 You lust and do not have; so you commit murder. You are *envious* and cannot obtain; so you fight and quarrel. You do not have because you do not ask. 3 You ask and do not receive, because you ask with *wrong* [κακῶς, *kakōs*] *motives*, so that you may spend it on your *pleasures* [ἡδονή, *hēdonē*]. 4 You adulteresses, do you not know that *friendship with the world is hostility toward God*? Therefore whoever wishes to be a *friend of the world makes himself an enemy of God*. 5 Or do you think that the Scripture speaks to no purpose: "He jealously desires the Spirit which He has made to dwell in us"? (G | J | H |)

Seeking wealth in order to be able to spend it on one's pleasures (plural of ἡδονή, *hēdonē*) is condemned as enmity (ἔχθρα, *echthra*) with God in Jas 4:1–5. This "friendship with the world" is a form of adulterous idolatry that makes oneself an enemy (ἐχθρός, *echthros*) of God (v. 4). By implication, asking so as to receive involves having the right motives (v. 3)—motives that involve spending one's wealth on things other than one's pleasures. Such spending would include helping the poor. This mandate also explicitly condemns lusting for that which one does not have (v. 2).

Covetousness Clarifiers

> 1 Tim 3:2–3 An overseer, then, must be above reproach, the husband of one wife, temperate, prudent, respectable, *hospitable*, able to teach, 3 not addicted to wine or pugnacious, but gentle, peaceable, *free from the love of money*. (C |)

---

142. Attridge, *The Epistle to the Hebrews*, 387. The OT quotation is most likely from Deut 31:6, 8. The present call to confidently rely on God's care and provision seems somewhat reminiscent of Matt 6:25–34 (Lane, *Hebrews*, 518).

1 Tim 3:8 Deacons likewise must be men of dignity, not double-tongued, or addicted to much wine or *fond of sordid gain*. (C |)

Titus 1:7–8 For the overseer must be above reproach as God's steward, not self-willed, not quick-tempered, not addicted to wine, not pugnacious, *not fond of sordid gain*, 8 but *hospitable*, loving what is good, sensible, just, devout, self-controlled. (C |)

First Timothy 3:2–3; 1 Tim 3:8; and Titus 1:7–8 affirm that elders and deacons must be free from the love of money and sordid gain.[143] In contrast they are to be hospitable to strangers by sharing their homes and meals. The overseer, a "functional title,"[144] appears to have been responsible for the distributions to the poor, akin to the apostles in Acts, at least in the context of the early church fathers.[145]

In summary, coveting is identified as a sin in the Decalogue and thus is forbidden in Rom 13:9 and explicitly mentioned as a sin in Rom 7:7–11. Jesus similarly warns that deeds of coveting and greed (Mark 7:22) are among the "evil things" that defile a person (Mark 7:23, 20). Because greed is something that *the depraved* are filled with (Rom 1:28–29), it "must not even be named among" believers (Eph 5:3). For no "covetous man ... has an inheritance in the kingdom" (Eph 5:5)—as coveting calls forth "the wrath of God" (Eph 5:6). To the extent that it affects interhuman action it results in injustice for it seeks to secure or withhold that which does not rightfully belong to it. In this sense, social gospel and liberation theology advocates are astute in recognizing that the alienation of greed is a sin.

GENEROSITY

Generosity is an indispensable component of helping the poor. As has already been noted in the discussions of Luke 16:1–13; 2 Cor 9:8–11; and 1 Tim 6:17–19, generosity is a common component of Christian obligation.[146] Two camouflaged but parallel generosity mandates will receive our attention here.

---

143. For seeking such gain is what those of a "depraved mind" seek (1 Tim 5:6).

144. Knight, *The Pastoral Epistles*, 290; N. White, *Titus*, 187.

145. By way of example note Ignatius's command to Polycarp to "vindicate your [Polycarp's] position by giving your whole attention to its material and spiritual sides" (Ignatius, *To Polycarp*, 1:2). See C. Richardson, *Early Christian Fathers*, 118.

146. The probable presence of generosity among the fruits of the Spirit in Gal 5:22 (NRSV) adds to its commonness ("ἀγαθωσύνη," BDAG 4; F. Bruce, *The Epistle to the Galatians*, 253–54; Rendall, *The Epistle to the Galatians*, 188; George, *Galatians*, 403).

Generosity Mandates

> Matt 6:22–23 The eye is the lamp of the body; so then if your *eye is clear* [ἁπλοῦς, *haplous*], your whole body will be full of light. 23 But if your *eye is bad* [πονηρός, *ponēros*], your whole body will be full of darkness. If then the light that is in you is darkness, how great is the darkness! (P | | |)

> // Luke 11:34–36 The eye is the lamp of your body; when your *eye is clear* [ἁπλοῦς, *haplous*], your whole body also is full of light; but when it is *bad* [πονηρός, *ponēros*], your body also is full of darkness. 35 Then watch out that the light in you is not darkness. 36 If therefore your whole body is full of light, with no dark part in it, it will be wholly illumined, as when the lamp illumines you with its rays." (P | | |)

The reference to the good (ἁπλοῦς, *haplous*) and evil (πονηρός, *ponēros*) eye in Matt 6:22–23 and Luke 11:34–36 is a mandate unto generosity. Alan M'Neile concludes, perhaps too strongly, that, in the NT, πονηρός (*ponēros*) is "nowhere found strictly of physical soundness."[147] Biblical usage does however support the connection between an evil eye and covetousness, envy, and greed.[148] It is indeed difficult to overlook the evidence for this connection as found in Deut 15:9; 28:54–58; Prov 23:6; 28:22; Matt 20:15; and Mark 7:22.[149] Singleness or simplicity (ἁπλότης, *haplotēs*) is used throughout the NT to refer to generosity and, correspondingly, the single or simple (ἁπλοῦς, *haplous*) eye refers to being generous and provides Matt 6:22–23 with an amiable fit within its Sermon on the Mount context. Jesus is not changing the subject.

The mandate is not to be greedy (which is a great darkness), but rather to pass the here excluded middle of contentment, and be generous. Contextually, by way of the Luke-paralleled (Luke 12:22–34) context of the Matthew passage (Matt 6:19–34), these generosity mandates have the poor as their recipients (Luke 12:33). Such mandates naturally

---

147. M'Neile, *The Gospel According to Saint Matthew*, 85.

148. This observation is by no means recent. John Lightfoot affirmed this—along with noting the concordant Jewish usage—for Latin and English readers in the seventeenth century (Lightfoot, *Horæ Hebraicæ et Talmudicæ*, 2:156–57). Jewish scholar Samuel Lachs supplies more recent agreement (Lachs, *A Rabbinic Commentary on the New Testament*, 127–28; *pace* Manson, *The Sayings of Jesus*, 93).

149. Extracanonical support is found in, for example, Sirach 14:3–10 and Tobit 4:7–10. For additional usage see Allison, "The Eye is the Lamp of the Body," 61–83.

flow into commands to give generously—such as those found in Luke 6:38 and 1 Tim 6:18.

The mandate of these two passages has often been obfuscated in translation precisely because it is integrally comprised of both an idiom and a metaphor. Relatively few NT texts experience such complex linguistic commingling. Unable to translate both, English translators have generally opted to translate the metaphor—to clearly preserve the relation of light and the eye.[150]

GIVE AND LEND

Mandates concerning giving and lending will naturally benefit those who have need of asking and borrowing. Thus the poor become the primary candidates for being the beneficiaries of such mandates.

Give and Lend Mandates

> Matt 5:42 *Give* to him who asks of you, and do not turn away from him who wants to *borrow* from you. (S | | | I/P)

> // Luke 6:29–30, 34–36 Whoever hits you on the cheek, offer him the other also; and whoever *takes away* your coat, do not withhold your shirt from him either. 30 *Give* to everyone who asks of you, and whoever *takes away* what is yours, do not demand it back.... 34 If you *lend* to those from whom you expect to receive, what credit is that to you? Even sinners lend to sinners in order to receive back the same amount. 35 But *love* your *enemies*, and *do good*, and *lend*, expecting nothing in return; and your *reward* will be great, and you will be sons of the Most High; for He Himself is kind to ungrateful and evil men. 36 Be *merciful* [οἰκτίρμων, *oiktirmōn*], just as your Father is *merciful* [οἰκτίρμων, *oiktirmōn*]. (SC | M | HS | I/P)

Matthew 5:42 and Luke 6:29–30, 34–36 contain Jesus' Sermon on the Mount and Sermon on the Plain mandates concerning giving and lending. But what does the "giving" refer to? The interpretive decision—between favoring almsgiving, lending (reiteratively), or demanded relinquishing—is incredibly difficult. And ultimately appropriately tentative. Both passages, by way of employing a general phrase and terminology,

---

150. But this translation choice has not been followed elsewhere. The most recent Czech translation, for example, opts to translate the idiom over facilely preserving the metaphor. See *Překlad 21. století* (21st Century Translation).

may mandate giving generally—in such a way as to subsume almsgiving.[151] Both could be about lending alone by way of a synonymous Semitic parallelism in Matt 5:42.[152] Or both passages could be about litigious or forceful demanding, as already surfaced in Matt 5:40 and Luke 6:29.[153] So Calvin prefers the litigious demanding interpretation in Luke, though he allows for understanding Luke 6:30 as "an exhortation to liberality in giving."[154] Additionally, as already evident within the citations, each passage may be understood as entailing a mandate different from the other. And, on top of all this variance, looking to biblical antecedents provides no relief. For Jesus also refers back to lending texts such as Deut 15:7–11 within the context of almsgiving (Matt 26:11 // Mark 14:7 // John 12:8).[155] Still, any particular decision here will not affect the range of our obligations as almsgiving is certainly mandated elsewhere.

What can we observe by way of whittling down the options? In terms of Matthew, the enfolding Matt 5:38–42 contextual unit addresses tit-for-tat reciprocity. Though commentators often assume, on the basis of the beginning of verse 39, that non-retaliation, nonresistance, or non-retribution is the encompassing context focus, such an assumption necessarily stumbles over verse 42.[156] For there is no mention of wrong-

---

151. Calvin, *Commentary on a Harmony of the Evangelists*, 1:301–2; Blomberg, *Matthew*, 113–14; France, *The Gospel of Matthew*, 222–23; Hagner, *Matthew*, 131; Keener, *A Commentary on the Gospel of Matthew*, 201–2; Morris, *The Gospel According to Matthew*, 128; Nolland, *The Gospel of Matthew*, 260–61; Bock, *Luke*, 593–94 (aiding indigent beggars but subsuming lending).

152. Lachs, *A Rabbinic Commentary on the New Testament*, 105; Davies and Allison, *Matthew*, 1:547–48; Bock, *Luke*, 594 (concerning Matthew); Danker, *Jesus and the New Age*, 146 (concerning Luke); Manson, *The Sayings of Jesus*, 52 (concerning Luke). The referral to lending in the gnostic *Gospel of Thomas* 95 is occasionally summoned as additional support. See Davies and Allison, *Matthew*, 1:547–48.

153. Nolland, *Luke*, 297; Marshall, *The Gospel of Luke*, 262; Stein, *Luke*, 208. The terminology of μὴ ἀπαίτει ("do not demand it back"), as found in Luke 6:30, is perhaps employed concerning theft in *Didache* 1:4 ("for you are not able to get it back anyway" from οὐδὲ γὰρ δύνασαι) but also with respect to lending and almsgiving in *Didache* 1:5 (which refers to the first part of Luke 6:30 as well). This almsgiving (ἐλεημοσύνη, *eleēmosynē*) is then explicitly referred to in the warning of *Didache* 1:6. But even the taking or receiving (λαμβάνω, *lambanō*) of *Didache* 1:4, in its context of relating to enemies, may be about litigation or possibly even lending as well.

154. Calvin, *Commentary on a Harmony of the Evangelists*, 1:301, 300.

155. For its part, Deut 15:7–11 will receive more detailed analysis in the Breadth of Recipients section of chapter 7.

156. Representative scholars include Davies and Allison, *Matthew*, 1:543, 547; France, *The Gospel of Matthew*, 220.

doing on the part of those asking and wanting to borrow. A considered consistency (with v. 42) and an amiable fit with Luke warmly commend the approach of Donald Hagner and Craig Blomberg—of seeing the treatment of enemies as the general theme.[157] But because this is not clear, I would like to argue for the *élan* of a broader possibility—all the while being very comfortable with both readings.

There are a number of reasons for going fishing with a wider net. Unlike in Luke, an explicit focus on enemies does not arrive in Matthew until the next "antithesis" segment (Matt 5:43–48). Because Matt 5:42 is not about responding to harming, we lose the non-retaliation component of verse 39 as a possible integrative theme for the present "antithesis."[158] Furthermore, this forbidden retaliation is textually bound up with the focus on evil people or possibly on "the evil deed" (v. 39).[159] So when we lose the former we lose with it its *explicit* focus on evil persons and treatments.[160] And so Hagner bears no finer integrating theme and Blomberg suggests it is about going beyond the letter of the law. But transcending a reciprocal tit-for-tat extrapolation of the *lex talionis* (v. 38) is the more immediate and fine-tuned textual possibility. Popular entailments of the *lex talionis* are, after all, what Jesus appears to be responding to—a principlized "reciprocity ethic."[161] For aside from the first example of the dishonoring slap to the face (v. 39), the remaining instances address living by like for like reciprocity more generally—for no physical injury is sustained. And so we have moved beyond the domain of the jurisprudence outlined in the OT *lex talionis* mandates. But not beyond their measure

---

157. Hagner, *Matthew*, 131; Blomberg, *Matthew*, 113.

158. So Hagner agrees that the issue of non-retaliation is confined to verse 39 (Hagner, *Matthew*, 131). While Blomberg, for his part, affirms that it does not extend as far as verse 42 (Blomberg, *Matthew*, 113–14).

159. Hagner, *Matthew*, 131.

160. Even before reaching verse 42, it is not altogether clear whether the person who wishes to legally sue and the Roman soldier who has a legal right to commandeer assistance (vv. 40–41) are evil or committing an evil deed—particularly if the suit is concerning a pledge for a loan. See Davis, *Lex Talionis in Early Judaism and the Exhortation of Jesus in Matthew 5:38–42*, 153. Still, this plaintiff and soldier are certainly being untoward and causing loss—and expectedly would be considered enemies (even if they were not so already). So while not unambiguously evil, the enemy possibility remains.

161. Nolland, *Luke*, 297.

for measure extrapolation—a common concern and expectation both in terms of commensurate harm and commensurate benefit.[162]

So how does this get showcased in the present "antithesis"? The slap on the "right cheek" (v. 39) was likely backhanded. Its recipient could ask for a "bruise for bruise" judgment (Exod 21:24–25) and have the perpetrator struck in turn or, if the Mishnah reliably records earlier tradition, receive a sizable financial judgment in its stead.[163] But Jesus, in this as yet unextrapolated but conspicuously least-physical-injury-possible instantiation, says forgo the remedial justice of seeking the *lex talionis* remedy—the tip for the tap—and rather be willing to take another dishonoring insult.[164] The next instance concerns the loss of a tunic (the inner garment) either as compensation or as a pledge—the collateral for a loan (v. 40).[165] Tit-for-tat reciprocity would incite the defendant to look forward to an occasion to sue the *plaintiff* back—at the first opportunity of securing *his* tunic. But Jesus commands that rather than seeking such payback, the defendant proffer his cloak (the outer garment) as well—the more essential bit of clothing. Though such a pledge was not permitted to be kept overnight (Exod 22:26–27; Deut 24:12–13), providing it would certainly cause the defendant daily hassle. The commandeered load-bearing of verse 41 would never be requited. The Roman soldier would never return such assistance in kind. With no hope of receiving equivalent reciprocation, Jesus nevertheless declares that the subjugating occupier should be assisted for double the legal distance. That the loss of time and labor should be borne even though no positive mutuality would ever come of it. So while Matt 5:42 is unambiguously about living beyond tit-for-tat reciprocity in terms of only providing benefit for expected benefit, the transition beyond solely

---

162. Phillips, "The Tilted Balance," 223–40; Stählin, "ἰσότης," *TDNT* 3:345.

163. Though four zuz was deemed a suitable recompense for a punch by some (a zuz being equivalent to a denarius which was a laborer's day's wage), Rabbi Judah claimed in the name of Rabbi Jose the Galilean that a hundred zuz was more appropriate for a cuff and 200 zuz for a slap—while a backhanded slap deserved 400 zuz (more than a laborer's year's earnings). See the Mishnah, *Bava Qamma* 8:6. And so a dishonoring slap was deemed twice as offensive as a punch while a backhanded slap deserved fourfold recompense.

164. Jesus' choice is conspicuous because it is the greater that subsumes the lesser and not the lesser, the greater.

165. Lachs, *A Rabbinic Commentary on the New Testament*, 104; Davis, *Lex Talionis in Early Judaism and the Exhortation of Jesus in Matthew 5:38–42*, 153.

harm for harm recompense appears to begin in the previous verse. This focus on expected recompense in the *positive* sense is happily backed up by the Lukan parallel concerning lending (Luke 6:32–35)—and also shows up within Matthew's next "antithesis" (Matt 5:46–47).[166] Thus Jesus' followers are to live beyond allotting measure for measure even in the benefit-bestowing sense.

The plausibility of taking tit-for-tat reciprocity as the integrating theme of the present "antithesis"—of taking it alone—entails that the treatment of enemies need not be the overarching concern. And when Hagner and Blomberg's suggestion does not win by default, we are freed to entertain a wider range of recipients—even the needy who are not our enemies. And so Matt 5:42, in its transcending of the "reciprocity ethic," may command us to give to those poor who will not be able to return in kind if we ever become impoverished—and to lend to those who cannot lend back.[167] Almsgiving to the immediately poor was certainly far from a tit-for-tat endeavor—and the broadness of the term employed for asking (αἰτέω, *aiteō*) is extensive enough to subsume begging (as in Acts 3:2).[168] This terminological broadness—in the face of our lacking more direct evidence—was perhaps not self-evidently constrictive enough for Matthew's hearers so as to indicate but lending alone.[169] Furthermore, a "synonymous parallelism" is not arguable here upon the basis of a perceived phraseological similarity between verses 42 and 40.[170] The change of phrasing in verse 42—in bypassing an "if/then" structuring and moving directly to the imperative—certainly does not *fit* the pattern of the previous verses (including the infinitive found after σοι in v. 40). Nor is there any problem with Matt 5:42 mentioning *both* giving and

---

166. Living by *do ut des* (I give so that you give back) is also Jesus' target when addressing who it is meritorious to invite to a luncheon or dinner (Luke 14:12–14).

167. Because lending to fellow Jews was done without charging interest (Lev 25:35–37), it was a favor to do so—for the lender derived no financial gain from it. But among the potentially poor, providing a loan to someone who was likely to be able to lend back in your own time of need provided, by way of inculcated reciprocity, some valuable communal security.

168. Similarly, the term for giving is also broad enough to subsume almsgiving unto the immediately poor (as in John 13:29). Hence the NRSV translation: "Give to everyone who begs from you."

169. Because it concerns itself with usury, something that does not fit either Gospel passage well, *Gospel of Thomas* 95 proves not direct enough. Pace Davies and Allison, *Matthew*, 1:547–48; Pao and Schnabel, "Luke," 297 (who perceive usury in Matthew).

170. As appears to be the intent of Davies and Allison, *Matthew*, 1:547.

lending—whether for the sake of clarity in distinguishing between the intended recipients or because one is bound to be asked to lend a larger sum than when giving alms.[171]

But there is another—less repetitious and perhaps more alluring—way of understanding the lending alone option. A like-minded interpretive possibility that sneaks itself in here. Perhaps the mandates of Matt 5:42, when found so contextually proximate, are prone to socioeconomic reconstruction as referring to two differing forms of reciprocity that are generally acknowledged as common in Jesus' day. In all, four reciprocity types are up for grabs. Of these, it is "balanced reciprocity" that refers to regular lending and debt—where repayment is expected as soon as the borrower is able or in a set interval of time. So while balanced reciprocity was of the "borrow now, repay shortly" variety, "general reciprocity" was rather "borrow now, repay sometime."[172] The latter was not lending in the contemporary Western sense for it took the form of "ritualized gift-giving and receiving."[173] Still, a "gift accepted" implied "an obligation owed."[174] For even general reciprocity entailed "a sort of implicit, non-legal contractual obligation, unenforceable by any authority apart from one's sense of honor and shame."[175] But honor and shame were a very big deal back then—somewhat akin to how they are taken to this day in traditional Arabic contexts. And so general reciprocity entailed that the initial recipient would help you out with an equivalent gift when the tables were turned. This was the communal security of "kinship" according to Hanson and Oakman—and it likely extended to friends as well.[176] For their part, Paul Achtemeier, Joel Green, and Marianne Thompson suggest that the obligation to give to kin was there, but not the strings. That "expectationless reciprocity"—general reciprocity *without* the reciprocity—was the proper entailment of kinship.[177] But even though this

---

171. In this sense, lending may be the "do more" aspect. Nevertheless, which aspect, if any, is intended to be greater here is unclear.

172. Hanson and Oakman, *Palestine in the Time of Jesus*, 116, 105, 186.

173. Noell, "A 'Marketless World?'" 86.

174. Oakman, "The Ancient Economy," 129; Malina, *The New Testament World*, 94–95.

175. Malina, *The New Testament World*, 94.

176. Hanson and Oakman, *Palestine in the Time of Jesus*, 186; Noell, "A 'Marketless World?'" 91.

177. Achtemeier et al., *Introducing the New Testament*, 172.

expectationless reciprocity is construed as a mutual expectation held by all kin, its historical existence is doubtful. Hanson's and Oakman's reconstruction has the distinct advantage of being a more apt characterization of even contemporary socioeconomic contextual equivalents. The final type, "patronage reciprocity," regulated patron-client relationships such that while repayment itself was never expected, the patron did receive back loyalty and appropriate honoring. Of these four reciprocity types, what I have been referring to as tit-for-tat reciprocity most readily encompasses the operation of the first two—both balanced and general reciprocity.[178] Precisely so due to their engendering the ability to borrow and receive back an equivalence in turn—to being given priority in our time of need. Lending for lending, and a gift for a gift.

While it is tempting to see all of Matt 5:42 as referring to general reciprocity, as Hanson and Oakman do in considering its Lukan parallel, the textual data deserves precedence.[179] For the terminology of lending (δανείζω, *daneizō*) found in its latter half simply does not fit with the gift giving of general reciprocity. Gifting and lending were not the same thing even then. And it is this same observation that torpedoes appropriating for Matthew the patronage reciprocity interpretation—as Achtemeier, Green, and Thompson draw in Luke.[180] In their reconstruction, Jesus sought to widen the expectationless reciprocity of kinship to all the needy, and to winnow the expectation of honor indebtedness and loyalty out of the patronage reciprocity of the wealthy.[181] So while patronage reciprocity was commonly extended toward non-kin and almost never toward the immediately poor, Jesus is taken as expanding it to such and at the same time transforming it into the expectationless reciprocity of kinship.[182] And so the lending terminology of Matt 5:42 becomes a thorn in the side for both of these reconstructions. For if the higher form—this expectationless patronage as unto kin—ought to be

---

178. Patronage reciprocity also achieves *do ut des*, but to a comparatively lesser extent—for while it receives back a benefit, it is not one that is materially equivalent. See Malina, *The New Testament World*, 100.

179. Hanson and Oakman, *Palestine in the Time of Jesus*, 117–18.

180. Achtemeier et al., *Introducing the New Testament*, 173.

181. Ibid., 172–73.

182. Regionalism aside, scholars tend to affirm the inherent utilitarianism of first century patronage while also noting that the indigent were not useful to wealthy patrons. See Stambaugh and Balch, *The New Testament in Its Social Environment*, 64; Esler, *Community and Gospel in Luke–Acts*, 176, 198; Hands, *Charities and Social Aid in Greece and Rome*; Waltzing, *Étude historique sur les corporations professionnelles*, 1:300–306.

made available to all, then why mention the vastly inferior option of lending as well? What place is there left for it? Especially in a context where lending was provided for the selfsame purpose of thwarting an otherwise inevitable collapse into immediate poverty? Furthermore, sourcing our reconstructions from Luke provides no reprieve, for the same terminology of lending occurs in Luke 6:34–35. Nor is it clear that wealthy patrons are the primary intended audience in either parallel. Jesus' immediate disciples do not easily fit that bill. Patronage reciprocity was not their ballpark. Even when we take into account that in Luke the woes upon the rich immediately precede the matter and that Jesus' immediate disciples no longer possess much to give and even less to lend, Jesus is still remembered as broadening the call of patronage to all believers—even the non-wealthy. So Luke, like Paul, knows that Jesus altered and "brought down" to *all* the patron maxim of preferring giving to receiving (Acts 20:35). Whereby blessing one-sided giving even on a more humble scale than patronage proper. And so Jesus' mandates here are just as easily addressed to the general multitude as to the rich that might be among them. What remains a possibility however is that Jesus in Matt 5:42 is mandating *both* the general reciprocity of giving to kin who ask it of us and the balanced reciprocity of lending to non-kin who wish to borrow from us. That His hearers not practice security-conscious self-interest in providing these two differing forms of what we may consider "lending." Precisely by extending them even to those who will not extend them in turn—in our time of need. Whereby incurring the loss of something very valuable for survival.[183] And so, as far as Matt 5:42 goes, the giving mentioned may refer either to almsgiving or to general reciprocity toward kin. It is the Lukan parallel, as we shall see, that makes the latter interpretation the less likely.

If Matthew does indeed allow for a giving beyond lending or general reciprocity, then its recipients will be the beggarly poor—those who ask.[184] Because taking the first part of verse 42 as a resurfacing of the de-

---

183. Due to their "subsistence-level farming" and the ever-present threat of natural calamity, the livelihood of the peasant farmer majority was always precarious (Harland, "The Economy of First-Century Palestine," 521).

184. Calvin, *Commentary on a Harmony of the Evangelists*, 1:302; Keener, *A Commentary on the Gospel of Matthew*, 201–2; Plummer, *An Exegetical Commentary on the Gospel according to St. Matthew*, 86. Additional support for this understanding is found in *Didache* 1:5–6—which moreover lays responsibility on both the giver and the receiver—that the latter be found in genuine need. So Craig Keener stresses Judaism's

manded relinquishing of verse 40 results in unexpected and unneeded repetition, this third interpretive option is as unlikely here as it is in Luke (despite the common terminology of "taking" in Luke 6:29–30). And so the spotlight returns to the immediately poor. And besides, even the lending being addressed here was intended, in the OT, to help sustain those whose means falter (Deut 15:7–8; Lev 25:35–37)—those spiraling into immediate poverty.

In the cumulate parallel, Luke 6:27–36, we can be quite certain of three things: that verse 30—either in part or as a whole—addresses lending, that living beyond measure for measure is what animates its mandates, and that the intended recipients in Luke are our enemies. The subsequent reiteration of the initial buildup (vv. 27–30) via the rhetorical questions concerning credit and reward (vv. 32–34) reveals that lending is at issue in verse 30. For nothing which precedes the rhetorical questions, save verse 30 (which is appropriately the concluding exemplar), can pertain to this reiterated lending. And this contextual symmetry is subsequently reaffirmed in verse 35. So lending is subsumed in the call of verse 30. And whether anything more may be subsumed is the open question.

It is rather likely that the latter part of Luke 6:30 concerns lending. Though the mentioned "taking away" (αἴρω, airō) is widely assumed to be forceful because the term may mean that—this is not certain. For it can just as readily indicate "taking up" or merely "taking" (as in Luke 19:21 and Mark 15:24). And the fit is better in taking it as referring to borrowing for it is indeed hard to imagine, as even dissenters such as John Topel confess, that one could somehow ask back what was forcibly stolen by a bandit or legally taken away by suit.[185] Despite the reminiscent terminology of "taking" (the same form of αἴρω, airō, as in Luke 6:29), a reiteration of demanded relinquishing would result in a conspicuously isolated and unnecessary repetition in its context.[186] And so demand-

---

"high work ethic" and the genuine neediness of most beggars (Keener, *A Commentary on the Gospel of Matthew*, 201). Still it is preferable to asynoptically suspend judgment concerning this giving until we reach the moment of integration (in the next chapter).

185. Danker, *Jesus and the New Age*, 146; Plummer, *A Critical and Exegetical Commentary on the Gospel according to St. Luke*, 186; Keener, *The IVP Bible Background Commentary*, 205; pace Bock, *Luke*, 594; Calvin, *Commentary on a Harmony of the Evangelists*, 1:300–301; Marshall, *The Gospel of Luke*, 262; Nolland, *Luke*, 296–97; Stein, *Luke*, 208; Topel, *Children of a Compassionate God*, 154.

186. Hence the assumed quandary over Luke's intent and source usage here. See Marshall, *The Gospel of Luke*, 262; Nolland, *Luke*, 297.

ing, whether in the form of forceful theft or in securing a pledge, is also not the most likely incitement for the "giving" mandated earlier in Luke 6:30.[187] And taking the final injunction of this verse as a referral to nagging about already receiving back what was lent (as in Sirach 20:14–15) struts the most tailor-made fit.[188] And so, for Jesus' followers, there is to be no persistent badgering but rather quiet waiting. If perchance the second part of verse 30 is not taken so, then certainly the giving of the first part must pertain to lending. Contextual symmetry would require it. But if the latter portion does indeed refer to lending, as I have argued, then the first part is perhaps free to stretch wider. It can function as an instantiation of "doing good," the second of the contextual triplets, rather than the third. It may embrace almsgiving.

Luke 6:32–34 connects the lending of Luke 6:30, like its giving, to living beyond calculated reciprocity. The return that is commonly "hoped" for (ἐλπίζω, *elpizō*, v. 34, ἀπελπίζω, *apelpizō*, v. 35) is receiving reciprocal lending in one's own prospective time of need. The symmetry of loving "those who love you" (v. 32) and doing good to "those who do good to you" (v. 33) indicates that lending only to "those who will lend to you" is what is being challenged in verse 34.[189] This is reaffirmed in verse 35 where showing love, doing good, and lending are *all* to be pursued with the same attitude—one which is not driven by a hope of equivalent reciprocation. Consequently it is the potentially poor who are signified as both the purveyors and receivers of this lending.[190] The interpretive suggestion that the believer should rather not hope to receive back what

---

187. Whether such demanded relinquishing is incidentally subsumed within this giving—rather than functioning as the main concern—is hard to discern. Yet the context does not require any repetition.

188. Danker, *Jesus and the New Age*, 146; Manson, *The Sayings of Jesus*, 52.

189. John Nolland similarly argues that this is the only meaning of receiving back (Luke 6:34) which makes sense in this context—and he is far from alone. See Nolland, *Luke*, 299; Bock, *Luke*, 601; Calvin, *Commentary on a Harmony of the Evangelists*, 1:302–3; Marshall, *The Gospel of Luke*, 263; Stählin, "ἰσότης," *TDNT* 3:344–45; Stein, *Luke*, 209. The suggestion that usury is what is hoped for similarly stumbles over verse 34.

190. During the first century it was these potentially poor that made up the vast majority of the population of Palestine and the Roman Empire. The recipients of this lending would have been those potentially poor now slipping over into immediate poverty—the able-bodied whose crop had failed and who now needed a loan to get through to the next harvest (both for planting and survival). If all fared better next season they would repay their loan and rejoin the ranks of the potentially poor.

was lent further stumbles over the intentionality intimated by ἵνα (*hina*, v. 34)—for it is quite unlikely that anyone, let alone "sinners," would lend specifically "for the purpose" of merely receiving back the principle.[191]

In Luke, our enemies are clearly the intended recipients of this lending—for our treatment of them is the explicit focus throughout Luke 6:27–36. As such, they are not likely to reciprocate our loaning to them. Such enemies are unfeeling enough to demand possession of the more important cloak rather than the lesser tunic (v. 29)—whether by force or possibly by suit. And I suspect that the inclusion of "everyone" in verse 30 is intended to stress that *even enemies* are to receive the benefit of our giving (just as they are to benefit from our lending).[192] It is this contextual focus on enemies that eliminates general reciprocity from the running in Luke. As having kin as enemies was unlikely, almsgiving to legitimate enemies—should they become immediately poor—is the more likely intent.[193] For if the general reciprocity of kinship was to be extended even to enemies, then why would other non-kin only be offered the balanced reciprocity of lending? Again, why speak of a lesser "deal" just after commanding a better one toward *all*? And so it is almsgiving, in the end, that most readily embraces Jesus' call to give (if it is not, after all, just a reiterating component of His call to lending).

So what are we to make of Matt 5:42 and Luke 6:29–30, 34–36 by way of a minimalist interpretation? In terms of integration, in taking what is clearly affirmed from both Gospels, our mandate minimally entails that believers should live beyond tit-for-tat in lending to their enemies.[194] This much is certain, and though both Synoptics could convey

---

191. Pace Hagner, *Matthew*, 131 (concerning both Matthew and Luke); Davis, *Lex Talionis in Early Judaism and the Exhortation of Jesus in Matthew 5:38–42*, 154; Lachs, *A Rabbinic Commentary on the New Testament*, 105 (though regarding loans given just before the Sabbatical Year). While this interpretation fits comfortably with the latter part of verse 30, demanding something back (as in Luke 12:20) and patiently waiting for it to be returned is not the same thing.

192. As does Heinrich Meyer. See Meyer, *Critical and Exegetical Hand-Book to the Gospels of Mark and Luke*, 336.

193. The theoretical possibility that not enemies but merely "ungrateful" (v. 35) kin are in play at the beginning of Luke 6:30—such that they might become "equal opportunity" recipients of one's general reciprocity—is precluded grammatically. For "the ungrateful and evil" (τοὺς ἀχαρίστους καὶ πονηρούς, v. 35) refer indivisibly to the same group—our enemies.

194. For in going to Luke for a clear focus upon enemies we indelibly get saddled with a clear tit-for-tat confirmation in the process.

these same components, acknowledging the generalness of Matthew's formulation may perhaps allow for non-enemies and alms besides. Minimalism aside, almsgiving is certainly the lead horse in Luke. Also certain is that loving enemies, doing good, and lending (along with the giving subsumed therein)—particularly because it will not be requited—is a matter of mercy which will be specifically rewarded. The mercy nature of the Lukan mandates is also confirmed semantically by the summary mandate to be merciful (οἰκτίρμων, *oiktirmōn*) unto one's enemies just like the Father is (Luke 6:36).[195] The giving and lending mandates of Matt 5:42 and Luke 6:29–30, 34–36 extend to Jesus' larger audience as His immediate disciples, after having forsaken their possessions, would not have that much of anything to give or lend. But beyond that, our foregoing considerations serve as a warning to not apportion too much constructive weight—in terms of a systematic theology—to some particular interpretation of these passages.

> Matt 7:1–2 Do not judge so that you will not be judged. 2 For in the way you judge, you will be judged; and *by your standard of measure, it will be measured to you.* (G | | |)

> // Mark 4:24 And He was saying to them, "Take care what you listen to. *By your standard of measure it will be measured to you*; and more will be given you besides." (G | | |)

> // Luke 6:38 *Give*, and it will be given to you. They will pour into your lap a good measure—pressed down, shaken together, and running over. *For by your standard of measure it will be measured to you in return.* (G | | |)

Luke 6:38 adds to the mandate to give the promise of proportional reward: "For by your standard of measure it will be measured to you in return" (Luke 6:38). The giving referred to here may perhaps be a call to general reciprocity (the language certainly fits)—or possibly even a call to considering almsgiving in those terms. In this sense it might also gather in the giving of Luke 6:30. The reciprocity gained is appropriately

---

195. While Richard Burridge argues that the difference in terminology between Luke 6:36 and Matt 5:48 is redactional and aimed at the two poles of inclusive mercy and moral perfection, the author contends that in Matthew the perfection being referred to is the perfection of mercy as previously described in Matt 5:45. This perfection of mercy mandates the hearer to move beyond living out of the tit-for-tat perspective of common justice. See Burridge, *Imitating Jesus*, 75–76.

not from people but rather from God.¹⁹⁶ While this general measure for measure principle is applied in different directions outside of Luke 6:38, Mark 4:24 suggests that its proportionality might include something akin to a multiplication factor.¹⁹⁷

> Rom 12:8 or he who exhorts, in his exhortation; he who *gives, with liberality* [ἁπλότης, *haplotēs*]; he who leads, with diligence; he who shows *mercy* [ἐλεέω, *eleeō*], with cheerfulness. (G | | |)

In Rom 12:8 Paul mandates that believers who share (μεταδίδωμι, *metadidōmi*) do so with generosity (ἁπλότης, *haplotēs*) and that cheerfulness accompany the doing of mercy (ἐλεέω, *eleeō*).¹⁹⁸

FIRST/LAST

Jesus' mandates concerning becoming first and greatest enjoin sacrificing social status (becoming the last and the least) and participating in lowly service unto fellow believers—being willing to serve even the least of them.¹⁹⁹

First/Last Mandates

> Matt 19:27–30 Then Peter said to Him, "Behold, we have left everything and followed You; what then will there be for us?" 28 And Jesus said to them, "Truly I say to you, that you who have followed Me, in the regeneration when the Son of Man will sit on His glorious throne, you also shall sit upon twelve thrones, judging the twelve tribes of Israel. 29 And everyone who has left

---

196. God is the intended referent of the third person plural δώσουσιν, "they will pour," by way of rabbinic periphrasis. See Bock, *Luke*, 607–8; Marshall, *The Gospel of Luke*, 267; Nolland, *Luke*, 301; Stein, *Luke*, 212. In this sense the result is similar to Prov 19:17.

197. In terms of the phrasing parallels, Matt 7:1–2 takes up the judging of others while Mark 4:24 revolves around correctly judging Jesus' message (as does its Luke 8:18 parallel).

198. Thomas Schreiner argues that helping the poor is likewise envisioned within this mandate unto mercy (Schreiner, *Romans*, 660).

199. While the first/last summation in Matt 20:16 may refer to the equality, in one sense, of the spiritually least worthy in the "kingdom of heaven" (v. 1)—those who do not labor and forsake as much as the immediate disciples (Matt 19:29–30)—this, or any of the other viable interpretation possibilities, does not address the interhuman treatment of the poor and so this text will not be covered here. See Hagner, *Matthew*, 572–73 (worthiness interpretation). The same is true for Luke 13:30.

houses or brothers or sisters or father or mother or children or farms for My name's sake, will receive many times as much, and will inherit eternal life. 30 But *many who are first will be last; and the last, first.*" (S | M | H |)

// Mark 10:28–31 Peter began to say to Him, "Behold, we have left everything and followed You." 29 Jesus said, "Truly I say to you, there is no one who has left house or brothers or sisters or mother or father or children or farms, for My sake and for the gospel's sake, 30 but that he will receive a hundred times as much now in the present age, houses and brothers and sisters and mothers and children and farms, along with persecutions; and in the age to come, eternal life. 31 But *many who are first will be last, and the last, first.*" (S | M | H |)

Matthew 19:27–30 and Mark 10:28–31 connect being truly first to forsaking one's possessions and relatives—and hence one's social status—in order to directly follow Jesus. A forsaking which also benefited the poor (Matt 19:21 // Mark 10:21 // Luke 18:22; Luke 12:33).

Matt 18:1–5 At that time the disciples came to Jesus and said, "Who then is *greatest* in the kingdom of heaven?" 2 And He called a child to Himself and set him before them, 3 and said, "Truly I say to you, unless you are *converted* [στρέφω, *strephō*, turn, change] *and become like children,* you will not enter the kingdom of heaven. 4 Whoever then *humbles* [ταπεινόω, *tapeinoō*] *himself as this child,* he is the *greatest* in the kingdom of heaven. 5 And whoever *receives one such child in My name receives Me.*" (CG | | |)

// Mark 9:34–37 But they kept silent, for on the way they had discussed with one another which of them was the *greatest*. 35 Sitting down, He called the twelve and said to them, "If anyone wants to be *first,* he shall be *last of all* and *servant of all.*" 36 Taking a child, He set him before them, and taking him in His arms, He said to them, 37 "Whoever *receives one child like this in My name receives Me*; and whoever receives Me does not receive Me, but Him who sent Me." (CG | | |)

// Luke 9:46–48 An argument started among them as to which of them might be the *greatest*. 47 But Jesus, knowing what they were thinking in their heart, took a child and stood him by His side, 48 and said to them, "Whoever *receives this child in My name receives Me,* and whoever receives Me receives Him who sent Me; for the *one who is least among all of you, this is the one who is great.*" (CG | | |)

Matthew 18:1–5 is perhaps the strongest scriptural call to making oneself lowly (ταπεινόω, *tapeinoō*) so as to be logically willing to serve even the least. Scholars agree that the "child's humility is its lack of status, not its actions or feelings of humbleness."[200] They are however somewhat less predisposed to connect this lack of status—though only in this passage and not in Mark 9:34–37 and Luke 9:46–48—to its outflow of being willing to serve even such socially least (Matt 18:5). I suspect that this is largely the case because they want to accentuate the unique nuances of this passage *vis-à-vis* the others, set up for a particular interpretation of the "little ones" (vv. 6, 10, 14), and because the entrance requirement to be "converted *and* become like children" (v. 3, italics added) becomes more troubling. For it, just like the need to forgive (Matt 6:15; 18:35), requires more of normative Christian obedience. But the parallel texts, as well as the linking presence of "whoever" in verse 4, and subsequently, "and whoever" in verse 5, strongly suggest the connection.[201]

To make oneself as lowly as a child entails social humbling—becoming as the last, the least, the youngest—so as to be logically required, and correspondingly willing, to even serve the least (here the example of the child, v. 5). The social status of children accounts for why the disciples want to keep them from Jesus. For they do not want to trouble the Master with such social insignificants. Jesus' response in Matt 19:14 (// Mark 10:14–15 // Luke 18:16–17) is to permit them "for the kingdom of heaven belongs to such as these."[202] Thus Jesus' encouragement to become "greatest in the kingdom of heaven" (Matt 18:4) entails being willing to serve even those of the lowest social status—and this would subsume the young, and similarly, the poor.

Mark 9:34–37 affirms that the lowly *service* of being the last of all in order to be the first (v. 35) involves *receiving* even the socially least (vv. 36–37).[203] Being the "servant of all" is not meant quantitatively in terms of serving everyone but rather qualitatively in terms of seeking to serve even the least—as Jesus reveals by showing the disciples an exemplar

---

200. Hagner, *Matthew*, 518, 517; Blomberg, *Matthew*, 273; France, *The Gospel of Mark*, 374; Gundry, *Matthew*, 361; Turner, *The Gospel of Matthew*, 236.

201. So some commentators nevertheless agree. See Davies and Allison, *Matthew*, 2:760–61; Gundry, *Matthew*, 361.

202. The children's lowliness is exemplary. See Cranfield, *The Gospel According to St. Mark*, 324; Stein, *Luke*, 453.

203. France, *The Gospel of Mark*, 374; Bock, *The Gospel of Mark*, 481; C. A. Evans, *Mark 8:27—16:20*, 61.

of the socially least and saying that welcoming (in the serving sense, δέχομαι, *dechomai*, v. 37) such socially least is actually welcoming Him.[204] Jesus' concern here is reminiscent of the parable of the sheep and the goats where serving the least of "these brothers of Mine" is a direct serving of Jesus (Matt 25:40, 45).

Luke 9:46–48 maintains this same concern for becoming greatest via receiving even the least.[205] By accepting for oneself the position that is expected to do just that. The unenvied position of being the least important among one's companions and associates. The concrete mandate remains, as in the parallels, to be willing to receive and hospitably serve a child. For such service is serving Jesus. And the greatest is the one who has this honor. The possibility of considering the child, rather than his receiver, to be the referent of "the least" (in v. 48) is against the consistent grain of Jesus' teaching on the subject—for it is not the one who receives the "great" that is receiving Him.[206]

> Matt 20:25–28 But Jesus called them to Himself, and said, "You know that the rulers of the Gentiles lord it over them, and their great men exercise authority over them. 26 "It is not so among you, but whoever wishes to become *great among you shall be your servant*, 27 and whoever wishes to be *first among you shall be your slave*; 28 just as the Son of Man did not come to be served, *but to serve*, and to give His life a ransom for many." (G | | |)
>
> // Mark 10:42–45 Calling them to Himself, Jesus said to them, "You know that those who are recognized as rulers of the Gentiles lord it over them; and their great men exercise authority over them. 43 But it is not this way among you, but whoever wishes to become *great among you shall be your servant*; 44 and whoever wishes to be *first among you shall be slave of all*. 45 For even the

---

204. This same sense of *all* is also intended in Mark 10:44.

205. The parallelism of the least one being "the one who is great" (v. 48) implies that great here signifies greatest (for if *the* least one is great then the others are not to the same degree). Pace Plummer, *A Critical and Exegetical Commentary on the Gospel according to St. Luke*, 258.

206. The train of thought here is akin to Matt 18:4–5 where the one who humbles himself as the least and consequently receives the child is the greatest. Thus agreement, though for additional or unsaid reasons, is available. See Nolland, *Luke*, 519–20; Plummer, *A Critical and Exegetical Commentary on the Gospel according to St. Luke*, 258; Stein, *Luke*, 293; pace Bock, *Luke*, 896–97; Marshall, *The Gospel of Luke*, 397–98 (though Marshall is very tentative and accommodating).

Son of Man did not come to be served, *but to serve*, and to give His life a ransom for many." (G | | |)

// Luke 22:24–27 And there arose also a dispute among them as to which one of them was regarded to be greatest. 25 And He said to them, "The kings of the Gentiles lord it over them; and those who have authority over them are called 'Benefactors.' 26 But it is not this way with you, but the one who is the *greatest among you must become like the youngest*, and the *leader like the servant*. 27 For who is greater, the one who reclines at the table or the *one who serves*? Is it not the one who reclines at the table? But I am among you as the *one who serves*." (G | | |)

Matthew 20:25–28; Mark 10:42–45; and Luke 22:24–27 renew this mandate to accept for ourselves the social status of the youngest, the servant, or even a slave. At such a status level, the level of the last and least, it will be only natural for us to be willing to serve *all* (Mark 10:44). And *all* subsumes the believing low class poor. Luke 22:24–27 explicitly engages what it means to become as a child—to become as the youngest. It is to become as the least, as a servant (v. 26), in order to become the greatest by serving all. Furthermore, in all three passages, Jesus also draws attention to His own example for our mimesis.

Matt 23:11–12 But *the greatest among you shall be your servant*. 12 Whoever exalts himself shall be humbled [ταπεινόω, *tapeinoō*]; and whoever *humbles* [ταπεινόω, *tapeinoō*] himself shall be exalted. (G | | |)

The same concern surfaces here. The only way to prevent ourselves from being made low by God in the *eschaton*, is to consider ourselves of low enough status now so as to be willing to take on the lowly role of a mere servant.

John 13:14 If I then, the Lord and the Teacher, washed your feet, you also *ought to wash one another's feet*. (G | | |)

Jesus Himself models and mandates such servanthood during the Last Supper (Luke 22:27; John 13:14). The mandate of John 13:14, also unto lowly service below one's true rank, appears to be a general mandate rather than a concrete one due to the reference to it within 1 Tim 5:10.

RECEIVE

The following receive mandates entail providing hospitality to believers. Such hospitality includes meeting their sustenance needs—and also entails doing this for those who are the socially least among the believers (Matt 18:5; Mark 9:36–37; Luke 9:48).

Receive Mandates

Matt 10:40–42 He who *receives* you *receives* Me, and he who *receives* Me *receives* Him who sent Me. 41 He who *receives* a prophet in the name of a prophet shall receive a prophet's reward; and he who *receives* a righteous man in the name of a righteous man shall receive a righteous man's reward. 42 And whoever in the name of a disciple gives to one of these little ones even a *cup of cold water to drink*, truly I say to you, he shall not lose his *reward*. (S | M | H |)

// Mark 9:41 For whoever gives you a *cup of water to drink* because of your name as followers of Christ, truly I say to you, he will not lose his *reward*. (S | M | H |)

Matt 18:5 And whoever *receives one such child in My name receives Me*. (CG | | |)

// Mark 9:36–37 Taking a child, He set him before them, and taking him in His arms, He said to them, 37 "Whoever *receives* one child like this in My name *receives* Me; and whoever *receives* Me does not receive Me, but Him who sent Me." (CG | | |)

// Luke 9:48 and said to them, "Whoever *receives* this child in My name *receives* Me, and whoever *receives* Me *receives* Him who sent Me; for the one who is least among all of you, this is the one who is great." (CG | | |)

As noted earlier, Matt 18:5; Mark 9:36–37; and Luke 9:48 echo the parable of the sheep and the goats in describing what receiving Jesus looks like. Receiving even the socially least and youngest believer, so as to meet his sustenance needs, entails receiving the Master. Matthew 10:42 and Mark 9:41 concretize such receiving by revealing that providing even a cup of cold water, which entails the least costly and most effortless meeting of a sustenance need, will be rewarded. But these latter two passages address a different instance of hospitality—another sort of welcoming. The intended consistency of the internal symmetry of Matt

10:41 reveals that the "little ones" of Matt 10:42 are disciples (as in Mark 9:41), or perhaps better still, the least among the disciples. And contextually, within Matthew 10, it refers to these disciples in their role as Jesus' emissaries—as His sent out messengers (Matt 10:5–6, 14). And so while the connection of this hospitality to receiving the disciples' message is not to be downplayed in either passage, still it is in the rewarded act of receiving the provisionless missionaries (vv. 9–10) that the acceptance is manifest.[207] And so all of Jesus' specific receive mandates are hamartiologically revealed to be issues of mercy.

> Rom 16:2 that you *receive* her in the Lord in a *manner worthy of the saints*, and that you help her in whatever matter she may have need of you; for she herself has also been a *helper* [προστάτις, *prostatis*] of many, and of myself as well. (CG | | |)

The receiving of Phoebe in Rom 16:2 is described as helping and reveals that providing hospitality and assistance for foreign believers should be done in a "manner worthy of the saints."

> Heb 13:1–3 Let *love* of the brethren continue. 2 Do not neglect to show *hospitality to strangers*, for by this some have entertained angels without knowing it. 3 Remember the *prisoners*, as though in *prison* with them, and those who are *ill-treated* [κακουχέω, *kakoucheō*], since you yourselves also are in the body. (SC | | |)

Such hospitality to visiting believers is also mandated in Heb 13:1–3. The mandate to "remember the prisoners" (v. 3) is added as a component of loving the brethren.[208] This remembering is to be sympathetic (v. 3) and entails the "visiting" described in the parable of the sheep and the goats—a visiting which provides sustenance care.[209] Consequently, such sympathetic care is an instance of mercy akin to the συμπαθέω (*sympatheō*) shown in Heb 10:34. Believers who are persecuted and mistreated (κακουχέω, *kakoucheō*), a category that subsumes those in prison, are to receive similar care—in accordance with their needs.[210] This mistreatment appears to have had physical dimensions for

---

207. Blomberg, *Matthew*, 182; Hagner, *Matthew*, 296.

208. The love of the brethren subsumes both the mandates to hospitality and prisoner care. See Lane, *Hebrews*, 511–13; Thurén, *Das Lobopfer der Hebräer*, 209–10; Attridge, *The Epistle to the Hebrews*, 385–87.

209. Lane, *Hebrews*, 513.

210. Ibid.

the believers are mandated to remember "those who are mistreated as if you yourselves were suffering bodily."[211]

In summary, receiving believers in a hospitable manner so as to meet their sustenance needs, whenever it is elucidated, is identified as an issue of mercy. Caring for imprisoned and mistreated Christians is a related aspect of brotherly love (φιλαδελφία, *philadelphia*, Heb 13:1). Hebrews 6:10 reveals that "God is not unjust so as to forget your work and the love which you have shown toward His name, in having ministered and in still ministering to the saints." Such service (διακονέω, *diakoneō*) to the brethren, which is analogous to receiving, is also rewarded—affirming the relation between διακονέω (*diakoneō*) and mercy.

FEEDING

Jesus' miraculous feedings were intended to meet the sustenance needs of the crowds that were following Him. In Matt 14:15–22 and Mark 6:34–44 Jesus explicitly commands the disciples to meet these sustenance needs.

Feeding Mandates

Matt 14:15–22 When it was evening, the disciples came to Him and said, "This place is desolate and the hour is already late; so send the crowds away, that they may go into the villages and buy food for themselves." 16 But Jesus said to them, "They do not need to go away; *you give them something to eat!*" 17 They said to Him, "We have here only five loaves and two fish." 18 And He said, "Bring them here to Me." 19 Ordering the people to sit down on the grass, He took the five loaves and the two fish, and looking up toward heaven, He blessed the food, and breaking the loaves He gave them to the disciples, and the disciples gave them to the crowds, 20 and they all ate and were satisfied. They picked up what was left over of the broken pieces, twelve full baskets. 21 There were about five thousand men who ate, besides women and children. 22 Immediately He made the disciples get into the boat and go ahead of Him to the other side, while He sent the crowds away. (C | | |)

---

211. Ibid., 507–8. So in terms of verse 3, our sympathy for the brethren should be as if we ourselves "were in (their) body" (Attridge, *The Epistle to the Hebrews*, 387).

// Mark 6:34–44 When Jesus went ashore, He saw a large crowd, and He felt compassion for them because they were like sheep without a shepherd; and He began to teach them many things. 35 When it was already quite late, His disciples came to Him and said, "This place is desolate and it is already quite late; 36 send them away so that they may go into the surrounding countryside and villages and buy themselves something to eat." 37 But He answered them, *"You give them something to eat!"* And they said to Him, "Shall we go and spend two hundred denarii on bread and give them something to eat?" 38 And He said to them, "How many loaves do you have? Go look!" And when they found out, they said, "Five, and two fish." 39 And He commanded them all to sit down by groups on the green grass. 40 They sat down in groups of hundreds and of fifties. 41 And He took the five loaves and the two fish, and looking up toward heaven, He blessed the food and broke the loaves and He kept giving them to the disciples to set before them; and He divided up the two fish among them all. 42 They all ate and were satisfied, 43 and they picked up twelve full baskets of the broken pieces, and also of the fish. 44 There were five thousand men who ate the loaves. (C | | |)

// John 6:4–15 Now the Passover, the feast of the Jews, was near. 5 Therefore Jesus, lifting up His eyes and seeing that a large crowd was coming to Him, said to Philip, *"Where are we to buy bread, so that these may eat?"* 6 This He was saying to test him, *for He Himself knew what He was intending to do.* 7 Philip answered Him, "Two hundred denarii worth of bread is not sufficient for them, for everyone to receive a little." 8 One of His disciples, Andrew, Simon Peter's brother, said to Him, 9 "There is a lad here who has five barley loaves and two fish, but what are these for so many people?" 10 Jesus said, "Have the people sit down." Now there was much grass in the place. So the men sat down, in number about five thousand. 11 Jesus then took the loaves, and having given thanks, He distributed to those who were seated; likewise also of the fish as much as they wanted. 12 When they were filled, He said to His disciples, "Gather up the leftover fragments so that nothing will be lost." 13 So they gathered them up, and filled twelve baskets with fragments from the five barley loaves which were left over by those who had eaten. 14 Therefore when the people saw the sign which He had performed, they said, "This is truly the Prophet who is to come into the world." 15 So Jesus, perceiving that they were intending to come and take Him by force to make Him king, withdrew again to the mountain by Himself alone. (C | | |)

> Matt 15:32–38 And Jesus called His disciples to Him, and said, "I feel *compassion* [σπλαγχνίζομαι, *splanchnizomai*] for the people, because they have remained with Me now three days and have nothing to eat; and *I do not want* [θέλω, *thelō*] *to send them away hungry, for they might faint on the way.*" 33 The disciples said to Him, "Where would we get so many loaves in this desolate place to satisfy such a large crowd?" 34 And Jesus said to them, "How many loaves do you have?" And they said, "Seven, and a few small fish." 35 And He directed the people to sit down on the ground; 36 and He took the seven loaves and the fish; and giving thanks, He broke them and started giving them to the disciples, and the disciples gave them to the people. 37 And they all ate and were satisfied, and they picked up what was left over of the broken pieces, seven large baskets full. 38 And those who ate were four thousand men, besides women and children. (C | M | S |)

Jesus' explicit commands in Matt 14:15–22 and Mark 6:34–44 as well as the implied mandates of John 6:4–15 and Matt 15:32–38 are localized mandates. They do not extend to everyone who would be able to accomplish them and, in addition, Jesus fully intends to meet these sustenance needs Himself (John 6:6). John 6:4–15, a parallel to Matt 14:15–22 and Mark 6:34–44, presents Philip as the spokesman and testee on behalf of the disciples.[212] Jesus' question, "Where are we to buy bread, so that these may eat?" (John 6:5), appears to imply a delegation of responsibility analogous to Jesus' wanting (θέλω, *thelō*), in Matt 15:32, to not send the crowd away hungry. Matthew 15:32 reveals that, in Jesus' eyes, providing for sustenance needs, even when He is in the role of an analogous host and the reason for the crowd's hunger, is a matter of compassionate empathy (σπλαγχνίζομαι, *splanchnizomai*). Jesus thus does not consider His ability to provide for these sustenance needs, even when in their direct presence, as a matter of justice akin to Nicholas Wolterstorff's sustenance rights. This lack of provision could have resulted in the collapsing of some of the crowd on the way (Matt 15:32)—the weak, elderly, and young would have been particularly susceptible. This passage suggests that Wolterstorff's approach, at minimum, must adopt a very strong human/divine disjunction.

In sum, the localized nature of Jesus' feeding mandates means that they are not pertinent to interhuman obligation.

---

212. Köstenberger, *John*, 203.

WIDOWS

The concern to help and not harm widows and the fatherless, who are considered orphans, is amply manifest throughout both testaments. The biblical mandates concerning widows entail that they not be unjustly harmed (Exod 22:21–24; Deut 24:17–18; 27:19; Job 24:3, 12; 29:12–14, 16–17; Ps 94:3, 6; Isa 1:23; 10:1–4; Jer 7:5–7; 22:2–5; Ezek 22:2, 6–7; Zech 7:9–10; Mal 3:5; [Matt 23:14] // Mark 12:38–40 // Luke 20:46–47), that they receive judicial assistance and protection (Isa 1:17, 19–20), that special assistive measures be provided to them (Deut 14:28–29; 16:9–17; 24:19, 20–22; 26:12–13; 1 Tim 5:3–16), and that they generally receive assistance (Job 22:5, 9–11; 24:19–21; 31:16–17; Jas 1:27). This well attested concern is thoroughly appropriate as defenselessness and poverty was the common plight of families that had lost their main provider.[213]

Widows Mandates

> [Matt 23:14 Woe to you, scribes and Pharisees, hypocrites, because you *devour widows' houses*, and for a pretense you make long prayers; therefore you will receive greater *condemnation*. (S | J | H | P)][214]

> // Mark 12:38–40 In His teaching He was saying: "Beware of the scribes who like to walk around in long robes, and like respectful greetings in the market places, 39 and chief seats in the synagogues and places of honor at banquets, 40 who *devour widows' houses*, and for appearance's sake offer long prayers; these will receive greater *condemnation*." (S | J | H | P)

> // Luke 20:46–47 Beware of the scribes, who like to walk around in long robes, and love respectful greetings in the market places, and chief seats in the synagogues and places of honor at banquets, 47 who *devour widows' houses*, and for appearance's sake offer long prayers. These will receive greater *condemnation*. (S | J | H | P)

Mark 12:38–40 and Luke 20:46–47 are the only NT mandates against injustice to widows (and are borne witness to by the later copyist

---

213. This assumption of poverty is evident, for example, in the mandates concerning the Feast of Weeks (Deut 16:9–12, 16–17) and the Feast of Booths (Deut 16:13–17).

214. Matthew 23:14 is not found in the earliest manuscripts but is included throughout merely for the sake of completeness.

addition that is Matt 23:14).²¹⁵ This injustice, which is hamartiologically indicated (being a specific source of condemnation), concerns devouring widows' houses. The means whereby this despoiling was accomplished is uncertain. Perhaps the property of widows who had dedicated their remaining days to the service of the temple was being managed in such a way as to take advantage of them.²¹⁶ Or, similarly, the widows were being cheated out of their estates by scribes in their capacity as guardians appointed by their husbands' wills.²¹⁷ Perhaps an abuse of hospitality is intended or the scribes provided the widows with unrepayable loans on the basis of the pledging of their houses.²¹⁸ It is also perhaps conceivable that they charged such high legal fees to widows that they became insolvent.²¹⁹ Less likely is the possibility that the scribes and Pharisees took "large sums" from widows in exchange for intercessory prayer.²²⁰ It is indeed difficult to discern whether an abuse of hospitality or some manner of defrauding is in view. As has been previously noted, defrauding is revealed to be a sin in the NT. Consequently, not much can be discerned from these passages except the tentative possibility that abusing the hospitality of the potentially poor is an interhuman injustice.²²¹

> 1 Tim 5:3–16 Honor widows who are widows indeed; 4 but if any widow has children or grandchildren, they must first learn to practice piety in regard to their own family and to make some return to their parents; for this is acceptable in the sight of God. 5 Now she who is a widow indeed and who has been left alone, has fixed her hope on God and continues in entreaties and prayers night and day. 6 But she who gives herself to wanton pleasure is dead even while she lives. 7 Prescribe these things as well, so that they may be above reproach. 8 But if anyone does not provide for his own, and especially for those of his household, he has denied the faith and is worse than an unbeliever. 9 A widow is to be put

---

215. The parable concerning how to pray without losing heart in Luke 18:1–5, while having a widow as its protagonist, provides no mandates.

216. Ellis, *The Gospel of Luke*, 239.

217. Derrett, "Eating Up the Houses of Widows," 1–9.

218. Jeremias, *Jerusalem in the Time of Jesus*, 114; Leaney, *A Commentary on the Gospel According to St. Luke*, 256.

219. Stählin, "χήρα," *TDNT* 9:448–49.

220. Nineham, *Saint Mark*, 333.

221. The widows in these passages are revealed to be potentially poor because they are susceptible to having their houses confiscated—such widows likely became immediately poor after they were despoiled.

on the list only if she is not less than sixty years old, having been the wife of one man, 10 having a reputation for good works; and if she has brought up children, if she has shown hospitality to strangers, if she has washed the saints' feet, if she has assisted [ἐπαρκέω, *eparkeō*] those in distress [θλίβω, *thlibō*], and if she has devoted herself to every good work. 11 But refuse to put younger widows on the list, for when they feel sensual desires in disregard of Christ, they want to get married, 12 thus incurring condemnation, because they have set aside their previous pledge. 13 At the same time they also learn to be idle, as they go around from house to house; and not merely idle, but also gossips and busybodies, talking about things not proper to mention. 14 Therefore, I want younger widows to get married, bear children, keep house, and give the enemy no occasion for reproach; 15 for some have already turned aside to follow Satan. 16 If any woman who is a believer has dependent widows, she must assist [ἐπαρκέω, *eparkeō*] them and the church must not be burdened, so that it may assist [ἐπαρκέω, *eparkeō*] those who are widows indeed. (S | | | I)

First Timothy 5:3–16 provides the most extensive NT treatment of mandates relating to the assistance of widows. This passage clarifies that the widows which should receive the corporate assistance of being put on "the list" (vv. 9, 11) are those that are "widows indeed" (vv. 3, 5, 16).[222] This definition of widowhood, which frames the beginning and ending of this text, means that a woman who has lost her husband is not considered a "widow" (in terms of church assistance) if she has any children or

---

222. The call to honor (τίμα, v. 3) those who are widows indeed appears to be an allusion to the fifth commandment (Exod 20:12; Deut 5:16). The issue of Corban, in Mark 7:9–13 and Matt 15:3–6, reveals that honoring parents involves helping them as they may have need. George Knight agrees (Knight, *The Pastoral Epistles*, 216). Other expected duties to parents, such as remaining with them and burying them, could be superseded by a higher obligation to respond to Jesus' call to become an immediate disciple during His earthly ministry (Matt 19:29 // Mark 10:29 // Luke 18:29; Matt 8:21–22 // Luke 9:59–60). Jesus, unlike the Pharisees and scribes, could commission such allegiance from His immediate followers (Matt 10:37 // Luke 14:26). Furthermore, the injunction to "allow the dead to bury their own dead" (Matt 8:22 // Luke 9:60) refers most easily to a deceased parent rather than to one still ill—for then the adherent's request might rather have been for healing. The phrase functions as a rhetorical call concerning the burial—to let that matter take care of itself. See Manson, *The Sayings of Jesus*, 73; Nolland, *Luke*, 543; Hagner, *Matthew*, 218; *contra* Marshall, *The Gospel of Luke*, 411. Arrangements can be made, others will do it. And so Jesus' command here is not necessarily an injunction to forgo allotting for one's aged parents if they should come into sustenance need.

grandchildren that could provide for her (v. 4). Eligible widows are those which are "left alone" (v. 5) and not a part of any "household" (οἰκεῖος, *oikeios*, v. 8) and therefore have no extended family to help provide for their needs (v. 16). Such widows are likely to be immediately poor. In terms of receiving the support of being on "the list," such "family-less" widows must also be God-trusting believers (v. 5) who have not given themselves "to wanton pleasure" (v. 6). The term translated "wanton pleasure," σπαταλάω (*spatalaō*), is a NT *dis legomenon*—appearing also in Jas 5:5 where it describes those who have "lived luxuriously on the earth." The term is also used to describe the arrogant pleasure seeking of Sodom which enjoyed an abundance of bread and wine (Ezek 16:49 LXX). In Sirach 21:15 it refers to an indulgent fool. Hence William Mounce asserts that the basic meaning of σπαταλάω (*spatalaō*) is to "live a luxurious, self-indulgent life, given to pleasure."[223] Because this term's economic meaning is unlikely to apply here, selfish pleasure rather than luxurious living appears to be in view.[224] Such "service-less" living (*contra* 1 Tim 5:10) would include being a busybody, engaging in gossiping, and "talking about things not proper to mention" (v. 13). Furthermore, in order to qualify, eligible widows must be no younger than "sixty years old, having been the wife of one man" (v. 9). Eligible widows must also have a previous record of devotion to "every good work" including the showing of hospitality to strangers, the humble service of the saints, the aiding of those in distress (θλίβω, *thlibō*), and likewise having "brought up children" (v. 10). Thus an eligible widow was "family-less," not self-indulgent, sixty or older, maritally faithful, and committed to serving other believers.[225] Younger widows could be expected to provide for themselves but, as sixty "was the recognized age in antiquity when one became an 'old' man or woman," such retirement-age widows were, provided they met the remaining prerequisites, eligible.[226]

---

223. W. Mounce, *Pastoral Epistles*, 283.

224. Ibid., 283.

225. The requirement for being a "one-man woman," ἑνὸς ἀνδρὸς γυνή, communicates, by elimination, marital fidelity (or possibly not having been divorced). For a prohibition against widow remarriage does not fit the context and polyandry was highly uncommon. See Knight, *The Pastoral Epistles*, 223; W. Mounce, *Pastoral Epistles*, 287; Lea and Griffin, *1, 2 Timothy, Titus*, 150. The requirement of motherhood (v. 10) may be intended as one exemplar of the manner of good works that such a widow is to have done.

226. Knight, *The Pastoral Epistles*, 223; Strack and Billerbeck, *Kommentar zum*

One who was a "widow indeed" appears to have become an intercessor or worker of the church—having taken a pledge of celibacy (vv. 11–12).[227] She may have been supported by living with other church members on a rotational basis (v. 13). Her support meant that she had to be careful to flee idleness (v. 13). The similarities between 1 Tim 5:13 and 2 Thess 3:11 are suggestive.

The term employed for the widow's church support, ἐπαρκέω (*eparkeō*), is a NT *tris legomenon*—appearing only in verse 10 and twice again in verse 16. This assistance is semantically identified as the provision of aid to someone.[228] The utilization of this term in verse 10 to describe the widow's own aid to those in distress connects ἐπαρκέω (*eparkeō*) to good works (ἔργοις καλοῖς and ἔργῳ ἀγαθῷ, v. 10) in non-familial contexts. Thus this relation may suggest that a mercy level of obligation is also in view as far as the church is concerned (v. 16). The inclusion of this aid alongside hospitality and humble service, which are both matters of mercy (as indicated elsewhere), likewise hints that the church provided assistance, as opposed to filial piety assistance, may be an issue of mercy. But with no hamartiological or semantic indicators present, such hinting, of itself, remains tentative. On the other side, the call to "honor" those who are "widows indeed" (v. 3) hints at a possible justice level of responsibility as honoring parents (to be discussed in the Family Responsibility section of chapter 6) and church elders (1 Tim 5:17), in this way, is justice.[229] So where do the chips fall after taking all of the textual clues into account? The distinction between the church, which must not be burdened, and the family, which must be (vv. 4, 8, 16), suggests a difference in obligation level—that the church's obligation is lower. The familial lines are drawn. And so *assisting* the "widows indeed" is a matter of mercy—a good work—for the church like it was for the widow herself toward non-family. The delimiting of the wid-

---

Neuen Testament aus Talmud und Midrasch, 3:653; W. Mounce, *Pastoral Epistles*, 286; Lea and Griffin, *1, 2 Timothy, Titus*, 150.

227. In *To the Smyrnaeans* 13:1, Ignatius extends his "greetings . . . to the virgins enrolled with the widows" (C. Richardson, *Early Christian Fathers*, 116). It appears that by Ignatius's time, the "order of widows" which was provided for by the giving of the church, had come to include virgins who had also committed themselves to celibacy.

228. "ἐπαρκέω," BDAG 359.

229. For a further defense of such honoring as entailing assistance when needed or remuneration for pastoral work see Knight, *The Pastoral Epistles*, 216; W. Mounce, *Pastoral Epistles*, 278–79.

ows—the fact that not all widows were to be helped—similarly portends that assisting widows is a matter of mercy for the church.

This passage also clarifies a believer's obligations to her dependent parents—in the extended family sense.[230] Such care is a piety (v. 4) that is required of a believer (vv. 7, 16). The strong language of verse 8 suggests that such care is likely an issue of justice, for "if anyone does not provide for his own, and especially for those of his household, he has denied the faith and is worse than an unbeliever." This mandate also implies the need, for the able-bodied, to work in order to support one's own. The reason for these mandates is that "the church must not be burdened." This concern, which is analogous to that expressed in 2 Cor 11:9; 12:13–14, 16; 1 Thess 2:9; and 2 Thess 3:8, informs the strict guidelines for providing church-based sustenance assistance to widows. Such exclusionary guidelines—where a person's age, character, and commitment to good works are determinative—are dissonant with Wolterstorff's conception of sustenance rights.

> Jas 1:27 Pure and undefiled religion in the sight of our God and Father is this: to *visit* [ἐπισκέπτομαι, *episkeptomai*] *orphans and widows* in their *distress* [θλῖψις, *thlipsis*], and to keep oneself unstained by the world. (S | | | I)

James confirms that visiting (ἐπισκέπτομαι, *episkeptomai*) "orphans and widows in their distress" (θλῖψις, *thlipsis*) is "pure and undefiled religion in the sight of our God and Father" (Jas 1:27).[231] This visiting, ἐπισκέπτομαι (*episkeptomai*), does not mean coming over in order to drink their coffee and have a bit of a chin-wag. It entails taking care of those distressed so as to alleviate their distress (as in Matt 25:36).[232]

Widows Clarifiers

> Acts 6:1 Now at this time while the disciples were increasing in number, a complaint arose on the part of the Hellenistic Jews

---

230. W. Mounce, *Pastoral Epistles*, 298.

231. James contrasts the untainted (ἀμίαντος, *amiantos*) religion of Jas 1:27 with the vain and worthless (μάταιος, *mataios*) religion described in Jas 1:26. This contrast, along with the subsumed mandate to "keep oneself unstained by the world" (Jas 1:27), indicates that this tainting does not needfully entail that caring for widows in their distress is a justice matter. For additional discussion, regarding this focus on religiosity, see Martin, *James*, 51–52.

232. Ibid., 44, 52.

against the native Hebrews, because their *widows* were being overlooked in the *daily serving of food*. (S | I/P)

Acts 9:36, 39–41 Now in Joppa there was a disciple named Tabitha (which translated in Greek is called Dorcas); this woman was abounding with *deeds of kindness and charity* [ἔργων ἀγαθῶν καὶ ἐλεημοσυνῶν] which she continually did. . . . 39 So Peter arose and went with them. When he arrived, they brought him into the upper room; and all the widows stood beside him, weeping and showing all the *tunics and garments* that Dorcas used to make while she was with them. 40 But Peter sent them all out and knelt down and prayed, and turning to the body, he said, "Tabitha, arise." And she opened her eyes, and when she saw Peter, she sat up. 41 And he gave her his hand and raised her up; and calling the saints and widows, he presented her alive. (S | I/P)

Acts 6:1, a passage formerly discussed, describes another example of corporately dispensed sustenance assistance to widows. Acts 9:36, likewise formerly engaged, affirms the goodness of giving alms to widows.

SATIATION

Deuteronomy 23:24–25 permits the satiation of one's hunger by partaking of a neighbor's produce: "When you enter your neighbor's vineyard, then you may eat grapes until you are fully satisfied, but you shall not put any in your basket. When you enter your neighbor's standing grain, then you may pluck the heads with your hand, but you shall not wield a sickle in your neighbor's standing grain." So while harvesting or taking enough for later is forbidden, immediate satiation is allowed.

This law is different from the gleaning laws of the OT (Lev 19:9–10; 23:22; Deut 24:19–22) in that it does not focus on regulating the leftovers of harvesting—on preventing owners from gleaning so as to allot what is left by the reapers to the poor, the widow, the orphan, and the alien. Rather than forbidding thorough harvesting, Deut 23:24–25 regulates how people are to pass through ripe agricultural areas. Perhaps this law was intended "to create an atmosphere of general grace and hospitality and to provide practical aid for the traveler who, in those ancient days, might not be able to carry sufficient food supplies for a long journey and who would have no way of preserving certain foodstuffs from spoilage."[233] But it seems to have permitted anyone who was hungry to satiate them-

---

233. Merrill, *Deuteronomy*, 316.

selves on their neighbor's produce as harvest time approached. As utilizing harvesting implements was forbidden, such labor-intensive satiation would have naturally attracted the poor in significantly greater proportion. For it would not generally have been worthwhile for landowners—as they could better invest their efforts into efficiently harvesting their own produce.

While not a mandated action, Jesus' approval and defense of this satiation practice, even on a Sabbath, reveals that He believed that this pre-harvest meeting of sustenance needs was still permitted (Matt 12:7).

Satiation Clarifiers

> Matt 12:1 At that time Jesus went through the grainfields on the Sabbath, and His disciples became *hungry and began to pick the heads of grain and eat.* (S | I/P)
>
> // Mark 2:23 And it happened that He was passing through the grainfields on the Sabbath, and His disciples began to make their way along while *picking the heads of grain.* (S | I/P)
>
> // Luke 6:1 Now it happened that He was passing through some grainfields on a Sabbath; and His disciples were *picking the heads of grain, rubbing them in their hands, and eating the grain.* (S | I/P)

A number of commentators have assumed that corn was being picked.[234] As all who have tried it can attest, Luke 6:1 dispels this possibility—for "rubbing" is required to loosen seeds of grain and serves no useful function when eating corn.[235] As noted, such labor intensive alleviation of hunger—as rubbing heads of grain is very intensive for the little that it yields—is most likely to benefit the poor at the outlay of wealthier landowners.

PARTIALITY

The practice of partiality, the preferring of the high to the low and the rich to the poor, is strictly forbidden in the NT. If anything, a reverse partiality is mandated within the concern for being first and greatest in the kingdom.

---

234. Marshall, *The Gospel of Luke*, 231; France, *The Gospel of Mark*, 144.
235. Bock, *The Gospel of Mark*, 423; Nolland, *Luke*, 255; Merrill, *Deuteronomy*, 316.

Partiality Mandates

> Rom 12:16 Be of the same mind toward one another; do not be haughty in mind, but *associate with the lowly*. Do not be wise in your own estimation. (CG | | |)

Paul's mandate in Rom 12:16 asserts that believers must associate with the "lowly." While status is certainly in view, poor believers would naturally be included in this commanded association.[236]

> Jas 2:1–7 My brethren, do not hold your faith in our glorious Lord Jesus Christ with an attitude of personal favoritism. 2 For if a man comes into your assembly with a gold ring and dressed in fine clothes, and there also comes in a *poor man in dirty clothes*, 3 and you pay special attention to the one who is wearing the fine clothes, and say, "You sit here in a good place," and you say to the *poor man*, "You stand over there, or sit down by my footstool," 4 have you not made distinctions among yourselves, and become judges with *evil* motives? 5 Listen, my beloved brethren: did not God choose the *poor* of this world to be rich in faith and heirs of the kingdom which He promised to those who love Him? 6 But you have dishonored the *poor man*. Is it not the *rich* who oppress [καταδυναστεύω, katadynasteuō] you and personally drag you into court? 7 Do they not blaspheme the fair name by which you have been called? (SP | J | S | I)

In Jas 2:1–7 James identifies partiality to the rich as an evil (v. 4)—a dishonoring of the immediately poor (v. 6). Participating in this injustice is particularly ironic because, in the big picture of things, it is the unbelieving (v. 7) "rich who oppress you and personally drag you into court" (v. 6). The oppression spoken of here, καταδυναστεύω (*katadynasteuō*), refers to the overpowering of those with less influence—even via the judicial system (v. 6). Also noteworthy is the reminder in Jas 2:5 that God has elected (ἐκλέγω, *eklegō*) the "poor of this world to be rich in faith"— that, for His part, He shows them special favor in terms of inheriting the kingdom through faith and love of Him.[237] But this favor functions as

---

236. While scholarly opinion is divided, the sense of associating with the lowly is to be preferred over the notion of engaging humble tasks. See Schreiner, *Romans*, 668–69.

237. This is not to say that all the poor believe. Still, attempts to understand the πτωχοί (*ptōchoi*) of verse 5 as referring generally to the pious are misguided—for they break the logic and argument of this passage (*contra* Martin, *James*, 64–65; Davids, *The Epistle of James*, 111). For the immediately impending contrast in verse 6 is with the poor man, τὸν πτωχόν, spoken of earlier (vv. 2–3). And so verse 5 is an integral part of

a deep comfort rather than as an interhuman mandate. For, as another poster child for the human/divine disjunction, the interhuman mandate is rather to make no distinctions (v. 4).²³⁸

> Jas 2:8–12 If, however, you are fulfilling the royal law according to the Scripture, "YOU SHALL LOVE YOUR NEIGHBOR AS YOURSELF," you are doing well. 9 But if you show *partiality*, you are *committing sin and are convicted by the law as transgressors*. 10 For whoever keeps the whole law and yet stumbles in one point, he has become guilty of all. 11 For He who said, "DO NOT COMMIT ADULTERY," also said, "DO NOT COMMIT MURDER." Now if you do not commit adultery, but do commit murder, you have become a transgressor of the law. 12 So speak and so act as those who are to be judged by the law of liberty. (SPI | J | H | I)

These verses, Jas 2:8–12, tie into the immediately preceding passage and assert that such partiality is a transgression of the command to love your neighbor as yourself. Such partiality is proscribed in Lev 19:15 which commands: "You shall do no injustice in judgment; you shall not be partial to the poor nor defer to the great, but you are to judge your neighbor fairly." The prohibition of Lev 19:15 is found in very close textual proximity to Lev 19:18—the source of James' "love your neighbor" quotation in Jas 2:8.²³⁹ Because such partiality is "committing sin" (v. 9), it is an instance of injustice.

> Jas 3:17 But the wisdom from above is first pure, then peaceable, gentle, reasonable, full of mercy and good fruits, *unwavering* [ἀδιάκριτος, *adiakritos*], without hypocrisy. (G | | |)

General impartiality is also mandated in Jas 3:17 which asserts that "the wisdom from above" is ἀδιάκριτος (*adiakritos*, impartial).²⁴⁰

James' argument—and thus the poor it refers to are indeed the immediately poor. And so some do agree. See K. Richardson, *James*, 115; Blomberg, "Wealth," *EDBT* 816.

238. *Pace* Martin, *James*, 57, 63–64. Correspondingly, James' aim here is to help us reorient our background perspective so as to make this goal readily embraceable. God values and honors the poor (v. 5), why should we dishonor them (v. 6)? It is rather the unbelieving rich who cause harm and actively dishonor God (vv. 6–7), so why should we hold the wealthy in any higher esteem?

239. The reference to becoming "judges with evil motives," in Jas 2:4, likewise appears to correlate this association.

240. Dibelius and Greeven, *James*, 214; Martin, *James*, 133.

OPPRESSION AND HIGH RESOLUTION JUSTICE

Oppression is the use of entrusted or financial power to perpetrate injustice with immunity. It refers to the injustice that one can get away with due to one's influence or occupation.

High resolution justice mandates are those which possess a "concrete" or better resolution. Concrete mandates naturally affect interhuman obligations to the poor but also extend beyond them. Unlike with the NT passages concerning oppression, only a representative selection of such justice mandates will be discussed below.

Oppression and High Resolution Justice Mandates

> Mark 10:19 You know the commandments, "DO NOT *MURDER*, DO NOT COMMIT ADULTERY, DO NOT *STEAL*, DO NOT BEAR FALSE WITNESS, Do not *defraud*, HONOR YOUR FATHER AND MOTHER." (C | | |)

Mark 10:19 (// Matt 19:18–19 // Luke 18:20) reiterates the Decalogue mandates against murder, adultery, theft, and false witness as well as affirming the honoring of parents in addition to forbidding fraud. Of these, murder, theft, bearing false witness, and defrauding are the most pertinent for the present purpose of identifying mandates which are most likely to be transgressed against the poor. These interhuman treatments are identified as issues of justice in other passages. In the OT, sanctions are prescribed for their transgression. Within the New, texts such as Mark 7:21–23 semantically identify murder and theft as evil (πονηρός, *ponēros*, v. 23). Romans 13:9–10 does the same by labeling these injustices as κακός (*kakos*, evil, v. 10). For its part, 1 Cor 6:8–10 relates defrauding to injustice and further identifies theft and swindling (which is itself a mix of robbery and defrauding) as injustice—and does so not only semantically but also hamartiologically on account of the consequences attached to them.

> Luke 3:12–13 And some tax collectors also came to be baptized, and they said to him, "Teacher, what shall we do?" 13 And he said to them, "*Collect no more than what you have been ordered to.*" (C | | |)

> Luke 3:14 Some soldiers were questioning him, saying, "And what about us, what shall we do?" And he said to them, "*Do not take money from anyone by force, or accuse anyone falsely*, and be content with your wages." (C | | |)

Luke 3:12–13 mandates that tax collectors not misuse their position to defraud while Luke 3:14 mandates soldiers not to steal through extortion or to bear false witness. To take an OT example, Deut 19:18–19 confirms, both hamartiologically and semantically, that refraining from such false accusation is a matter of justice obligation.

> Rom 13:8 *Owe nothing to anyone* except to love one another; for he who loves his neighbor has fulfilled the law. (C | | |)

> Rom 13:9–10 For this, "YOU SHALL NOT COMMIT ADULTERY, YOU SHALL NOT *MURDER*, YOU SHALL NOT *STEAL*, YOU SHALL NOT *COVET*," and if there is any other commandment, it is summed up in this saying, "YOU SHALL LOVE YOUR NEIGHBOR AS YOURSELF." 10 Love does no *wrong* [κακός, *kakos*] to a neighbor; therefore love is the fulfillment of the law. (C | J | S |)

The Rom 13:8 mandate to "owe nothing to anyone" entails the repayment of debts.[241] The parable of the unforgiving servant (Matt 18:23–34) clarifies that forgiving a debt is a matter of mercy (σπλαγχνίζομαι, *splanchnizomai*, v. 27, ἐλεέω, *eleeō*, v. 33) while repaying it is a matter of justice (vv. 25, 34).[242] Romans 13:9–10, as already noted, forbids murder, stealing, and coveting (with the latter aspect having received our attention earlier). Carrying out these justice mandates is a part of interhuman love—a vital component of loving our neighbors as ourselves (v. 9).

> Jas 5:1–6 Come now, you rich, *weep and howl* for your *miseries which are coming upon you*. 2 Your riches have rotted and your garments have become moth-eaten. 3 *Your gold and your silver have rusted*; and their rust will be a witness against you and will

---

241. Moo, *The Epistle to the Romans*, 812; Schreiner, *Romans*, 691.

242. In terms of obligation level, the forgiveness of debts behaves like forgiveness itself—the ultimate referent of the parable. Also significant is Jesus' explicit articulation of sin as debt here (Matt 18:21–23). So while some have taken the Lord's prayer (Matt 6:12 // Luke 11:4) as a mandate unto the forgiveness of financial or honor debts—particularly those of the peasant farmers—this interpretation is not a good match for what is really a "made-to-order" prayer for Jesus' immediate disciples (Luke 11:1). *Pace* Hanson and Oakman, *Palestine in the Time of Jesus*, 111; Achtemeier et al., *Introducing the New Testament*, 173. The internal symmetry of these petitions is also problematic. For we, like the disciples, do not *all* owe God money—that He should forgive us our tithes, redemptions, vows, and debts of honor (Matt 6:12). And besides, "sins" also come up in Luke 11:4—and the resultant terminological equivalency of sin and debt is noted. See Marshall, *The Gospel of Luke*, 460–61; Bock, *Luke*, 1055. And to cap it off, Matt 6:14–15 confirmingly asserts that it is the forgiveness of "transgressions" that is the topic at hand.

consume your flesh like fire. It is in the last days that you have stored up your treasure! 4 Behold, the *pay of the laborers who mowed your fields, and which has been withheld by you,* cries out against you; and the outcry of those who did the harvesting has reached the ears of the *Lord of Sabaoth.* 5 You have lived luxuriously on the earth and led a life of wanton pleasure; you have fattened your hearts in a *day of slaughter.* 6 You have *condemned and put to death the righteous man* [δίκαιος, *dikaios*]; he does not resist you. (C | J | H |)

The previously noted oppression by the rich in Jas 2:6–7 does not add any concrete resolution level information.[243] On the other hand, Jas 5:1–6, likewise previously discussed, does. It contributes a justice level prohibition against defrauding one's employees, in this case field harvesters, and against committing judicially proxied murder. The oppression the rich had been getting away with. For the sake of clarification, it may also be worth noting that causing someone to stumble, especially the "little ones," in Matt 18:6; Mark 9:42; and Luke 17:1–2 refers to tempting rather than wronging.[244] Hence it will not garner our attention.

PASTORAL

Three additional aspects of the NT data—those concerning pastoral support, healing, and Jesus' mission—overlap with the data we have already considered. While these scriptural concerns do not ultimately contribute any additional mandates or clarifiers to the data set pertaining to helping the poor, they are nevertheless noteworthy for the continuities they highlight or the attention they receive in the theological material concerning poverty.

The pastoral and missionary support mandates found within the epistles of Paul are a continuance of Jesus' affirmation that a worker is worthy of his support (Matt 10:10). These mandates entail a continuation of the support of those, who like Jesus and His band of disciples, engaged in pastoral and missionary ministry. This continuity is made

---

243. This is not to say that suggestions—of legal persecution, of legal pressures over rents, wages, debts, and securing usury, or of defrauding—have not been offered. See Davids, *The Epistle of James*, 112; Martin, *James*, 66; Ropes, *A Critical and Exegetical Commentary on the Epistle of St. James*, 195–96; K. Richardson, *James*, 116. But that they remain but surmisals.

244. Keener, *A Commentary on the Gospel of Matthew*, 449; Gould, *A Critical and Exegetical Commentary on the Gospel according to St. Mark*, 177–78; Bock, *Luke*, 1385–86.

explicit in 1 Cor 9:14 which affirms that "the Lord directed those who proclaim the gospel to get their living from the gospel." And so Paul clarifies throughout 1 Cor 9:4–18 that pastoral and missionary workers have a right (ἐξουσία, *exousia*, vv. 4, 6, 12, 18) to receive support. This just support is also mandated in Gal 6:6, though its obligation level is not revealed there.

But Paul himself, though he is certainly a pastoral and missionary worker, does not wish to make use of this justice provision (1 Cor 9:15, 18) for the sake of being able to "offer the gospel without charge" (v. 18). And this explains why he does not consider the Philippians' aid (Phil 4:14–17) as a matter of justice even when he is experiencing the distress of immediate poverty (θλῖψις, *thlipsis*, v. 14). Even when he is imprisoned and thus cannot maintain his *modus operandi* of working secularly (in tandem) in order to earn sustenance. So Paul identifies the Philippians' sharing (συγκοινωνέω, *synkoinōneō*, v. 14 and κοινωνέω, *koinōneō*, v. 15) as a gift (δόμα, *doma*, v. 17) that will be rewarded and thus as a mercy.[245] In this he affirms that even when he takes on the state of a poor brother—even when it is persecution that is the cause of his immediate poverty—receiving sustenance assistance is a matter of mercy. That this is how things stand when pastoral and missionary support is not in play.

But whenever pastors and missionary workers do not willfully set aside this right they are to be treated like anyone else in being justly paid for their work (in a Rom 4:4 sense).

HEALING

It is not uncommon to find that Jesus' healings of the beggarly disabled are held up as impetuses unto helping the poor. Nevertheless, Jesus' healings, even when they transform the non-able-bodied into the able-bodied, and thus enable a rise out of poverty, are not universally mandated.[246]

In terms of the obligations in play, Jesus' healing of the leper in Mark 1:40–42 is semantically identified as an issue of having mercy (σπλαγχνίζομαι, *splanchnizomai*, v. 41). Jesus is similarly "moved with compassion" (σπλαγχνίζομαι, *splanchnizomai*, v. 34) to act on behalf of the two blind men in Matt 20:30–34. The healing of the demoniac of the

---

245. The specific reward of verse 17 is from God (O'Brien, *The Epistle to the Philippians*, 538–39).

246. While Jesus does authorize and command the twelve of Matt 10:8 and the seventy others of Luke 10:9 to heal, such an empowering is recognized to be a non-universal gifting after His earthly ministry (1 Cor 12:28–30).

country of the Gerasenes is also identified as an act of mercy (ἐλεέω, *eleeō*) by Jesus (Mark 5:19). His healing of the woman who had hemorrhaged for twelve years (Matt 9:20–22 // Mark 5:25–34 // Luke 8:43–48) also provided economic relief—for her pursuit of physicians had cost her "all that she had" (Mark 5:26). And the raising of the widow's only son in Luke 7:12–13, which would have resulted in the alleviation of her (likely) potential or immediate poverty, is semantically disclosed as an act of compassion (σπλαγχνίζομαι, *splanchnizomai*, v. 13). Furthermore, Jesus is not constrained to heal—as in Nazareth (Matt 13:54–58 // Luke 4:23–27). Even when in the immediate presence of many who are longing to be healed, Jesus sometimes chooses to heal but one. And so, of the "multitude of those who were sick, blind, lame, and withered" (John 5:3), only one non-able-bodied man is healed by the pool of *Bēthzatha* (John 5:2–9). All this affirms that providing healing is a matter of mercy—even for Him who is most able. Correspondingly, Jesus' many healings (Mark 3:9–10) are related to doing good, εὐεργετέω (*euergeteō*), in Acts 10:38. And we have no reason to think that the remaining healings in the NT are any different. As in Jesus' case (Matt 9:2–8; 11:4–5; 15:30–31; 21:14; Luke 5:18–26; 7:22; John 5:3–9), Peter's healing of the immediately poor lame man in Acts 3:2–8 would have enabled him to leave behind his dependence on begging.

In summary, when textually revealed, the healing and exorcism described in the healing passages, even when it helps to alleviate immediate poverty, is categorized as a matter of mercy. Even for Jesus. Furthermore it is also not universally mandated. And as we have already noted, Jesus provides healing to more than just the immediately or potentially poor.

JESUS' MISSION

Jesus' self-claimed mission also receives extensive scholarly attention with respect to its impact on Christian obligations to the poor. While very noteworthy and informative, this mission is spoken of in terms of fulfillment rather than in terms of mandated obligation and thus will receive only brief attention here.

Jesus' Mission Clarifiers

> Matt 11:4–5 Jesus answered and said to them, "Go and report to John what you hear and see: 5 the BLIND RECEIVE SIGHT and the lame walk, the lepers are cleansed and the deaf hear, the dead

are raised up, and the POOR HAVE THE GOSPEL PREACHED TO THEM." (S | I)

// Luke 7:22 And He answered and said to them, "Go and report to John what you have seen and heard: the BLIND RECEIVE SIGHT, the lame walk, the lepers are cleansed, and the deaf hear, the dead are raised up, the POOR HAVE THE GOSPEL PREACHED TO THEM." (S | I)

Matt 12:18, 20 BEHOLD, MY SERVANT WHOM I HAVE CHOSEN; MY BELOVED IN WHOM MY SOUL is WELL-PLEASED; I WILL PUT MY SPIRIT UPON HIM, AND HE SHALL PROCLAIM *JUSTICE* TO THE GENTILES. . . . 20 A *BATTERED REED* HE WILL NOT BREAK OFF, AND A *SMOLDERING WICK* HE WILL NOT PUT OUT, UNTIL HE LEADS *JUSTICE* TO VICTORY. (I |)

Luke 4:18–21 "THE SPIRIT OF THE LORD IS UPON ME, BECAUSE HE ANOINTED ME TO *PREACH THE GOSPEL TO THE POOR*. HE HAS SENT ME TO PROCLAIM RELEASE TO THE CAPTIVES, AND RECOVERY OF SIGHT TO THE BLIND, TO *SET FREE THOSE WHO ARE OPPRESSED*, 19 TO PROCLAIM THE *FAVORABLE YEAR* OF THE LORD." 20 And He closed the book, gave it back to the attendant and sat down; and the eyes of all in the synagogue were fixed on Him. 21 And He began to say to them, "Today this Scripture has been *fulfilled* in your hearing." (S | I)

Luke 13:19 It is like a mustard seed, which a man took and threw into his own garden; and it grew and became a tree, and THE BIRDS OF THE AIR NESTED IN ITS BRANCHES. (G |)

In appropriating Isa 61:1–2 and Isa 58:6 in Luke 4:18–21, Jesus claims that the fulfillment of the year of Jubilee is connected to preaching to the poor, the release of captives, the returning of sight to the blind, and the setting free of the oppressed.[247] Because Jesus nowhere mandates the property-returning decree of the Jubilee provisions themselves (Lev 25:10–15, 28–33, 40, 50–54; 27:17–24; Num 36:4) nor apparently engaged in the release of any prisoners or oppressed (including John the

---

247. Bock, *Luke*, 410–11. The part about returning sight to the blind is from the LXX. The Hebrew here, "an opening to those imprisoned," can be read both ways for the opening may perhaps be that of the eyes (Watts, *Isaiah*, 299, 300). And blindness is an imprisonment from the visible world. Still, freedom for prisoners is the more likely Hebrew meaning. Perhaps Luke adds the setting free of the oppressed, a phrase from Isa 58:6, precisely in order to cover both possible meanings—freedom from the binding of blindness and for the imprisoned.

Baptist), it is helpful to understand this mission in terms of miracles, exorcism, proclamation, and the spiritual liberation of the "day of salvation" described in Isa 49:8 and 2 Cor 6:2.[248] Matthew 11:4–5 and Luke 7:22 confirm the fulfillment and affirm that the poor, if anyone, deserve to be given the good news.[249] Though part of the same harmony, the justice and mercy of Matt 12:18 is of a low resolution akin to the apparent sheltering and shading nature of the kingdom in Luke 13:19.[250]

IMPETUSES

The extent to which a mandate is not "specific" or "concrete," or even of a "principle" or "general" resolution, is the extent to which it does not add to the domain of our obligations. Said another way, the lowest resolution level, the level of moral impetuses, does not serve to define the domain of believer obligation but rather merely reminds us of the necessity of pursuing these subsumed obligations. Consequently, the NT impetuses unto justice, mercy, and love will receive only a representative tabulation below.

It is safe to assume that no believer will want to argue against any of these three impetuses. They are the umbrella under which all of the preceding mandates keep dry. The goal here is merely to remind ourselves that biblical mandates are even provided at this low resolution, but nevertheless conceptually significant, moral summary level. For such impetuses are the glue that gives us reason to believe that conceptual integration is both permissible and possible. For impetuses assume

---

248. For more extensive argumentation see, for example, Bock, *Luke*, 404–11.

249. The focus here is no more on spiritual poverty than it is on spiritual blindness, lameness, leprosy, deafness, and deadness. See Marshall, *The Gospel of Luke*, 291; Stein, *Luke*, 228. Luke's omission of the phrase "to bind up the brokenhearted" from Isa 61:1 (MT and LXX) in Luke 4:18 is also suggestive—perhaps he was, in this manner, trying to preserve the focus on the literal poor (Kim, *Stewardship and Almsgiving in Luke's Theology*, 19). Furthermore, a literal rather than spiritualized intention—at minimum in terms of miracles—is required from Luke 4:18–21 in order to preserve the logic of what happens next. For Jesus claims that while His anointing is fulfilled, it will nevertheless not be manifested in Nazareth (Luke 4:23–27 // Mark 6:1–6). And so He gives two OT prequels. A reminder that the prophet Elijah was sent to the poor widow of Zarephath during a widespread famine and that Elisha healed a diseased Syrian called Naaman rather than their acting upon the needs of their home turf (vv. 25–27). Jesus' explanatory focus here on miracles for immediately poor widows and the non-ablebodied sick is also highly suggestive. And so Jesus leaves His home turf having healed only "a few sick people" (Mark 6:5).

250. It is difficult to discern if sustenance provision is possibly intended here (Bock, *Luke*, 1225–27).

that their hearers will know how to fill out their broad non-specificity. How to heed their call in higher resolution circumstances. So that their call has, after all, some discernable, and obeyable, content. This is merely another way of saying that single rule, or few rule, ethical systems are dependent upon a multi-rule subsystem to provide higher resolution—so as not to slide into moral subjectivity and situationalism.

Impetuses to Justice

Matt 23:23–25 Woe to you, scribes and Pharisees, hypocrites! For you tithe mint and dill and cummin, and have neglected the weightier provisions of the law: *justice* [κρίσις, *krisis*] and *mercy* and faithfulness; but these are the things you should have done without neglecting the others. 24 You blind guides, who strain out a gnat and swallow a camel! 25 Woe to you, scribes and Pharisees, hypocrites! For you clean the outside of the cup and of the dish, but inside they are full of *robbery* and self-indulgence. (GI | J | S |)

// Luke 11:39–42 But the Lord said to him, "Now you Pharisees clean the outside of the cup and of the platter; but inside of you, you are full of *robbery* and *wickedness* [πονηρία, *ponēria*]. 40 You foolish ones, did not He who made the outside make the inside also? 41 But give that which is within as *charity*, and then all things are clean for you. 42 But woe to you Pharisees! For you pay tithe of mint and rue and every kind of garden herb, and yet disregard *justice* [κρίσις, *krisis*] and the love of God; but these are the things you should have done without neglecting the others." (GI | J | HS |)

Rom 12:9 Let love be without hypocrisy. Abhor what is *evil* [πονηρός, *ponēros*]; cling to what is good. (I | J | S |)

1 Tim 6:11 But flee from these things, you man of God, and pursue *righteousness* [δικαιοσύνη, *dikaiosynē*], godliness, faith, love, perseverance and gentleness. (I | J | S |)

2 Tim 2:19 Nevertheless, the firm foundation of God stands, having this seal, "The Lord knows those who are His," and, "Everyone who names the name of the Lord is to abstain from *wickedness* [ἀδικία, *adikia*]." (I | J | S |)

1 John 5:17 All *unrighteousness* [ἀδικία, *adikia*] is *sin*, and there is a sin not leading to death. (I | J | HS |)

Impetuses to Mercy

Matt 5:7 Blessed are the *merciful* [ἐλεήμων, *eleēmōn*], for they shall receive *mercy* [ἐλεέω, *eleeō*]. (I | M | S |)

Matt 9:13 But go and learn what this means: "I DESIRE COMPASSION [ἔλεος, *eleos*, from חֶסֶד, *khesed*], AND NOT SACRIFICE," for I did not come to call the righteous, but sinners. (I | M | S |)

Matt 12:7 But if you had known what this means, "I DESIRE COMPASSION [ἔλεος, *eleos*, from חֶסֶד, *khesed*], AND NOT A SACRIFICE," you would not have condemned the innocent. (I | M | S |)

Matt 23:23 Woe to you, scribes and Pharisees, hypocrites! For you tithe mint and dill and cummin, and have neglected the weightier provisions of the law: *justice* and *mercy* [ἔλεος, *eleos*] and faithfulness; but these are the things you should have done without neglecting the others. (I | M | S |)

Rom 1:31 without understanding, untrustworthy, unloving, *unmerciful* [ἀνελεήμων, *aneleēmōn*]. (I | M | S |)

Col 3:12 So, as those who have been chosen of God, holy and beloved, put on a heart of *compassion* [οἰκτιρμός, *oiktirmos*], kindness, humility, gentleness and patience. (I | M | S |)

Jas 2:13 For judgment will be merciless [ἀνέλεος, *aneleos*] to one who has shown no *mercy* [ἔλεος, *eleos*]; *mercy* [ἔλεος, *eleos*] triumphs over judgment.[251] (I | M | S |)

Impetuses to Love

Love, like righteousness, subsumes both justice and mercy. So it is no surprise that the mandates to love one's neighbor span obligations both just and merciful (Rom 13:8–10; Luke 10:27–37).[252]

---

251. The internal structure of this transitional verse affirms that its main referent is clemency. Still its transitional nature confirms that such mercy, like the justice obligations noted earlier (Jas 2:9–11), is a subset of the law of neighborly love (Jas 2:8, 12). So, in this sense, it functions as a call to go beyond impartiality. See Davids, *The Epistle of James*, 118–19. *Pace* Martin, *James*, 71–72. James also appears to employ this verse as a lead-in into the sustenance assistance mandate of the immediately following verses (Jas 2:14–17). As such it implies that this feeding and clothing mandate is most likely a matter of mercy.

252. This plenteous mandate is also found in Matt 19:19; 22:39; Mark 12:31; Gal 5:14; and Jas 2:8.

Matt 5:44–48 But I say to you, *love* your enemies and pray for those who persecute you, 45 so that you may be sons of your Father who is in heaven; for He causes His sun to rise on the evil and the good, and sends rain on the righteous and the unrighteous. 46 For if you *love* those who *love* you, what reward do you have? Do not even the tax collectors do the same? 47 If you greet only your brothers, what more are you doing than others? Do not even the Gentiles do the same? 48 Therefore you are to be perfect, as your heavenly Father is perfect. (GI | M | H |)

// Luke 6:27–28, 32–33 But I say to you who hear, *love* your enemies, do *good* to those who hate you, 28 bless those who curse you, pray for those who mistreat you. . . . 32 If you *love* those who *love* you, what credit is that to you? For even sinners *love* those who *love* them. 33 If you do *good* to those who do *good* to you, what credit is that to you? For even sinners do the same. (I | M | H |)

John 13:34–35 A new commandment I give to you, that you *love* one another, even as I have *love*d you, that you also *love* one another. 35 By this all men will know that you are My disciples, if you have *love* for one another. (I | | |)

Rom 1:31 without understanding, untrustworthy, *unloving* [ἄστοργος, astorgos], *unmerciful*. (I | | |)

Rom 12:9 Let *love* be without hypocrisy. Abhor what is *evil* [πονηρός, ponēros]; cling to what is good. (I | | |)

Rom 13:8–10 Owe nothing to anyone except to *love* one another; for he who *loves* his neighbor has fulfilled the law. 9 For this, "YOU SHALL NOT COMMIT ADULTERY, YOU SHALL NOT MURDER, YOU SHALL NOT STEAL, YOU SHALL NOT COVET," and if there is any other commandment, it is summed up in this saying, "YOU SHALL *LOVE* YOUR NEIGHBOR AS YOURSELF." 10 *Love* does *no wrong* [κακός, kakos] to a neighbor; therefore *love* is the fulfillment of the law. (CI | J | H |)

1 Cor 13:4–6 *Love* is patient, *love* is kind and is not jealous; *love* does not brag and is not arrogant, 5 does not act unbecomingly; it does not seek its own, is not provoked, does not take into account a wrong suffered, 6 does not rejoice in *unrighteousness* [ἀδικία, adikia], but rejoices with the truth.[253] (GI | | |)

---

253. The command itself, to live this love, arrives in 1 Cor 14:1.

1 Cor 16:13–14 Be on the alert, stand firm in the faith, act like men, be strong. 14 Let all that you do be done in *love*. (I | | |)

Gal 5:6 For in Christ Jesus neither circumcision nor uncircumcision means anything, but faith working through *love*. (I | | |)

Gal 5:13 For you were called to freedom, brethren; only do not turn your freedom into an opportunity for the flesh, but through *love* serve one another. (I | | |)

Phil 2:1–4 Therefore if there is any encouragement in Christ, if there is any consolation of *love*, if there is any fellowship of the Spirit, if any *affection and compassion* [σπλάγχνα καὶ οἰκτιρμοί], 2 make my joy complete by being of the same mind, maintaining the *same love*, united in spirit, intent on one purpose. 3 Do nothing from *selfishness* or empty conceit, but with humility of mind regard one another as more important than yourselves; 4 *do not merely look out for your own personal interests, but also for the interests of others*. (GI | M | S |)

Love is something which is very difficult to consider briefly. It rightfully earns many book-length treatments.[254] But only a few comments will suffice for our purposes. Once shorn of its hyperbolic and *eros*-oriented usage, love showcases its affective and purposive components. The affective component subsumes the relational and emotive connection while the purposive element is eloquently highlighted in the parable of the good Samaritan. In terms of this purposive component, the love mandates of the NT connect love to *seeking another's good* (and benefit) in a manner analogous to Rom 15:2: "Each of us is to please his neighbor for his good, to his edification." So loving one's enemies means doing good to them (Luke 6:27). Accordingly, love does no evil to others (Rom 13:10) and is set against injustice (1 Cor 13:6). For interhuman love, in its purposive sense, is not something other than justice and mercy. And Wolterstorff is right in being opposed "to those who see *agape* as something other than justice, or worse yet, as pitted against justice," for "*agape* rightly understood incorporates the doing of justice."[255] When remedial or retributive justice is set aside, as we have done in seeking our

---

254. Clark, *The Word Hesed in the Hebrew Bible*; Piper, "Love Your Enemies"; Outka, *Agape*; Furnish, *The Love Command in the New Testament*; Carson, *The Difficult Doctrine of the Love of God*; Carson, *Love in Hard Places*; Morris, *Testaments of Love*; Getz, *Loving One Another*.

255. Wolterstorff, "How Social Justice Got to Me and Why It Never Left," 665.

non-judicial obligations, "general justice"—what I have called preceptive justice—is never at odds with mercy. Interhuman love swallows them both without chocking.

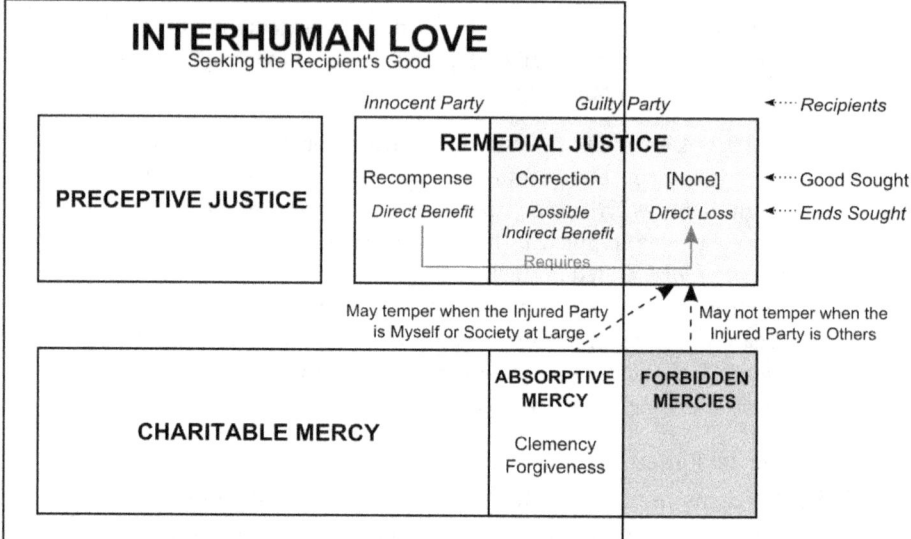

FIGURE 5: The Purposive Component of Interhuman Love[256]

Now that we have surveyed all of the NT mandates and their accompanying clarifiers concerning the moral treatment of the poor, from high resolution prescriptions unto almsgiving to low resolution moral impetuses, we are ready to bring them together within a non-destructive integration.

---

256. By way of explanation, absorptive mercy may absorb the direct loss justly coming to the guilty party provided that the injured party itself is granting this clemency. In instances where the injured party is society at large, where the harm caused did not specifically impact any concrete individuals or has broadly affected all, a judge generally assumes this injured party role on behalf of society. But whenever the injured party is concrete others, decreeing absorptive mercy upon the guilty party is injustice and hence an instance of forbidden mercy. For its part, remedial justice seeks the end of directly benefiting the injured party while necessarily causing direct loss to the guilty party. Sometimes this process brings about the indirect benefit of facilitating moral correction among the guilty—where consequences achieve a pedagogical effect.

SIX

Hearing the Witness
Data Integration

CONTOURS OF NT OBLIGATION

AND SO WE ARRIVE at the synoptic moment. It is time for the resolution principle's grandest performance. What can we ascertain concerning social justice and charity by way of the NT? We are looking for three main results in pursuing a conceptual integration of the data patterns: a cumulative contour summary of NT justice and mercy, an evaluation of the core contention (the extent to which justice is means or ends-based), and an evaluation of the recent theological influences upon evangelical understandings of the moral treatment of the poor. All of these results, from their own angle, serve to address our particularities—to address the extant theological impasse.

Procedurally, it is helpful to divide the contours of NT obligation unto the poor into those treatments which are textually revealed as being a matter of mercy and those which communicate a justice status. The presentation of these contours entails the individual and mutual integration of our previously encountered data aspects. Correspondingly, this contour summary will generally engage the biblical data as grouped along these lines.

DOMAIN OF MERCY

What sorts of moral treatments of the poor are revealed as matters of mercy in the NT? To integrate this domain, we will pursue the data as it increases in detail with respect to what is mandated—from lower to higher resolution. From broadly encompassing to more distinct. In this arrangement the data will also generally increase in detail with respect to its intended recipients—from low to high recipient resolution.

Our aim is to narrow in on what kind of help is specified as a matter of mercy—and to whom.

Doing Good

Doing good, which ultimately encompasses "all people" among its recipients (Gal 6:10), is also contextually related to the mercy of lending to the potentially poor (now falling into immediate poverty) who may not return the favor—particularly one's enemies who likely would not return the favor even if they could (Luke 6:30, 34–36).[1] Accepting the seizure of one's property by one's enemies is similarly a matter of mercy (Luke 6:29, 36; Heb 10:34). This is hardly surprising.

A few other similarly narrowed emphases occur within the broad NT concern for doing good.[2] Jesus' healings are one such emphasis (Matt 12:12–13 // Mark 3:4–5 // Luke 6:9–10; Acts 10:38)—and were semantically classified as instances of mercy by Jesus Himself. Jesus also subsumes the mercy of almsgiving under the doing of good (Mark 14:7). Feeding hungering believers is another manifestation of it (2 Thess 3:6–13). And in 1 Tim 6:17–19 doing good is related to participating in good works, being generous, and being ready to share with the immediately (or possibly potentially) poor. Such focused doing of good is revealed to be a matter of mercy for it stores up future reward (v. 19). Hebrews 13:16 similarly connects doing good with sharing. And so whenever it is presented in a higher resolution manner and its obligation level is revealed, doing good is consistently identified as a matter of mercy.

Good Works

Like doing good, good works are at times related to specific acts of mercy such as almsgiving (Acts 9:36) and the Jerusalem collection (2 Cor 9:8). Galatians 6:9–10 prioritizes the doing of such good works to believing recipients. So good works extend to humbly serving the brethren—including showing hospitality to strangers and assisting those in distress (1 Tim 5:10). Sharing with needy believers (1 Tim 6:18) and providing hos-

---

1. This is the minimalistic entailment—the reach of the mandate which is textually certain. Luke 6:29–30, 34–36 may perhaps also mandate almsgiving to enemies experiencing immediate poverty—but this is contestable.

2. In a few passages, such as Rom 2:7, 10; 3:12; 7:21, "doing good" refers to the broader notion of doing good and doing right—for Paul's usage here is concerned with being wide enough to subsume the requirements of the law.

pitality and travel assistance to Christian missionaries (Titus 3:13–14) are also instances of good works.[3] These are all treatments that we, as believers, are to be careful to engage in (Titus 3:8), and are to be zealous to do (Titus 2:14), for we are saved *unto* them (Eph 2:10). Nevertheless, whenever their obligation level is revealed, good works are related to mercy.

Receiving and First/Last

The mandates concerning receiving and hospitality enjoin, in part, providing for the needs of visiting believers (Rom 16:2; Heb 13:2). Matthew 10:40–42 and Mark 9:41 intimate that even the least troublesome and most basic of sustenance provision, the providing of a cup of water to drink, is an instance of mercy. Consequently, even the smallest outlay—the smallest provision of sustenance aid—is identified (as best as we can gather) as a matter of mercy. Though these passages are mixed texts—where receiving the messengers and their message is also in play—the rewarded manifestation nevertheless subsumes the helpful act.

The hospitable provision of shelter and, more so, sustenance is to be extended to brethren who are imprisoned or experiencing injustice and persecution (Heb 13:1–3). While the needs which are to be met by such receiving are not fully specified, the provision of sustenance *is* mandated along with the expected provision of shelter which is part of hospitality.

Yet there is also another, often overlooked, sense in which receiving is mandated within the NT. The encouragement to seek to become first and greatest in the kingdom is bound up with serving even the least significant believer. And so believers are mandated to shelve their social status and consider themselves the last and the least so as to be logically willing to participate in lowly service unto fellow believers of truly lowly social status. Being willing to serve even the least among us entails serving the young, perhaps the spiritually insignificant, and also the low class poor along with those experiencing immediate poverty. Such receiving of the poor so as to serve them would entail helping to meet their needs.

In sum, whenever it is textually specified, receiving is revealed to be a matter of mercy. Even when it is the receiving of believers. And even when it is likely to be the receiving of believers of the lowest social status.

---

3. So while pastoral and missionary remuneration is a matter of justice, providing travel assistance and hospitality to traveling ministry workers is a merciful supplement to this support.

Giving and Generosity

Giving, at minimum in terms of lending, is likewise subsumed under mercy in Luke 6:30, 34–36—where it is related to doing good—and similarly mandated in Matt 5:42. Although only lending is certain in both of these passages, Matt 5:42 might possibly call those who have experienced a surplus to not only lend to non-kin who would otherwise slip into immediate poverty, but to also provide general reciprocity to kin in the same circumstances. For it is logical that it would be those with a harvest or income surplus that would be "asked" to give and "wanted" as potential lenders (Matt 5:42). A contemporary context of severe economic depression or famine would prove similar in calling believers to give and lend to prevent kin and non-kin from starving due to a lack of sustenance or "workstuffs" such as plantable seed. And both parallels may conceivably even subsume almsgiving. Whatever the case, such giving is divinely rewarded in accordance with the donor's own generosity (Luke 6:38). Generosity is likewise mandated in Luke 16:1–13; 2 Cor 9:8–11; and 1 Tim 6:17–19 where it is similarly revealed to be an instance of mercy. Matthew 6:22–23 and Luke 11:34–36 also mandate generosity and, by way of the Luke-paralleled context of the Matthew passage, connect it to giving alms to the immediately poor (Luke 12:33). The parable of the unjust steward (Luke 16:1–13) is noteworthy for it mandates generosity with "our" possessions and wealth—which are properly understood as belonging to God—and hamartiologically reveals that such generosity is a matter of mercy. These generosity mandates tend to be overwhelmingly focused toward the immediately poor when taken in their context. So while some may choose to extend them more broadly, at minimum the almsgiving-related mandates noted above are themselves firmly intended unto the beggarly poor.

Sharing

The NT mandates concerning sharing are focused on κοινωνία (koinōnia) among the brethren but, particularly within the Gospel of Luke, stretch to include all the immediately needy among the intended recipients (Luke 3:11; 10:27–37; 14:12–14). Romans 12:20–21 even extends the sustenance provision of food and drink to one's enemies. Both the wider reaching and the brethren focused mandates are textually revealed to be instances of mercy whenever obligation indicators are present.

Accordingly, the parable of the good Samaritan mandates mercy unto someone who is a partial enemy when he is befallen by injustice. The meeting of such a victim's sustenance and medical needs is identified as an act of mercy upon his immediately poor condition. This is particularly surprising to those who would adopt a sustenance rights position. This focus on the provision of sustenance to the immediately needy is echoed in Luke 3:11 which mandates the sharing of clothes or food with "him who has none." Correspondingly, Luke 14:12–14 mandates the merciful inviting to dinner of the non-able-bodied and immediately poor who "do not have the means to repay you" (v. 14)—rather than those who have the means to return the invitation. This focus on the immediately poor as the proper recipients of such sharing is affirmed in the parable of the sheep and the goats (Matt 25:31–46) which identifies the needy as those who are dependent upon the provision of sustenance and sustaining assistance. Such passages connect the πτωχοί (*ptōchoi*, plural of *ptōchos*) to those possessing the sustenance needs entailed in hunger, thirst, being an alien, being sick, diseased, or feeble, and experiencing nakedness or imprisonment. The sharing inherent in the Jerusalem collection was also intended to bring relief to the immediately poor among the Judean believers. The sharing mandated in Jas 2:15 likewise concerns the sustenance provision of "what is necessary for their body" unto "a brother or sister . . . without clothing and in need of daily food."

The sharing entailed in the "love feasts" (Jude 1:12) is also intended to benefit the immediately poor who had nothing to contribute to the common meals (see also 1 Cor 11:21–22, 33–34; Acts 2:44–46). Accordingly, the NT data reveals that sharing, whenever it is elucidated, is bound up with alleviating the sustenance needs of the immediately poor. Whenever its obligation level is communicated, sharing is semantically or hamartiologically identified as a matter of mercy.

Almsgiving

Almsgiving is both semantically and hamartiologically revealed to possess a mercy level of obligation. The recipients of alms are identified, whenever this identification is provided, as the immediately poor (Matt 19:21–24 // Mark 10:19–23 // Luke 18:22) and as immediately or potentially poor widows (Acts 9:36, 39–41). This former connection of almsgiving, ἐλεημοσύνη (*eleēmosynē*), to its immediately poor recipients is readily visible within the overlap of Luke 12:33 and Luke 18:22 (// Matt

19:21 // Mark 10:21). While our previous chapter, in appreciating the passages in an isolated manner, allowed for the theoretical possibility of some of the almsgiving mandates extending to the potentially poor, the integrated witness and the socio-historical context argue for ἐλεημοσύνη (*eleēmosynē*) as being unto the immediately poor. This is also the case with the remote almsgiving of the Jerusalem collection. And so even small gifts to the beggarly poor in sustenance need, whether they be immediately present or remote, are matters of mercy.

Selling Possessions and Wealth

But what about large gifts? What about giving it all to the immediately poor? This is perhaps the most evident issue within the mercy domain. Is Jesus' mandate to His immediate disciples—to sell their possessions and give the proceeds as alms to the poor—universally applicable or localized? The data reveals that, even during His ministry, Jesus did not extend this mandate to all believers. Examples of the non-obligated include Zaccheus, Joseph of Arimathea, Martha, Mary, Lazarus, the demoniac of the country of the Gerasenes, and those who supported Jesus' ministry. These examples affirm that the domain of those who could be saved was wider than the domain of those obligated to sell their possessions and immediately follow Jesus. Jesus' mandate was aimed at His broader group of disciples and apparently subsumed the seventy of Luke 10:1–4. Correspondingly, Luke 12:13–21 intimates that the crowd and the disciples are differently obligated as Jesus merely warns the former against greed (v. 15) while commanding the latter to sell their possessions (Luke 12:33). This high resolution differentiation agrees with Jesus' affirmation that the "laborer is worthy of his wages" (Luke 10:7) and that, consequently, those participating—as pastoral and missionary workers—within His ministry are to be supported on the basis of their spiritual profession (as was Jesus Himself).

Obeying this mandate, to sell all for the benefit of the poor, was nevertheless required of Jesus' immediate disciples.[4] Still their obedience

---

4. Colin Brown, Philip Esler, and John Nolland are among the recent thinkers who have also come to the same conclusion. See C. Brown, "πτωχός," *NIDNTT* 2:825; Esler, *Community and Gospel in Luke–Acts*, 169; Nolland, *Luke*, 764. Many in the history of the Christian church have held this view, often coupled with a conviction of continued present applicability. Even at the time of the Reformation, Waldensians and proto-Reformers such as John Wycliffe and Jan Hus passionately advocated this understanding.

is hamartiologically identified as a matter of mercy. This obligation level is likewise attested by the resulting donation being referred to as almsgiving (Luke 12:33). The recipients of the benefits of this mandate are identified, whenever an identification is made, as the immediately poor.

But this possessions mandate is not attested beyond the confines of Jesus' earthly ministry. While a practical perspective of detachment from possessions is mandated (1 Cor 7:29–31) along with a parallel mindfulness concerning their inherent transience (Jas 1:9–11), the selling of possessions within the nascent church of Acts is unmandated and partial. Correspondingly, Jesus' conjoined mandate to forsake family ties (Luke 18:29) in order to follow Him is likewise understood by the disciples themselves to not apply beyond His ministry (1 Cor 9:5). The clarifiers of Acts reveal that the partial selling of one's possessions was voluntary (Acts 5:1–11) and hence also a matter of mercy—even when it served to alleviate the sustenance needs of immediately present believers (such as providing food for widows in Acts 6:1). This mercy of partial selling is identified as being intended to meet the needs of immediately poor brethren. Additionally, 1 Cor 13:3 confirms that the selling of one's possessions in order to provide for the needs of the poor is extraordinarily worthy precisely because it is no longer normative. Even for apostles such as Paul. Even when it may sustain the immediately poor.

A broad set of NT texts affirm the ownership of possessions among believers, including 2 Cor 12:14 which affirms the propriety of parents engaging in saving up for their children. A few more data points are worth considering. Most revealingly, the ownership of possessions was similarly permitted for those in missionary and pastoral ministry roles. Philip the evangelist, one of the original seven deacons of the nascent church, owned a house large enough to host guests (Acts 21:8). Nor had he forsaken his family ties (Acts 21:9). The requirements for elders (and deacons) also do not stipulate the forsaking of wives, families, or possessions. On the contrary, elders must manage their households well and be hospitable to strangers—and such hospitality assumes possessing a dwelling. Additionally, living with abundance is affirmed in Phil 4:11–13—even for an apostle—as well as in 3 John 1:2.[5] Tellingly, 2 Cor 8:11–13 mandates that participation in the Jerusalem collection ought

---

5. Though, admittedly, we ought not argue for an affirmation of retaining large amounts of wealth on the basis of these passages. See F. Bruce, *Philippians*, 125; O'Brien, *The Epistle to the Philippians*, 525–26.

not to usher the donors themselves into need. And this entails a retention of possessions. Thus 1 Tim 6:17–19 applies Jesus' mandate concerning storing up treasure in heaven to the rich so as to enjoin them unto generosity and sharing rather than unto the complete renunciation of their possessions. Such mandate passages provide explicit support for the post-Jesus'-ministry transition we have been observing.

Two tie-ins are worth a brief mention. Jesus presents four different notions of being genuinely first on the basis of being last. But only two of these impinge on our treatment of the poor.[6] The most common notion, noted earlier, subsumes the general (and concrete) level mandates regarding humble service even unto the lowliest of believers. The specific resolution notions, located in Matt 19:27–30 and Mark 10:28–31, are intertwined with Jesus' mandate to His disciples to forsake their possessions and relations—whereby becoming last in the eyes of the world—in order to follow Him (Matt 19:27 // Mark 10:28). As such, these specific mandates are mercy mandates that benefited the immediately poor and were, unlike their more common general resolution cousins, localized to the duration of Jesus' ministry.

What about the second tie-in? The NT witness concerning pastoral and missionary support provides a continuation of Jesus' and His disciples' acceptance of ministry provision (Luke 8:2–3). But because this provision is semantically identified as a matter of justice, it will receive further consideration when we turn our attention to the Domain of Justice.

In summary, the obligator set of Jesus' mercy level mandate to sell all in order to become His immediate disciple envelopes only His immediate followers—and even these, apparently, solely for the duration of His earthly ministry. It is not surprising then that subsequent to Jesus' ministry, believers who are not pastoral or missionary workers are even commanded to be self-sufficient (1 Thess 4:11–12). As a result, this integration concerning the selling of one's possessions is accomplished on the basis of the textual delimitation of the domain of its proper obligators. As a result we have observed that selling all in order to aid the immediately poor is a matter of mercy, that partial selling is considered a mercy, as is any almsgiving—no matter how small.

---

6. The parable of the workers in the vineyard (Matt 20:1–16) is not related to the treatment of the poor and so will not receive our attention. The same is true of the warning to the Jews in Luke 13:30.

Jerusalem Collection

The main Jerusalem collection is explicitly (2 Cor 9:7) and semantically (Acts 24:17) identified as a matter of mercy and a form of almsgiving. The recipients of this gracious sharing and generosity are the immediately poor (Rom 15:25–27; compare 2 Cor 9:12) among the remote believers of Judea. The two collections affirm that when the cause of believers' immediate poverty is either general calamity (like the famine of Acts 11:28–30) or general economic hardship, even remote believers are to participate in the alleviation of these needs. This extension of obligation to remote believers is logical because, under such circumstances, it is unlikely that local believers would be adequately well off in sufficient numbers to assist their local needy brethren without themselves becoming immediately poor. Thus the surplus of the remote believers is to mercifully provide for the lack among the immediately poor of Judea during their distress. And reciprocity among believers may be expected (2 Cor 8:14).[7]

High Obligation Mandates

James 2:14–17 and 1 John 3:16–18, along with Matt 25:31–46, reveal that helping an immediately accessible and immediately poor believer with his or her immediate sustenance needs, particularly in terms of food and clothing, is a matter of very high obligation.[8] In both James 2 and 1 John 3 the respective writers have demonstrated that they have no inhibitions in calling a spade a spade and sin a sin—and that they will do so in order to make their point come across as strong as possible. And yet when addressing the meeting of other believers' sustenance needs, such as when they are experiencing nakedness and lacking daily food (Jas 2:15–16), James talks about cultivating a useful living faith and John about loving with deeds rather than with mere lip service. We would expect sin language and a strong condemnation. But are only given an appeal to loving

---

7. While some disagreement exists concerning whether this reciprocity is to be taken in spiritual or material terms (if the need should arise), it is certainly possible to perceive the latter. See Garland, *2 Corinthians*, 384–85; Bernard, *The Second Epistle to the Corinthians*, 88.

8. While some argue that favorably receiving the believing messenger is in view in Matt 25:31–46 (as akin to some of the other receiving mandates), this supposition is not ultimately determinative because this postulated message acceptance is nonetheless manifest in meeting such a believing messenger's sustenance needs.

like Jesus did (1 John 3:16) and to demonstrating our living faith by our works (Jas 2:18).[9] Furthermore, mercy terminology surfaces in 1 John 3:17, where believers are mandated not to shut off their compassion, and in the serving terminology of Matt 25:44.[10] All these observables (along with parallels to the broader mercy of the good Samaritan) intimate that these high obligation mandates are nevertheless of a mercy level. And that they were understood to be so. They function nonetheless as a normative manifestation (Matt 25:31–46) of a living faith (Jas 2:14–17) and having the "love of God abide" in oneself (1 John 3:16–18). This mercy obligation to provide for the immediate sustenance needs of an immediately poor "brother or sister" (Jas 2:15), while not a matter of justice, is a natural and inalienable part of genuine faith and Christian love (1 John 3:16–18).

And so these mandates spotlight the normative deeds of love and faith. They highlight that our responsibilities, even though they be of a mercy status, increase with respect to aiding immediately present believers who are experiencing the specific lack of food and covering.[11] Believers with such needs have a prioritized entitlement to our merciful attention. Incidentally, having the "world's goods" (1 John 3:17) does not entail living in luxury but rather possessing *something* to live on (as in Mark 12:44).[12] All believers who are not immediately poor themselves, and therefore can help, are addressed by this mercy mandate. The needs of their brethren in this instance are indeed dire.

Work and the Proper Recipients of Giving

The aforementioned provision of pastoral support and a continuing involvement in sharing and almsgiving logically requires that non-pastoral believers engage in "secular" work. This implication is confirmed via the NT mandates concerning participation in legitimate employment. Acts

---

9. Our expected mimesis is also affirmed in 1 John 3:17. See Smalley, *1, 2, 3 John*, 197.

10. In referring to it as shutting off one's compassion, the KJV and NET capture John's reference to closing off one's inward parts (σπλάγχνον, *splanchnon*), the seat of compassion, very accurately. See R. Brown, *The Epistles of John*, 450; Smalley, *1, 2, 3 John*, 195–97; Akin, *1, 2, 3 John*, 160.

11. Food and covering are the lowest common denominator as 1 John 3:16–18 is somewhat undefined. The mandates of Matt 25:31–46 mark out a wider scope.

12. Smalley, *1, 2, 3 John*, 196.

20:33–35 connects not working for one's living to coveting the possessions of others and reveals that the indigent which are to be given aid (in the regular sense—when no general calamities intrude) are the non-able-bodied poor. This category of the weak includes the disabled, the diseased, and the feeble—all those who are impotent to work on physical grounds (those with mental handicaps are presumably included). This constraint, which is also echoed in 1 Thess 5:14, prevents the work mandates from undermining themselves in their aim to aid those with sustenance needs. This category of the weak is parallel to many of the immediately poor who are contextually related to the πτωχοί (*ptōchoi*) in the Gospels: the blind, the lame, the crippled, the diseased, the leprous, and the deaf. Such would have commonly experienced immediate poverty in the first century. Able-bodied believers are to give to (Acts 20:35) and share with (Eph 4:28) such non-able-bodied brethren out of what the able-bodied earn from their hard work (Acts 20:35).[13] Ephesians 4:28 asserts that this sharing is to be based on need and thus affirms that alleviating immediate poverty is in view. These work passages, when integrated, mandate providing for the immediately poor that are in need due to personal calamity. And so, for the able-bodied, seeking to work so as to be independent is correspondingly part of "behaving properly" (1 Thess 4:12) and not burdening others (2 Thess 3:8).

Additional resolution is provided in 2 Thess 3:6–15 which mandates that only the non-indolent ought to have their outstanding sustenance needs met by other believers. When work is available, those "not willing to work" (v. 10) are not to have their immediate sustenance needs met by brethren seeking to do good (v. 13). This mandated treatment confirms that sustenance assistance is not an inalienable right. When considered a right at all, it can most certainly be lost, or suspended, via indolence in the face of opportunity to work. But it is better still, in keeping with the NT data, to classify this provision of sustenance aid to non-indolent believers as a matter of mercy. For the sharing of sustenance with needy brethren is suggested to be of a mercy obligation level even within Acts 20:33–35, where it is related to blessing, and in 2 Thess 3:13 where it is identified as a higher resolution instance of doing good. The conceptual overlap with providing alms and, to an even greater degree, with the

---

13. By implication, non-able-bodied brethren are the primary beneficiaries of these work-to-share mandates. See Lincoln, *Ephesians*, 304.

sharing entailed in κοινωνία (*koinōnia*) also affirms that such help—even when it is to needy brethren—is a mercy.

Moreover, indolence even appears to be understood as an injustice toward others for it results in the consequence of being disassociated (2 Thess 3:6, 14) and is likewise included within what is apparently a sin list in Titus 1:12–13. And so providing help to the indolent is enabling injustice. Applying the resolution principle entails that the high resolution mandate of 2 Thess 3:6–15, to provide sustenance aid to only the non-indolent needy—those who cannot work so as to eat their own bread (vv. 8, 12)—is to inform the lower resolution mandates concerning providing for the immediately poor. Our present passage possesses the highest resolution as it incorporates both components: a call to help as well as mandates concerning when not to help. The other lower resolution passages only subsume the former component. This delimiting integration is not only driven by the entailments of the resolution principle but is likewise required to avoid contradiction. This passage, along with the parallel trajectories entailed in the mandates to work so as to provide aid to the physically weak, prescribes that only the non-able-bodied or non-indolent believer receive sustenance provision. And in most contexts—the non-exceptional ones—those legitimately not working were the non-able-bodied. If, however, the lower resolution mandates to give to believers experiencing sustenance needs were to be considered all-encompassing and unqualifiable, a contradiction would arise. Correspondingly, delimiting texts, such as 2 Thess 3:6–15, are the most apparent candidates for the application of the resolution principle. For it is the means whereby their detail can be preserved rather than suppressed.

The high obligation mandates entail providing, at minimum, food and covering to a starving and naked (γυμνός, *gymnos*) believer (Jas 2:15). The work mandates clarify that, even when lacking food (2 Thess 3:10), indolent believers in immediate sustenance need are not to receive sustenance assistance from their brethren. As such the work mandates clarify the sub-case of believer indolence—even in an otherwise high obligation context.

Integrating the NT data concerning giving to the poor results in the following set of contours. Giving alms and sharing is identified as a matter of mercy which consistently aims to alleviate the sustenance needs of those who are experiencing immediate poverty due to causes other than their own indolence. Generosity, like much of the higher resolution doing of good, has the same aim. Helping indolent believers is explicitly forbidden. It is one of Scripture's forbidden mercies. For it enables sin.[14] Though our giving is to be generous (Rom 12:8) and our κοινωνία (*koinōnia*) is to be a genuine form of fellowship that contributes "to the needs of the saints" (Rom 12:13), our mercy ends where indolence begins. Though we are to forsake alienation and even consider ourselves as "members one of another" (Rom 12:5; Eph 4:25) and even though the "love of God" does not abide in us if we do not meet the needs of our brethren when we can (1 John 3:17), indolence severs this assisting fellowship. The willfully indolent have no moral claim against believers. Not even to their mercy.

The proper recipients of giving are those who are non-able-bodied due to personal calamity, those who are in immediate poverty as a result of natural calamity (such as a famine) or general economic distress (such as with the main Jerusalem collection or a great depression), and those who are in immediate need due to injustice (such as in the parable of the good Samaritan).[15] These are the poor whom the NT mercy mandates aim to help—the non-indolent in sustenance need. For in all the passages that are non-ambiguous with respect to identifying their recipients, the recipients are consistently revealed to be the immediately poor (or those now becoming so). No non-ambiguous mandates are provided unto aiding those, believing or otherwise, who are not experiencing immediate poverty—or its imminent arrival. Thus Jesus' lending mandates (Matt 5:42 // Luke 6:29–30, 34–36) are, by all historical indications, intended to thwart the otherwise imminent fall of the potentially poor into immediate poverty. And the textual data concurs. Luke 6:34–35 testifies that the common expectation in lending was to secure the future benefit of being able to borrow in turn. Such a future benefit would only have

---

14. Both the indolence itself and its begotten sins such as busybody meddlesomeness and gossiping (2 Thess 3:11; 1 Tim 5:13).

15. Immediately needy brethren such as retirement-age widows (who have been left alone due to calamity or unjust forsaking), shelterless aliens, and the imprisoned are therefore also to be aided. Imprisoned brethren were very likely to be so due to injustice. Showing hospitality to traveling brethren and itinerant pastors and missionaries, while an important NT focus, participates in a slightly broader constellation of obligations than providing for the shelter needs of alien but needy believers. But the latter may be the contextual focus of Matt 25:31–46, and so its shelter mandate may be aimed at the immediately needy.

been of interest to those among the potentially poor majority. And could only be provided back by those who were themselves ordinarily—except for their present spiral into sustenance want—potentially poor. Thus this lending would have targeted the able-bodied who possessed a fair likelihood of rejoining the potentially poor after plowing through their present crisis. But Jesus ups the ante by calling His followers to extend their lending to even the bad prospects—such as their enemies. We may justifiably consider these intended recipients as among the immediately poor in the sense that, barring outside assistance, nothing else could now stop the imminent arrival of sustenance want—if it had not gripped them already. They were seeking to borrow precisely because it was now certain that they could no longer provide for all of their sustenance needs until the next harvest or payday.[16] And so, in the end, it is clarifiers concerning the support of widows (as in Acts 6:1; 9:36, 39–41) that comprise the only remaining mercy instances that are uncertain. Instances where the potentially poor *per se* might also be among the recipients. But the ambiguity of these few remaining passages is not sufficient to expand the NT focus away from aiding the immediately poor. We would need to possess a very good textual argument for allowing the ambiguous to qualify the consistent testimony of the clear. So which poor are we mandated to help? The non-able-bodied and the non-indolent who find themselves in immediate poverty as a result of calamity, economic distress (such as insufficient available work), and injustice. To borrow from the widow terminology of 1 Tim 5:3, 16, we are to assist those who are "poor indeed." These, along with those who are "widows indeed," are the proper recipients of our mercy.

Support of Widows

Supporting believing widows is another instance of specific help, akin to that entailed in the work mandates, but unto recipients of an even higher resolution. The daily provision of food to Christian widows (Acts 6:1) was the only other corporate ministry unto the poor that the nascent church engaged in beyond the distribution of proceeds to needy brethren.[17] Coming a little later on, 1 Tim 5:3–16 provides greater reso-

---

16. The possible call unto general reciprocity in Matt 5:42 would have benefited kin in the very same circumstances—those in the midst of their potential poverty degrading into immediate sustenance want.

17. The support of pastoral and missionary workers was not seen on the same terms

lution regarding the delimiting of those widows which are to receive the church's systematic corporate aid. An eligible widow had to be believing, "family-less," not self-indulgent, sixty or older, maritally faithful, and committed to serving other believers. Such a resourceless widow was a "widow indeed" and apparently became an intercessor or worker of the church—having taken a lifelong pledge of celibacy (vv. 11–12). It appears that she may have been supported by living with other church members on a rotational basis (v. 13). In conceptual agreement with 2 Thess 3:11, such supported widows had to be careful to flee idleness (1 Tim 5:13). Only believing, retirement age widows without other means of support were to receive this corporate aid as, whenever possible, "the church must not be burdened" (1 Tim 5:16). Consequently, the resolution principle affirms that the corporate church support of widows was intended to be significantly delimited to meeting the sustenance needs of resourceless widows who were known for service. Widows not fulfilling the stipulated requirements were not to be helped in this corporate church manner—a helping which is implied to be a matter of mercy.

Aside from this corporate support, Jas 1:27 mandates individual assistance to widows and orphans in their distress—this assistance certainly entailed meeting immediate needs and perhaps implied the meeting of their protection needs. The provision of clothing, as exemplified by Tabitha (Acts 9:36, 39–41), similarly appears to have been of individual persuasion as no corporate delegation is intimated in the text. Such aid on Tabitha's part is semantically identified as an act of mercy.

Helping Unbelievers

One important "near field" extrapolation—or perhaps logical implication—deserves our attention even now. Believers experience a particularly high mercy obligation to aid other immediately accessible believers who are in immediate need of food and clothing (and possibly other needs such as shelter). It is normative for Christians, if they are however able, to help, at minimum, such an immediately accessible fellow believer if he is not indolent. For such indolence would have already resulted in a break of fellowship with the indolent believer. And this "disfellowshipping" would have meant that he no longer had access to

---

for it was understood as wages due for services rendered. As such, this support was not identified as a component of providing for the immediately poor.

the assistive benefits of the believing community. Because believers have a higher obligation to the "household of the faith" (Gal 6:10), if even fellow believers—those with whom believers are "members one of another" (Rom 12:5; Eph 4:25), to whom the sharing of κοινωνία (*koinōnia*) is enjoined, and to whom they have the highest levels of mercy obligation (Matt 25:31–46; Jas 2:14–17; 1 John 3:16–18)—are not to be aided in their indolence, it is enormously improbable that indolent unbelievers are intended to receive such sustenance aid.

Still, the NT data does mandate the doing of good to both believers and unbelievers (Gal 6:10). This ends up being related to giving to those who ask—at minimum in terms of lending to those spiraling into immediate poverty even when they cannot or will not out of hostility return the favor (Matt 5:42 // Luke 6:30, 34–35). It also includes providing food and clothing to those who have none (Luke 3:11). Even enemies are to receive sustenance provision when in immediate need of food and drink (Rom 12:20). These mandates, which include unbelievers as part of their recipient set, are identified as matters of mercy whenever their obligation level is specified. Nevertheless as we have noted, the application of the resolution principle, and the logic of believers possessing a greater obligation to fellow believers, entails that such immediately poor are not to be helped if their poverty arises out of their own unwillingness to participate in work.

DOMAIN OF JUSTICE

So what do our comprehensive constraint obligations encompass? The domain of the NT justice mandates concerning the moral treatment of the immediately and potentially poor encompasses four main areas of emphasis. We will progress through these from the wider-reaching emphases toward those specifically unto the poor *qua* poor. The first two emphases, pastoral support and family responsibility, are somewhat exceptional because they are bound up with the special role of their recipient. It is best to get these two "mixed" obligations out of the way first. The following emphasis is on general justice and oppression and, as such, subsumes the general justice obligations concerning non-work, satiation, partiality, and covetousness.[18] The final emphasis is our long sought prize—the special obligation of social justice.

---

18. The terminology of "general justice," as it is being used here, refers to the set of

Pastoral Support

Pastoral and missionary support continues throughout the NT on the basis of Jesus' assertion that His ministry workers are worthy of their support (τροφή, *trophē*, Matt 10:10). Thus 1 Cor 9:14 confirms that "the Lord directed those who proclaim the gospel to get their living from the gospel." Paul further identifies such support as a matter of justice in 1 Cor 9:4–18—for pastoral and missionary workers have a right (ἐξουσία, *exousia*, vv. 4, 6, 12, 18) to their support. First Timothy 5:17–18 asserts that, while those who are widows indeed are to be honored with church support, the elders "who rule well" and "who work hard at preaching and teaching" are "worthy of double honor" (v. 17). This mandate unto pastoral support is likewise framed out of Jesus' assertion that "the laborer is worthy of his wages" and additionally supported by the OT mandate against muzzling a threshing ox (v. 18).[19] The recipients of this corporate support are the ruling elders, especially those engaged in preaching and teaching, and non-tent-making itinerants and missionaries (1 Cor 9:4–11). The extent of the support is not clarified except that it should provide for the worker's sustenance needs (τροφή, *trophē*, Matt 10:10) to the extent that he may "refrain from working" in additional employment (1 Cor 9:6) and still be able to support his family (1 Cor 9:5).[20]

Sometimes, as with Jesus and His disciples during His ministry and in Paul's missionary efforts, such pastoral workers also experience immediate poverty. But normatively, this is not to be the case. Furthermore, receiving their "wages" (Luke 10:7) is not reckoned a matter of justice on account of their experiencing any such need. Rather it is reckoned on account of their labor in ministry.

Family Responsibility

Jesus' fiery rebuke of the Pharisees and scribes in Matt 15:3–9 and Mark 7:9–13 asserted that honoring one's parents involved helping to take care of them, provided they needed such care, presumably when they

---

preceptive justices that nevertheless are not "special obligations" aimed uniquely at the poor. This will be the common usage throughout this chapter and the next.

19. This OT mandate, likewise appearing in 1 Cor 9:9, is connected to the benefit that the ox's owner receives when it is lent out to others in order to thresh their grain (Verbruggen, "Of Muzzles and Oxen," 699–711).

20. Normatively, each assembly is to provide the wages of its pastor or pastors (2 Cor 11:8).

are older. Failing to provide such assistance is identified as a transgression, παραβαίνω (*parabainō*), of the Law (Matt 15:3). First Timothy 5:4 subsumes taking care of one's widowed mother and grandmother under the mandate to make some return to one's parents. This assumes that such children are old enough to provide so as not to be classifiable as "orphans." It appears that widowers, by implication, had to work to provide for themselves if they had no offspring to assist them. Furthermore, 1 Tim 5:8 clarifies that failing to provide for one's own, especially for those of one's own extended household, constitutes denying the faith and being "worse than an unbeliever."[21] And 1 Tim 5:15 reaffirms that even daughters, rather than merely sons, were responsible for assisting any widows which were dependent upon them. Consequently, providing for the immediately and potentially poor dependents (when they have need) in one's extended family is identified as a matter of justice. This mandate explicitly subsumes widows and dependent parents—particularly when they are aged. It is safe to assume that other dependents in the household, such as the handicapped, would attempt to offset this familial aid with their own begging (when from a non-wealthy family). It is also safe to assume that all who could work would—for it would be an injustice against the family not to do so. Interestingly, John Calvin argues that committing indolence is an injustice for all, even those who need not work to support themselves, while 2 Thess 3:10 only intimates that it is an injustice for those who would be supported by others.[22]

General Justice and Oppression

The NT texts affirm that general justice, the keeping of which benefits all persons, is to be kept for the sake of the poor and non-poor alike. This includes the proscription of murder, theft, defrauding, swindling, not repaying debts, bearing false witness, failing to pay employees, and unjust, judicially-enabled summary execution (Jas 5:1–6).[23] These in-

---

21. One's household was not limited to one's immediate family as presently understood in the West, but extended to parents and grandparents (who would have been cared for under the same roof). This understanding is required to maintain the logical force of Paul's argument here. See Lea and Griffin, *1, 2 Timothy, Titus*, 148; *contra* Knight, *The Pastoral Epistles*, 221; W. Mounce, *Pastoral Epistles*, 284.

22. Calvin, *Commentaries on the Epistle of Paul to the Philippians, Colossians, and Thessalonians*, 355.

23. There has been a renewed interest to also include the "injustice of domination" as a component of NT concern. See Stassen and Gushee, *Kingdom Ethics*, 360–61. But

justices can be summarized under the notions of murder, defrauding theft, and the false accusation of bearing a false witness. All of these may be transgressed against the poor—often with greater ease due to their vulnerability.

All of these general injustices can become matters of oppression in instances where one party is placed into a position of relative power whereby it can expect to overpower another party so as to prevent the securing of remedial justice for the former party's preceptive injustices. Oppression may thus be helpfully conceptualized as the use of entrusted or financial power to perpetrate injustice with virtual immunity. It refers to the injustice that one party can get away with due to its influence or occupation.

Within the NT, oppression (καταδυναστεύω, katadynasteuō) is mentioned by name, as it relates to interhuman treatment, only in Jas 2:6. In this verse the unbelieving rich are identified as those who have the power to oppress believers and personally drag them into courts where the oppressors will prevail. The withholding of pay from the hired workers of Jas 5:1–6 also appears to be an instance of oppression because the workers appear to have no recourse but to cry out to "the Lord of Sabaoth" (Jas 5:4). And so the oppressors will ultimately have the Lord of armies to deal with. The judicially enabled murder of the righteous man by the unjust rich in Jas 5:6 also bears the markings of oppression because the courts have permitted his condemnation and "he does not

---

the passages commonly cited to support this addition are unfortunately less than satisfying. For Jesus' conflicts with the Jewish religious leaders, while revolving around His authority, are ultimately tied up with His claims for Himself. The conflict arises because the religious leaders, in seeking to carry out their not illegitimate responsibilities, wrongly reject the rightful heir of the vineyard (and further transgress in how they seek to be rid of Him). Their authority, in itself, is not the focal issue in these texts—but rather their mistaken misuse of it. This misuse included the adding of the burdens of the Oral Torah (Matt 23:2–4; Luke 11:46). See Hagner, *Matthew*, 659. The other commonly referenced texts fare no better. For while beating other believers rather than serving them and living wildly (possibly at their loss and expense) is condemned (particularly for church leaders), few would argue that such violent mistreatment is not proscribed by general justice *itself* (here carried out as oppression: Matt 24:49 // Luke 12:45). Still the proper treatment of those over whom one has authority is commended in the very same texts (Matt 24:45–46 // Luke 12:42–43). Similarly, Jesus' remarks concerning giving to Caesar what is his, the poll-tax, do not clearly condemn the injustice of Roman domination. And so domination, particularly as general authority, does not receive as clear a NT challenge as is sometimes hoped.

resist."²⁴ Such oppression is hamartiologically identified as a matter of injustice in Jas 5:1–6. The smaller scale oppression of being defrauded by a tax collector is proscribed in Luke 3:12–13. Similarly, the oppression enabled by a soldier's occupation, the ability to extort and bear false witness in relative security, is likewise proscribed in Luke 3:14.

While noted briefly in the Widows Mandates section of the preceding chapter, the options for what the unjust devouring of widows' houses entailed must now needfully receive further attention. John Nolland contends that, of all the possible options, either inappropriate estate guardianship or the abuse of hospitality is most likely to be in view.²⁵ But being pressed into offering hospitality does not appear to the author as likely grounds for becoming insolvent—for if the widow did not have much, there would not be much to share.²⁶ It is apparently best to understand Jesus' mandate in terms of the inappropriate guardianship identified in *Gittin* 52a–52b of the Babylonian Talmud.²⁷ This defrauding of widows' estates is, at minimum, a matter of injustice ([Matt 23:14] // Mark 12:40 // Luke 20:47) and appears to have been carried out with the occupational privilege entailed in oppression.²⁸

If this interpretation is correct, this despoiling of a widow's property joins the above noted NT data as a form of oppression. These oppression mandates together form the boundaries of what may be identified as systemic sin toward the poor within the NT corpus. Revealingly, these institutionally-permitted transgressions contravene the prohibitions against murder, defrauding theft, and the bearing of false witness—proscriptions which benefit all persons generally. Consequently, the NT data does not support a notion of the hamartiosphere which entails non-volitional injustice. What about being a part of the system? The soldiers and tax collectors of Luke 3:12–14, while participating in the mainte-

---

24. Ralph Martin agrees that, as conceived in this passage, "the poor do not resist because they cannot" for "they are helpless" (Martin, *James*, 181–82).

25. Nolland, *Luke*, 976.

26. Becoming significantly indebted to neighbors in order to provide such hospitality, via the borrowing of foodstuffs, also seems unlikely.

27. Though this testimony is comparatively late, Duncan Derrett and Robert Stein agree that it is still to be preferred, and Joseph Fitzmyer is similarly inclined. See Derrett, "Eating Up the Houses of Widows," 1–9; Stein, *Luke*, 507; Fitzmyer, *The Gospel According to Luke*, 1318.

28. As noted earlier, Matt 23:14 is not found in the earliest manuscripts but is listed throughout merely for the sake of completeness.

nance of an occupational and often unjust regime, were not mandated to cease their involvement in this hamartiosphere but rather to desist from the concrete doing of injustice—the injustice over which they had control. All this is not to say that sin is not present in institutions or that "top management" and societal rulers do not choose injustice as a means and unjust goals as ends. But rather that each "cog" is responsible for their own sphere of activity. The forms of oppression mentioned in the NT texts are purposeful and intended. They are enabled by the privilege of occupation or the manipulative influencing enabled by wealth and, consequently, would not be achievable against the oppressor's peers. So such oppression is merely concrete injustice safely pursued from behind the protections of financial power and occupational privilege. And the poor are commonly the easiest targets.

Our integration of general justice and oppression reveals that oppressive injustice, as far as it is indicated in the NT, is not something systemically hidden from the obligator but rather concerns the protected transgression of clear justice obligations. The poor are easier to oppress but it is still a transgression of general justice—not a special obligation to the poor alone.

Non-Work

Several additional general justice mandates, which also apply toward our treatment of the poor, are noted in the NT. These mandates concern being able-bodied and unwilling to work, harvest time satiation, renouncing partiality, and forsaking covetousness.

Being unwilling to work, as has been noted, is likewise identified as an injustice against those who would be requested to support such indolence. Titus 1:12–13 mandates against indolent laziness and includes it among the sins of lying, evil viciousness, and gluttony. Correspondingly, indolence is to result in the consequence of being shamed and disassociated from fellow believers (2 Thess 3:14).

Satiation

The hand-picking of another's standing grain for the purpose of satiating one's hunger is not mandated but allowed by Jesus in the parallel texts of Matt 12:1; Mark 2:23; and Luke 6:1. This limited and labor-intensive pre-harvest meeting of a person's sustenance needs is accorded in Deut

23:24–25. This Deuteronomy mandate is a non-sanctional casuistic command and consequently its obligation status remains undisclosed. In any case, such labor intensive alleviation of hunger—which is most likely to benefit the poor at the outlay of wealthier landowners—is defended by Jesus in His Judean context. This satiation provision, despite its uncertain obligation status, entails that the hungry may satiate themselves (at a significant outlay of labor) in the brief window of time between the ripening and harvesting of the harvest.[29]

It is noteworthy that this OT satiation mandate is not limited toward the poor like the OT gleaning mandates were. Anyone, no matter their socioeconomic situation, could benefit from its provision. While its obligation status remains uncertain in both testaments by way of our semantic and hamartiological criteria, logical inference cautiously tilts the scales in favor of perceiving this as a justice matter. If such satiation was permitted, it would have been perceived as a right by the one passing through the field, and consequently as a provision of justice. It is for this reason that satiation cautiously appears here—under our discussion of justice. Nevertheless the window of opportunity was likely to be very limited for the landowners could harvest as soon as the produce was ripe.

Partiality

While many scriptural texts, including Jas 3:17, forbid partiality against anyone, Jas 2:1–12 specifically forbids partiality toward the rich at the expense of the immediately poor (v. 3). While the partiality proscribed here merely concerns displays of honor in the assembly, it is hamartiologically and semantically identified as the transgression of a justice level obligation. If even this is unjust and transgresses the royal law (Jas 2:4, 8–9), then any greater displays of partiality are all the more evil and guilt-worthy (vv. 4, 10). If anything, Scripture calls us to the mercy of the social inversion—of being most careful to serve even the least and to bestowing "more abundant honor" on those "we deem less honorable" (1 Cor 12:23). So as to elevate them to the same standard of treatment as the others naturally receive. The underlying concern for not showing partiality in the way the world does is nevertheless a matter of general

---

29. The wielding of a sickle as well as any gathering for later is specifically forbidden in Deut 23:24–25.

rather than social justice—for it is intended to benefit the poor and rich alike.[30]

Covetousness

Being greedy or covetous, like being unwilling to work, is identified as a cause for being disassociated from other believers (1 Cor 5:9–11). As noted earlier, Acts 20:33–35 relates these two injustices. The believer is to "beware, and be on . . . guard against every form of greed" (Luke 12:15). Jesus evaluates, on God's behalf, the rich man who stores up only for himself as a "fool" (Luke 12:20). To the extent to which avarice affects interhuman treatment it results in idolatrous injustice for it seeks to secure or withhold that which does not rightfully belong to it. The arrangements of 2 Cor 9:5 are intended to thwart the possible negative affects that avarice might play in the giving toward the Jerusalem collection. In this sense, the sin of covetousness can act in the opposite direction of the mercy of sharing with the immediately poor. As such, covetousness results in a form of "alienation" which hardens its host against the needs of the poor. But in addition to having an affect upon our willingness to engage in merciful aid to the immediately poor, covetousness also results in interhuman injustices such as rapacious swindling and defrauding. This unjust rapaciousness is a concrete and willed component of the hamartiosphere.

The Special Obligation of Social Justice

So to what extent is justice a function of need? Does the NT contain any mandates that are intended to benefit the poor *alone* and that are nonetheless identified as matters of justice? Or asked another way: what obligations rightfully belong to the domain of social justice?

The mandates that govern the proper use of wealth subsume Jesus' parable of the rich man and Lazarus (Luke 16:19–31).[31] This text identifies being rich and using one's surplus solely for the purpose of self-indulgence in the face of immediate, calamity-caused, non-able-

---

30. As in Lev 19:15—itself present at the initial bestowing of the royal law (in Lev 19:18).

31. While the parable of the rich fool within Luke 12:13–21 provides some somewhat ambiguous but suggestive background support for the parable of Lazarus, its mandate is nevertheless not clearly presented as benefiting the poor *alone*. And the same is the case with the parable of the unjust steward (Luke 16:1–13).

bodied poverty when the alleviation of the sustenance needs involved is a matter of donating one's scraps (v. 21)—as a matter of sin requiring repentance (v. 30).[32] The obligators of this justice mandate are the appreciably rich who habitually dress "in purple and fine linen, joyously living in splendor every day" (v. 19). This delimiting of the obligator set, aside from being an integral part of Jesus' mandate, is entailed by the resolution principle in integrating this text with Matt 25:31–46 (as well as the almsgiving mandates and the parable of the good Samaritan).[33] The parable of the sheep and the goats depicts the sharing of sustenance with those who are diseased and feeble (ἀσθενέω, *astheneō*, in Matt 25:36, 39 and ἀσθενής, *asthenēs*, in Matt 25:43–44), in a manner that is conceptually analogous to Luke 16:19–31, as a matter of mercy. At least as best as we can tell.[34] Consequently, a non-contradicting, resolution-based integration requires that Matt 25:31–46 be understood as communicating the mercy obligation level of such sustenance provision to obligators generally—and specifically to those who are not themselves appreciably rich. Said another way, the rich are obligated by a justice mandate which is superimposed on top of the generally applicable mercy mandate. This obligator-limiting integration similarly extends to all analogous mercy mandates, such as those entailed in the parable of the good Samaritan, which befittingly do not identify their intended obligator set as appreciably wealthy. The parable of Lazarus identifies a unique, ends-based justice level obligation which obligates those at the greater levels of wealth. The self-indulgent rich who behave analogously to the rich man in the parable of Lazarus rightly receive the warning woes of Luke 6:24—for they are presently receiving their "comfort in full" and can therefore expect no further comfort in the life to come.

32. As noted previously, Luke 16:20–21 reveals that the poor man was non-able-bodied for he was defenseless and had to be "laid," ἐβέβλητο, at the rich man's gate.

33. Methodologically put, in observing the present parable's conspicuous lack of fit within its helping category (due to its discordant level of obligation) it therefore becomes necessary to seek out what is uniquely different about its mandate in order to achieve non-destructive integration. And the only singular facet that is forthcoming is its explicitly pared domain of obligators.

34. Even if we were to consider Matt 25:31–46 to be an uncertain passage—one which does not fully identify its mandates as a matter of mercy—its overlaps with the sharing, receiving, and almsgiving passages would nevertheless still tip the scales in favor of perceiving the parable of the sheep and the goats as pertaining to mercy. And so, even if we prefer to keep Matt 25:31–46 neutral, our integration would merely be carried out in a wider circle.

Scholarly agreement affirms that Jesus' parable of Lazarus was intended as an additional response to the covetousness of the Pharisees "who were lovers of money" (Luke 16:14). Jesus had already condemned their greed as an abomination in the sight of God (Luke 16:15). For covetousness is always a sin. The parable of Lazarus clarifies that in the face of immediate, calamity-caused, non-able-bodied poverty, when the alleviation of the sustenance needs involved is a matter of donating one's scraps, for the rich not to do so is but a matter of greed. Under such circumstances, not providing sustenance aid from their castoffs is a sure matter of pure covetousness on the part of such rich. And so for rich obligators abounding in scraps, what is otherwise a matter of merciful almsgiving, becomes a matter of justice via the superimposition of another obligation—their obligation to avoid such pointless greed. For such rich, not being sinfully greedy means donating their leftovers.[35]

So the justice superimposition is that of avoiding a unique tangible instance of greed. But where do we draw this justice line—how rich do we have to be in order to be obligated? The purposeful contrast of the passage—between the desperate non-able-bodied poverty of Lazarus and the significant wealth of the rich man—can be perceived in three ways. Perhaps the contrast is intended to be that of *perception*—of highlighting that what "is highly esteemed among men" is nonetheless "detestable in the sight of God" (Luke 16:15). And so while the immediately poor are not esteemed among men (Prov 14:20, 19:4) this is nevertheless not their genuine evaluation before God. Or perhaps the contrast serves to underscore the appropriateness of the rich man's *punishment* and the poor man's ultimate comfort (Luke 16:25). But it is also possible that the contrast is a purposeful component of the passage's *mandate* intention.

---

35. While Bruce Malina reconstructs greed as the desire to increase one's wealth and accompanying status (at the perceived zero sum expense of others), all that the NT clearly conveys (beyond condemning rapaciousness and lusting after riches) is that greed entails having surplus and not giving anything away—not even donating one's scraps (Malina, *The New Testament World*, 97–99). Rather than depicting greed as any effort to earn some more financial resources than one was born into, the NT mandates target gaining *or* possessing wealth without putting *any of it* into "circulation" for the benefit of others (Luke 12:13–21; 16:1–13). For the rich could well lend to the potentially poor that are spiraling into immediate poverty, or act as patrons, or do some almsgiving (even though the parables of the rich fool and the unjust steward do not clearly delimit their intended recipients). Not providing one's scraps nevertheless remains the unambiguous summit of such greed. And the only mandate that incontrovertibly has the poor *per se* as its intended beneficiaries.

The passage itself supplies an emphasis on the appropriateness of the punishment and so it is best to recognize this as the main intent of the contrast employed. But the appropriateness of the punishment is nonetheless intricately tied up with the mandate itself—for it generates it. As such, the substantial wealth of the rich man is an integral constituent of the mandate.

But how are we to quantify this richness? In absolute or relative terms? What about in terms of non-alienation or *shalom*? In keeping with the argument of chapter 2, it is preferable to adopt an absolute quantification. It is certainly morally safer in any case. And so an absolute measurement of the rich man's wealth entails that those who can afford an ornate home (if the gate meant anything), the very expensive clothing brands, and to dine finely every day are obligated. The extent of those obligated by this justice mandate can similarly be identified as those who are wealthy enough to be able to provide for the immediate sustenance needs which exist in their immediate presence out of the scraps and leftovers which fall from their table—the food which "would have been thrown out anyway" or perhaps given to the dogs (Matt 5:27 // Mark 7:28).[36] For not donating such scraps and leftovers to the non-able-bodied in immediate poverty, when such poor are in the rich person's immediate vicinity, is a matter of injustice. And so while a relative understanding (when wedded to the very high end of the rich man's possible wealth) may tempt us to only obligate people such as King Bhumibol of Thailand, Queen Elizabeth II, Carlos Slim, and Bill Gates, an absolute, "scraps level," understanding extends much wider. Are we, as contemporary Westerners, as rich as the rich man? What amounted to being extraordinarily wealthy back in the first century is much more commonplace now. If we are enjoying a fine home, fine clothes, and fine food, our castoffs—to paraphrase Basil of Caesarea—belong to the poor.[37]

This absolute understanding is the safer one. We dare not gamble with God's possible recompense by opting for a relative quantification that would exclude all who are as wealthy as the rich man, in absolute terms, from obligation. But the practical issues involved quickly surface. If we happen to be this rich then we are obligated by justice to feed the calamity-caused, non-able-bodied immediately poor in our immediate

---

36. Bock, *Luke*, 1367; Nolland, *Luke*, 828–29.

37. Avila, *Ownership*, 66. Basil of Caesarea, also known as Saint Basil the Great, was a bishop in Caesarea in the fourth century.

vicinity. What if a larger number of them show up? Are we to provide until all of our scraps are gone or until we are not so appreciably rich? The passage would suggest that we are to give, at minimum, while we still have scraps. That distributing our castoffs is the confine of our justice obligation. This contextual delimitation dovetails very well with Paul's mandate to the rich to not "be conceited or to fix their hope on the uncertainty of riches" (1 Tim 6:17) but rather to "do good, to be rich in good works, to be generous and ready to share" (1 Tim 6:18). Since enjoying what God supplies is permitted (1 Tim 6:17), and Paul's mandate unto generous sharing is revealed to be a matter of mercy even for the rich (1 Tim 6:19), we can conclude that being ready to generously share one's goods is a mercy while withholding one's scraps is unjust greed. That social justice has a right to our castoffs.

EVALUATING THE CORE CONTENTION

The above integrated contours of NT obligation outline how we are to be just, merciful, and loving in our treatment of the poor. The only ruler related treatment discovered—outside the incidental condemnation of judicially enabled oppression—encompasses the noting of the satiation provisions of Deut 23:24–25. The hamartiosphere, as it is demarcated in the NT with respect to its effects upon the poor, was found to be composed of known and personally willed sins.

So how broad is the reach of social justice? To what extent is justice a regulator of means and to what extent is it a regulator of ends? Where is the proper locus of the applicability of justice? In evaluating this core contention it is necessary to isolate the justice mandates that are intended to benefit the poor *alone*.

As church support for pastors is not granted as a function of their possible poverty, this role dependent provision is not a matter of social justice. For it is rather a matter of the general justice of paying a worker his due wages. Providing old-age help to one's parents is also intertwined with their relational role. Rather than having such obligation extend to a whole category of obligators—as is normally the case—only relatives are constrained. So even other believers are not obligated to support your parents. As this significant obligator delimitation is distilled through specific relation ties, providing old-age help is not a matter of social justice. For society (and its members generally) is not obligated. The same can be said with respect to providing for the other dependents, whether young or non able-bodied, in one's extended household. Furthermore, matters of general justice and oppression were found to be, in either manifestation, issues of general justice. Consequently, the parable of Lazarus (Luke 16:19–31) furnishes the only mandate that is concerned with social justice. This unique instance mandates that the sufficiently wealthy donate their scraps to alleviate the sustenance needs of the calamity-caused, non-able-bodied poor within their immediate vicinity.

It is perhaps possible that this mandate unto the rich may be extrapolated beyond the personal calamity of disease and disability to encompass other calamity causes such as those noted in the almsgiving texts—general calamities such as famine as well as experiencing dependent widowhood. Similarly, vicinities have changed significantly since the first century—giving to the third world is now often as accessible as giving on our block. But the consideration of such extrapolations is best left for the next chapter.

Nonetheless we are left with precious little wiggle room for the justice obligation level of this mandate is hamartiologically revealed. Still Jesus' parable of Lazarus constitutes the sole *clear* instance of (non-familial) ends-based justice obligation within the NT. Under such conditions justice is concerned with the results of the game. In this constellation of rich obligators and non-able-bodied, immediately poor recipients, justice is a function of need. And so the covetousness of the rich in the face of such poverty transgresses the totality of social justice in the NT. All other assistance of the poor is a matter of mercy. Save the special justice obligation of familial assistance.[38] And justice, in all other instances but these two, is concerned with the means—the rules—of the game.[39]

As a result of our considerations, the relationship between need and obligation, in terms analogous to figure 1 of chapter 1, may be presented in the form of figure 6 below.

---

38. Familial assistance has already been identified as a unique case for it constrains only a limited few and its resulting provision is a matter of mercy for all the unrelated.

39. The only tentative exceptions are the parables of Luke 12:13–21 and Luke 16:1–13, where the breadth of recipients is regrettably uncertain—though the intended recipients are quite possibly the poor. Despite their taunting ambiguity, these parables should nonetheless remain in the back of our minds.

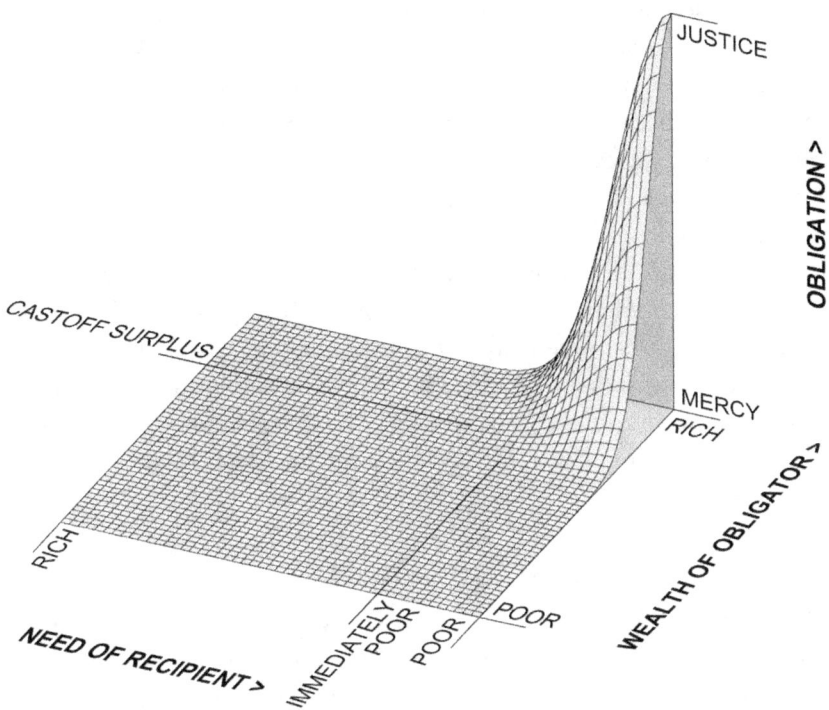

FIGURE 6: NT Justice as a Function of Need

Figure 6 portrays the NT relationship between mercy and justice unto the poor as a sloped step function. It affirms that justice, as it is delineated in the NT, is predominantly means-based except in the instance of the rich who are able to provide, out of their surplus scraps, for the sustenance needs of the readily accessible, calamity-caused, immediately poor. The special ends-based obligation of familial assistance is not represented here for it would require one more dimension and, more so, because it is not a matter of social justice.

All the other helping treatments of the poor are explicitly, semantically, or hamartiologically identified, whenever such identification is textually provided, as possessing the contingent obligation level of mercy. Whether the contribution is small or the proceeds of selling all of one's possessions, whether to believers or unbelievers, whether to local saints or remote ones, whether the cause of the poverty was calamity or general economic distress, all such assistance is a matter of mercy. Except in the case of the indolent—toward whom assistance is forbidden.

And so social justice is not after all a Siren or Medusa, but Helen of Troy. The sufficiently wealthy must provide their castoffs as a matter of social justice and those without such leftovers are called to merciful charity. And because social justice is a complimentary superimposition, both obligations levels can coexist without diluting or subverting each other. The strict libertarian and the strict egalitarian can buy each other a drink tonight.

But it is also noteworthy to reaffirm that in terms of charity's recipients, no explicit mandates were found for helping the potentially poor as such (and that the same is true with social justice). All non-ambiguous mandates identify their intended recipients as among the immediately poor (or the imminently so). And so the category of the potentially poor recedes from view as far as the helping mandates (and figure 6) are concerned.

EVALUATING THE RECENT THEOLOGICAL INFLUENCES

Now that the core contention has been evaluated, the additional key challenges raised by the more recent theological influences upon evangelical ethics may receive a brief NT evaluation as well. All three of these influences, in their own way and particularly in their own intended context, are certainly appealing.

Social Gospel

The main contentions raised by Rauschenbusch's social gospel concern the proper domain of the biblical concept of oppression and systemic evil, the isolation of its biblical remedies, and the clarification of whether notions of common property are subsumed under biblical justice.

The NT data identifies only a few instances of systemic evil and oppression. These instances of oppression are revealed to be merely matters of general injustice as safely pursued from behind the protections of financial power and occupational privilege. The identified oppressions may be subsumed under the general justice categories of murder, defrauding theft, and the bearing of false witness. In terms of greater detail, the textual instances refer to an oppressive abuse of the judicial system (Jas 2:6), defrauding hired workers of their pay (Jas 5:4), the committing of judicially-enabled murder (Jas 5:6), defrauding during tax collection (Luke 3:12–13), as well as extortion and false accusation (Luke 3:14).

The defrauding of a widow's property also appears to be a matter of oppression ([Matt 23:14] // Mark 12:40 // Luke 20:47). The NT data does not entail or support any notion of a hamartiosphere which consists of non-volitional injustice—where one is guilty merely by association (Luke 3:12–14). The forms of oppression identified within the NT texts are revealed to be purposeful and intended. This communicated domain does not incorporate notions of corporate responsibility but rather communicates that individuals are responsible for the evil that they personally will against those who are vulnerable before them.

Accordingly, the NT response to such oppression includes the assertion of mandates to cease and desist from participating in such injustice (Luke 3:12–14) as well as warnings concerning divine recompense upon the oppressors (Jas 5:1–6; [Matt 23:14] // Mark 12:40 // Luke 20:47). Furthermore, believers are perhaps mandated to bear up under theft and defrauding (in Luke 6:29) and even commended for joyfully accepting the seizure of their property (Heb 10:34). These acceptance mandates do not serve to diminish the sinfulness of oppression but reveal that seeking mutual Christian support (Heb 10:34) rather than vengeance upon one's legitimate enemies (Rom 12:17–21; Matt 5:43–45) is understood to be the path of Christian obedience. Particularly when justice cannot be secured.[40]

The NT data concerning common property reveals that the sharing pursued in the nascent church of Acts, and likewise during the Jerusalem collection, is not a matter of justice but rather mercy. This merciful sharing was furthermore intended to voluntarily "shave off" the surplus of comparatively well-off brethren for the sake of meeting the immediate poverty needs of other believers. It was not intended to produce the equality of uniform distribution, but rather the "equality" of enabling the immediately poor to have their needs met. In addition, 2 Thess 3:6–15 mandates that indolent believers were not to be included in any such sharing. While joyfully used for the common good, Judean believers still owned their possessions and properties—at least until they perchance chose to sell them and donate the proceeds to the church.[41]

---

40. When it can, there is nothing wrong with seeking it (Acts 16:35–39). With the caveat that believers are to have their mutual disputes settled before believers alone (1 Cor 6:1–8).

41. The collectivization of labor, "the means of production," and natural resources is not addressed.

Liberation Theology

Liberation theology, particularly Gutiérrez's formulation of it, raises three additional but nevertheless key contentions. These main emphases concern the preferential option for the poor, the delineation of the domain of unjust alienation, and ascertaining whether all of the poor are necessarily so due to oppression.

James 2:5 is perhaps the only clear articulation of a preferential option for the poor in the NT—for Luke 6:20 is explicitly directed at Jesus' possessionless disciples—and it is certainly the only one past Jesus' earthly ministry. But even it speaks in terms of allotted faith—in terms of divine favor rather than in terms of generating an interhuman mandate. Quite on the contrary. For it is given in the context of mandated impartiality (Jas 2:1–12)—where it is purposefully intended to reinforce the mandate that no distinctions are to be made among ourselves (v. 4). To hammer home that interhuman preferentiality (προσωπολημψία, *prosōpolēmpsia*, v. 1, προσωπολημπτέω, *prosōpolēmpteō*, v. 9) is vehemently forbidden.[42] So while God, in terms of electing unto faith, is "impartially partial," believers, for their part, carry out no such function.[43] And so, despite Gutiérrez's advocations, God's preferential option of Jas 2:5 does not furnish an interhuman partiality mandate. Our special obligations and our unique, poor-focused charitable concerns are driven by other passages (such as the parable of Lazarus and Jesus' calls to serve the least). By an impartially partial commitment to meeting sustenance needs.

In terms of unjust alienation, the NT affirms that covetousness, insatiability, avarice, and rapaciousness are indeed matters of sinful injustice. Such alienation, when it affects interhuman treatment is a matter of transgressing a justice level obligation. Thus defrauding, swindling, withholding one's scraps, giving away *nothing*, and being unwilling to work are related to the injustice of covetous greed. Nevertheless generosity, the polar opposite of covetousness, is revealed to be a matter of mercy—even when it is extended to the immediately poor who are so due to hav-

---

42. The OT antecedent to this impartiality is found very near to the source of James' "love your neighbor" quotation (Jas 2:8 from Lev 19:18). And it too affirms bidirectional interhuman impartiality—for in our judgments we must "not be partial to the poor nor defer to the great" (Lev 19:15).

43. Miroslav Volf is hugely perceptive in expressing God's fair favoring in this way (Volf, *Exclusion and Embrace*, 222).

ing suffered calamity, economic distress, or injustice. Consequently, the NT data suggests that the justice domain of alienation, as it is proposed by Gustavo Gutiérrez, is too broad. The NT does not affirm that all forms of alienation are themselves unjust for even the mutuality of Christian κοινωνία (*koinōnia*) is identified as a matter of mercy. Furthermore, 2 Thess 3:6–15 even mandates alienation from immediately poor believers whenever this poverty is caused by their own indolence. Providing care for the unrelated poor, in all circumstances but those described in the parable of Lazarus, is a matter of mercy. Consequently Gutiérrez's contention, that failing to provide such care is a manifestation of sinful alienation, is contradicted by the NT data. Due to Gutiérrez's emphasis on alienation, he contends that sin is systemically pervasive and must never be perceived as solely privatized. The NT, in all its concerned texts, as has been noted, is at odds with this conclusion. So in summary, the NT domain of unjust alienation is limited to concrete sins such as covetousness—including the injustice decried in the parable of Lazarus. Beyond familial responsibility, this domain does not clearly extend its reach to any other provision of aid to the poor.

Gutiérrez's blanket identification of the poor with the oppressed is also difficult to maintain in light of the NT data. While his setting makes such a focus readily understandable, it nevertheless remains at odds with the textual witness. Second Thessalonians 3:6–16 mandates, for example, that those who are in immediate need due to indolence are not to be treated like those who are unjustly imprisoned or mistreated (Heb 13:3). The NT data also affirms that calamity, personal as well as general, can result in poverty. Furthermore, even in the parable of the good Samaritan, mercy rather than justice is at stake in responding to the (not strictly oppressive) injustice that had already taken place. Oppression is not the only forwarded cause of sustenance need. But Gutiérrez's strategy in identifying the poor with the oppressed is intended to increase the obligation level of all those participating in the hamartiosphere—at least in his conception of it. For if all poverty is due to oppression, and everyone plays a part in this oppression, then everyone is obligated at a justice level of obligation to assist the poor (as a matter of remedial justice). As a result of this move, not only is the set of those classically referred to as the "undeserving poor" completely emptied, as all of the poor are automatically reclassified as "deserving," but the communicated obligation level of the mercy mandates unto helping the poor is automatically overridden—in defiance of the biblical text.[44]

Sustenance Rights

Are Wolterstorff's three duties—to avoid depriving people of sustenance, to help protect the vulnerable from such deprivation, and to sustain the victims if deprivation does occur—matters of justice obligation? Because Wolterstorff considers all practicable aspects of helping the poor as matters of justice, except perhaps when the poor are indolent in the face of "decent" work, these three duties are intended to cover the breadth of our moral treatment of the poor.

Wolterstorff frames his first duty, to avoid depriving people of sustenance, in active terms. His assertion that the objective victimization of the poor is a matter of justice is most certainly supported by the NT data. His second duty, to help protect the vulnerable from sustenance deprivation, is not well attested within the NT corpus—as either a justice or a mercy. Wolterstorff frames this second duty in structural terms and thus would suggest that influencing unjust structures is a matter of justice obligation. While Jesus and James speak out on behalf of the oppressed, it is unclear whether the trajectory of such engagement is a matter of justice or mercy obligation. Because no NT mandates are attested in this regard, the justice or mercy nature of this second duty remains uncertain. Wolterstorff formulates his third duty, to sustain the victims of deprivation, in very broad terms. He argues that the provision of sustenance, except perhaps when the poverty is caused by indolence, is "not an issue of generosity" but rather a matter of justice obligation.[45] Correspondingly, he considers those who do not receive sustenance as having been unjustly deprived.[46] By way of evaluation, except in the unique instance of the mandate contained in the parable of Lazarus, helping the poor in the NT (when they are not of one's household) is textually revealed to be a matter of mercy rather than justice obligation. Consequently, Wolterstorff's third duty is, for the most part, contradict-

---

44. At least since the sixteenth century, the "deserving poor" has referred to those who were to receive help while the "undeserving poor" has referred to those who were not to be helped for fear of enabling their indolence (akin to the differentiation mandated in 2 Thess 3:6–15). See also Richards et al., *Helping the Poor*, xxv, 151–83.

45. Wolterstorff, *Until Justice and Peace Embrace*, 82.

46. Ibid., 85.

ed by the textual data. For it only extends to the castoffs of the wealthy and to familial assistance. The testimony of 2 Thess 3:6–15 furthermore confirms that in the case of indolence even the remaining obligations entailed by merciful charity are annulled.

With the contours of NT obligation behind us, how are we now to proceed in making textually informed extrapolations? The following chapter will, in its pursual of practical implications, take up these issues.

SEVEN

Drawing Conclusions, Sketching Extrapolations

SO WHAT HAVE WE done? Our hands are covered with the blood of our nighest presuppositions. We have shaken our fist not at heaven but at ourselves. The passage level *discrimen* has whittled down our particularities—the same, variously conditioned particularities that we needed to publicly expose in order to begin our premeditated malefaction against them. We have found our nerve. Building on the assumption that, methodologically, determinism is preferable to indeterminism, we melted down our plowshares and forged the resolution principle. And this resolution principle allowed passages containing greater detail to stream this detail to passages possessing a lower level of resolution so that we could avoid contradiction within our process of data integration. We have been cold and calculating—we have shamelessly spotlighted *how* we have come to identify various biblically mandated treatments as matters of justice or not. And we heartily recommend such full disclosure to others.

Our driving intention was to uncover our comprehensive constraint obligations. So what have we discovered? What does the NT mandate regarding our moral treatment of the poor? That social justice is Helen of Troy. That a great deal of breathing room has been left for charity beyond the distributive justice mandated in the parable of Lazarus. Indeed, this mandate, located in Luke 16:19–31, is the sum content and complete delineation of NT social justice. Jesus thereby constrains the appreciably rich to donate their scraps to alleviate the sustenance needs of the non-able-bodied immediately poor found within their immediate vicinity. Dealing justly with our scraps is not out of our reach. Mennonite Gleaners Societies gather unharvested and blemished foodstuffs—what is either not economically profitable to harvest or cannot be sold—and dehydrate and ship this sustenance to the developing world. While this provision does not fully mirror the gleaning mandates of the OT—where the able-bodied poor gleaned the most difficult portions of the harvest at a great expenditure of their own effort—it does embody the concern for justly distributing our castoffs. We will critically reengage the breadth of our individual responsibilities in this important regard when we turn our full attention to extrapolation.

While this is where NT social justice ends its domain, one other instance of helping the poor is identified as a matter of justice level obligation. Providing for the possible needs of those in one's extended household, such as one's aged parents, is also comprehensively required. This familial assistance, while also ends-based, is relationship dependent and hence not a matter of social justice. For the members of society at large are not constrained. For it is not a matter of justice on the basis of the need *alone* but rather on the basis of the familial relationship. So only a limited few are constrained by this justice obligation and the resulting provision is a matter of mercy for all the unrelated. And so the parable of Lazarus and familial assistance is the extent to which justice is a function of need within the NT—but with the latter piety not being a function of need alone. This is the end of comprehensive constraint—what we are unrelentingly obligated toward by justice.

And the remainder is charitable mercy. The remaining mandates to help the poor all find their home here.[1] While this is where mercy begins, there is nevertheless also a place where mercy ends. For we are mandated not to engage in forbidden mercies. For we are only to give to the non-indolent immediately poor—the "poor indeed." I recognize that this calls some of our aid into question. Particularly our indiscriminate handouts. But then our complaint is with the biblical mandates. For Scripture is "uncompassionate" when it comes to enabling injustice. When it comes to encouraging sin. And, when we think about it ethically, it is hard not to come to agree that this is how it should be. And so, in terms of the psychological models of helping and change, the NT

---

1. And it is helpful to remember that this demarcation of obligation levels was inspired under comparatively much direr circumstances than what the developed world presently experiences. That it was given in a context where the livelihood of the potentially poor majority was perpetually precarious—where slipping into immediate poverty was ever one small-scale financial setback away (Harland, "The Economy of First-Century Palestine," 521). And yet assisting the poor even under such desperate circumstances is not—except for the rich abounding in scraps—disclosed as a matter of justice.

data affirms the Existentialist and Behavioralist approaches to behavior modification by mandating both reproof and consequences for indolent behavior—for living in a disorderly manner.² For love, in its purposive sense, requires seeking the other's good. It requires the seemingly arrogant but biblically furnished disclosure of knowing what the other's good is. It requires recognizing, perhaps reluctantly, that enabling able-bodied indolence is not for the other's good. That, despite how good it can personally make us feel, such enabling is not love but harming. For love always means aiming at the other's benefit rather than assuaging our own guilt or placating our own psychological needs. For the latter is merely sinful self-love in the self-centered, φίλαυτος (philautos), sense that we are generally warned against (2 Tim 3:2).

Still, we will briefly consider some of the complicating cases when we turn to extrapolation. For now it is sufficient to conclude this summary of our obligations by noting that addressing the tangential fallout of experiencing need—the side effects that are nonetheless not the need itself—is in one instance identified as an issue of general justice. So while mitigating the tangential side effects of poverty is generally, if anything, a mercy matter—one which is not distinctly mandated in the NT—showing impartiality in allotting respectful treatment is nevertheless a matter of general justice.³ Thus demonstrating favoritism toward the non-poor or treating the non-indolent poor disfavorably, even in terms of showing mere signs of respect, is a transgression of general justice.⁴ While people are much more prone, due to self-interest, to disrespect the poor than the rich, this mandate nonetheless remains a subset of our general justice obligation to impartiality. If anything, believers are to pursue the polar opposite—the inversed favoring of mercifully allocating more honor and concern to those the world considers the unseemly

---

2. And these shunning and shaming consequences were of a very serious nature within their more communal cultural context. Indeed, this is the greatest punishment mandated for believers to carry out within the NT. Its sting would have been greater than just the loss of the sustenance provision.

3. The call to receive and serve the least may entail treating the poor in a way that is above what their worldly status demands—and so, in this respect, it mitigates the low esteem that they generally receive. Still the overt emphasis of these mandates nevertheless remains on willfully taking upon oneself a comparable status so as to serve the socially lowly as one who is below them. The focus is on the lowering.

4. The indolent on the other hand—especially when they be believers—are to be shamed, not associated with, and admonished (2 Thess 3:14–15).

Drawing Conclusions, Sketching Extrapolations 279

and the least. For in this way our natural tendencies toward partiality and social ranking will be counterbalanced so that we may come to have a genuinely equal concern for one another (1 Cor 12:25). For us, there are to be no outcasts—no Dalits or Burakumin.

IMMEDIATE PRACTICAL IMPLICATIONS

So what does this NT synthesis of our justice and mercy obligations provide for us? Some firm bearings for mapping a way out of the theological impasse over social justice. Some biblical incitement to be able to resist tempting but forbidden treatments. And some immediate practical repercussions beyond uncovering our comprehensive constraint. To these immediate aftershocks we now turn.

Help Competition

For the sake of continuity it is preferable to consider these implications—one at a time—in the order in which they were originally raised in the Introduction. The first of these concerns help competition. Wherever a multiplicity of Christian helping ministries exists, developing agreement around the NT mandate to not provide help to the able-bodied but willfully indolent—those for whom such provision would discourage change—would eliminate help competition in its most undermining sense. A common stance against indiscriminate handouts, among individual believers and their helping ministries, is a worthy aim.[5] One which the NT enjoins. While some such agreement may still allow for assistance that ties skill development and lifestyle change to its receipt—

---

5. This goal surfaces some practical issues that are beyond our present scope. It may nonetheless be helpful to note briefly the main concern. Where beyond enfeebling physical and mental disability do we draw the line regarding the non-able-bodied? What about psychological issues? Especially ones which are the results of inflicted injustice? What about those who have been victims of debilitating abuse? Unlike with physical and mental disability, the NT contains no plain mandate to aid such. But perhaps these too may be considered as part of the weak—though, it is to be steadfastly hoped, only transiently so. Praxis-wise, victims of significant abuse are, for the most part, readily distinguishable along the spectrum of those who merely aim to have others support them in their indolence and those who are so traumatized as to be enfeebled. Such high degrees of trauma are difficult to counterfeit convincingly. It is not difficult to feel empathy here. And so the practical boundary of the non-able-bodied may perhaps be temporarily stretched to assist the victims of obvious mental trauma so long as the help offered aims to address the debilitation and does not support indolence via enabling such victims to become more self-supporting.

such constructive help is itself beyond what is mandated within the NT. It is not a manner of mercy to which believers are called. This may initially appear surprising, but with no safety net in place, the NT mandates a focus on engaging more pressing needs—those of the non-indolent. So help toward lifestyle change remains beyond the call of the NT, and it may be, as we consider extrapolation, that other unfulfilled involvements—whenever practical limitations make them mutually exclusive—may take precedence over this unmandated manner of helping.

All such reduction of help competition—any commitment to collectively shun indiscriminate handouts—any such common stance is dependent on acknowledging that feeding the able-bodied indolent is not a matter of social justice. Or of any form of scriptural justice. Even the scrap-laden rich are to aid the non-able-bodied.[6] Such aid can be withheld from the indolent specifically because providing it is not a matter of constraining justice. And so, as far as ethics is concerned, the indolent cannot demand anything of believers—and withholding assistance is not merely another manner of thinly veiled oppression. It is not a manner of structural evil or even bitty patronizing. Nor even a matter of legitimate mercy—for it is forbidden.

Because helping the indolent is not a matter of justice, not doing so is guilt-free. The only guilt that may be found is rather in providing handouts to the able-bodied indolent for such enables injustice—the coveting and wanting of what belongs to others and of enabling busybody-ness and gossip. Believers are to assist the "poor indeed" and it is precisely this ethical agreement that permits meaningful cooperation to exist among Christian ministries.

Help Prioritization

The disambiguation of the domains of justice and mercy also allows us to prioritize our treatments of the poor. When limited resources force on us mutually exclusive choices over how and where to help, doing justice must take precedence. Two justice mandates, which are not likely to come into conflict amongst themselves, are enjoined upon us. Providing for our aged parents, should they come into need, as we provide for

---

6. Attempts to extrapolate the parable of Lazarus to encompass even the able-bodied indolent among its rightful recipients appear rather infelicitous. How are we to reconcile a forbidden mercy becoming a demanded justice? When even the lower obligation is proscribed, why would we consider the higher one to be enjoined?

other dependents within our family is demanded by justice of all their grown descendents.[7] Furthermore the parable of Lazarus constrains the rich to donate their scraps to the non-able-bodied immediately poor within their immediate vicinity. It is not necessary to ponder the precise prioritization of these two justice mandates for, as mentioned, they are very unlikely to conflict. It is no great task for the rich to help their aged forbearers. They can easily afford to do so and still give their scraps away to the non-able-bodied poor in immediate need around them. Still, the conglomerate precedence of these two mandates matters. For fulfilling these two justice obligations is required of us before we may turn our attentions to any mercy. This means, for example, that the rich must help these poor from their scraps before pursuing other beneficent involvements. That the immediately needy non-able-bodied around them are to be fed from their castoffs in precedence over their dogs—or even other people's dogs. That the rich cannot permit themselves to become too involved in some patronage at some community or service club organization so as to not give their foremost attention to this justice requirement. Such is the nature of justice.

What comes next after our justice obligations? The mandated mercies that the NT enjoins upon us. By this I mean those that are mandated at a higher than impetus resolution—and particularly the specific and concrete ones. All things being equal—and we will allot some brief attention to possible sources of inequality below—mandated mercies take priority over the unmandated. For these mercies are what the NT explicitly emphasizes and calls believers to.

Some of these mandated mercies seem to take precedence over the rest by communicating a very high level of mercy obligation. Whenever we come across an immediately present believer in dire and urgent sustenance need—at minimum one lacking clothes and daily food—it is *normative* for us to provide merciful aid if we are however able (Jas 2:14–17; 1 John 3:16–18; Matt 25:31–46). Showing such mercy is just something that genuine believers do.

The most structured of the mandated mercies that remain is the mandate to provide for those who are "widows indeed." The delimiting

---

7. Not even Corban—a vowed prioritization of giving to God—is permitted to override this assistive aspect of honoring one's parents (Mark 7:9–13). Even in the case of needy widows, the church should not be burdened when children or grandchildren are available to provide (1 Tim 5:4, 8, 16).

of this mandate to care for worthy *believing* widows is permitted precisely because it is a matter of mercy rather than justice. It is not unjust of believers to provide for these widows alone.

Mercy is likewise mandated toward the non-able-bodied. The handicapped, the physically weak, the diseased, and the unjustly clobbered to physical incapacitation are to receive the merciful assistance of non-rich able-bodied believers as well. The able-bodied are to work so that—avoiding immediate poverty themselves (1 Thess 4:11–12)—they can share what they earn and give alms. Here too believers are called to assist other believers first. But the parable of the good Samaritan and the almsgiving mandates reveal that this mercy is not limited to benefitting believers alone—a topic that we will return to shortly.

But before we do so, one other group of recipients deserves note for they too are to benefit from the mercy mandates. The immediately poor who are brought to this state by way of an economic depression, a lack of available work, famine, or persecution (Heb 13:3) are to likewise receive assistance from even non-rich believers. Though the emphasis of the NT with respect to these causes is predominantly upon believers helping remote believers (the Jerusalem collections), the Jerusalem church furthermore provided such aid to its local believers (from the proceeds of land sales such as that of Barnabas). The concern for aiding the persecuted and imprisoned in Heb 10:32–34 and Heb 13:3 is likewise directed toward local believers.

These three "less dire" subcategories of mandated mercy, differentiated by the causal circumstances of their respective recipients, are difficult to place in a more precise prioritization on the basis of the textual data. It is hard to say which subcategory, if any, should take precedence in our pursuit of doing mercy. Perhaps the corporately structured mandate toward those who are "widows indeed" is to take pole position here. They and their orphaned children certainly ride shotgun in Jas 1:27.[8] Furthermore, such an emphasis would carry over rather well the established OT priority to be concerned to provide for them and landless aliens. With Gentiles no longer being landless in Israel during NT times (Matt 8:8 // Luke 7:6; Acts 10:28), perhaps widows and their children remain the contracted version of this OT prioritization.[9] Still

---

8. As previously noted, in Scripture, the fatherless are appropriately considered as orphans for they too suffer from the loss of the primary provider.

9. Jack Pastor provides additional treatment of Gentile land ownership during this era (Pastor, *Land and Economy in Ancient Palestine*, 100–102).

the otherwise poor do sometimes occur along with widows and orphans in the OT recipient lists—as in Job 31:16–17, 32, and Zech 7:10. Also sometimes included is the daily wage earner (שָׂכִיר, *sakir*, in Mal 3:5 and Deut 24:14–17) who is potentially poor but with the prospect of experiencing immediate poverty if not paid at the end of the workday (Deut 24:15). And so while a tendency may be perceived, it is still hard to elicit from it a firm prioritization—particularly within the bounds of the NT. So thus far into our consideration—it appears best to deem the various "less dire" subcategories of the mandated mercies as generally equal in priority.

It seems helpful at this point to turn back and consider the extent or non-extent to which believers become the delimited recipients or obligators of the mandated justices and mercies of the NT. The justice mandate to care for one's aged forbearers when they come into need obligates both Christians and non-Christians, for not to do so makes one "worse than an unbeliever" (1 Tim 5:8). This explicit demarcation of the obligator domain also implies that unbelievers are included within the recipient domain of the mandate—for unbelieving obligators are likely to have unbelieving parents and grandparents (a good portion of the time).

The parable of Lazarus, like the parable of the good Samaritan, obligates even the unbeliever to carry out its mandate. The logical push is that if even the nominally believing rich or the generally despised Samaritans who worship what they "do not know" (John 4:22) are obligated, how much more are believers. And so all the rich—whether unbelieving and especially those considering themselves believing—are constrained by the parable of Lazarus. But what about the intended recipient? Lazarus is certainly identified as a believer within the parable—for he is comforted in Abraham's bosom. But the parable itself hints at a broader recipient set. The rich man would have known better had he listened to "Moses and the Prophets" (Luke 16:29, 31). And these have a lot to say about aiding even the resident alien (גֵּר, *ger*) who was generally not part of the people for his unbelief.[10] And so the net of recipients draws wider.

---

10. Resident aliens were, for example, not permitted to celebrate Passover unless they were willing to become as the natives in circumcision and so confirm their change of allegiance (Exod 12:48). Furthermore, as with the common OT widow, orphan, and alien listings, even the context of Job 31:16–28—a passage which will soon receive greater attention—has a reference to aiding the alien within its immediate context (v. 32).

In terms of the mandated mercies, the parable of the good Samaritan also casts a wide net. For it answers the question of who is our neighbor. And the half dead man was different in ethnicity and belief from the unfavorably seen Samaritan who aided him. And so even the ethnically and religiously other—even when hated—are our neighbors and the appropriate recipients of such merciful love.[11] In terms of obligators, as mentioned, in moving from the lesser to the greater, from the lesser shaming the greater, how much more should believers consider themselves obligated in this regard. While the mandated mercies of the NT are often aimed at aiding fellow believers, the alms mandates also move beyond this believing obligator and recipient matrix. The disciples were mandated to give alms to the beggarly poor who may not—and likely often did not—believe in Jesus. And so the benefits of interhuman mercy extend, in part, to more than just believers.

With these recipient and obligator considerations behind us, we may return to the prioritization of our helping. What may become our priority after we have given attention to our mandated justice and mandated mercy obligations? It is safe to assume that there are no unmandated justices for us to heed (especially after we have integrated in our OT justice obligations) for we would never know them to be so without biblical prodding. So this leaves unmandated mercies as our third priority in helping the poor. Merciful love may move us to compassionately assist the poor in areas that are not intimately related to their sustenance needs. Kindnesses that do not address immediate poverty all belong in this category. And so any assistance provided to the potentially poor—or even to those, such as the relatively poor, who are better off still—belongs here. Such unmandated mercies include, for example, providing education, infrastructural help, know-how assistance, and advocating for the receipt of remedial justice in instances where it is being denied to the poor[12]—in other words, any other non-forbidden mercy unto the immediately and broadly poor.

---

11. While the recipient in this parable is a Jew, and hence presumed to be God-fearing to an extent, the expansion to unbelievers—while not strictly demanded by logic—is confirmingly affirmed in the mandates to love one's enemies and to do good to even them (Luke 6:27, 35). For this subsumed even the occupiers—the pagan Roman soldiers who could legally demand that one carried their equipment or some other load for them for one mile (Matt 5:41).

12. So while the NT speaks up for and affirms the universal application of general justice and the application of remedial justice in instances of the former's transgres-

Drawing Conclusions, Sketching Extrapolations

If we are to judge the unmandated mercies by their nearest relative, the mandated mercies, then it is most probable—in the sore absence of any available evidence (they being unmandated)—that they too are to be extended to believers first and additionally to unbelievers as well. Perhaps they may fall under the lengthening shadow of the umbrella of doing good (Gal 6:10).

Few would argue that we can neglect our justice obligations to the poor for the sake of pursuing mercy. In terms of priority, justice comes before mercy. The same cannot so easily be said of the boundary between the mandated and unmandated mercies. Earlier I affirmed that—all things being equal—mandated mercies are to take precedence over the unmandated. This deserves to be defended and unpacked some more. Why should we consider this to be the case?

Being careful and cautious here is warranted. What are we to make of all these troubling instantiations of mercy that we can so readily think up but that go unmandated in the text itself? Perhaps we are to consider them to be of an equivalent priority to the biblically mandated mercies. Or perhaps these unmandated mercies should not be considered of any priority at all. Or maybe they should be considered as located in between these two options.

The mandated mercies provide a focus. They are concerned with relieving immediate poverty. The immediate poverty of the non-able-bodied or the working poor that are experiencing immediate sustenance need due to natural catastrophes such as famine or due to economic depression. This is the express call of mercy in the NT. The "poor indeed" are to receive a believer's attention. Their serious and dire immediate poverty deserves to be the focus of our helping.

For even when considering the broader biblical mandates to love and demonstrate mercy, it is hard to find contextual hints of a specific calling that stretches beyond the meeting of such needs. And so the golden rule of Matt 7:12 is recounted without any more specifying context than the motivational connection to God promising to provide for our own needs (Matt 7:7–11). Additionally, with Luke 6:31, this same

---

sion, it does not mandate pursuing it on behalf of the wronged as a non-judicial third party—beyond the general justice responsibility to not bear false witness (Matt 15:19; Matt 19:18 // Mark 10:19 // Luke 18:20). Interestingly, the OT mandate to sustain general and remedial justice is a matter of justice obligation for societal rulers and judicial functionaries—those in a position of responsibility to see it accomplished—but not clearly so for un-enmeshed third parties.

"doing unto others" is contextually concretized to loving one's enemies, doing good, and lending to those now needy who will not return the favor later (Luke 6:34–35). This context connects the golden rule to choosing to do good where it will not be requited rather than to intimating a broader range of sustenance assistance specifics.[13] Moreover, this is the manner of mercy that the mandate to "be merciful, just as your Father is merciful" is calling for in Luke 6:36. As a summation of the Law and the Prophets, the golden rule is also a restatement of the second greatest commandment to love our neighbors as ourselves. Both of these calls to loving others are thus chaperoned and defined by the content of the Law and the Prophets and not merely subject to situational interpretation like some acontextual principle. So while these broad calls to loving others leave room for a broader doing of good, they do not mandate any additional specifics (from a NT perspective) in this regard—particularly toward the poor.

Other mercy passages share the same fate. The broadly stated calls to mercy in Jas 2:13 and Matt 5:7 are contextually identified as mandates unto clemency and so do not provide additional specifics with respect to helping the poor.[14] Seeking the good of others before our own, particularly when they are brethren, is mandated in Rom 15:2 and 1 Cor 10:24. Yet in both cases the contextual focus is on not causing these same others to stumble over issues of weakened conscience—such as what a believer may eat. While the good works of Tabitha in Acts 9:36 were broader than merely giving money to the poor, they were nevertheless intended to meet their sustenance needs. Rather than merely providing money to buy cloth, Tabitha put in the additional labor of making clothes for poor widows. Her actions are not mandated beyond the semi-mandating approval of being referred to as works of goodness and almsgiving. Still her low-radius extrapolation of the Gospel call to almsgiving—in terms of merely adding some additional labor to her gift—shows that such low-radius extrapolations of doing good are welcome with respect to meeting sustenance needs. Still, her example does not entail a broadening leap into the unmandated mercies. The same is true of the call to the rich

---

13. At least as far as interpretive certainty is concerned. Luke 6:30 might also subsume a call to almsgiving when we find our enemies in a state of beggarly poverty, but this possibility is uncertain.

14. Though if Jas 2:13 is also taken as a lead-in to what follows, it serves to roll out the red carpet for a well-known poor-benefiting mandate (Jas 2:14–17).

in 1 Tim 6:17–19 to abound in the good works associated with generous giving and sharing. Such doing of good is intended to benefit those experiencing need. So it is also in Titus 3:14, where believers are to "learn to engage in good deeds to meet pressing needs" which are, in this case, the provision of hospitality and aid to needy missionary workers (v. 13). And so it is that many NT passages, which at first remembrance seem to encourage a leap to the unmandated mercies, do not in the end provide any additional focus but rather find themselves narrowed to noncontribution by their context (in terms of not adding anything new) or remaining unspecifyingly broad.[15] And so consequently, addressing the causes of poverty, things such as a lack of education, socioeconomic instability, and planning to mitigate the effects of drought, is not specifically enjoined. In fact, no explicit mandate to address the causes of poverty, as opposed to its resultant needs, is given.

This brings us to the tricky notion of being careful to avoid adding to Scripture. Legalism tends to get defined along these lines—as demanding of others what is not in Scripture itself. Cognizant of Jesus' woes, we must be careful to avoid developing a new Oral Torah (Luke 11:46). At minimum it seems that we cannot judge those who do not make the unmandated mercies a priority—especially of an equal priority to the mandated—for we cannot call them to it on the basis of Scripture itself. On first glance this may appear quite troubling. But whenever resources are limited as such that we cannot accomplish the mandated mercies along with unmandated kindnesses, it is not hard to come to agree that the mandated are to be carried out first. For lives, rather than sustainability or general welfare improvement, hang in the balance.

Even Augustine's famous dictum, to "Love, and do what thou wilt" readily becomes an albatross around the neck of him who is not familiar with the prescriptive content of love and is relying merely on good intents.[16] For we do not know what love is if we do not know what it mandates. If we do not care for love's internal structure, its foci, or its priorities. Only such a circumspectly self-conscious *charitas* can love, and do what it wills.

The other end also deserves to be argued. The unmandated mercies are a non-forbidden form of doing good. While not its focus, they are

---

15. All we have really done here is to have given ourselves a more fine-grained feel for the biblical tautology—that the realm of the unmandated mercies is unmandated.

16. Augustine, *Ten Homilies on the First Epistle of John*, 7:8 (NPNF[1] 7:504).

not against Scripture. Most of the time they are logical extrapolations to addressing the causes of the need that the mandated mercies seek to meet. Still, they do not find explicit support in the mandates of the NT, so they remain merely logical high-radius extrapolations.[17] But ones which Scripture does not forbid.

So what are we to make of the legitimacy of the unmandated mercies? Scripture allows for, but does not specifically call unto them. The broad stroke mandates, such as the golden rule and the second greatest command seem to allow for such mercies without much specifying their boundaries. The mandates unto serving even the least among the brethren (such as Matt 20:26–28; 23:11; Mark 9:35; 10:43–45; and Luke 22:26–27) and unto looking out "for the interests of others" (Phil 2:3–4) so as to be willing to become as their slave (δοῦλος, *doulos*, Phil 2:7) also create space for the unmandated mercies of doing good by, for example, helping to mitigate the probable causes of a possible future submergence into indigence (at least among believers). The same broad call to serving one another may be found in Gal 5:13–14. The connection of Jesus' healings and exorcisms to "doing good" in Acts 10:38, while not commanded, nevertheless makes space for the unmandated mercy of seeking to provide medical aid. Though Jesus' healings benefited both the poor and the non-poor, providing medical aid to the potentially and immediately poor would appear to fall under this unmandated interhuman treatment of doing good. The short-term medical convalescence that the good Samaritan provided for the half dead victim articulates a mandated subset which also provides a little precedent toward allowing for broader medical assistance. Additionally, those who are "widows indeed" were to have devoted themselves "to every good work" (1 Tim 5:10). The examples cited include raising children, showing hospitality to visiting strangers, washing the saints' feet, and assisting those in distress. These illustrations intimate that, while the focus is often upon helping the immediately poor, a variety of specifics can be subsumed under good works. To this Gal 6:10 adds the broad, contextually unspecified mandate that "while we have opportunity, let us do good to all people, and especially to those who are of the household of the faith."

---

17. High-radius refers here to the leap distance of the extrapolation. The fewer characteristics that are carried over from a mandate to its extrapolation, the greater its "radius." Accordingly, the greater the radius of the extrapolation, the lower the certainty of its obligation. More detailed definitions are to come. And it is possible to leap too far.

And so the broad mandates allow for the existence of the unmandated mercies, though, without bequeathing to them the higher prioritization of the explicitly mandated mercies.

Some may be surprised that the NT does not place an emphasis on "teaching people to fish"—on education, on sharing expertise, and on infrastructural assistance. That this assistance is but a logical periphery may, at first glance, threaten to give the development worker palpitations. And so a number of explanations have been offered. Anthropologists of a primitivist tendency, such as Bruce Malina, tend to draw attention to the then supposedly common perception of material goods as being finitely limited.[18] Somewhat akin to what is presently known as a zero sum understanding of economics—that in order for any to become better off others must become comparatively worse off. Working toward longer term economic improvement—moving a group of people out of potential poverty—would appear self-defeating under such perceived conditions—for it just moves the need elsewhere.[19] Still, this reconstructed understanding is not universally affirmed.[20] Or perhaps the church knew that it was too small and socially powerless to affect macroeconomic factors (though this apprehension would not have thwarted micro-projects). Additionally, with less technological ability to control the environment, there was also less that could be effectually planned for and improved in the first century in terms of agricultural output—arguably the main economic activity.[21] And moreover, perhaps the church did not possess enough means to be able to accomplish more—for it too suffered from poverty.

While all of these factors may have played some role, they are not sufficient to overthrow, with any level of decisiveness, the possibility that God intended that meeting the needs of the non-indolent immediately poor take precedence—and that this be the mandated aim of charitable obligation. For the NT surfaces this as the normative domain and goal of mercy unto the poor. The deepest and most urgent needs are to be at-

---

18. Malina, *The New Testament World*, 97–98, 105.

19. This thinking however did not apparently thwart a concern to aid the immediately poor.

20. Fuller mention of the various reconstruction possibilities is provided in the Cultural Containment section of chapter 3.

21. Other causes of poverty, such as becoming non-able-bodied or a widow, were also hard to affect—as they are to the present.

tended to—the flashpoint rightfully garners more of our attention than the periphery.

Still, when injustice impedes the provision of the mandated mercies—such as when oppression, defrauding, or theft is permitted to remove sustenance aid from the immediately poor—such conditions might serve to "bring forward" the unmandated concern for seeking remedial justice for the unjustly treated.[22] The seeking of justice for these immediately poor is brought forward, in terms of priority, as it becomes a helpful means of seeking the mandated mercy ends of sustaining the indigent in their distress. Seeking such justice thus garners a higher *functional* priority—but this escalation remains instrumental and derivative. This seeking moves forward to participate in the mandated mercies because the perpetrated injustice is undermining *their* intended effect.

Still this is not so clearly the case with other unmandated mercies. These, by and large, remain merely high-radius extrapolations of the intent to meet the needs of the potentially indigent by heading off the potential causes of their future need. These high-radius extrapolations are allowed for by the general callings to love, to do good, and to show mercy—but they are merely logical extrapolations nonetheless. They remain in last place in terms of biblical priority.

Acknowledging these unmandated means of poverty prevention is not a matter of principlizing appropriation as there is no focus on addressing the developmental causes of poverty present within the mandate texts. It is an—after the fact—extrapolation. A paradigmatizing step beyond the text. It is an extrapolation from meeting the need to, when greater resources allow, helping to prevent the need from occurring—an extrapolation to mitigating the humanly-affectible contributing causes of immediate and potential poverty. And so trying to economically stabilize a region so that its own people can take over responsibility for consistently meeting their own sustenance needs is a good deed for it aims at their good. It is helping an area or country to provide for its own people.

And so the unmandated mercies are permitted but we should seek to accomplish the higher priority helpings first. To let the text set and keep the mandated matters as our primary focus, aim, and priority. And, when we wish to be pragmatic besides, the unmandated mercies should

---

22. The NT affirms such justice while not calling those that are not in a ruler position to achieve it.

only be engaged in at the same level of priority as the mandated if their pursuit results in a net benefit for the immediately poor. For those to whom mercy is mandated. Said another way, believers should, as best as we can, aim to avoid a net loss for the most needy when pursuing the unmandated mercies. Any non-forbidden help is good help, but providing help to the most needy is the best help. Thus when we pursue the unmandated mercies at the same level of priority as the mandated it is because we perceive them as functioning as a means—a means for achieving a net benefit for the biblical mandates' recipients. In all other instances the unmandated mercies function as a comparatively lower priority good. And so, in these other instances, those in danger of sickness or worse due to being immediately poor as a result of being non-able-bodied, calamity, economic depression, or being without means in retirement age take precedence over those with lesser needs and over less pressing mercies. Even helps such as literacy training maintain a lower priority. In circumstances where a net benefit cannot be reasonably anticipated, it is recommendable that we help to secure the mandated mercies before we move on to the unmandated.

While most of the world does not, at present, experience immediate poverty *en masse*, and the United Nations and other non-governmental organizations (NGOs) strive to step in quickly for refugees and famine victims, immediate poverty is still commonly experienced in pockets around the globe—on a micro-scale that is often harder to locate and affect. And so hardworking parents, enslaved to a brick kiln owners in Bangladesh, have to watch their infants die of starvation before their own eyes because they do not earn enough to feed them too.[23] And the orphaned street kids of Rio de Janeiro are forced to scavenge for survival while being preyed on by gangs and police. And potentially poor rural parents in Thailand—in order not to become immediately poor—send their daughters, only semi-aware of their likely fate, to the cities where they become youth and child prostitutes. And non-able-bodied Ukrainian widows die without any medical attention in their derelict houses. Such immediately poor remain numerous—and their plight the biblical priority. And when we are not able to do more, we should not fail to seek to do something about this.

I have said that we should avoid helping the less needy at the expense of the more needy. To pursue the mandated mercies before the

23. J. Lingenfelter, "Why Do We Argue over How to Help the Poor?" 163.

unmandated. But perhaps the most important part of this discussion concerning prioritization is whether local sustenance needs are to take precedence over remote ones. Does the NT support any such sub-prioritization? Should mercy begin at home and only afterwards consider the sustenance needs of persons of other nationalities and ethnic groups? Jesus' band of disciples certainly gave alms to the immediately poor who were in their vicinity, and the local churches were to support those who were "widows indeed" amongst their own number, but the NT also contains some indications concerning how believers are to perceive helping those who are not immediately present to them. Even though it was undoubtedly simpler and more common to be aware of the needs in a person's local vicinity.

The prioritizing of need over vicinity is described in the first Jerusalem collection and mandated in the second. The first, the Antiochene collection, was taken in response to a prophecy about the coming of "a great famine all over the world" that later "took place in the *reign* of Claudius" (Acts 11:28). Being warned of the coming famine's esurient reach—that it would be, from their perspective, worldwide and encompass the whole of the Roman empire—the church in Antioch could have acted to insulate themselves and prepare for local needs. After all, they too were a part of the known world that would be hit. They could have thought about and prioritized preparing for the needs of their own locality. But they rather considered that the need in Judea would arguably be made greater by the impending approach of its Sabbatical Year of 47–48.[24] Anticipating a greater—a more aggravated—need in Judea, the brothers and sisters in Antioch prepared a collection for the coming needs of the Jerusalem church. They did this for brothers and sisters of a different nationality and descent (Acts 11:19–21) who were, furthermore, geographically removed from them.[25] This "proto-collection," unlike the main Jerusalem collection, carries with it no indication that it was carried out for mixed or blended reasons. The Antiochene brethren allotted their aid on the basis of the degree of anticipated need rather than on considerations of location or nationalistic kinship—on considerations of proximity or ethnic affinity.

---

24. Barrett, *Acts*, 563; Witherington, *The Acts of the Apostles*, 80.

25. For argumentation on taking τοὺς Ἑλληνιστὰς (Acts 11:20) as referring to Greeks rather than Hellenistic Jews see Barrett, *Acts*, 550–51.

Drawing Conclusions, Sketching Extrapolations

This was not for them a matter of following the generally affirmed sub-prioritization of helping believers before unbelievers. They could have stored up means to benefit the more vulnerable among their local brethren but chose to take up a collection for those who were remote. Thus it was not just an issue of choosing remote believers over the local unbelieving indigent. They chose the greater anticipated neediness of their remote brethren over their own anticipated distress. The honorable and praiseworthy giving of the Macedonians during the second collection—in giving out of their own "deep poverty [πτωχεία, *ptōcheia*]"—similarly affirms that proximity did not serve to increase obligation, for they could have used the gathered funds to help alleviate their own "affliction" (θλῖψις, *thlipsis*) of immediate poverty (2 Cor 8:2).

The main Jerusalem collection is, in the end, no different. While admittedly pursued with a plurality of motives that included a desire to make for good relations between Jewish and Gentile believers (Rom 15:27, 31), it too affirms that the greater sustenance needs of remote brethren were to take precedence over merely local ones. The example of the selflessness of the Macedonians has already been mentioned. How they chose to aid their remote brethren even over their own spiritual community—over themselves. Paul similarly admonished the Corinthians to give to their remote brethren in Judea even though they may have been concerned about endangering their own self-sufficiency (αὐτάρκεια, *autarkeia*, 2 Cor 9:8) in doing so. God would provide. And so they were mandated to seek an equality that meant that the greater needs of their remote brethren were to take priority over their own lesser sustenance concerns (2 Cor 8:13–15). The level of need determined priority. So while the desire to allow the Gentile churches to show their care for their Jewish brethren is present throughout, Paul confirms that if the tables were turned—if the need changed hands—that their Jewish brethren would prioritize the Gentiles' remote distress and do likewise (2 Cor 8:14).[26]

So what may we conclude? In terms of all of the applicable data, whenever the topic of remote need surfaces in the NT, as long as remote mandated mercies are possible, they should take precedence over a local expansion into the unmandated. That mandated mercies, even at a dis-

---

26. For a further defense of perceiving the mentioned reciprocity as not a matter of solely spiritual blessing, as it is in Rom 15:27, see M. Harris, *The Second Epistle to the Corinthians*, 591–92.

tance, maintain their priority. Because the nascent church prioritized its help to the more needy—even when remote—we can deduce that proximity does not increase obligation. That localness does not for higher priority make. The mandates of the main Jerusalem collection showcase this—that remote and local impoverishment is seen equally and the deciding prioritization factor is the depth of need. And so, need triumphs over vicinity even amongst the mandated mercies and certainly over against any local but unmandated ones. Perhaps we may extrapolate that the priority of the unmandated mercies is analogous—that the degree of comparative need usurps, even here, any consideration of local or remote. But this remains a guesswork extrapolation by way of next of kin—for the lack of any extant textual warrant.

The Jerusalem collections prioritize the most acutely immediately poor. They understand the greatest need, whether local or remote, as the highest priority. And so, to summarize our mercy obligations, we may engage in the other good deeds—the unmandated mercies—but biblically speaking, mandate-driven wise, we are to try to find a way to do the mandated mercies first—not to leave the weightier provisions undone for the sake of the lesser. And beyond that, a greater responsibility to our brethren and the comparative depth of need is what molds priority—and not relative proximity.

These considerations allow us to mull over one final category of the unmandated mercies more incisively. For actively helping the able-bodied indolent to become non-indolent is not mandated. So providing opportunities to learn life skills—such as learning to get up in the mornings at a sufficiently early time, learning to keep appointments and to fulfill initially small responsibilities, learning social skills—is not enjoined of believers within the NT. How needy are the first world's indolent on the global scale? So providing such help comes to occupy the tail end of the unmandated mercies because such indolent are not—within a safety-net system where they are provided for—experiencing acute need. They are rather the comparatively least needy of our help. For their level of need is substantially self-caused rather than externally caused. They are generally not poor due to their socioeconomic context. Compared to them, the potentially poor in non-safety-net settings lack the opportunity to better their circumstances. And so it is the non-welfare state poor—those not willfully indolent—that experience a comparatively greater context of need, and a higher priority. But there are likely to be some exceptions.

For the children of the indolent, even when in a safety-net state, may experience an elevated context of need when their parents fail to take care of their own. This is often the case in the context of addiction. Such kids experience potential or, at times, even immediate poverty through no willing of their own. Thus their plight is of a higher priority than that of their parents.

All things being equal, first is justice, then the mandated mercies, and then the unmandated mercies. Still Scripture does result in one additional category—or perhaps better said, one additional non-category of obligation. For the sake of completeness, the forbidden mercies need to be placed as the lowest possible priority. There is a lot for believers to do before we even begin to theoretically contemplate doing the forbidden. For we are mandated not to enable indolence—as it encourages sin. To help untangle our mixed sensitivities we may need to remember that the situation of the willfully indolent was much more severe in the first century than in contemporary safety-net states—and that, even then, believers were forbidden from helping the able-bodied indolent where work was available. Even when the indolent otherwise claimed to be fellow brethren. Such helping was, even then, a strict non-priority.[27]

This then is the prioritization of our helping.

Help Goals and Values

Still, the distinction between justice and non-justice—between justice and mercy—remains the most pivotal distinction. Because most of the helping Christians are mandated to provide to the poor, provided they are not rich, is a matter of mercy, believers can carefully consider the goals and values of each helping context—without fearing an immediate fall into moral transgression if they do not provide aid on a rigidly "first come, first serve" basis. This mercy nature of much of our helping also allows us to prioritize our assistance to those who are most needy—rather than to those who present themselves first. Each context can be evaluated for ways whereby to accomplish the most good with the limited means at our disposal. The mandated mercies can thus be prioritized over the unmandated. No transgression occurs in such an

---

27. For the sake of additional clarity, there is a significant difference between the tail end of the unmandated mercies and the forbidden ones. The former engage in helping the indolent by addressing their indolence itself while the latter by meeting their resultant need—and there is to be no aid for that.

application of wisdom and the potential recipients have no moral claim against the giver to act otherwise. The believer's moral obligation unto mercy is comparatively conditional and driven rather by a response of gratitude to God who "loves a cheerful giver" (2 Cor 9:7).

Ownership of Possessions

Similarly, because non-rich believers are motivated by mercy rather than justice to help the immediately poor—and by a lower level of prioritization to help the potentially poor—followers of the Way may own possessions. Even though Jesus demanded a higher commitment and a greater renunciation during His earthly ministry, believers and even the apostles themselves understood that they were able to own possessions after Jesus' crucifixion.[28] Provided, of course, that the possessions did not function as a master to them, that they remained on their guard against every form of greed, that they would not permit the deceitfulness of riches to choke out the seed that was in them, and that they continued to act to store up their treasures in heaven rather than on earth while demonstrating that they were living so as to serve God rather than mammon. For this unrighteous mammon is for making friends for the kingdom—for we are not its owners but mere stewards of it. For its only rightful owner is the One whom we rightly serve. With such an understanding it is possible for believers to own possessions without hypocrisy. Even in the presence of poverty.[29] But the ownership of scraps is another matter.

For the believer with scraps the obligation is higher—justice demands that these scraps be given to, at minimum, the non-able-bodied immediately poor in her immediate vicinity. The rich person does not own his scraps—these possessions belong to such immediately poor. And so in this case—the case of justice—the ownership of some of what

---

28. Technically after the Last Supper (Luke 22:35–36). During Jesus' earthly ministry He did mandate a greater commitment that included forsaking all of one's possessions—thus more was expected as normative of His immediate disciples. While the Lord is certainly still positioned to ask this of any of His followers as a personal and discriminate mandate, it is revealed as no longer normative—while still being commendably supererogatory (1 Cor 13:3).

29. Here too it is helpful to remember that these mandates and clarifiers were given in a context that we would consider third world. A context where need is more acute. If even in such a comparatively severer context the ownership of possessions was permitted, we may have less doubt in fairer circumstances.

we may consider to be our own possessions is forbidden. And so while rich believers are to be rich in good works and ready to share generously "their" riches, they must *always* be ready to give away their castoffs. And even for the non-rich, in their hard work, it is to be our goal to labor in willful part for the purpose of sharing with those who have need (Eph 4:28). For all are to conscientiously store up their treasure in heaven, for though presently entailing a somewhat lesser degree of requirement, Jesus' mandate remains undeprecated.

Social Activism

Because morally authoritative social activism is predicated on—and molded by—the demarcated content of social justice, biblical justice guides a believer's engagement in social change. Our mercy obligations do not carry such social potency. For it is not a matter of demandable justice that they be carried out. For its part, the NT presents a justice understanding which implies that seeking a social environment where children and grandchildren are responsible to provide for their aged forbearers, should they come into (legitimate) need, is just. Additionally, any social engagement which has as its aim a desire that no disrespect come to the immediately poor also has the tacit approval of the NT—likewise on the basis of our justice obligations. And finally, a recognition of the obligation, on the part of the rich, to give their castoffs to the non-able-bodied immediately poor around them may be pursued with the backing of biblical social justice. And so this mandate extrapolates to provide the moral basis for a graduated tax system where the more affluent pay more for the functioning of contemporary society. For some of this taxation is redistributed to the non-able-bodied and those amidst calamity. And perhaps, as an addition, it may also be that advocating and developing a culture of conscientiously understanding our scraps and castoffs as belonging to the immediately poor would further the cause of social justice. And make Helen smile.

And so, by demarcating these obligations—the distinction between justice and mercy, between social justice and charity—we are furnished with the moral ground for social change. With this we arrive at the end of the immediate practical implications. It is with these considerations in mind, and with having gotten our feet somewhat wet already, that we may now dive into further extrapolations.

DEFENDING SOCIAL JUSTICE

Extrapolation, particularly when it is not low-radius extrapolation, must always be acknowledged to be speculative—even when it is relegated to the very final step of practical interpretation. For it takes what is not explicit in a passage and scurries it up the ladder of abstraction. And while it is indispensable, it remains but composed of our best guesses. But there are nonetheless some precautions that we can entertain to make these guesses more probable than their rivals.

Still, there are a few more things to nail down before we apply it to the parable of Lazarus. The foremost is to defend this parable's textual mandate as indeed a matter of justice obligation—and furthermore to defend the shape of its prescriptive content. For what if the mandate is altogether different? Theologians from places such as Tübingen and others, like Ernest Renan, have in the past contended that the proper mandate here is that one must not be wealthy.[30] That the rich are condemned *qua* rich while the poor are delivered *qua* poor. Claims such as these can be aggregated together as the exegetical approaches that perceive the "great reversal" of Luke 16:25 as the interpretive crux of the parable. On this construal the mandate is altogether different: be immediately poor to be saved. On first glance, this appears to be a viable interpretive option. For it fits well with Jesus' woes of Luke 6:24–25, and the anticipated reversals of Luke 1:52–53 and perhaps Luke 2:34. It even fits well into its immediate context as an elaborating condemnation of the "Pharisees, who were lovers of money" (Luke 16:14). Perhaps even the earlier call, to "make friends for yourselves by means of the wealth of unrighteousness" in Luke 16:9, may mean: do not remain rich. In terms of retaining any possessions, it certainly meant that toward Jesus' immediate disciples. Perhaps it could be seen as wider-reaching. Up to this point, the meaning can go both ways. But it is the parable's explicit intertextuality that breaks the contextual stalemate. For the rich man and his brothers would have been warned and known better if they had but listened to "Moses and the Prophets" (Luke 16:28–29, 31). And the OT does not bring such a mandate—it does not condemn possessing wealth

---

30. See, for example, the distrustfully revisionistic but trendsetting Renan, *Vie de Jésus*, 174–75. Some more recent advocates of this view include Hock, "Lazarus and Dives," *ABD* 4:267; Johnson, *Sharing Possessions*, 15; Mealand, *Poverty and Expectation in the Gospels*, 32; Pilgrim, *Good News to the Poor*, 113–19; Schottroff and Stegemann, *Jesus von Nazareth*, 38–40.

per se. It does not teach a "great reversal" of this blanketing sort. Rather the opposite. Wealth is often seen as a divine blessing. For the patriarchs, Abraham included, were all significantly rich. And so "Moses and the Prophets" could not have provided the necessary warning concerning the existence of a "be immediately poor" mandate.[31]

While there are some "reversals" mentioned in the OT, that the parable's rich man was no villain, but "merely a commonplace wealthy man," focuses the mandate's attention on his treatment of the poor Lazarus.[32] The rich man was but a general wealthy Jew, he too was a "child" of Abraham (Luke 16:25). Since then the "great reversal" of Luke 16:25 is not intended to teach that receiving good things in this life results in receiving agony in the next—because "Moses and the Prophets" do not teach this—what does it communicate? It is best to read it as a euphemism for the rich man's involvement in Lazarus receiving bad things. It is as if Abraham is saying "you had lots while Lazarus suffered; you didn't change his lot and now he cannot alter yours"—a genteelism for the lack of just treatment on the rich man's part; a nice way of saying "you were unjust in your greed and now things have been set to right."

Incidentally, some commentators appear to infer from the rich man's plea to Abraham—to have mercy on his present agony—that his former treatment of Lazarus was also a matter of mercy.[33] This assumes a rather strong parallel within the parable. But the repentance language of verse 30 indicates that more is at issue. Nor is there any indication in the passage that this is a reciprocal instance of not showing mercy and thus not receiving mercy for the rich man's other sins. For no other sins are intimated. And so it is wise to go with the clear over the assumption—

---

31. And so evangelical commentators tend to agree that it is the rich man's actions, his treatment of the poor, rather than his economic condition that brings about his "great reversal." See Bock, *Luke*, 1372–73; Nolland, *Luke*, 830; Marshall, *The Gospel of Luke*, 636, 639; Stein, *Luke*, 425; Spence, *St. Luke*, 2:69–70. For even in the broader context of Luke, to say nothing of Acts, salvation is not granted on the basis of economic status or hardship but on faith. So, for example, in Luke 7:50 it is received on the basis of faith and love for Jesus and in Luke 8:12 on the basis of believing. And the Lukan passages that might be interpreted as granting salvation to the poor indiscriminately are buffeted either by their immediate context (as with Luke 6:20 and 6:22–23) or by diverging requirements (as with the rich young ruler and Zaccheus).

32. Spence, *St. Luke*, 68.

33. Though their terminological usage may be somewhat malleable, Darrell Bock describes it in terms of compassion language and I. Howard Marshall in terms of charity. See Bock, *Luke*, 1372, 1377; Marshall, *The Gospel of Luke*, 636.

for we may no more infer a justice mandate on the basis of the internal justice parallelism in verse 25 alone.

And so, due to its OT intertextuality, the parable of Lazarus does not teach a general "reversal." Nor does it mandate that one may not be rich. This is affirmed by the broader context of Luke–Acts and by the mistreatment detail present within the parable itself. Nor does it intimate that the transgressed mandate was a matter of mercy. So since the parable is not about economic position it is therefore about something else. What if it is about the concrete treatment described *and* faith in Christ?

This too has been a popular interpretation. It allows us to dilute the justice nature of the treatment described by moving this obligation level over onto the shoulders of faith. The main issue here is the most obvious. There is no indication in this parable that faith in Christ is being addressed. The repentance needed is better understood as specific, rather than general, due to the explicit subject matter and because we cannot identify any contextual hint of belief in Jesus as a present focus. Except perhaps in the notion of someone rising from the dead. But even here, if we read this passage in light of what is as yet unknown at that time, we are more likely to think of Lazarus' rather than Jesus' coming resurrection.[34] Even for the very redactionally inclined, cognizant that Luke is writing after the resurrection, the broader context he chooses for this parable remains the proper use of wealth—and not faith in the one to be resurrected. The parable is indeed addressed at the Pharisees of Luke 16:14—at their abominable love of money. It reprimands them again for this sin—a transgression like the adultery mentioned in Luke 16:18. Furthermore, the one to rise from the dead is to do so in order to be sent back to give the warning against living as the rich man did (Luke 16:27–28) rather than concerning belief in the resurrected one. That is the end of the rising being sought.

The deference to the OT witnesses in kind. For upon Christ's coming, one can no longer salvifically believe upon the basis of the OT alone anyway. Though it speaks of Him, it does so in a prophetic and preparatory manner. And here too Luke–Acts concurs.

---

34. For it is probably safe to assume that Lazarus' resurrection was a known tradition—even among Luke's hearers. H. K. Luce agrees (*The Gospel according to St. Luke*, 172). See also Schnackenburg, *Das Johannesevangelium*, 429–30; Marshall, *The Gospel of Luke*, 635.

Drawing Conclusions, Sketching Extrapolations

The concern that often fuels this interpretation is the worry that a focus on a particular obedience—the rich man's specific mistreatment of Lazarus—if taken as a holistic totality, would imply salvation by works—that merely not committing this injustice results in salvation. But there is no reason to take the passage thus exhaustively. It is about a concrete serious sin, not the whole extent of salvation. We are not jumping from the fire into the frying pan for relief. Just as people are not saved by way of their economic condition *per se*, this particular obedience also does not save *per se*. Though its transgression is enough to condemn. And that is Jesus' contextual warning. In many ways this concern is to be had with a number of parables including the immediately previous one: the parable of the unjust steward. It may be had with any parable that eschatologically covers a particular mandate rather than salvation more generally. The immediately preceding verse to the parable bespeaks the needed perspective—for it condemns the transgression of another mandate—the one against adultery. And so Jesus does not intend the parable to be taken in exhaustive holistic isolation. The broader context of His teaching, its other components, assures of that. And faith in Him is part of that broader canvas. It is just not the subject matter here—that place belongs to the condemned mistreatment.

Craig Blomberg's approach may be taken as representative of one final alternative. He agrees that the parable of Lazarus is not about faith in *Christ*. But he contends that it is about a broader repentance toward *God* and the moral folly of an indulgent lifestyle.[35] This approach also thins the parable's express mandate, but to a lesser degree than the other options we have considered. Blomberg connects his take on the repentance mentioned in Luke 16:30—that of general repentance—as leading into the specific repenting away from not helping the poor.[36] He affirms that those "who accumulate wealth with no thought for God or the destitute around them will be eternally condemned."[37] And summarizes

---

35. Others share the same interpretive perspective—at least in part. Robert Stein agrees concerning the broader repentance while David Pao and Eckhard Schnabel regarding the hard-hearted lifestyle. See Stein, *Luke*, 425; Pao and Schnabel, "Luke," 345.

36. So he claims: "All this strongly suggests that the rich man realized that his problem was that he had never truly repented and become right with God. He knew the Old Testament teaching about caring for the needy, yet never lifted a finger to help poor Lazarus right on his doorstep" (Blomberg, *Neither Poverty nor Riches*, 123). See also Blomberg, *Interpreting the Parables*, 205.

37. Blomberg, "Wealth," *EDBT* 815.

the parable's mandate as militating against the "greedy and indulgent lifestyles that wealth can often spawn."[38] Such "self-centered lifestyles" are what Jesus condemns.[39] Blomberg's interpretation is carried along by a sympathetic concern to get out of range of the haunting echoes of Tübingen. Beyond hearing the rich condemned *qua* rich.[40] The irony is that his broader repentance and focus on lifestyles similarly deemphasizes, though to a lesser extent, the concrete behavior of the rich man. Blomberg's general repentance does come with the side benefit of deftly circumventing the possibility of salvation by works. Still, the main issue is as with the previous attempt to commingle faith in Christ. No textual or contextual indicator of a general repentance is forthcoming. The rich man undoubtedly considered himself a believing Jew—a child of Abraham. And so while any specific disobedience may be theoretically interpreted as an indicator of a broader, overarching need, it is much harder to prove that this broader need is the primary, intended focus. Jesus crafted this parable as a rejoinder to the Pharisees' greed.[41] Internally, it is about the rich man's spelled-out mistreatment of Lazarus. The burden of proof remains upon those who would perceive more. For nothing else is intimated—nothing else was the target. The concern for a broader repentance is thus a systematic, integrative consideration rather than one sprung from the passage content—a foreign infusion, rather than a contextual effusion.

Accordingly, it is far better to view the repentance required as a concrete repentance for the specific transgression being described. This may not be the only repentance people need, but it is the only repentance described in this parable. And so we also find no hint of a general repentance on Lazarus' part. This is not the focus here. Rather it is on the type of transgression that can send a person into punishment. Thereby confirming its severity—how detestable such love of money is in the sight of God. That such treatment, as described, on the part of the rich,

---

38. Blomberg, *Neither Poverty nor Riches*, 224.

39. Ibid., 225.

40. Ibid., 123; Blomberg, *Interpreting the Parables*, 205. This concern extends, for him, beyond the parable of Lazarus (Blomberg, *Neither Poverty nor Riches*, 225).

41. I. Howard Marshall is correct in pointing out the unbroken and sustained focus of Jesus here upon addressing the Pharisees (Marshall, *The Gospel of Luke*, 632). In this sense, the rich man's cry to "father Abraham" (Luke 16:30, 24, 27) likely functioned as another barb at the Pharisees who were, like the rich man, hiding behind their descent (Matt 3:7–9 // Luke 3:7–8).

is damnable. For the focus of the parable is the just damnation of the rich man—and those like him—for their unjust greed.

Blomberg's additional principlization of the parable as a mandate against a self-centered and indulgent lifestyle is more benign—for he is careful to connect it to concrete helping. Still it is better to maintain the parable's focus upon the just treatment of the poor to begin with—on what listening to "Moses and the Prophets" entails.[42] On what Jesus concretely describes. While it is unlikely to be Blomberg's intention, a shift in focus to an "adjectified" lifestyle is easier to rationalize away. Jesus is more specific. Even upon forgoing the general repentance, Blomberg's lifestyle approach readily becomes both broader and less forceful at the same time. Forsaking self-centered lifestyles among the rich is mandated—yet all the while the concrete obligation to give away their scraps is forgotten. Even if we were to accept the principlization, without the concrete mandate, how would we objectively measure our indulgence or self-centeredness? The heart is deceitful. At the same time the principlized mandate is unspecific enough to appear to entail a much broader social justice obligation. One which could not be defended on the basis of the passage alone. For so much could be the opposite of self-centeredness and indulgence. And so the parable of Lazarus remains, explicitly, not about a general repentance, and not about a nebulous lifestyle, but about a concrete justice mandate aimed at the rich.

EXTRAPOLATING SOCIAL JUSTICE

So what does this mandate look like close up? Will we still like it without the makeup? For how wide is the set of intended obligators? What exactly must be given to the intended recipients? And how wide can we extrapolate these recipients? The last of these domains, because it allows for the possibility of a wider radius of extrapolation, will needfully take up a greater portion of our reflection. By comparison, the first two domains are more so limited, for the purposes of extrapolation, by the resolution principle—the self-conscious and yet textually sensitive desire to avoid adding in contradiction.[43]

---

42. Happily, this is a concern picked up on by a number of commentators. See Bock, *Luke*, 1375; Pao and Schnabel, "Luke," 345; Nolland, *Luke*, 831; Spence, *St. Luke*, 69–70.

43. While caution is warranted, and biblical theology must take appropriate precedence, the parable of Lazarus does not by its content or detail demand an interpretation that is irreconcilably contradictory to the rest of the NT witness.

Breadth of Obligators

The first matter, the extent of the obligated, has already been broached in previous chapters. It is morally safest to transpose the rich man's wealth to our present day in absolute terms. If we can afford an ornate home (or one with a gate), expensive clothing brands, and to dine well every day, we are indeed obligated. If we are wealthy enough to be able to provide for the immediate sustenance needs which exist in our immediate presence out of the scraps and leftovers which fall from our table, we are surely constrained. For what amounted to being extraordinarily wealthy back in the first century—having a fine home, fine clothes, and fine food—is so much more commonplace now. How much further may we go and extrapolate the range of the obligated? Perhaps as wide as those who are wealthy enough to have other scraps, not just food, which they can treat lightly and dispense with with little thought. Various scraps which could nevertheless be made to aid the most immediately poor. Certainly this mandate is not just for millionaires—the rich and famous—for the Pharisees were "lovers of money" (Luke 16:14) but they were not all very rich. This provides a little encouragement to extrapolate wider. Historically reconstructing the Pharisees is not all that easy either. A complex and somewhat tentative picture is all we can hope for at present. For the Pharisees were a variegated group and Jesus was not always confronting them all.[44] This diversity is acknowledged even in Luke 16:18, immediately prior to the parable of Lazarus, where Jesus—particularly in light of His broader teaching on divorce—condemns the Pharisaic school of Hillel, while affirming the Pharisaic school of Shammai.[45] As to their economic condition, history seems to bear out that while "some Pharisees were part of the governing class, most Pharisees were subordinate officials, bureaucrats, judges, and educators."[46] Generally retained as literate assistants of the governing class. So they were not all very wealthy, yet they were also not part of the

---

44. Silva, "The Place of Historical Reconstruction in New Testament Criticism," 115.

45. The Hillel school taught a liberal approach that allowed for a great many reasons as justifying divorce—including, as illustrative, if a wife even displeased her husband by spoiling a meal (Mishnah, *Gittin* 9:10). The house of Shammai only allowed for adultery. Interestingly, the Talmudic rabbis went on to conceive of Hillel as their founder, giving him preference—particularly in the Babylonian Talmud—preserving his material while Shammai's teaching is only extant where it was being opposed by Hillel.

46. Saldarini, "Pharisees," *ABD* 5:301–2.

poorer lower classes.⁴⁷ The Pharisees also consistently sought influence with the wealthy and governing class in their effort "to gain access to power and to influence society."⁴⁸ And so they needfully affirmed the potency and influence of wealth. So who was Jesus addressing? Those among them who were very wealthy and did such things as the parable's rich man or all of the Pharisees for what they respected, allowed for, and likely even defended in their seeking of "power over society"?⁴⁹ Or even the broader portion of them that had scraps to spare? The Pharisees were not unconcerned about the poor—but Jesus' mandate would still have condemned them. Or at least a portion of them. Or at very minimum what they permitted for others. So Jesus' focus on the Pharisees does not allow us to extrapolate too widely with much confidence. Still a low-radius extrapolation to include the wealthy with dispensable scraps other than food may be entertained. Indeed, the parable's explicit gaze upon those who have scraps logically contains the possible extrapolations and sets limits on the breadth of the domain of obligators. And it does so in fruitful tandem with the awareness that similar helping of the poor is communicated to be a matter of mercy for the non-rich.

Breadth of Giving

So we may move from who all is obligated to what they are, in turn, obligated to give. What is owed? What degree of giving is required by this mandate? What exactly does the avoidance of a superimposition of greed demand from the well-off? The parable of Lazarus requires their leftovers, their scraps, their castoffs.⁵⁰ Because the description of what fell (πίπτω, *piptō*) from the rich man's table employs the passive of the verb meaning "to throw" (βάλλω, *ballō*), Joachim Jeremias has suggested that it refers to bread being used as a finger napkin and then thrown to the floor rather than food which unwittingly fell there or was just brushed aside.⁵¹ Such bread would have been thrown there for the dogs. This adds the possibility that the rich owe what they would otherwise

---

47. Ibid., 5:301.
48. Ibid.
49. Ibid., 5:302.
50. Bock, *Luke*, 1367; Nolland, *Luke*, 828; Stein, *Luke*, 423.
51. Jeremias, *The Parables of Jesus*, 184.

throw away as dog food.⁵² That what they do not want, at least in terms of food, rightfully belongs to the immediately poor.

But some have suggested that the rich man's scraps might have indeed been given to Lazarus—because he remained and was not chased away from the "ornate" gate.⁵³ But this argument is not sufficient because Lazarus may have remained either in misplaced hope or to beg from the rich man's visitors and acquaintances—who were also likely to be well off. So other commentators who nonetheless suggest this possibility are more tentative and provide no argument.⁵⁴ And so it is better to agree with Irenaeus that Lazarus received nothing.⁵⁵ For that is what the parable indicates by piling on the description of Lazarus' misery, for worse still than his unfulfilled longing—"even the dogs" were tormenting him (Luke 16:21). Correspondingly, we are informed that during his life it was "bad things" that Lazarus received (Luke 16:25). And furthermore, the upcoming general parallelism, where the rich man does not receive even a drop of water in his own agony (vv. 23–26), similarly highlights his former lack of any response.⁵⁶

Similarly, molding broader interpretations upon the basis of the suggested folktale parallels also turns out to be less than faithful to the parable itself.⁵⁷ Not unexpectedly, a number of contemporaneous yarns address the general theme of reversal and recompense in the afterlife. The Egyptian folktale of Si-Osiris's and Setme Chamoïs's journey to the netherworld to see the reversal of a rich and poor man's fortunes is likely

---

52. Particularly noteworthy in this regard is the identical phrasing found in Matt 15:27 and Luke 16:21: τῶν πιπτόντων ἀπὸ τῆς τραπέζης (what fell, or was thrown, from the table). This similarity was conspicuous enough that most later manuscripts add the immediately preceding τῶν ψιχίων (the crumbs) of Matt 15:27 to Luke 16:21. So the dogs received the leftovers that the servants threw away after the repast or which possibly fell from the table during the meal (Reiling and Swellengrebel, *A Handbook on the Gospel of Luke*, 570–71).

53. Luce, *The Gospel according to St. Luke*, 172; Plummer, *A Critical and Exegetical Commentary on the Gospel according to St. Luke*, 392.

54. I. Howard Marshall is careful and very tentative (*The Gospel of Luke*, 632, 635–36). Henry Spence provides no argument (*St. Luke*, 66). And Alexander Bruce presents the possibility as merely suppositional (*Luke*, 588).

55. Irenaeus, *Against Heresies*, 2.34:1.

56. Arndt, *The Gospel according to St. Luke*, 364; Bock, *Luke*, 1367; Schweizer, *The Good News According to Luke*, 260.

57. The most influential of these treatments being Gressmann, *Vom reichen Mann und armen Lazarus*.

the oldest of these. The Palestinian story of Bar Ma'yan, the rich tax collector, and the poor student of the Torah also contains a reversal and was later even incorporated into the Palestinian Talmud (*Sanhedrin* 6.23c // *Hagigah* 2.77d). Lucian's Greco-Roman tales in *Gallus* and *Cataplus* portray Micyllus, a poor shoemaker, and Megapenthes, a tyrannical rich man, experiencing reversal in Hades.[58] Perhaps Lucian drew upon tales known prior to his own time.[59] But in each case the specifics of the folktales are quite different from the parable of Lazarus. With Si-Osiris, no specific misdeed is mentioned on the rich man's part. His punishment and the poor man's felicity are based upon a comparative weighing of their own individual good and evil deeds.[60] Bar Ma'yan, for his part, makes it to paradise but is punished there (while the poor scholar is at ease) since his unspecified sinful deeds too were much more numerous than his good.[61] While poor Micyllus is insulted and beaten by the powerful, and Megapenthes's life is an experiment in evil, their ultimate reversal is predicated rather upon their disparate levels of self-control.[62] Lucian was a cynic after all. And so even by a criterion of dissimilarity, the rich man's concrete mistreatment of Lazarus stands out. As his particular evil deed. The folktale parallels turn out to be not particularly helpful—particularly when they are used to shift the meaning away from the content and context of Jesus' parable.[63] Jesus may have altered a well-known folktale, possibly for the sake of the resulting mnemonic value, but His own wording remains the best context for its interpretation. And so we are again left to Jesus' parable itself—as is appropriate.

So, the castoffs still belong to the immediately poor. In terms of extrapolating what social justice compels the rich to give, the action is

---

58. Ronald Hock has advocated this as the most suitable parallel ("Lazarus and Micyllus," 447–63).

59. The most likely antecedent is Menippus the cynic's *Nekyia* from the third century BC (Hock, "Lazarus and Dives," *ABD* 4:267). Incidentally, the traditional name for the rich man, Dives, is but drawn from the Latin Vulgate's adjective—the term for rich. But the rich man has also borne many other names: Neues, Nineveh, Phineas or Finees, and Amenophis (Metzger, *A Textual Commentary on the Greek New Testament*, 140–41).

60. Griffith, *Stories of the High Priests of Memphis*, 44–50.

61. For an English translation see Neusner, *The Talmud of the Land of Israel: Sanhedrin and Makkot*, 181–82.

62. For a wider discussion see Eck, "When Patrons Are Not Patrons," 347.

63. Additional suggested parallels, such as 1 Enoch 22, only serve to acknowledge Jewish background understanding concerning the abode of the dead.

around defining castoffs. Food that is left over is required giving, but can we extrapolate to other castoffs? What about clothing we no longer want—other types of scraps that can meet immediate sustenance needs? Though Tabitha's foray into clothing was a mercy matter, may we pursue a similar low-radius extrapolation here? The parable's mandate to give the food that the rich do not want to finish, or wipe their hands in, or give to their dogs, resurfaces the extent of the poverty being addressed—the plight of the starving poor. If we have not given this, how about a low-radius extrapolation to equivalents? That we would give an amount equivalent to what was thrown out or used as pet food. The key question is: What level of uselessness to us must a castoff possess that, if we no longer want it, it must be used to aid the poor? What level of potential benefit must we forgo? If we do not want it, and would receive no benefit from it, then it is owed. If we would throw it away anyway or could not monetize it then, like the produce given to the Mennonite Gleaners, it belongs to the poor. But what about the castoffs that we no longer want but could benefit from in their disposal or liquidation? For even our meal leftovers could always be used for some personal benefit—to make compost or feed our pets. And so even things that we no longer want, but could derive a *low* benefit from, are for the poor. Perhaps it is safest to keep nothing of a lower worth than an "equivalent to dog food" amount. Something which, over the course of a given year, is actually a significant amount. But some things we may no longer want entail a large potential benefit—such as a property—such things are beyond the mandate of this parable. And are identified as matters of mercy in Acts. Still the proceeds of a typical garage or yard sale, while not identical to food leftovers, are within a low-radius extrapolation as such scraps generate but a low benefit. In fleeing the sin of greed, the parable of Lazarus sternly warns against not helping out of our scraps. Any wider extrapolation, a move beyond scraps and castoffs, is contained by 1 Tim 6:17–19 which describes the broader sharing of the rich as a matter of mercy. And so non-scraps are not in play.

Breadth of Recipients

So who is obligated? Those with scraps. What are they obligated to give away? Their scraps. But who are they obligated to give to? Who are the rightful instigators of the mandate? When does it kick in? How far can "near field" extrapolation take us here? To those enduring incapacitating ailment or disease—wider than just the crippled and ulcerated; wider than merely starving beggars with a skin disease.[64] And so we may extrapolate, as we have, to the immediately poor in our immediate presence who are non-able-bodied from various causes. But can we go any wider? In this regard, the parable's explicit intertextuality deserves our attention first. Yet because it is contested, this intertextuality is a question that will require some detail—an excursus of sorts.

Some have perceived in the parable of Lazarus a referral back to Deut 24:6–15.[65] But this text warns against taking inappropriate pledges (such as millstones) for loans, against oppressing a poor hired laborer by, for instance, not paying his daily wages by sunset, and against other injustices—such as kidnapping. Indeed, these mandates are matters of justice obligation for their transgressions follow a trend—they are identified as matters of sin (v. 15), evil, and punishment (v. 7).[66] But they are not about giving sustenance aid to the immediately poor like Lazarus. Neither is the call to not pervert the judicial justice (מִשְׁפָּט, *mishpat*) due to aliens and the fatherless that is mentioned in verse 17. Nor are the gleaning laws of verses 19–22. For the non-able-bodied would not be able to take advantage of them. And so the rich man could not have known better on the basis of Deuteronomy 24.

David Seccombe is among those who have argued for accepting Isa 58:7 as the intended background.[67] This passage holds more promise:

> Isa 58:6–10 Is this not the fast which I choose, To loosen the bonds of wickedness, To undo the bands of the yoke, And to let the oppressed go free And break every yoke? 7 *Is it not to divide your bread with the hungry And bring the homeless poor into the house; When you see the naked, to cover him; And not to hide*

---

64. Not likely to have been leprosy for Lazarus was begging in public. See Bock, *Luke*, 1366; Marshall, *The Gospel of Luke*, 635; Fitzmyer, *The Gospel According to Luke*, 1131.

65. C. A. Evans, *Luke*, 250; C. F. Evans, "The Central Section of St. Luke's Gospel," 49. Though I. Howard Marshall readily confesses that "the links are not very strong" (Marshall, *The Gospel of Luke*, 632).

66. The righteousness (צְדָקָה, *tsedaqah*) of verse 13, in this context of blessing, may perhaps possess a broader meaning than interhuman justice alone—as the similarity of wording to Deut 6:25 may also perhaps suggest. Consequently it is the sin language of verse 15 that settles the issue (at least concerning the wages).

67. Seccombe, *Possessions and the Poor in Luke–Acts*, 176–77; Bornhäuser, "Zum Verständnis der Geschichte vom reichen Mann und armen Lazarus Luk. 16,19–31," 835–36.

yourself from your own flesh? 8 Then your light will break out like the dawn, And your recovery will speedily spring forth; And your righteousness will go before you; The glory of the LORD will be your rear guard. 9 Then you will call, and the LORD will answer; You will cry, and He will say, "Here I am." If you remove the yoke from your midst, The pointing of the finger and speaking wickedness, 10 And if you give yourself to the hungry And satisfy the desire of the afflicted, Then your light will rise in darkness And your gloom will become like midday.

The text mandates what is, in God's eyes, an appropriate fast—an appropriate humbling. How to become like water in places that have seen only mirages (Isa 58:11). It proscribes wicked injustice and oppression—such as driving hard all one's workers (נָגַשׂ, *nagas*, Isa 58:3) and striking with a wicked fist (Isa 58:4). It also enjoins sharing food with the hungry, hospitably hosting the homeless, and giving clothes to the naked (v. 7). This is what makes righteousness (צֶדֶק, *tsedeq*, v. 8) and light (vv. 8, 10) shine forth. Still it is not certain here that aiding the hungry, homeless, and naked is a matter of justice obligation. The righteousness mentioned in verse 8 may be broader. In verses 6–8, and their 9–10 restatement, an enveloping call unto *both* justice and mercy may be intended—as in Mic 6:8—though the justice there be more concerned with right judgment (מִשְׁפָּט, *mishpat*) and the mercy with lovingkindness (חֶסֶד, *khesed*).[68] God may be concerned to mandate *both* as is suggestively permitted by the separating repetition of "is it not" (הֲלוֹא) in verses 6 and 7. And so here too the rich man may claim ignorance concerning comprehensive constraint—though he has not fasted as he should.

Others widen their search. Robert Stein appends Exod 22:21–24 and Amos 6:1–7 to the passages we have already considered.[69] But the former only addresses oppression and the latter focuses on condemning pampered arrogance—as made explicit in Amos 6:8.[70] Darrell Bock advocates distilling the precedent from still a broader range of OT texts.[71]

---

68. This same enveloping call is also given in Zech 7:9.

69. Stein, *Luke*, 425.

70. An arrogance that does not care if Joseph, their kinsmen in the southern kingdom, face calamity or go into exile (Amos 6:6–7). See Harper, *A Critical and Exegetical Commentary on Amos and Hosea*, 149.

71. He suggests Deut 14:28–29; 15:1–3, 7–12; 22:1–2; 23:19; 24:7–15, 19–21; 25:13–14; Isa 3:14–15; 5:7–8; 10:1–3; 32:6–7; 58:3, 6–7, 10; Jer 5:26–28; 7:5–6; Ezek 18:12–18; 33:15; Amos 2:6–8; 5:11–12; 8:4–6; Mic 2:1–2; 3:1–3; 6:10–11; Zech 7:9–10; Mal 3:5 (Bock, *Luke*, 1375). This is a list adopted by others. See Pao and Schnabel, "Luke," 345.

But these mostly concern matters such as loan and pledge provisions, they forbid usury, mandate general justice and the proper treatment of hired hands, condemn oppression, theft, defrauding, and keeping the poor, the alien, the widow, and the fatherless from receiving judicial justice. Indeed, there is a lot of ethical concern for not harming, taking advantage of, or committing crimes against the vulnerable poor *throughout* the OT. It is a matter of justice that they have unhampered access and are able to avail themselves of the procedural benefit of judicial enforcement—to be able to plead their cause and receive judicial protection. But only two of the proposed passages, beyond Isa 58:6–10, appear, at least initially, to address giving unto the poor.

The first of these interesting possibilities is also from Isaiah:

> Isa 32:5–7 A fool will no longer be called noble, nor a villain said to be honorable. 6 For fools speak folly, and their minds plot *iniquity*: to practice ungodliness, to utter error concerning the LORD, *to leave the craving* [נֶפֶשׁ, nefesh, soul] *of the hungry unsatisfied, and to deprive the thirsty of drink.* 7 The villainies of villains are evil; they devise wicked devices *to ruin the poor with lying words, even when the plea of the needy is right.* (NRSV)

But we are left with three interpretive options. The preceding chapters of Isaiah, all the way back to chapter 28, have catalogued what bad governance looks like. But Isa 32:1–5 looks forward to a change. It anticipates, with perhaps partial messianic overtones, what good rulers will be like in contradistinction.[72] Such proper governance will be carried out by the truly noble (vv. 5, 8) and not by fools and scoundrels. So perhaps Isa 32:6 is a warning against "the consequences of allowing a fool to rule."[73] That governance by a fool results in there not being enough food for the worst off and a harmful "failure to take care of water resources in a dry country."[74] But the intentionality language of this verse suggests that more than just the indirect, unintended consequences of "bumbling" folly are in play.[75] And so the second interpretation perceives a social

---

72. Oswalt, *The Book of Isaiah*, 579–80.

73. Watts, *Isaiah*, 413. Marvin Sweeney adopts a similar interpretation and agrees that the fool brings hunger and thirst—for that is what his utterances lead to (*Isaiah 1–39*, 410–11).

74. Watts, *Isaiah*, 413.

75. Ibid. John Watts's argument in favor of the younger Masoretic Text and thus against the preferable reading found in the Great Isaiah Scroll (1QIsa^a of the Dead

justice mandate—on the basis of the sin terminology—that is aimed at rulers, at their obligation to satisfy the hungry with food and the thirsty with drink. This is the understanding suggested by all translations that perceive the fool's wickedness to be that of *leaving* the hunger unsatisfied.[76] But the underlying Hebrew sounds more active, literally the fool's iniquity is "to empty out [make empty] the throat [soul] of the hungry, and the drink of the thirsty he causes to lack."[77] So this third approach also identifies injustice in the actions of the fool, but the resulting mandate is rather to not "snatch food from the hungry soul and drink from the thirsty."[78] A mandate against an active design to take food out of the throat of the already hungering and drink away from the already thirsting.[79] An affirmation of Wolterstorff's first duty. Rather than his third. So Carl Nägelsbach sees the fool's actions as "for the purpose of enriching one's self by robbery of the poor and weak" whereby "this is figuratively

---

Sea Scrolls), the Septuagint, and the early Aramaic translation of Isaiah (the Targum Jonathon) is ultimately inconsequential (the targumic *toseftot* do not play a role in Isaiah 32). See ibid., 411. Even if we were to accept "his mind does wickedness" as preferable to "his mind devises wickedness," the fool's evildoing, from his "mind dedicated to wickedness," is still a willed moral affair (ibid., 410, 413). It is not merely the result of the "unpurposed" consequences of lacking good sense. And so it does not matter if the wickedness is explicitly premeditated or merely willed with much mental dedication.

76. Among English translations see, in addition to the NRSV, the ESV, NET, NIV, HCSB, NKJV, NJPS, NAB, CEV, NCV, TEV, RSV, BBE, and MOFFATT.

77. לְהָרִיק נֶפֶשׁ רָעֵב וּמַשְׁקֵה צָמֵא יַחְסִיר. This becomes: "They deprive the hungry of food" in the NLT, and "to make empty the soul of the hungry, and to cause the drink of the thirsty to fail" in the ASV. In agreement are the KJV, JPS, YLT, DARBY, and DOUAY-RHEIMS. The NASB attempts to straddle the fence by translating "To keep the hungry person unsatisfied And to withhold drink from the thirsty" while adding that it is literally "*make empty the hungry soul*" and "*he causes to lack*" in the margins. It also suggests that Isa 3:15 and 10:2 be compared with this verse though the content and context of both these verses speak to oppression and plundering—to *making* empty rather than *leaving* empty.

78. A transgression that John Calvin here calls "the worst and most flagrant of all cruelty" (Calvin, *Commentary on the Book of the Prophet Isaiah*, 2:411).

79. Concerning the metaphorical referral to the throat or stomach of the hungry—the part of the "soul" which can feed and feel hunger—see "נפש," BDB 660; "נֶפֶשׁ," HALOT 712; Watts, *Isaiah*, 410–11. Due to the term "soul" being somewhat ambiguous in this context, the meaning of "craving" (NRSV, RSV, ESV) has sometimes been suggested. See "ריק," *TDOT* 13:482. But the possibility of this meaning is dependent upon firstly adopting the second interpretation—something which is up for grabs.

expressed: to make empty the soul of the hungry (i.e., to take away what can satisfy the need of the hungry . . .)."⁸⁰

Having shunned the first interpretation—whose mandate is merely not to let fools rule—what are we to make of the latter two? Noticeably, with very few exceptions—the NLT and, in small part, the NASB— English translations after 1917 (when the JPS was published) have opted for *leaving* the hungry empty. But before then, and for quite a long time, the third interpretation enjoyed broad dominance within translation. Though the church fathers make little comment about this portion of Isa 32:6, by the time of the Reformation translations the third interpretive approach is widely affirmed.[81] The tide changed, in the English world, with James Moffatt's translation of 1926. If we were to wager but a quick guess we may wonder if the change came through the deserved influence of Wilhelm Gesenius.[82] Gesenius's lexical work in the 1800s provided the basis for the BDB of 1906—and the newer English lexicons, with the exception of the *TWOT*, have largely remained in agreement.[83]

---

80. Nägelsbach, *The Prophet Isaiah*, 345. George Rawlinson, in terminology similar to the YLT, agrees that the fool's wickedness is "making empty the soul of the hungry— yea, the drink of the thirsty will he cause to fail" (Rawlinson, *Isaiah*, 1:522).

81. Unfortunately, Cyril of Alexandria does not get any further into the verse than "the fool speaks folly" (McKinion, *Isaiah 1–39*, 225). In the days of the Reformation the Wycliffe Bible of 1395 translated "and he schal make voide the soule of an hungry man, and schal take awei drynke fro a thirsti man." The Lutherbibel of 1545 had "so that [in the sense of: in order that] he starves out the hungry souls, and denies drink to the thirsty" (author's translation of "damit er die hungerigen Seelen aushungere vnd den Dürstigen das trincken were"). This is a translation the Lutherbibel of 1912 maintains. The Geneva Bible of 1587 agreed: "to make emptie the hungrie soule, and to cause the drinke of the thirstie to faile." As did the KJV of 1611: "to make emptie the soule of the hungry, and hee will cause the drinke of the thirstie to faile." A translation that remains to the present with only minor adjustments having been made in the ERV of 1885.

82. Gesenius's work provided a *leave empty* understanding of Isa 32:6. See "רוּק," *Lexicon manuale hebraicum et chaldaicum in Veteris Testamenti libros*, 852; Gesenius, "רוּק," *Hebräisches und Aramäisches Handwörterbuch über das Alte Testament*, 779; Gesenius, *Der Prophet Jesaia*, 75. This was a change from other contemporaneous lexicons such as Wigram, "רוּק," *The Englishman's Hebrew and Chaldee Concordance of the Old Testament*, 1165.

83. "רִיק," BDB 937–38. The KBL, for its part, seems to speak out of both sides of its mouth—affirming both interpretations by way of one's preferred language. In German it affirms "leave empty, leave to starve or in want" (author's translation of "leer lassen, darben lassen" where the latter is emphasized), while the immediately succeeding English has "*cause to suffer want*" ("רִיק," KBL 890). *HALOT* agrees with the BDB and has "to leave empty, in want" ("רִיק," *HALOT* 1228). Jerry Shepherd contends that "the wicked fool leaves the hungry empty" while acknowledging that literally "he empties the soul

This is a formidable array of support for the second interpretive option. Furthermore, commentaries have mostly gone the way of the lexicons—with the occasional surprise.[84] Among the few dissenters, aside from the aforementioned, is John Oswalt who sees in Isa 32:6 the active oppression of the weak.[85] Despite resulting in a significant difference in terms of ethical import, most commentators, with the exception of Carl Nägelsbach, do not wager any argument for their interpretation—apparently choosing to merely adopt a lexical reading without feeling compelled to provide any explanation or defense. Some even make no comment at all on the mandate.[86]

The recent lexicons, for their part, also tend to avoid offering any support for their *leave empty* rendering of Isa 32:6 (including Gesenius)—even though such a translation is a sole occurrence, a conceptual *hapax*, in terms of meaning. So *HALOT*, as a representative example, provides no explanation for it even though this rendering is at semantic odds with the rest of the hiphil instances of meaning for ריק (*resh-yod-qof*): to emp-

---

... of the hungry" (Shepherd, "רִיק," *NIDOTTE* 3:1106). The *TDOT* is consistent in supporting a *leave empty* interpretation ("רִיק," *TDOT* 13:482; Fabry, "חָסֵר," *TDOT* 5:81, 85; Seidl, "רָצֵב," *TDOT* 13:536). James Swanson is a bit more difficult to decipher, but his "go without food" is likely to be taken in the *leave empty* sense (Swanson, "רִיק," *Dictionary of Biblical Languages with Semantic Domains*). The *TWOT*, as noted, does not suggest any additional meaning beyond "make empty, empty out"—though it does not mention the passage explicitly (W. White, "רִיק," *TWOT* 2:846). Nevertheless, when the passage is cited it is understood more so in terms of the first interpretive option—that hunger is the result of God's disfavor toward faithless fools (J. B. Scott, "חָסֵר," *TWOT* 309).

84. Hence the second interpretation is adopted by Beuken, *Isaiah* 2/2, 216; Blenkinsopp, *Isaiah*, 1:428; Goldingay, *Isaiah*, 181; Grogan, *Isaiah*, 206; Keil and Delitzsch, *Commentary on the Old Testament*, 7:331; Motyer, *The Prophecy of Isaiah*, 259; Ridderbos, *Isaiah*, 259–60; G. Smith, *Isaiah*, 1:541. Hans Wildberger agrees but, interestingly, defends the wickedness of such withholding on the basis of Job 22:7 (Wildberger, *Isaiah 28–39*, 241). Walter Brueggemann also adopts the *leave empty* interpretation and thereupon quotes Calvin's strong condemnation—though Calvin, for his part, is condemning something else (Brueggemann, *Isaiah*, 1:253, 255).

85. Oswalt, *The Book of Isaiah*, 578, 581, 582. The commentaries of Samuel Widyapranawa and Edward Young appear, by their language, to agree (though Young's take is perhaps a little more passive). See Widyapranawa, *The Lord Is Savior*, 198; E. J. Young, *The Book of Isaiah*, 2:388, 390. John Skinner similarly sees the offense as "to deprive the destitute of their scanty subsistence" (Skinner, *The Book of the Prophet Isaiah*, 241). While allowing for both interpretations are—with the latter interestingly being pre-Gesenius—Alexander, *Commentary on the Prophecies of Isaiah*, 2:3; and Henry, *An Exposition of All the Books of the Old and New Testaments*, 3:289.

86. Childs, *Isaiah*, 240; Seitz, *Isaiah 1–39*, 228–33.

ty out, to pour out, to pour out the sword or sheath, and to pour out—in terms of sending forth—one's soldiers.[87] But why should we perceive a *leave empty* in Isa 32:6 when all the other scriptural occurrences speak to actively emptying out or pouring out? To *making empty* rather than to leaving some emptiness—some *status quo*—unchanged? Happily James Swanson and the *TDOT* are exceptions to this lexical silence. So Swanson contends that to "go without food" can be taken as the "figurative extension of pouring out a mass from a container."[88] But though Swanson admits to employing a "figurative extension," he provides no reason to choose the metaphorical extrapolation over a more literal meaning. For why should we opt for metaphor when the non-metaphorical makes sufficient sense? Heinz-Josef Fabry, while affirming that with respect to the thirsty "the hiphil appears with a transitive causative meaning 'cause to lack, deprive,'" nevertheless takes "leave unsatisfied" as appropriate with respect to the hungry—though he acknowledges the latter as parallel to the former.[89] His argument for this interpretation is that this portion of the verse is "a Wisdom interpolation" similar in intent to Wisdom of Ben Sira 4:3 (the Hebrew Sirach).[90] While Sirach 4:1–3 is also about not harming the poor and hungry, the תמנע מתן of Sirach 4:3 does warn not to keep back the gift. But this approach is more hopeful groping than argument, for why should we assume that Sirach elucidates Isaiah's intent—that it functions as a "parallel passage"?[91] Holding such an assumed "parallel" as determinative for the present meaning lacks the necessary weight. And so these arguments against the third interpretation achieve much less than they intend.

Furthermore, we have some reason to prefer the *make empty* understanding. In terms of the immediate context, the symmetry of the end of Isa 32:6 argues for seeing the needy actively *deprived* not only of drink but, in like fashion, of food as well.[92] While the hiphil infini-

---

87. "ריק," *HALOT* 1228.

88. Swanson, "רִיק," *Dictionary of Biblical Languages with Semantic Domains.*

89. Fabry, "חָסַר," *TDOT* 5:81, 85.

90. Ibid., 5:85. A referral to Wisdom of Solomon is unlikely—for it does not engage hunger, thirst, or poverty in a commensurate manner.

91. Even Fabry's constituent claim that Isa 32:6 is an interpolation is tentative—Isaiah was likely familiar with the wisdom movement (Prov 25:1) and such phrasing is certainly "eminently worthy of the great prophet" (Kelley, *Isaiah*, 282–83).

92. So Edward Young, though he speaks of the mandate with mercy terminology, also identifies a chiastic symmetry in: "to make empty the soul of the hungry, and the drink of the thirsty he makes to fail" (E. J. Young, *The Book of Isaiah*, 2:390).

tive construct of ריק (*resh-yod-qof*) in Isa 32:6 is indeed a biblical *hapax legomenon*, it is not an absolute *hapax*. Other forms of the stem occur. But none of them, as mentioned, convey a *leave empty* meaning. And so the burden of proof remains squarely with those who would perceive something outside the causative *emptying out* idea so overwhelmingly prevalent with this root. Moreover the Septuagint maintains an active causal understanding in its translation of both phrases as: "to scatter hungry souls, and he will cause the thirsty souls to be empty."[93] So in considering how to translate "to pour out the souls of the hungry," the LXX apparently adopted a meaning akin to Abraham pouring out his trained men in Gen 14:14—in the send out and send forth sense. And so sending forth the hungry became scattering the hungry. But the meaning remained active and causal. It maintained the sense of actively doing something to the hungry rather than just letting them alone.

Similarly, the Targum Jonathon, though it interprets Isa 32:6 metaphorically—in terms of hungering for instruction and thirsting for the words of the Law—also keeps the verbs active and causal. The fool weakens (שלהי) the soul of the righteous and tries to make the Law to cease (בטל).[94] The targum understands "emptying out the soul" as something that weakens it—so rather than leaving the soul the same the targum speaks of making it worse off. This too hints at the third approach more so over the second. For it intimates more than merely not helping. So at the turn of the first millennium the famed Rashi (Rabbi Shlomo Yitzhaki), while acknowledging the targum, nonetheless contended concerning the fools in Isa 32:6 that, "According to the simple meaning, they rob the poor."[95]

---

93. Brenton, *The Septuagint with Apocrypha*. Alfred Rahlfs's critical edition differs from the Codex Vaticanus, which Brenton employs, only in accepting ποιῆσαι over ποιήσει in τοῦ διασπεῖραι ψυχὰς πεινώσας καὶ τὰς ψυχὰς τὰς διψώσας κενὰς ποιῆσαι (Rahlfs, *Septuaginta*). In the Göttingen-based NETS translation this becomes "in order to scatter hungry souls and to make empty the souls that thirst."

94. The Aramaic paraphrase of the whole verse is: "For the wicked will talk wickedness, and in their heart they meditate violence, to practise falsehood, and to speak revolt against the Lord, to weary the soul of the righteous, who long after instruction, as the hungry after bread; and after the words of the law, which are like water to him that is athirst, they purpose to make to cease" (Pauli, *The Chaldee Paraphrase on the Prophet Isaiah*, 105). See also Chilton, *The Isaiah Targum*, 63; "שלהי," *Targum Lexicon*; "בטל," *Targum Lexicon*.

95. Rashi, *Commentary on the Tanakh*.

Encouragingly, the critical text of Jerome's Vulgate agrees and adds its voice in favor of the third interpretation (as does the traditional Clementine text). The fool works his iniquity "and he makes empty the soul of the hungry, and the drink of the thirsty he takes away [by force]" (author's translation of *et vacuefaciat animam esurientis et potum sitienti auferat*).[96] Perhaps the contemporary Western preponderance toward the *leave empty* interpretation results from a tendency to take "hungry" as a categorical absolute. For if the referents are absolutely without any food, as opposed to living in undernourished poverty with recurrent hunger, then there can be nothing to snatch from them. But Isa 32:6 can just as well be paraphrased as condemning any effort "to empty out the throat of the already hungering, to take away whatever drink the thirsting have left"—as a condemnation of active oppression and defrauding of the poor.[97] Thus we have no reason to accept a possible metaphor or a hypothetical interpolation when what is written makes good sense in itself. So, out with the new, in with the old.

So, thus far at least, the rich man of the parable of Lazarus may still claim that he has not transgressed. The second plausible passage surrounds Ezek 18:12–18:

> Ezek 18:4–18 Behold, all souls are Mine; the soul of the father as well as the soul of the son is Mine. The soul who *sins* will die. 5 But if a man is *righteous* and practices *justice and righteousness*, 6 and does not eat at the mountain shrines or lift up his eyes to the idols of the house of Israel, or defile his neighbor's wife or approach a woman during her menstrual period—7 if a man does not *oppress anyone*, but restores to the debtor his pledge, does not commit robbery, *but gives his bread to the hungry and covers the naked with clothing*, 8 if he does not lend money on interest or take increase, if he *keeps his hand from iniquity and executes true justice* [מִשְׁפָּט, mishpat] *between man and man*, 9 if he walks in My statutes and My ordinances so as to deal faithfully—he is *righteous* and will surely live, declares the Lord GOD. 10 Then he may have a violent son who sheds blood and who does any of these things to a brother 11 (though he himself did not do any of these things), that is, he even eats at the mountain shrines,

---

96. Quote taken from the Stuttgart Vulgate (fourth edition): *Biblia Sacra iuxta vulgatam versionem*.

97. This is akin to what is condemned in the following verse—that the scoundrel subverts judicial justice against the vulnerable poor. And Isa 32:7 is not anywhere near as interpretively contentious. For it confirms a common OT mandate.

and defiles his neighbor's wife, 12 *oppresses the poor and needy*, commits robbery, does not restore a pledge, but lifts up his eyes to the idols and commits abomination, 13 he lends money on interest and takes increase; will he live? He will not live! He has committed all these *abominations*, he will surely be put to death; his blood will be on his own head. 14 Now behold, he has a son who has observed all his father's *sins* which he committed, and observing does not do likewise. 15 He does not eat at the mountain shrines or lift up his eyes to the idols of the house of Israel, or defile his neighbor's wife, 16 or *oppress anyone*, or retain a pledge, or commit robbery, *but he gives his bread to the hungry and covers the naked with clothing*, 17 he *keeps his hand from the poor*, does not take interest or increase, but *executes* My ordinances, and walks in My statutes; he will not die for his father's iniquity, he will surely live. 18 As for his father, because he *practiced extortion*, robbed his brother and did what was not good among his people, behold, he will die for his *iniquity*.

The primary concern here is that sons not be punished for the sins of their fathers (Ezek 18:1–3, 19–20), but the matter occasions an enumeration of sin and righteousness. And the sin language continues on in verses 19–22. The passage is about three generations: a righteous grandfather, a sinful father, and a righteous grandson. The characterization of the righteous is the same in both cases, except that "he keeps his hand from iniquity" (v. 8) becomes "he keeps his hand from the poor" (v. 17). And so the iniquity originally spoken of is specified and connected to the mandate to not "oppress anyone" (vv. 6, 16). The description of the sinful father is different however in that it is missing three components.[98] There is no explicit mention of what his hand gets into. But such mention is here unnecessary for we are told that he "oppresses the poor and needy" (v. 12)—and that subsumes his dirty hand. Furthermore, his having "practiced extortion" (v. 18) is also likely to do with oppressing the poor—as both are listed prior to robbery—if the ordering within verses 12 and 18 is intended to be consistent. Not executing true judicial justice nor walking in God's statutes and ordinances (vv. 8–9, 17) is also not reiterated. As it is in the broader summary of the grandfather's and grandson's righteousness. For the father does the opposite—that he does not walk in the statues and ordinances is clear enough from the

---

98. And possesses one added component, that the father is "violent" and "sheds blood" (v. 10).

other specifics already covered, and his oppression and extortion means that he has no inclination toward seeing "true justice between man and man" be done (v. 8). It is the third difference that is most striking—and the most relevant for assessing the contribution of this passage. For the father's sin list does not include not giving "his bread to the hungry" and not covering "the naked with clothing" (vv. 7, 16). And engaging in such treatments cannot be subsumed under executing judicial justice, renouncing extortion, or avoiding oppression. Nor under restoring pledges, not committing robbery, and not taking interest or increase on loans. Nor is this treatment a broad summary statement. And so this third difference is peculiar. Is such giving therefore not a matter of justice but rather mercy? Does it critique injustice by way of passing over the "excluded middle"? Is this why it is not included in the father's sins but rather in the broader righteousness of the others (vv. 5, 9, 19)? This is certainly possible on the basis of the text. And so the rich man, though his righteousness is incomplete, remains largely untouched—and certainly uncertain regarding any comprehensive constraint.

While not ironclad, these two passages are certainly above-average possibilities for the intertextuality affirmed in the parable of Lazarus—the best thus far. But they, along with the others, demonstrate how difficult it is to identify an OT prequel to the mandate in Luke 16:19–31.[99] The commonly referred to texts do not appear to contain the appropriately analogous elements—the most troublesome of which is that they are not clearly instances of the same obligation level. Instances where giving food to the immediately poor is a matter of justice. Or they are not about feeding the poor at all. And so the search for conceptual parallels to Jesus' parable of Lazarus needfully leads elsewhere. In looking for the scriptural antecedents to the rich man's obligations, it is natural to contemplate the mandates given unto the distinctively wealthy: the patriarchs, kings, and Job. It is the last of these that most readily oblige.

> Job 31:16–28 *If I have kept the poor from their desire,* Or have caused the eyes of the widow to fail, 17 *Or have eaten my morsel alone, And the orphan has not shared it* 18 (But from my youth he grew up with me as with a father, And from infancy I guided her), 19 *If I have seen anyone perish for lack of clothing, Or that the needy had no covering,* 20 *If his loins have not thanked me,*

---

99. So a number of commentators make no concrete suggestions at all—including Nolland, *Luke*, 831, 833; Spence, *St. Luke*, 2:68–70.

And if he has not been warmed with the fleece of my sheep, 21 *If I have lifted up my hand against the orphan, Because I saw I had support in the gate,* 22 *Let my shoulder fall from the socket, And my arm be broken off at the elbow.* 23 For calamity from God is a terror to me, And because of His majesty I can do nothing. 24 If I have *put my confidence in gold,* And *called fine gold my trust,* 25 If I have gloated because *my wealth was great,* And because my hand had *secured so much*; 26 If I have looked at the sun when it shone Or the moon going in splendor, 27 And my heart became secretly enticed, And my hand threw a kiss from my mouth, 28 That *too* would have been an *iniquity calling for judgment,* For I would have denied God above.

Job, like the rich man, was also extraordinarily wealthy (vv. 24–25) for he possessed "7,000 sheep, 3,000 camels, 500 yoke of oxen, 500 female donkeys, and very many servants" so as to be "the greatest of all the men of the east" (Job 1:3).[100] But is the mandate that is presented here—to give to the poor what they desire, food for the fatherless and widow (vv. 16–17), and clothing to the one perishing of nakedness (vv. 19–20)—a matter of justice? Oppressing and denying judicial justice to the orphan (v. 21) certainly is—for it calls for suitable punishment.[101] The hand lifted up against the vulnerable is to be broken and completely enfeebled (v. 22).[102] While this punishment, in itself, due to its fastidious appropriateness, may not extend a justice level of obligation to the earlier mentioned help, the broader context conspires to affirm just such a classification. For not helping the poor "too would have been an iniquity" (v. 28) for Job because it is, like the other matters, purposely brought up within Job's "avowal of innocence" against sins.[103] Structured as a unit, his "if I" and "if my" maledictions, starting in verse 5 and continuing through the end of Job 31, compose his oath that he has not

---

100. More precisely, Job was comparatively a sure bit greater and wealthier than the rich man.

101. The gate of the city was where judicial process was carried out.

102. Becoming partially non-able-bodied suits the crime, just like earlier with respect to adultery (Job 31:9–10) and later with respect to Job's tenant workers (Job 31:38–40). See Alden, *Job*, 304–5. Carl Keil and Franz Delitzsch see a further reach, for they subsume, as under this appropriate punishment, even not aiding the naked (Keil and Delitzsch, *Commentary on the Old Testament*, 4:590–91).

103. Habel, *The Book of Job*, 429; Alden, *Job*, 297; Driver and Gray, *A Critical and Exegetical Commentary on the Book of Job*, 261.

committed these crimes.[104] That he has not committed anything worthy of punishment. That he is not guilty of anything deserving of his present circumstances. And so Job's "oath of innocence" lists matters of justice obligation—at the least for rich obligators—and the rich man should have listened. Furthermore, as a concern for aiding the alien and traveler also surfaces within the context (Job 31:32), Job's concern is shown to have extended to more than just locals and compatriots.

But is it reasonable to consider Job as part of the intertextuality, and do we have reason to expect that Luke was familiar with the book? The Hebrew Bible is commonly known by the acrostic *Tanakh* which represents its traditional tripartite arrangement: *Torah* (the Law), *Nebhi'im* (the Prophets), and *Kethubhim* (the Writings or Hagiographa). This tripartite division is suggested by Ben Sira (Greek Prologue), possibly as early as *circa* 130 BC, affirmed by Josephus in the first century AD, and similarly suggested by Melito of Sardis *circa* AD 170.[105] But a bipartite scheme, the Law and the Prophets, is known at Qumran.[106] And as the NT employs both arrangements (Luke 24:27, 44 and Acts 26:22; 28:23 for example), it appears that both means of referring to the OT were in use at the time.[107] So where did Job belong? Among the prophets in the bipartite referral. And for the tripartite, whether the book of Job was considered one of the prophets, as a number ascertain upon the basis of Josephus, or was part of a proto-writings division, it would still have been included in the idiomatic "Moses and the Prophets" (Luke 16:29, 31).[108] And so Job is game as part of the parable's intertextuality.

---

104. Norman Habel provides an extensive and culturally contextualized discussion of the nature and function of Job's oath of innocence—as a way of clearing his name in the absence of ready witnesses. See especially Habel, *The Book of Job*, 427–31.

105. So the prologue of Sirach refers to "the law, and the prophets, and other books of our fathers" (KJV Apocrypha). Josephus, *Against Apion*, 1:37–42; Archer, *A Survey of Old Testament Introduction*, 80.

106. J. Smith, *The Books of History*, 14; Dunbar, "The Biblical Canon," 311. This is particularly interesting because the earliest biblical targum, the fragments of the Targum Job (4QtgJob, 11QtgJob) were found there.

107. J. Smith, *The Books of History*, 14; L. Harris, *Inspiration and Canonicity of the Bible*, 140–48.

108. For Job as among the prophets, see Dunbar, "The Biblical Canon," 304; J. Smith, *The Books of History*, 14. Job is similarly referred to as "among the prophets" in Sirach 49:9 (though some reconstruction is necessary). See Charles, *The Apocrypha and Pseudepigrapha of the Old Testament in English*, 1:505.

Furthermore, Luke, like Paul with whom he traveled, knew Job. So while only Jas 5:11 refers to Job by name (and assumes familiarity with the book), and only 1 Cor 3:19 (from Job 5:13) and Rom 11:35 (from Job 41:11) quote Job, Luke is among those who nevertheless allude to Job (in Luke 22:31–32). The allusion, which is on Jesus' lips, warns Simon that he, and the rest of the apostles, will be sifted by Satan who has demanded it in a manner reminiscent of Job 1:6–12.[109] The allusion is very likely, and so, Jesus, and Luke, were familiar with Job.[110]

So our attentions may happily return there. For Job's "avowal of innocence" in Job 31:16–28 is a response to earlier accusations.

> Job 22:5–11 Is not your *wickedness* great, And your *iniquities* without end? 6 For you have taken pledges of your brothers without cause, And stripped men naked. 7 *To the weary you have given no water to drink, And from the hungry you have withheld bread.* 8 But the earth belongs to the mighty man, And the honorable man dwells in it. 9 *You have sent widows away empty, And the strength of the orphans has been crushed.* 10 Therefore snares surround you, And sudden dread terrifies you, 11 Or darkness, so that you cannot see, And an abundance of water covers you.

In considering Job's present circumstances as a just judgment from God (מִשְׁפָּט, *mishpat*, Job 22:4), Eliphaz logically deduces that Job must have sinned. That his wickedness and iniquities must have been numerous and great (v. 5). And so he postulates a sin list which includes not giving drink to the weary, failing to feed the hungry, sending widows away empty, and crushing the fatherless (vv. 7, 9).[111] And he takes it that it is for these transgressions that Job is now being afflicted (vv. 10–11). And so Job 22:7 is not like Isa 32:6 in that it does not condemn an active removal of sustenance but rather, in going further, condemns a lack of

---

109. Larkin, *Luke's Use of the Old Testament in Luke 22–23*, 241–43; Marshall, *The Gospel of Luke*, 820–21; Fitzmyer, *The Gospel According to Luke*, 1424; Beale and Carson, *Commentary on the New Testament Use of the Old Testament*, 384.

110. The only other viably probable allusion to Job from Luke is found in Acts 2:24. Here the matter concerns the recurrence of the LXX word ὠδῖνας (pangs) which occurs only within Job 39:2. Still, Luke's text appears more concerned with alluding to Ps 18:4–5 (Ps 17:5–6 LXX). For additional detail see Beale and Carson, *Commentary on the New Testament Use of the Old Testament*, 536–37.

111. Whether the last two transgressions do not address giving, but rather condemn turning a widow out of her home and treating fatherless laborers very harshly, does not diminish the earlier given mandate to provide water and bread to the needy. See Hartley, *The Book of Job*, 327.

Drawing Conclusions, Sketching Extrapolations

assistance on Job's part. The connection to wealth is tangible. For Job is accused of behaving like a rich ruler "who thinks he owns everything" (v. 8).[112] Who has become coldly arrogant in his status and success so as to only be able to love himself now.[113] And so, even here, the rich man is put on notice about his justice obligations to the likes of Lazarus.

Perhaps one more passage should be mentioned for the sake of completeness—though it does not, upon closer scrutiny, clearly address giving to or feeding the poor.

> Job 29:11–17 For when the ear heard, it called me blessed, And when the eye saw, it gave witness of me, 12 *Because I delivered the poor who cried for help, And the orphan who had no helper.* 13 *The blessing of the one ready to perish came upon me, And I made the widow's heart sing for joy.* 14 I put on righteousness, and it clothed me; My *justice* [מִשְׁפָּט, mishpat] was like a robe and a turban. 15 *I was eyes to the blind And feet to the lame.* 16 *I was a father to the needy, And I investigated the case which I did not know.* 17 *I broke the jaws of the wicked And snatched the prey from his teeth.*

Though this text initially appears broader, it nonetheless maintains a focus on judicial process throughout. Job, in his judicial role, carefully investigated cases so as to thwart the designs of the wicked and to deliver the otherwise helpless poor (vv. 12–13, 16–17). For he assumed judicial roles when at the gate (Job 29:7)—the court of justice in his time.

Correspondingly, a concern for not unjustly wronging the poor is maintained throughout Job. So theft, taking forbidden pledges, and even seizing a house which one has not built (Job 20:19) is forbidden against the poor. Thus the list of evils in Job 24:3–11 highlights, at minimum, taking forbidden pledges, perhaps even enslaving the fatherless, and not paying the workers.[114] But no additional justice mandates concerning providing sustenance aid to the poor are to be found.

If Job accounts for the intertextuality of the Prophets and Writings, assuming that "Moses and the Prophets" is not merely a catchall for the OT—which it may well be—then what may we find in the Law? In

---

112. Ibid., 326.
113. Alden, *Job*, 232; Keil and Delitzsch, *Commentary on the Old Testament*, 4:478.
114. Job 24:21 returns to the theme of doing no good to the widow but does not elaborate.

this regard, Deut 14:28-29; 26:12; and Deut 15:7-11 seem to look most promising.

Deuteronomy 14:28-29 and its conceptual parallel in Deut 26:12 mandate that the tithe of every third year, excluding the Sabbatical Year, be given to the Levite, alien, orphan, and widow.[115] Thus not counting the fallow Sabbatical Year—when everything that grows is intended for the poor—we may infer, for our modern way of accounting, that, on average, 3.33% was given to the poor when taken per annum. This would have been the minimum amount as these poor were also to benefit from the offerings shared during the yearly feasts (Deut 16:1-17). This mandate unto giving to the poor, were it to be considered a matter of justice, could perhaps have jogged the rich man's forgetful conscience.[116] At least remotely.[117]

But perhaps the most potential, though admittedly indirect, resides in Deut 15:7-11—a passage, that like Deut 14:28-29, was earlier suggested by Darrell Bock.

> Deut 15:7-11 If there is a *poor man* with you, one of your brothers, in any of your towns in your land which the LORD your God is giving you, you shall not harden your heart, *nor close your hand from your poor brother*; 8 *but you shall freely open your hand to him, and shall generously lend him sufficient for his need in whatever he lacks.* 9 Beware that there is no *base* [בְּלִיַּעַל, beliyya'al, wicked] thought in your heart, saying, "The seventh year, the year of remission, is near," *and your eye is hostile* [רָעָה, ra'a', evil] *toward your poor brother, and you give him nothing*; then he may cry to the LORD against you, and it will be a *sin* in you. 10 You shall *generously give* to him, and your heart shall not be grieved when you give to him, *because for this thing* the LORD your God will *bless you* in all your work and in all your undertakings. 11 For the poor will never cease to be in the land; therefore I command you, saying, *"You shall freely open your hand to your brother*, to your *needy and poor* in your land."

While Jesus refers back to Deut 15:11 in the context of almsgiving (Matt 26:11 // Mark 14:7 // John 12:8), this passage is initially about

---

115. For further discussion, see Christensen, *Deuteronomy*, 305, 641.

116. The divine blessing of Deut 14:29 may be an expression of general eudemonia and so may not preclude a justice level of obligation.

117. For, in being presented as a typical Jew, he may have dutifully given his tithes to the temple and, in expecting them to do the rest, felt justified even in this regard.

doing the good of lending. For one is to generously lend from a willing heart (vv. 7–8, 10) rather than to give nothing (v. 9). This is why the Sabbatical Year figures so prominently in such giving (v. 9)—for that is the year in which all debts were to be forgiven (Deut 15:1–3). To lend the poor man nothing as the Sabbatical Year approached is but unjust greed—having an "evil eye"—and a sin (v. 9). If circumstances degraded to the point that selling oneself into indentured servanthood would bring benefit in terms of securing sustenance, this too was an option for an indentured duration of six years (Deut 15:12–18).[118] Interestingly, Hillel abrogated the debt remission mandate in his famous *prozbul*—out of a concern for the poor.[119] For the rich of his day were refusing to lend to the needy out of fear of the Sabbatical Year. Because this increased the desperation of the poor, Hillel decreed that debts that were transferred to the court may continue to be collected for they are no longer private debts.[120] But even so, Lazarus, being non-able-bodied, would not have been able to repay and so would have had trouble procuring a loan—nor would he have been able to secure an indentured servant position. Giving to Lazarus would not have been a loan—he could not repay or work it back. And so the rich man, while not lending to Lazarus for what he lacked, was unlikely to have considered this a lending situation. Still, Jesus, in referring to this passage in the context of almsgiving, may have perceived a broader call upon those able to give to a poor man.[121]

---

118. The Hebrew is ambiguous here, the kinsman may have been sold or sells himself (see also Exod 21:2–6; Lev 25:39–43; and Jer 34:14). See ibid., 320.

119. Mishnah, *Shevi'it* 10:3–7. Though the *prozbul* is attributed to Hillel, some find this attribution uncertain.

120. Urbach, *The Sages*, 373.

121. The astute reader may have noticed that Deut 15:7–11 incorporates both sin and reward language. This is a complexity—already noted in the Generosity section of chapter 5—that is inherent in passages which address both greed and generosity. So it may be that to greedily lend *nothing* is injustice, to lend the excluded middle of *something* is justice, and to lend a *generous amount* is mercy. Indeed generosity is highlighted in verses 8 (וְהַעֲבֵט תַּעֲבִיטֶנּוּ) and 10 (נָתוֹן תִּתֵּן)—with the latter possessing the mercy language. The middle may indeed be excluded from discussion as we move from injustice, past justice, to beyond injustice's ethical negation—to the "supra" level of obligation. Additionally, it may also be that the language of blessing may perhaps refer to the general eudemonia (as in Deut 30:16) attached to keeping the mandates concerning the poor (as in Deut 14:29; 23:20; 24:19). Though this is made somewhat less likely here by the statement that it is "on this account" that the blessing is given (v. 10 NRSV)—still even this phraseological inclusion is not sufficiently dissuasive.

So while the possibilities in the Torah are more tangential, the strongest non-judicial, non-oppression-related, and non-general justice obligations to the poor are to be found in Job. For it distinctly communicates an ends-based social justice obligation concerning giving to poor widows and fatherless orphans as well as to the remainder of the immediately poor—the hungry, thirsty, and naked (Job 22:7; 31:19–20). And, conspicuously, Job is a rich man. So we are right to wonder if this mandate is aimed specifically at the rich. That is certainly all that the specific mandate contexts affirm with certainty. For wealth is alluded to within both of the concerned mandate passages (Job 22:5–11; 31:16–28). Furthermore, the potentially poor could not afford to take in the fatherless (Job 31:18) and to feed and clothe the immediately poor—and so this obligation is needfully aimed at those, like Job, who could. And so Job, in itself, does not broaden this domain of obligators beyond the rich—for it is concerned with Job's moral obligations.

While some may argue that perhaps everyone with anything to give is obligated in like manner—that this was the assumed culture of those times—the lack of consistent parallels throughout the OT portends otherwise. For such giving is not indicated to be a matter of justice for everyone—or even for everyone better off than the potentially poor—in any OT passage. Even if we were to somehow consider the aforementioned Isaiah texts (Isa 32:5–7; 58:6–10) to be about giving rather than non-oppression, the mandates themselves are likewise aimed at the rulers, the rich landowners, and the influential wealthy. Moreover, it is much more probable that the cultural expectation was addressed uniquely at the rich anyway.[122]

And so with all of these considerations under our belt we may return to our primary concern: what does the explicit intertextuality claimed within the parable of Lazarus allow us to extrapolate with respect to the recipients, the instigators, of its mandate? The Job mandates suggest an extrapolation beyond the strictly non-able-bodied to the immediately poor more generally—to hungry widows and their children, to the naked, to the thirsty and hungry from a variety of causes. Deuteronomy 15:7–11 is similarly broad in mandating lending to a poor man without specifying the manner in which he came to be in need of a loan. And so personal and general calamity as well as economic depression become

---

122. J. C. Scott, *The Moral Economy of the Peasant*, 11, 27, 51.

Drawing Conclusions, Sketching Extrapolations 327

allowable causes for the sustenance needs that the rich are constrained to address. And the domain of recipients receives some broadening.

Additionally, the mandate in Job is also broader in terms of what is given—not just castoffs. Though Job did not aid the poor with but table scraps, he may still perhaps have been able to meet their needs out of what was, for him, an "equivalent to scraps" amount. But perhaps not. And so the giving mandates of Job may entail a broader obligation upon the rich than the parable of Lazarus alone. And so while Craig Blomberg is accurate in observing that the "New Testament is less positive about wealth than the Old Testament," the wealthy, in turning to the OT for comfort, will find their justice obligations unto the poor increased nonetheless.[123] And so even those tempted to see progressive revelation run backwards—to have the OT modify and deprecate the New—will still find greater moral constraint. Will find things panning out not quite as "well" as expected.[124]

Though I have argued for Job as the most probable intertextuality behind the parable of Lazarus, such a systematic deduction, whenever the referent is not made explicit, nevertheless remains speculative to some degree. And so a NT attempt at extrapolation should also be considered as a secondary avenue—if only to describe the process of hermeneutically managing such an attempt. Because the social justice mandate given in the parable of Lazarus is a NT singularity, a sole instance, the resolution principle has nothing to work on.[125] Except thwarting contra-

---

123. Blomberg, "Wealth," *EDBT* 816.

124. So in terms of our present focus, NT theology, the NT only indicates that justice owns our castoffs. But in terms of an OT theology, justice appears to own more than just the scraps of the rich. And the systematically inclined are bound to wonder what a *gesamtbiblische Theologie* would look like. Though not the present focus, a whole-Bible theology would likely perceive this OT justice obligation as pertaining to a giving which is nevertheless below the generosity threshold of being most ready to share (εὐμετάδοτος, *eumetadotos*) and demonstrating the sharing fellowship (being κοινωνικός, *koinōnikos*) that is identified as a mercy for the rich in 1 Tim 6:18. It would pertain to justly meeting the needs of the immediately poor who are immediately present out of one's wealth without demonstrating the higher generosity of NT *koinōnia*—without moving beyond the minimal provision of Job 22:7–9. For some level of generous giving is a mercy even for the rich.

125. As noted in chapter 5, Luke 12:13–21 does furnish some somewhat vague but suggestive background support for the social justice highlighted in the parable of Lazarus. But its contribution is unfortunately not beyond argument—and so it does not provide for another stable data point. This parable of the rich fool mandates the need to justly give something merely by implication—via the negation of using one's abundance

dictions and reminding us to compare mandates given at the same level of resolution. How then are we to tame Richard Hays's metaphorical leap?[126] For he is correctly aware that metaphor-making is what pastors and theologians often do—even at the passage level. And as in mathematics, so in theology: extrapolation on a single data point is indeterminate. Particularly so when there "are no foolproof procedures" for validating any metaphorical appropriation.[127] So while Hays is correct that leaping is common practice, he is less correct to contend that there is nothing more that we can do (aside from deferring to the interpretive community and to focal motifs) to limit the initial indeterminacy.

So how can we increase the probability of our extrapolations—even in the last mile? How can we add some more data points—even if they come with large error bars—to our interpretive graph? By allowing a comparative similarity in equivalent resolution mandate components to generate the domain of extrapolative possibilities while harnessing a commitment to non-contradiction to delimit these possibilities. So that non-contradiction delimits what the conceptual "parallels" allow. We are looking for biblical precedent among mandates that are somehow similar—whether via an overlap in terms of *obligator* (rich person), *recipient* (non-able-bodied immediately poor), the *type of need* met (hunger), the *manner of help* provided (food), and the *scope of what is given* (castoffs). To be hermeneutically impartial, we are initially looking for what any conceptual "parallel" (when considered one at a time) may allow for in terms of extrapolation. Only the obligation level cannot be somehow extrapolated to change—for that would generate its own immediate ethical contradiction. Justice and mercy are simply not of the category of entities that can be thus extrapolated. For they are, unlike the other component ranges mentioned, mutually exclusive in this sense (in terms of their obligation level).

---

just for oneself. While this rich man's justly required giving would have likely issued from more than his literal castoffs in coming from his bumper-crop harvest (vv. 16–18), his giving of something more than *nothing* may have corresponded to—or even been less than—what was for him an "equivalent to scraps" amount. Nonetheless, for its part, just to stay on the safe side of this particular parable, if we have an abundance we might wish to make sure that we are giving something of it to the poor. As Luke 16:1–13 plays the same wispy but provocative tune.

126. R. Hays, *The Moral Vision of the New Testament*, 298–304.
127. Ibid., 304.

Drawing Conclusions, Sketching Extrapolations 329

So what does this extrapolative method generate for us in terms of the parable of Lazarus? Here the obligation level differentiation is tied to the scope of what is given—to castoffs. For none of the other aspects of this mandate can account for it being a matter of justice. This is the only thing that differs, by way of elimination, from comparable mercy mandates. And so the scope of what is given is what distinguishes this mandate in terms of moral impetus and ultimately also in terms of its obligators—those with leftovers. Thus, methodologically, everything must be kept from contradicting with this scope as it constitutes the mandate's justice characteristic. It polices all of the "parallel"-generated possibilities. And needfully prevails. Only compatible extrapolations are allowed.

This determines which mandate *components* can be extrapolated from the conceptual "parallels." There can be no widening of the obligators—by definition—for they all must possess castoffs. Nor can there be, as noted, any widening of the scope of what is given. But an extrapolative broadening of the recipients, the type of need met, and the manner of help provided is permissible.

Furthermore, in canvassing the conceptual "parallels" of the NT, we find that certain components—now in terms of their linking overlap rather than any subsequent component extrapolation—do not generate any castoff-congruent "extrapolatables."[128] In terms of the rich (obligators), the parable of the rich fool adds no specifics while 1 Tim 6:17–19 is our delimiting text for it affirms that generously giving more than castoffs is a matter of mercy even for the rich. And being "rich in good works," "generous," and "ready to share" (v. 18) does not sound like donating but castoffs to begin with. And so the obligators component does not generate any options to extrapolate from. The same is true with respect to the recipient "parallels." For even though the non-able-bodied immediately poor are to receive alms, aid out of our paychecks (Acts 20:33–35), and nice meal invitations (Luke 14:12–14), neither the monetary gift nor the banquet is likely to be made from castoffs.[129] In terms

---

128. The viewing angle has now changed to the components in their role of surfacing the possible "parallels" and away from their other role in subsequently regulating which component data can be extrapolated from these same "parallels." These are the components which feed in the passages by way of overlap rather than those which feed extrapolations out of these sourced passages—with the latter not necessarily being identical to the former. The vectors in versus the vectors out.

129. While Jesus heals the non-able-bodied immediately poor, there are no generally-reaching NT mandates attached to this.

of the castoffs themselves (the scope of what is given), there is no textual recurrence—this scope is not mentioned elsewhere. And this elimination leaves but the remaining two interrelated components—the type of need and the manner of help—as the extrapolation possibilities to be tabulated in figure 7.

Mandate Components	Parable of Lazarus Data	Uneliminated Components Parallels	Extrapolatable Components	Extrapolation
obligator	rich person	-	-	-
recipient	non-able-bodied immediately poor	-	-	-
type of need	hunger	Matt 25:31–46; Rom 12:20–21	manner of help	drink, clothing, aiding the weak and imprisoned
		Rom 12:20–21	recipient	personal enemy
manner of help	food (enough to meet the immediate need)	Luke 3:11; Jas 2:14–17	manner of help	clothing
		2 Thess 3:6–13	recipient	non-indolent
scope of what given	castoffs	-	-	-

FIGURE 7: "Parallel"-Generated Extrapolation

Looking for unambiguous precedent requires a focus on equivalent resolution extrapolations. It means taking up only what is explicitly mentioned in the "parallel" passages rather than taking components that are left open-ended as a wider warrant. Luke 3:11 and Jas 2:14–17 convey that supplying clothing to the naked is a manner of help conjoined to providing food. This conjoined helping is also reiterated in Matt 25:31–46—as among other connected helpings. And Rom 12:20–21, for its part, similarly stretches the manner of help to be provided by mandating the conjoined provision of drink to the thirsty. And because the type of need met and the manner of help provided are closely interrelated, these "parallel" passages similarly stretch the types of need that are to be met. And so helping to provide drink to the thirsty, clothing to the naked, and aid to the weak and imprisoned—provided these are non-indolent and even if they be personal enemies—becomes the "parallel"-generated extrapolation. All of these things can be done out of our leftovers. What is tabulated can come from castoffs.

Drawing Conclusions, Sketching Extrapolations 331

In order to simplify subsequent referral, it is helpful to consolidate our "parallel"-generated extrapolations by transposing them down to a single degree of articulation. By transposing them into the recipient component. And so the rich, by way of NT extrapolation, are to provide for the thirsty, the clothesless, the variously physically enfeebled, and the persecuted imprisoned *in addition to* the hungry—out of their castoffs. This recipient set stretches to subsume personal enemies, but not the indolent. And if we take it as helpful to mull over the clarifiers too, then those suffering from general calamity (λιμός, *limos*, famine, in Acts 11:28), remote brethren (Acts 11:28–30), and widows (Acts 6:1) similarly join the set. And so we may extrapolate beyond the non-able-bodied immediately poor to the non-indolent immediately poor from a number of causes. And, similarly, remote recipients join the ranks of the immediately present Lazarus by way of these "parallels."

And so, in querying only one variable at a time, we have eliminated down to a single interrelated angle of "parallel"-generated extrapolation. Delimiting the possibilities via either contradiction or having nothing new added. So need (hunger) and its concordant address via the manner of help provided (food) becomes the instigator of the possible extrapolations. Extrapolations which broaden the domain of recipients both in terms of the causes of their indigence and their vicinity with respect to the obligator (if clarifiers are heeded). So, why are we not mandated for example, by way of extrapolation, to give to the non-able-bodied rich? Because no such "parallel" mandates are revealed—even in terms of mercy. And the component "parallels" do not forward this possibility. Thus, in looking to the mercy mandates, one component at a time, we have distilled the "parallel"-generated possibilities of NT extrapolation for the parable of Lazarus.[130]

What is the resulting radius of such an extrapolation? If low-radius extrapolations keep the obligators and recipients the same while keeping the mandated helping very similar and high-radius ones keep the obligators the same while substantially expanding the recipients and helping provided, mid-radius extrapolations keep the obligators and helping

---

130. I am well aware that some biblical theologians will object to this type of integration on principle, but having a single NT data point to extrapolate from forces upon us a certain amount of wanton recklessness. And there are component-"parallel" mercy mandates and clarifiers to be found in Luke–Acts. Certainly it is better than nothing—and better than assuming contradiction or incommensurability.

(such as the provision of castoffs) the same while adjusting the recipients by way of component "parallels."[131] So our mid-radius NT extrapolation of Luke 16:19–31 adjusted the recipients by adding additional poverty causes and broadening their proximity to the obligator. And low-radius extrapolations adjust the concrete medium of the help given—such as goods rather than money with Tabitha and the various forms that our castoffs take. Similarly the good Samaritan could have taken the robbery victim to a doctor and footed the bill rather than doing the bandaging himself or taken him to his own home (had it been nearby) rather than paying the innkeeper. So such things as the concrete medium of the help, the location where it is provided, and whether one meets the need personally or has it met at one's behalf and expense (primary or secondary causation) may change. For all this—the concrete medium and its delivery—does not change the need that is addressed. In contradistinction, high-radius extrapolation moves boldly from addressing needs to preventing their causes, from helping the immediately poor toward assisting the potentially poor. So while the obligation level of low and mid-radius extrapolations remains the same, this cannot be so easily claimed for high-radius extrapolations. For they abstract much, much wider from the text.

Sadly, even our NT extrapolation is somewhat tentative. All we can continue to say with total certainty is that those with scraps are to give them to the non-able-bodied immediately poor within their immediate vicinity as a matter of justice. Nevertheless, our present extrapolation is probable—particularly as it is backed up by the probable OT intertextuality claimed within the parable itself. Furthermore, Christians carry out such mid-radius extrapolations on other passages, though perhaps with less methodological rigor, with blissfully frightful regularity. Do we really want to argue that God would have us stop such mid-radius extrapolations? If not, then justice demands that the low-benefit castoffs from those with scraps be given to those who are immediately poor from causes other than indolence, whether they be local or remote.

So the mandate widens—without leaping to metaphor-making, paradigmatic, virtue-based, or principlizing appropriation. And if the earlier noted observations about the Jerusalem collections are anything to go by, it is the greater responsibility to our brethren and the compara-

---

131. And high-radius is the limit of reasonable extrapolation—anything beyond it is just reading in.

tive depth of need that should mold our priority. Perhaps—as we have no other indication to go by but our mid-radius extrapolation—even in matters of justice. As our world has become globalized, giving overseas is now as accessible and easy as giving downtown. And it may be that the greater need (and frequently even the higher incidence of faith) is found beyond the shores of the first world; that, aside from the children of the addicted, the non-welfare state poor face a greater context of want; that this context should have priority access to our castoffs; and that justice should begin where the need is greatest and most urgent.

Taming extrapolation—like taming wild Leviathan—is a lot of work, perhaps this is why it is seldom attempted, and dissonance is given the freer reign. I have provided the foregoing interpretive detail in the hope of raising and sorting through some of the complexity present in working through the particulars.

PLAYING WITH EXTRAPOLATIONS

But alas, our extrapolations will not leave us alone. We have ethical questions that appear not to be spoken to directly—or as directly as we may wish—but are nevertheless important for our practical obedience. While addressing the complexity of the issues surrounding structural sin and addiction is beyond the present scope, a few brief observations seem more appropriate than pensive silence. What, as a minimum, can we say with some certainty about these matters on the basis of the NT?

Considering Structural Sin

Beyond affirming general justice for all, the NT does not specifically mandate the addressing of systemic evil—the reconstructive claims of K. C. Hanson and Douglas Oakman notwithstanding.[132] Everyone, even a soldier or tax collector propping up an extractive occupational regime, is made responsible for the choices over which they have control—rather than the deeds of the "apparatus" they participate in. Perhaps this is because they were powerless to affect the system. So though they functioned in and even benefited from the "hamartiosphere," justice demanded that they not will any sin themselves. And so the paucity of NT societal mandates will necessarily chasten our extrapolations.

---

132. Hanson and Oakman, *Palestine in the Time of Jesus*, 117–20, 144–45.

Structural sin occurs whenever and wherever politico-socioeconomic arrangements permit general justice to be broken by the privileged with relative immunity. It is but structurally sanctioned oppression. It occurs when those possessing entrusted or financial power can reasonably expect to get away with defrauding, theft, extortion, or worse—to get away with concrete injustices against the less powerful. Thus such oppression is not hidden from the obligator in some "great cloud of unknowing." Oppression, in terms of theft, also occurs whenever coercion is employed in economic dealings—a "near field" extrapolation. It occurs when some are coercively forced to accept a one-sided dictation of terms. Whenever coercive power is used to get a better "deal" than one could secure between equally positioned players.

Though the NT speaks predominantly to local oppression, is it possible to extrapolate to a broader transnational context—to broader economic relations? To business dealings toward everyone—even those over the border? What reason do we have to consider our general justice obligations discontinuous in this regard? Has systemic injustice been denied a passport? For we are dealing with the same justice obligations though the recipients are but a little further away—a mid-radius extrapolation for the most part. The OT mandate that aliens in one's country receive general justice suggests a cross-boarder and cross-ethnicity concern that is similarly intimated by the Jerusalem collections—though the latter were matters of mercy unto brethren. However, the most telling NT mandate concerns the soldiers of Luke 3:14. Though commentators generally agree that these soldiers were Jewish, and perhaps assisted and protected the tax collectors, they worked on behalf of an occupying empire.[133] They were locals working for a foreign interest. And so even those working for foreign entities, at very minimum when they are local employees, are mandated to refrain from oppression within the host nation.

So what are we to make of all this in an age of globalized economies? Bullies, whether in the schoolyard or internationally, are always tempted to pick on the vulnerable. So what falls under using power to get a better "deal"? Aside from coercive practices and forced bundling, unilateral protectionism and one-way trade barriers are the most com-

---

133. Bock, *Luke*, 312–13; Fitzmyer, *The Gospel According to Luke*, 471; Marshall, *The Gospel of Luke*, 143; Nolland, *Luke*, 150; Plummer, *A Critical and Exegetical Commentary on the Gospel according to St. Luke*, 92.

mon forms of exploitation. Protectionism cannot hope to be instituted between equals. But the rich nations can keep their market closed to the poor nations through subsidies and import tariffs. And the less powerful cannot threaten reciprocal economic damage. They cannot force a fairer deal. And so national interests collude to exclude and to thwart a freer world market. Those who have the power protect themselves from their poorer competitors. There is some palpable irony in the propensity of our poor-friendly political parties to be protectionistic. Apparently, despite all good intentions, only *our* poor are endowed with moral worth. But admittedly, all such oppression considerations are clouded by the complexity of every country doing what it can get away with in jostling for access to resources and markets. Still, all things being equal, the wealthy should flee any semblance of theft and forge their economic "deals" on the level—if such a thing is possible in our world.

So outsourcing has become a great blessing to the third world—for it has, in effect, removed some of the protective barriers placed upon the job markets of the developed nations. And perhaps even a call to "buy from a poor country" would be more merciful than exhortations to buy Canadian, European, or American—if we wanted to go that far. Furthermore, if Wolterstorff is right that Western Europe created the underdeveloped countries during its time of coercive control, then some remedial amends are appropriate for the damage done.[134] So it may be that some of what we consider our charity, like any of Britain's charity to Bangladesh, is to some extent but a matter of remedial justice.[135] This is, admittedly, a tentative extrapolation from a biblical concern for remedy between individuals. In any case, we should be careful to not do any more of that kind of coercive damage.

Besides not participating in local or remote oppression, what are our obligations with respect to systemic injustice? Speaking up for the injured party, when we are in a third party position, is demonstrated but not mandated within the NT. James is perhaps the most strident in advocating the cause of the oppressed (Jas 5:1–6). So seeking to expose structural sin and advocating for its victims is an unmandated mercy

---

134. Wolterstorff, *Until Justice and Peace Embrace*, 89.

135. Wolterstorff contends that colonial rule and the East India Company self-servingly destroyed the indigenous economy and well-being of Bangladesh by acts of power (ibid., 86–92). Incidentally, his argument is not beholden to zero sum thinking—that we are better off because others are worse off—but is about concrete acts of injustice.

with respect to the NT. In terms of impetus, working to draw attention to such failures is a high-radius mercy extrapolation—one which moves from addressing outcomes to affecting their causes. And so battling the coercion, corruption, and protectionism of others remains an unmandated instance of loving our neighbors.

But why are we not free to extrapolate more widely? Because, aside from general justice, the NT offers no passages concerning systemic evil. And so we are left with more or less mid-radius justice extrapolations and high-radius mercy ones. And these are tentative enough already.

Considering Addiction

Addiction is an acute issue as it is a common cause of immediate poverty in safety-net states. It superimposes another challenge on top of the poverty it reinforces—a poverty which is seldom completely desperate on account of the government assistance. As addiction poisons the will, should the addicted be seen as non-able-bodied of mind? It is a tempting thought—for addiction can be completely debilitating.

As with structural sin, addiction considerations readily warrant their own book-length treatment. Only a few observations can be attempted here. For its part, the NT furnishes no mandates unto helping the addicted while providing sufficient warnings against the only addictive substance common in those days. All are forbidding from giving in to it—for drunkards "will not inherit the kingdom of God" (1 Cor 6:9, 10; Gal 5:21). Furthermore, believers are commanded "not to associate with any so-called brother if he is . . . a drunkard . . . not even to eat with such a one" (1 Cor 5:11). Rather Christians are to remove wicked persons such as these from among themselves (1 Cor 5:13). And this shaming removal would also lead to receiving no sustenance help. So if such "brethren" are to be shunned and not helped, then unbelieving alcoholics (though they are not judged by the church) could expect even less assistance.

Is providing sustenance assistance to drunkards a forbidden mercy? It is not explicitly forbidden, but we would not necessarily expect it to be as this drunkenness surfaces within a list of sins that do not automatically entail sustenance need (1 Cor 5:9–11; 6:9–10; Gal 5:19–21). For neither does drunkenness always entail immediate poverty. With no explicit prohibition and only the implication of the mandated shunning—and after weighing the impetus to do good and yet not enable sin—the prohibition against helping the indolent still appears to provide the closest analogy to this instance of personal sin and weakness. Particularly when the addiction leads to indolence itself.

Helping the addicted rise from their bondage is not mandated in the NT. It is an unmandated mercy. And when it is pursued, like when helping the indolent to become self-sufficient, the emphasis should be on addressing the addiction rather than on enabling it. The focus must be on facilitating change and encouraging choices away from the addiction and what vortexes its sufferers into it. Aid should only be provided when the addicted choose to pursue leaving the addiction. For the resultant need of addiction is its sanity check. For addiction is so strong that it often needs something equally stubborn to oppose it. Still, helping the addicted, like helping the indolent, lives at the tail end of the unmandated mercies. And so such assistance (to the comparatively less needy) carries a lower priority than helping the non-able-bodied, calamity-caused, or working immediately poor.[136]

CONFIRMING THE DISCRIMEN

Having surveyed the final conclusions and extrapolations of our study, now is probably a good time to reconsider how we got here. The main windfall of our methodology is that whereas an interpreter's variously conditioned presuppositions concerning the domains of justice and mercy are generally unevaluable on the basis of the biblical text, the employed approach allows for just such a textual level evaluation. Furthermore, this evaluation permits a textually-based assessment to be rendered concerning the currently extant theological dissonance over believers' moral obligations unto the poor: a path around the *impasse*.

We are comprehensively constrained not to sin. And so the hamartiological *discrimen*, when coupled with the resolution principle, is able to demarcate the NT domains of justice and mercy obligation, as these relate to the treatment of the poor, in a consistent and non-contradicting manner.[137] This amiable consistency is likewise apparent between the

---

136. There are exceptions of course. Those born with fetal alcohol syndrome, children, and those who are forced into addiction against their will as part of being forged into child soldiers or as part of being forced into prostitution are certainly another matter entirely.

137. Perhaps it is helpful here to note again that because the mandates within the parable of the sheep and the goats (Matt 25:31–46) conjoin the righteousness of faith

discrimen itself and the semantic indicators extant within the NT texts. Not only do the semantic and hamartiological indicators overlap within many of the NT data aspects, but several passages exhibit this overlap within their own bounds. And this overlap is evident within the boundaries of *both* justice and mercy level mandates: Matt 6:1–4 (almsgiving), Luke 6:29–36 (lending), Luke 11:39–42 (robbery and wickedness), Luke 12:22–34 (almsgiving), 1 Cor 6:7–10 (covetousness and defrauding), and 1 John 5:17 (interhuman injustice).[138] This textual affirmation of the proposed *discrimen*, on the basis of its semantic fidelity, corroborates its heuristic textual fit. Or perhaps the other way around, if we trust the *discrimen* but not the terminology. It is noteworthy, particularly in terms of biblical theology concerns, that the confirming fit spans not one but a number of authors: Matthew, Luke, Paul, and John. Much of the NT was penned by these men.

Aside from the logical compatibility present between comprehensive moral constraint and justice, the heuristic *discrimen* discovered also has the amiable competitive advantage of being well attested within the biblical data concerning the moral treatment of the poor. Identifying a textual level thread with greater scriptural attestation than the proposed hamartiological *discrimen* is likely to be significantly challenging—for the notions of sin, punishment, and reward are very common within the biblical text.

It is indeed important for the disambiguation of justice and mercy that our approach was textually-driven rather than extra-textual and that, furthermore, it pursued its differentiation at the passage level. It is on this basis alone that it can contribute toward the fostering of greater theological agreement concerning our justice and mercy obligations unto the materially poor. So perhaps we can have a change in the conversation: a move toward boldly addressing our particularity and to defending the hermeneutical "how" of our ethical proclamations concerning justice. Perhaps we may reap greater unity and spur on more inter-ministry cooperation.

---

with the works of faith, this text does not indeed threaten, particularly from a Protestant perspective, the noted consistency.

138. 1 John 5:17 even claims that all injustice is a matter of sin: πᾶσα ἀδικία ἁμαρτία ἐστίν. Walther Günther agrees that, in this verse, ἀδικία (*adikia*) most likely refers to "unjust deeds and injustice amongst men" (Günther, "ἀδικία," *NIDNTT* 3:575). For additional discussion of this text see R. Brown, *The Epistles of John*, 619; Bultmann, *The Johannine Epistles*, 87; Smalley, *1, 2, 3 John*, 297–301.

WHERE TO FROM HERE?

The hermeneutical methodology that was developed in this book was purposely formulated so as to be readily applicable to the whole of Scripture. The approach anticipates a subsequent evaluation of the OT textual data as well. The *Tanakh* has a lot more to attest concerning ruler and societal obligation than the NT. It has more to forbid such as adding "house to house" and joining "field to field, until there is room for no one but you, and you are left to live alone in the midst of the land" (Isa 5:8 NRSV).[139] For those who do not consider the OT deprecated *in toto*, the domain of justice and mercy obligations stands to gain a few more specific mandates. And as for the rich retreating to the OT for relief, Job is but one hiccup. Wealthy residents of the first world will find that our obligations can bear further increase.

ARGUING WITH MERCY

Biblical social justice is not always what we want. And when it is, it may be so only because we have submitted to our variously conditioned particularity rather than to Scripture itself. Because our moral constructs are deeply held, disappointment with biblical justice is common: for some, it incorporates too much; for others, way too little. But perhaps we can avoid a Kübler-Ross-like trek through "the five stages of disappointment" if we recognize that the NT has opened up for us a lot of room for joyful mercy. We may not be able to call it justice, but there remains a lot for us to do in heeding mercy's call. And even mercifully seeking that injustices be made right, by speaking up for the wronged, is part of that.

Additionally, a few mercy passages carry with them a high level of mercy obligation. Just like forgiveness does. When believers encounter a dire immediate sustenance need that they can meet—*especially* an utter lack of food and clothing—it is normative for them to show such mercy—*particularly* among the brethren. It remains a *normal* thing for Christians to do—even if it is not a matter of justice obligation. For it is how we demonstrate that "the love of God" abides in us (1 John 3:17) and show our faith by such works (Jas 2:18). For such treatment, like aiding "orphans and widows in their distress," is not more than but "pure

---

139. Such covetous hoarding rightfully receives woes (v. 8) and divine punishment (vv. 9–10). See Watts, *Isaiah*, 60; Keil and Delitzsch, *Commentary on the Old Testament*, 7:108.

and undefiled religion in the sight of *our* God and Father" (Jas 1:27)—the normative deeds of love and a *living* faith.[140]

Furthermore, Jesus spurs us on to be the greatest through a willingness to lower our status in our own eyes enough so as to be willing to serve even those we consider to be the least socially significant, those least beneficial and significant *to us*. For some that is the dirty but non-indolent poor, for others it is the insignificance that they attach to the suffering of other nationals. But Jesus mandates that we rethink our own importance to the point of pursuing the service of those, especially among the brethren, that we consider to be the lowest rung. To, among other things, willfully cultivate an attitude of helpfulness toward the non-indolent immediately poor—toward the needs of distant and insignificant outsiders. To be intentionally ready to "receive" the least.

On top of this we are firmly mandated to avoid greed and to not seek "wanton pleasure" (1 Tim 5:6; Jas 5:5). We are not to have an "evil eye" or, worse still, to kid around about it to ourselves. For "how great" is our darkness then (Matt 6:23)! Much rather are we to go past the middle of contentment into the generosity of the "single eye." To love helping the "deserving" poor more than money. To use "our" "unrighteous mammon" to make friends for the kingdom (Luke 16:9, 11–12). For all that we think we own is actually God's. And we are to seek the reward of the unjust steward.

And we should not think lightly of the rewards that He offers (Matt 6:2–4). If anything, we should call them to mind more often for they long to spur us on "to love and good works" (Heb 10:24 NET). And who can be callous in the face of such a generous offer of "true riches" (Luke 16:11)?

So mercy has a lot to speak to. And even so, while not all helping of the poor is a matter of social justice, biblical justice still extends to obligate a lot of us Westerners. If we possess castoffs, they belong to the non-indolent immediately poor. We are obligated in this with comprehensive constraint. This is not conditional. We dare not do injustice before our God. And if we are not providing for the sustenance needs of the immediately poor of the world, let us hope it is because the most

---

140. Craig Blomberg is astute in observing that using "our" material possessions to provide such help "is often the most important test-case of one's profession of discipleship" (Blomberg, *Neither Poverty nor Riches*, 126–27).

Drawing Conclusions, Sketching Extrapolations 341

needy are already being taken care of. For the immediately poor have a right to our efforts before the potentially poor.

And beyond that, the sky is the limit. Or perhaps our faith is the limit. Mercy knows few bounds. It is not limited in its expressions except by justice—that in our seeking to do good we repay our debts, provide for our parents, pastors, and dependents, live in non-dependence ourselves, and do not enable indolence. The mandate to give all, though still commendable (where it does not cause hardship for others), is now beyond the normative call of mercy (1 Cor 13:3). Still one may even give all with love—like the Moravian missionaries were ready to in going to live among lepers when that was still a dangerous thing to do.[141] And there is nothing wrong with living dangerously.

---

141. A. Thompson, *Moravian Missions*, 387–89.

APPENDIX

Passages Concerning the Moral Treatment of the Poor in the NT

Matthew

5:3
5:5–6
5:7
5:42
5:44–48
6:1–4
6:11
6:12
6:19–21
6:22–23
6:24–34
7:1–2
8:20
9:13
10:9–10
10:40–42
11:4–5
12:1
12:7
12:18
13:22
13:44–46
14:15–22
15:2–6
15:36–38
16:24–27
18:21–35
19:21–25
19:27–30
20:1–16
20:25–28
23:11–12
23:14
23:23–25
25:31–46
26:6–13
27:57

Mark

2:23
4:18–19
4:24
6:8–9
6:34–44
7:9–13
7:22
8:34–37
9:34–37
9:41
10:19
10:21–26
10:28–31
10:42–45
12:38–40
12:41–44
14:3–9
15:43

Luke

1:52–53
3:11
3:12–13
3:14
4:18–21
6:1
6:20
6:24
6:27–28
6:29–30
6:32–33
6:34–36
6:38
7:22
8:1–3
8:14
9:3
9:23–25
9:46–48
9:58
10:4
10:27–37
11:4

Luke (cont.)
11:34–36
11:39–42
12:13–21
12:22–34
13:19
14:12–14
14:18–23
14:33
15:14
16:1–13
16:14–15
16:19–31
18:11
18:22–26
18:28–30
19:2
19:8–9
20:46–47
21:1–4
21:34
22:24–27
22:35–36
23:50–51

John
6:4–15
6:27
12:3–8
12:25
13:14
13:29
13:34–35
19:38

Acts
2:44–46
4:32–37
5:1–11
6:1
9:36
9:39–41
10:2
10:4
10:31
11:28–30
16:14–15
20:33–35
24:17

Romans
1:29
1:31
12:8
12:9
12:11
12:13
12:16
12:20–21
13:8
13:9–10
15:25–27
15:31
16:2

1 Corinthians
4:11–13, 16
5:9–11
6:7–10
7:29–31
11:21–22
11:33–34
13:3
13:4–6
16:1–3
16:13–14

2 Corinthians
6:10
8:2–5
8:6–8
8:9
8:11–12
8:13–15
8:19–20
8:24
9:1
9:5–6
9:7
9:8–11
9:12–13
11:8–9
11:27
12:14

Galatians
2:10
5:6
5:13–14
5:22

Ephesians
4:28
5:3
5:5

Philippians
2:1–4
4:11–13
4:14–17

Colossians
3:5–6
3:12

1 Thessalonians
2:5

Passages Concerning the Moral Treatment of the Poor in the NT

1 Thessalonians (*cont.*)
4:11–12
5:14

2 Thessalonians
2:17
3:6–15

1 Timothy
2:9–10
3:2–3
3:8
5:3–16
6:5–11
6:17–19

2 Timothy
2:19

Titus
1:7–8
1:12–13
3:13–14

Hebrews
11:37
13:1–3
13:5–6
13:16

James
1:9–11
1:27
2:1–7
2:8–12
2:13
2:14–17
3:17
4:1–5
5:1–6

1 Peter
4:9

2 Peter
2:3
2:14

1 John
3:16–18
5:17

3 John
1:2

Jude
1:12

Revelation
2:9
3:17–18

Bibliography

Achtemeier, Paul J. *1 Peter: A Commentary on First Peter*. Hermeneia: A Critical and Historical Commentary on the Bible. Edited by Eldon J. Epp. Minneapolis: Augsburg Fortress, 1996.
Achtemeier, Paul J., Joel B. Green, and Marianne Meye Thompson. *Introducing the New Testament: Its Literature and Theology*. Grand Rapids: Eerdmans, 2001.
Ahlstrom, Sydney E., ed. *Theology in America: The Major Protestant Voices from Puritanism to Neo-Orthodoxy*. Indianapolis: Bobbs-Merrill, 1967.
Akin, Daniel L. *1, 2, 3 John*. NAC. Nashville: Broadman & Holman, 2001.
Alden, Robert L. *Job*. NAC. Nashville: Broadman & Holman, 1994.
Alexander, Joseph A. *Commentary on the Prophecies of Isaiah*. 2 vols. Rev. ed. Edited by John Eadie. Edinburgh: Andrew Elliot and James Thin, 1865.
Allison, Dale C., Jr. "The Eye is the Lamp of the Body (Matthew 6:22–23 = Luke 11:34–36)." *New Testament Studies* 33.1 (1987) 61–83.
Alter, Chen Martha, and Donald Snodgrass. "An Assessment of the Impact of SEWA Bank in India: Baseline Findings." Paper for the Harvard Institute for International Development. Washington, DC, August 1999.
Archer, Gleason L. *A Survey of Old Testament Introduction*. 3rd. ed. Chicago: Moody, 1998.
Aristotle. *Nicomachean Ethics*. Translated by W. D. Ross. Kitchener: Batoche, 1999.
Arndt, W. F. *The Gospel according to St. Luke*. St. Louis: Concordia, 1956.
Assmann, Hugo. *Theology for a Nomad Church*. Maryknoll: Orbis, 1976.
Attridge, Harold W. *Hebrews*. Hermeneia: A Critical and Historical Commentary on the Bible. Edited by Helmut Koester. Philadelphia: Fortress, 1989.
Aune, David E. *Revelation*. 3 vols. WBC. Dallas: Word, 1998.
Avila, Charles. *Ownership: Early Christian Teaching*. Maryknoll: Orbis, 1983.
Bahnsen, Greg L. "Helping the Poor without Feeding the Beast." *Antithesis* 1.2 (March–April 1990). No pages. Accessed 22 November 2001. Online: http://www.reformed.org/webfiles/antithesis/v1n2/ant_v1n2_poor.html.
Bahnsen, Greg L., et al. *Five Views on Law and Gospel*. Edited by Stanley N. Gundry. Grand Rapids: Zondervan, 1993.
Balanoff, Elizabeth. "Norman Thomas: Socialism and the Social Gospel." *ChrCent* (30 January 1985) 101–2.
Balz, Horst, and Gerhard Schneider, eds. *Exegetical Dictionary of the New Testament*. Grand Rapids: Eerdmans, 1993.
Barrett, C. K. *Acts*. 2 vols. ICC. London: T. & T. Clark, 2004.
———. "The House of Prayer and the Den of Thieves." In *Jesus und Paulus: Festschrift für W. G. Kümmel*, edited by E. Earle Ellis and Erich Grässer. Göttingen: Vandenhoeck & Ruprecht, 1975.
Barth, Karl. *Church Dogmatics*. 2/2. Translated by Geoffrey W. Bromiley et al. Edinburgh: T. & T. Clark, 1957.

Bauer, Walter, F. W. Danker, W. F. Arndt, and F. W. Gingrich, eds. *A Greek-English Lexicon of the New Testament and Other Early Christian Literature*. 3rd ed. Chicago: University of Chicago Press, 2000.

Beale, Gregory K. *The Book of Revelation: A Commentary on the Greek Text*. NIGTC. Grand Rapids: Eerdmans, 1998.

Beale, Gregory K., and D. A. Carson, eds. *Commentary on the New Testament Use of the Old Testament*. Grand Rapids: Baker Academic, 2007.

Ben Sira. *Wisdom of Ben Sira: Portions of the Book of Ecclesiasticus from Hebrew Manuscripts in the Cairo Genizah Collection Presented to the University of Cambridge by the Editors*. Edited by Solomon Schechter and Charles Taylor. Cambridge: Cambridge University Press, 1899.

Bernard, J. H. *The Second Epistle to the Corinthians*. EGT. Edited by W. Robertson Nicoll. New York: Armstrong, 1903.

Bernbaum, John A., ed. *Economic Justice and the State: A Debate between Ronald H. Nash and Eric H. Bevesluis*. Grand Rapids: Baker, 1986.

Berryman, Phillip. "Church and Revolution." *NACLA Report on the Americas* 30.5 (March 1997) 10–15.

Beuken, Willem A. M. *Isaiah*. 2/2. Historical Commentary on the Old Testament. Leuven: Peeters, 2000.

Birch, Bruce C. "Hunger, Poverty and Biblical Religion." *ChrCent* 92 (June 1975) 593–99.

Blenkinsopp, Joseph. *Isaiah: A New Translation with Introduction and Commentary*. 3 vols. AB. Garden City: Doubleday, 2003.

Blomberg, Craig L. "The Globalization of Hermeneutics." *JETS* 38.4 (December 1995) 581–93.

———. *Interpreting the Parables*. Downers Grove: InterVarsity, 1990.

———. *Matthew*. NAC. Nashville: Broadman & Holman, 1992.

———. *Neither Poverty nor Riches: A Biblical Theology of Possessions*. Downers Grove: InterVarsity, 2001.

Blount, Brian K. *Revelation: A Commentary*. New Testament Library. Louisville: Westminster John Knox, 2009.

Bock, Darrell L. *Acts*. BECNT. Edited by Robert W. Yarbrough and Robert H. Stein. Grand Rapids: Baker Academic, 2007.

———. *The Gospel of Mark*. Cornerstone Biblical Commentary. Carol Stream: Tyndale, 2005.

———. *Luke*. 2 vols. BECNT. Edited by Robert W. Yarbrough and Robert H. Stein. Grand Rapids: Baker Academic, 1996.

Bonino, José Míguez. *Doing Theology in a Revolutionary Situation*. Philadelphia: Fortress, 1975.

Bornhäuser, Karl. "Zum Verständnis der Geschichte vom reichen Mann und armen Lazarus Luk. 16,19–31." *Neue Kirchliche Zeitschrift* 39 (1928) 833–43.

Botterweck, G. Johannes, Helmer Ringgren, and Heinz-Josef Fabry, eds. *Theological Dictionary of the Old Testament*. Translated by Geoffrey W. Bromiley et al. 15 vols. Grand Rapids: Eerdmans, 1977–2006.

Brenton, Lancelot C. L., ed. *The Septuagint with Apocrypha*. Peabody: Hendrickson, 1986.

Brock, Brian. *Singing the Ethos of God: On the Place of Christian Ethics in Scripture*. Grand Rapids: Eerdmans, 2007.

Brooks, James A. *Mark*. NAC. Nashville: Broadman & Holman, 1991.

Brown, Colin, ed. *New International Dictionary of New Testament Theology*. 4 vols. Grand Rapids: Zondervan, 1986.
Brown, Francis, S. R. Driver, and C. A. Briggs, eds. *A Hebrew and English Lexicon of the Old Testament with an Appendix Containing the Biblical Aramaic*. Oxford: Clarendon, 1907.
Brown, Raymond E. *The Epistles of John*. AB. Garden City: Doubleday, 1982.
Brown, Robert McAfee. *Gustavo Gutierrez: An Introduction to Liberation Theology*. Maryknoll: Orbis, 1990.
———. *Gustavo Gutierrez: Makers of Contemporary Theology*. Atlanta: John Knox, 1980.
———. *Unexpected News: Reading the Bible with Third World Eyes*. Philadelphia: Westminster, 1984.
Bruce, Alexander B. *Luke*. EGT. Edited by W. Robertson Nicoll. New York: Armstrong, 1902.
Bruce, Frederick F. *1 and 2 Thessalonians*. WBC. Dallas: Word, 1982.
———. *The Book of the Acts*. NICNT. Rev. ed. Grand Rapids: Eerdmans, 1988.
———. *The Epistle to the Galatians: A Commentary on the Greek Text*. NIGTC. Grand Rapids: Eerdmans, 1982.
———. *Philippians: A Good News Commentary*. San Francisco: Harper, 1983.
Brueggemann, Walter. *Isaiah*. 2 vols. Westminster Bible Companion. Louisville: Westminster John Knox, 1998.
———. *Theology of the Old Testament: Testimony, Dispute, Advocacy*. Minneapolis: Fortress, 1997.
Brunner, Emil. *Christentum und Kultur*. Zurich: Theologischer Verlag, 1979.
———. *Justice and the Social Order*. Translated by Mary Hottinger. New York: Harper, 1945.
Bultmann, Rudolf K. *The Johannine Epistles*. Hermeneia: A Critical and Historical Commentary on the Bible. Edited by Robert W. Funk. Translated by R. Philip O'Hara et al. Philadelphia: Fortress, 1973.
Burridge, Richard A. *Imitating Jesus: An Inclusive Approach to New Testament Ethics*. Grand Rapids: Eerdmans, 2007.
Callahan, Kennon L. "The New Reality in Motivation." *Leadership* (Fall 1999) 31–32.
Calvin, John. *Commentaries on the Epistle of Paul to the Philippians, Colossians, and Thessalonians*. Translated by John Pringle. Edinburgh: The Calvin Translation Society, 1851.
———. *Commentary on a Harmony of the Evangelists: Matthew, Mark, and Luke*. 3 vols. Translated by William Pringle. Edinburgh: The Calvin Translation Society, 1846.
———. *Commentary on the Book of the Prophet Isaiah*. 4 vols. Translated by William Pringle. Edinburgh: Calvin Translation Society, 1847–1850.
Campbell, J. Y. "ΚΟΙΝΩΝΙΑ and Its Cognates in the New Testament." In *Three New Testament Studies*. Leiden: Brill, 1965.
Caputo, John D. *Against Ethics: Contributions to a Poetics of Obligation with Constant Reference to Deconstruction*. Bloomington: Indiana University Press, 1993.
Carson, D. A. *The Difficult Doctrine of the Love of God*. Wheaton: Crossway, 2000.
———. *The Gospel According to John*. The Pillar New Testament Commentary. Grand Rapids: Eerdmans, 1991.
———. *Love in Hard Places*. Wheaton: Crossway, 2002.
———. *Matthew*. The Expositor's Bible Commentary. Edited by Frank E. Gaebelein et al. Grand Rapids: Zondervan, 1984.

Carson, D. A., et al., eds. *Justification and Variegated Nomism: The Paradoxes of Paul.* Grand Rapids: Baker, 2004.

Chantraine, Pierre. *Dictionnaire étymologique de la langue grecque: Histoire des mots.* 4 vols. Paris: Klincksieck, 1980.

Charles, Robert H. *A Critical and Exegetical Commentary on the Revelation of St. John.* 2 vols. ICC. Edinburgh: T. & T. Clark, 1920.

Charles, Robert H., ed. *The Apocrypha and Pseudepigrapha of the Old Testament in English: With Introductions and Critical and Explanatory Notes to the Several Books.* 2 vols. Oxford: Clarendon, 1913.

Charlton, Mark. "Sharing Food: Charity or Justice?" Paper presented at the conference of Gifts of the Earth: An Ecumenical Forum. Winnipeg, MB, November 2000.

Chhokar, Jagdeep S., et al., eds. *Culture and Leadership Across the World: The GLOBE Book of In-Depth Studies of 25 Societies.* Hillsdale: Lawrence Erlbaum, 2007.

Childs, Brevard S. *Isaiah.* OTL. Louisville: Westminster John Knox, 2001.

Chilton, Bruce D. *The Isaiah Targum: Introduction, Translation, Apparatus and Notes.* The Aramaic Bible 11. Wilmington: Michael Glazier, 1987.

Chilton, David. *Productive Christians in an Age of Guilt-Manipulators: A Biblical Response to Ronald J. Sider.* Tyler: Institute for Christian Economics, 1981.

Christensen, Duane L. *Deuteronomy.* 2 vols. WBC. Dallas: Word, 1999.

Claerbaut, David. *Urban Ministry in a New Millennium.* Federal Way: World Vision, 2005.

Clark, Gordon R. *The Word Hesed in the Hebrew Bible.* Sheffield: Sheffield Academic, 1993.

Colson, Charles W. *Justice that Restores.* Wheaton: Tyndale, 2001.

Cone, Orello. *Rich and Poor in the New Testament.* New York: Macmillan, 1902.

Conn, Harvie M., ed. *Planting and Growing Urban Churches: From Dream to Reality.* Grand Rapids: Baker, 1997.

Cranfield, C. E. B. *The Gospel According to St. Mark.* The Cambridge Greek Testament Commentary. New York: Cambridge University Press, 1963.

Curtis, Susan. *A Consuming Faith: The Social Gospel and Modern American Culture.* Baltimore: John Hopkins University Press, 1991.

Danker, Frederick W. *Jesus and the New Age: A Commentary on St. Luke's Gospel.* Rev. ed. Philadelphia: Fortress, 1988.

D'Arms, John H. *Commerce and Social Standing in Ancient Rome.* Cambridge: Harvard University Press, 1981.

Davids, Peter H. *The Epistle of James: A Commentary on the Greek Text.* NIGTC. Grand Rapids: Eerdmans, 1982.

Davies, William David, and Dale C. Allison, Jr. *A Critical and Exegetical Commentary on the Gospel According to Saint Matthew.* 3 vols. ICC. Edinburgh: T. & T. Clark, 1988.

Davis, James F. *Lex Talionis in Early Judaism and the Exhortation of Jesus in Matthew 5:38–42.* Journal for the Study of the New Testament, Supplement Series. London: T. & T. Clark, 2005.

Derrett, J. Duncan M. "'Eating Up the Houses of Widows': Jesus's Comment on Lawyers?" *Novum Testamentum* 14.1 (January 1972) 1–9.

Derrida, Jacques. "Force of Law: The 'Mystical Foundation of Authority.'" *Cordoza Law Review* 11.5 (1990) 920–1045.

Dibelius, Martin, and Hans Greeven. *James.* Hermeneia: A Critical and Historical Commentary on the Bible. Edited by Helmut Koester. Translated by Michael A. Williams. Philadelphia: Fortress, 1964.

Diehl, William E., et al. *Wealth & Poverty: Four Christian Views of Economics*. Edited by Robert G. Clouse. Downers Grove: InterVarsity, 1984.
Donald, Trevor. "Semantic Field of 'Folly' in Proverbs, Job, Psalms, and Ecclesiastes." *Vetus Testamentum* 13.3 (July 1963) 285–92.
Donfried, Karl P., ed. *The Romans Debate*. Rev. ed. Peabody: Hendrickson, 1991.
Doriani, Daniel M. *Getting the Message: A Plan for Interpreting and Applying the Bible*. Phillipsburg: Presbyterian and Reformed, 1996.
Douglas, James D., ed. *New Bible Dictionary*. 2nd ed. Wheaton: Tyndale, 1982.
Driver, Samuel R., and George B. Gray. *A Critical and Exegetical Commentary on the Book of Job*. ICC. Edinburgh: T. & T. Clark, 1958.
Dunbar, David G. "The Biblical Canon." In *Hermeneutics, Authority, and Canon*, edited by D. A. Carson and John D. Woodbridge, 295–360. Grand Rapids: Baker, 1995.
Dunn, James D. G. *The New Perspective on Paul*. Rev. ed. Grand Rapids: Eerdmans, 2007.
———. *Romans*. 2 vols. WBC. Dallas: Word, 1988.
Duvall, J. Scott, and J. Daniel Hays. *Grasping God's Word: A Hands-On Approach to Reading, Interpreting, and Applying the Bible*. Grand Rapids: Zondervan, 2005.
Eck, Ernest van. "When Patrons Are Not Patrons: A Social-Scientific Reading of the Rich Man and Lazarus (Lk 16:19–26)." *HTS Teologiese Studies/Theological Studies* 65.1 (September 2009) 346–56.
Eglash, Albert. "Beyond Restitution: Creative Restitution." In *Restitution in Criminal Justice*, edited by Joe Hudson and Burt Galaway. Lexington: Lexington Books, 1977.
———. "Creative Restitution: A Broader Meaning for an Old Term." *Journal of Criminal Law, Criminology and Police Science* 48 (1958) 619–22.
Ela, Jean-Marc. *Le cri de l'homme africain*. Paris: L'Harmattan, 1980.
———. *De l'assistance à la liberation: les tâches actuelles de l'Eglise en milieu africain*. Paris: Centre Lebret, 1983.
Ellis, E. Earle. *The Gospel of Luke*. The New Century Bible Commentary. 2nd ed. Edited by Matthew Black. Grand Rapids: Eerdmans, 1974.
Elliston, Edgar J., ed. *Christian Relief and Development*. Dallas: Word, 1989.
Elwell, Walter A., ed. *Evangelical Dictionary of Biblical Theology*. Grand Rapids: Baker, 1996.
Engels, Donald. *Roman Corinth: An Alternative Model for the Classical City*. Chicago: University of Chicago Press, 1990.
Engen, Charles van, and Jude Tiersma, eds. *God so Loves the City: Seeking a Theology for Urban Missions*. Monrovia: MARC, 1994.
Enns, Paul P. *The Moody Handbook of Theology*. Chicago: Moody, 1989.
Erickson, Millard J. *Christian Theology*. 2nd ed. Grand Rapids: Baker, 1998.
Esler, Philip. *Community and Gospel in Luke–Acts: The Social and Political Motivations of Lucan Theology*. Cambridge: Cambridge University Press, 1989.
Evangelical Fellowship of Canada. "Issue Summary: Poverty & Homelessness." No pages. Accessed 7 September 2003. Online: http://www.evangelicalfellowship.ca/social/issue_viewer.asp?Issue_Summary_ID=21.
———. "Resources: Good News to the Poor." No pages. Accessed 7 September 2003. Online: http://www.evangelicalfellowship.ca/resources/resource_viewer.asp?Resource_ID=34.
Evans, Christopher F. "The Central Section of St. Luke's Gospel." In *Studies in the Gospels: Essays in Honour of R. H. Lightfoot*, edited by D. E. Nineham, 37–53. Oxford: Blackwell, 1955.

Evans, Craig A. *Luke*. NIBCNT. Peabody: Hendrickson, 1990.

———. *Mark 8:27—16:20*. WBC. Dallas: Word, 2001.

Fee, Gordon D., and Douglas K. Stuart. "The Problem of Cultural Relativity." In *How to Read the Bible for All Its Worth*, 3rd ed., 80–86. Grand Rapids: Zondervan, 2003.

Ferm, Deane W. *Contemporary American Theologies: A Critical Survey*. New York: Seabury, 1981.

Fiensy, David A. *The Social History of Palestine in the Herodian Period: The Land is Mine*. Studies in the Bible and Early Christianity. Lewiston: Edwin Mellen, 1991.

Finegan, Edward, and Niko Besnier. *Language: Its Structure and Use*. San Diego: Harcourt Brace Jovanovich, 1989.

Finley, Moses I. *The Ancient Economy*. 2nd ed. London: Hogarth, 1984.

Fitzmyer, Joseph A. *The Gospel According to Luke*. 2 vols. AB. Garden City: Doubleday, 1985.

Fletcher, Joseph. *Situation Ethics: The New Morality*. London: SCM, 1966.

Forrest, Robert W. E. "An Inquiry into Yahweh's Commendation of Job." *Studies in Religion* 8.2 (1979) 159–68.

Foster, George M. *Tzintzuntzan: Mexican Peasants in a Changing World*. 2nd ed. New York: Elsevier, 1979.

France, Richard T. *The Gospel of Mark: A Commentary on the Greek Text*. NIGTC. Grand Rapids: Eerdmans, 2002.

———. *The Gospel of Matthew*. NICNT. Grand Rapids: Eerdmans, 2007.

Freedman, David Noel, ed. *The Anchor Bible Dictionary*. 6 vols. New York: Doubleday, 1992.

Freyne, Sean. *Galilee from Alexander to Hadrian*. Wilmington: Michael Glazier, 1980.

Funk, Franz X., and Karl Bihlmeyer, eds. *Didache, Barnabas, Klemens I und II, Ignatius, Polykarp, Papias, Quadratus, Diognetbrief*. Die Apostolischen Väter. Tübingen: Mohr, 1924.

Furnish, Victor Paul. *The Love Command in the New Testament*. Nashville: Abingdon, 1972.

Gapp, K. S. "The Universal Famine under Claudius." *Harvard Theological Review* 28 (1935) 258–65.

Garland, David E. *1 Corinthians*. BECNT. Edited by Robert W. Yarbrough and Robert H. Stein. Grand Rapids: Baker Academic, 2003.

———. *2 Corinthians*. NAC. Nashville: Broadman & Holman, 1999.

Garrett, Duane A. *Proverbs, Ecclesiastes, Song of Songs*. NAC. Nashville: Broadman & Holman, 1993.

Geffcken, Johannes. *Zwei Griechische Apologeten*. Leipzig: Teubner, 1907.

George, Timothy. *Galatians*. NAC. Nashville: Broadman & Holman, 1994.

Gesenius, H. F. Wilhelm. *Hebräisches und Aramäisches Handwörterbuch über das Alte Testament*. Leipzig: F. C. W. Vogel, 1886.

———. *Lexicon manuale hebraicum et chaldaicum in Veteris Testamenti libros: Post editionem germanicam tertiam latine elaboravit multisque modis retractavit et auxit Guil. Gesenius*. Leipzig: F. C. W. Vogel, 1847.

———. *Der Prophet Jesaia: Uebersetzt und mit einem vollständigen philologisch-kritischen und historischen Commentar begleitet*. Leipzig: F. C. W. Vogel, 1829.

Getz, Gene A. *Loving One Another*. Wheaton: Victor, 1981.

Goldingay, John. *Isaiah*. New International Biblical Commentary on the Old Testament. Peabody: Hendrickson, 2001.

Gorrell, Donald K. *The Age of Social Responsibility: The Social Gospel in the Progressive Era, 1900-1920*. Macon: Mercer University Press, 1988.
Gould, Ezra P. *A Critical and Exegetical Commentary on the Gospel according to St. Mark*. ICC. New York: Charles Scribner's Sons, 1912.
Gray, Sherman W. *The Least of My Brothers: Matthew 25:31-46: A History of Interpretation*. Society of Biblical Literature Dissertation Series. Atlanta: Scholars Press, 1989.
Green, Joel B. "Good News to Whom? Jesus and the 'Poor' in the Gospel of Luke." In *Jesus of Nazareth: Lord and Christ: Essays on the Historical Jesus and New Testament Christology*, edited by Joel B. Green and Max Turner, 59-74. Grand Rapids: Eerdmans, 1994.
———. *The Gospel of Luke*. NICNT. Rev. ed. Grand Rapids: Eerdmans, 1997.
Gressmann, Hugo. *Vom reichen Mann und armen Lazarus: eine Literargeschichtliche Studie*. Berlin: Verlag der Königlichen Akademie der Wissenschaften, 1918.
Griffith, Francis L. *Stories of the High Priests of Memphis: The Sethon of Herodotus and the Demotic Tales of Khamuas*. Oxford: Clarendon, 1900.
Grigg, Viv. *Companion to the Poor*. Rev. ed. Monrovia: MARC, 1990.
———. "Sorry! The Frontier Moved." In *Planting and Growing Urban Churches: From Dream to Reality*, edited by Harvie M. Conn, 150-64. Grand Rapids: Baker, 1997.
Grogan, Geoffrey W. *Isaiah*. The Expositor's Bible Commentary: Isaiah-Ezekiel. Grand Rapids: Zondervan, 1986.
Grudem, Wayne. *Bible Doctrine: Essential Teachings of the Christian Faith*. Grand Rapids: Zondervan, 1999.
———. "Should We Move Beyond the New Testament to a Better Ethic? An Analysis of William J. Webb, Slaves, Women and Homosexuals: Exploring the Hermeneutics of Cultural Analysis." *JETS* 47.2 (June 2004) 299-346.
Gundry, Robert H. *Matthew: A Commentary on His Literary and Theological Art*. Grand Rapids: Eerdmans, 1982.
Gustafson, James M. "The Place of Scripture in Christian Ethics: A Methodological Study." *Int* 24.4 (October 1970) 430-55.
Guthrie, Donald. "The New Testament Approach to Social Responsibility." *Vox Evangelica* 8 (1973) 40-59.
Gutiérrez, Gustavo. *A Theology of Liberation: History, Politics and Salvation*. Rev. ed. Maryknoll: Orbis, 1988.
Habel, Norman C. *The Book of Job: A Commentary*. OTL. Philadelphia: Westminster, 1985.
Hafemann, Scott J., and Paul R. House. *Central Themes in Biblical Theology*. Grand Rapids: Baker Academic, 2007.
Haggard, Ted, and Jack Hayford, eds. *Loving Your City into the Kingdom: City Reaching Strategies for a 21-Century Revival*. Ventura: Regal, 1997.
Hagner, Donald A. *Matthew*. 2 vols. WBC. Dallas: Word, 1993.
Hamel, Gildas H. "Daily Bread." In *Poverty and Charity in Roman Palestine*, rev. ed. 2008, 1-46. Accessed 19 May 2010. Online: http://humweb.ucsc.edu/gweltaz/courses/history/hist_196/texts/root_poverty.pdf.
———. "Limited Good." Paper presented at the annual congress of the Society of Biblical Literature. San Diego, CA, 17 November 2007.
———. *Poverty and Charity in Roman Palestine, First Three Centuries C.E.* Berkeley: University of California Press, 1990.

———. "Poverty in Clothing." In *Poverty and Charity in Roman Palestine*, rev. ed. 2008, 47–81. Accessed 19 May 2010. Online: http://humweb.ucsc.edu/gweltaz/courses/history/hist_196/texts/root_poverty.pdf.

Hands, Arthur R. *Charities and Social Aid in Greece and Rome*. Ithaca: Cornell University Press, 1968.

Handy, Robert T., ed. *The Social Gospel in America: 1870–1920*. New York: Oxford University Press, 1966.

Hanks, Thomas D. *God so Loved the Third World: The Bible, the Reformation, and Liberation Theology*. Maryknoll: Orbis, 1983.

Hanson, K. C., and Douglas E. Oakman. *Palestine in the Time of Jesus: Social Structures and Social Conflicts*. Rev. ed. Minneapolis: Fortress, 2008.

Harland, Philip A. "The Economy of First-Century Palestine: State of the Scholarly Discussion." In *Handbook of Early Christianity: Social Science Approaches*, edited by Anthony J. Blasi, Jean Duhaime, and Paul-Andre Turcotte. Walnut Creek: AltaMira, 2002.

Harper, William R. *A Critical and Exegetical Commentary on Amos and Hosea*. ICC. New York: Charles Scribner's Sons, 1905.

Harris, J. Rendel. *The Apology of Aristides on Behalf of the Christians*. 2nd ed. Cambridge: Cambridge University Press, 1893.

Harris, Murray J. *The Second Epistle to the Corinthians. A Commentary on the Greek Text*. NIGTC. Grand Rapids: Eerdmans, 2005.

Harris, R. Laird. *Inspiration and Canonicity of the Bible*. Grand Rapids: Zondervan, 1969.

Harris, R. Laird, Gleason L. Archer, Jr., and Bruce K. Waltke, eds. *Theological Wordbook of the Old Testament*. 2 vols. Chicago: Moody, 1980.

Hartley, John E. *The Book of Job*. NICOT. Grand Rapids: Eerdmans, 1988.

Hauerwas, Stanley. *Character and the Christian Life: A Study in Theological Ethics*. San Antonio: Trinity University Press, 1975.

———. *A Community of Character: Toward a Constructive Christian Social Ethic*. Notre Dame: University of Notre Dame Press, 1986.

———. *The Peaceable Kingdom: A Primer in Christian Ethics*. Notre Dame: University of Notre Dame Press, 1983.

Hawtrey, Kim. "Economic Justice: A Twin Axiom Framework." *Reformed Theological Review* 50.3 (September 1991) 98–105.

———. "Evangelicals and Economics." *Association of Christian Economists Journal* 2 (1986) 47–60.

Hays, J. Daniel. "Applying the Old Testament Law Today." *Bibliotheca Sacra* 158 (January–March 2001) 21–35.

Hays, Richard B. *The Moral Vision of the New Testament: Community, Cross, New Creation*. San Francisco: Harper, 1996.

———. "Salvation by Trust? Reading the Bible Faithfully." *ChrCent* 114 (26 February 1997) 218–23.

Henry, Carl F. H. *Aspects of Christian Social Ethics*. Grand Rapids: Eerdmans, 1964.

Henry, Matthew. *An Exposition of All the Books of the Old and New Testaments*. 5 vols. London: W. Baynes, 1805.

Hervey, A. C. *I Timothy*. The Pulpit Commentary. Edited by H. D. M. Spence and Joseph S. Exell. Grand Rapids: Eerdmans, 1950.

Hock, Ronald F. "Lazarus and Micyllus: Greco-Roman Backgrounds to Luke 16:19–31." *JBL* 106.3 (Summer 1987) 447–63.

Hoekema, Anthony A. "Two Poles or One Goal?" *The Banner* 105 (November 1970) 4–6.
Hoppe, Leslie J. *Being Poor: A Biblical Study.* Wilmington: Michael Glazier, 1987.
———. *There Shall Be No Poor Among You: Poverty in the Bible.* Nashville: Abingdon, 2004.
House, Paul R. "Biblical Theology and the Wholeness of Scripture: Steps Toward a Program for the Future." In *Biblical Theology: Retrospect and Prospect*, edited by Scott J. Hafemann, 267–80. Downers Grove: InterVarsity, 2002.
House, Robert J., et al., eds. *Culture, Leadership, and Organizations: The GLOBE Study of 62 Societies.* Thousand Oaks: Sage, 2004.
Houten, Mark E. van. *God's Inner-City Address: Crossing the Boundaries.* Grand Rapids: Zondervan, 1988.
Hron, Ondrej. "Demarcating Biblical Justice: Can Hamartiology Be Conscripted into Providing a Textual Discrimen?" Paper presented at the annual meeting of the Evangelical Theological Society. Providence, RI, 20 November 2008.
———. "Hamartiological Heuristics as a Hermeneutical Key to Justice, Mercy and the Moral Treatment of the Poor in the New Testament." PhD dissertation, Universitas Carolina Pragensis, 2008.
———. "Is Helping the Poor a Matter of Justice or Mercy? Deciphering the Contours of the New Testament Witness." Paper presented at the annual meeting of the Evangelical Theological Society. New Orleans, LA, 19 November 2009.
———. "Seeking Compassion: A Methodology for Locating and Evaluating the Biblical Mandates for Helping the Poor." MTS thesis, Associated Canadian Theological Schools at Trinity Western University, 2004.
———. "Why Do We Argue over What Biblical Justice Demands? Particularity, Hermeneutics and the Necessary Characteristics of a Successful Textual Resolution." Paper presented at the annual meeting of the Evangelical Theological Society. San Diego, CA, 14 November 2007.
Hutchison, William R. *The Modernist Impulse in American Protestantism.* New York: Oxford University Press, 1976.
Jackson, Timothy P. *The Priority of Love: Christian Charity and Social Justice.* Princeton: Princeton University Press, 2003.
Jennings, Theodore W., Jr. *Reading Derrida / Thinking Paul: On Justice.* Stanford: Stanford University Press, 2005.
Jeremias, Joachim. *Jerusalem in the Time of Jesus: An Investigation into Economic and Social Conditions during the New Testament Period.* Translated by F. H. Cave and C. H. Cave. Philadelphia: Fortress, 1969.
———. *The Parables of Jesus.* London: SCM, 1963.
———. *Rediscovering the Parables.* New York: Charles Scribner's Sons, 1966.
Johnson, Luke T. *The Literary Function of Possessions in Luke–Acts.* Missoula: Scholars Press, 1977.
———. *Sharing Possessions: Mandate and Symbol of Faith.* Overtures to Biblical Theology. Philadelphia: Fortress, 1981.
Jones, David Clyde. *Biblical Christian Ethics.* Grand Rapids: Baker, 1994.
Josephus, Flavius. *The Works of Josephus: Complete and Unabridged.* Translated by William Whiston. Peabody: Hendrickson, 1996.
Kaiser, Walter C., Jr. "A Comparison of a Paradigm Approach to Biblical Law with a Principled Approach." Paper presented at the annual meeting of the Evangelical Theological Society. Valley Forge, PA, 16 November 2005.

———. "The Law as God's Gracious Guidance for the Promotion of Holiness." In *Five Views on Law and Gospel*, edited by Stanley N. Gundry, 177–200. Grand Rapids: Zondervan, 1993.

———. *Toward Old Testament Ethics*. Grand Rapids: Zondervan, 1983.

Kammer, Charles L. *The Kingdom Revisited: An Essay on Christian Social Ethics*. Washington: University Press of America, 1981.

Karris, Robert J. "Poor and Rich: The Lukan Sitz im Leben." In *Perspectives on Luke–Acts*, edited by Charles H. Talbert. Edinburgh: T. & T. Clark, 1978.

Kautsky, John H. *The Politics of Aristocratic Empires*. Chapel Hill: University of North Carolina Press, 1982.

Keener, Craig S. *A Commentary on the Gospel of Matthew*. Grand Rapids: Eerdmans, 1999.

———. *The Gospel of John: A Commentary*. 2 vols. Peabody: Hendrickson, 2003.

———. *The IVP Bible Background Commentary: New Testament*. Downers Grove: InterVarsity, 1993.

Keil, Carl Friedrich, and Franz Delitzsch. *Commentary on the Old Testament*. Peabody: Hendrickson, 2002.

Keller, Timothy J. *Ministries of Mercy: The Call of the Jericho Road*. Grand Rapids: Zondervan, 1989.

Kelley, Page H. *Isaiah*. Broadman Bible Commentary. Nashville: Broadman, 1971.

Kelsey, David H. *Proving Doctrine: The Uses of Scripture in Modern Theology*. Harrisburg: Trinity, 1999.

Khandker, Shahidur R. *Fighting Poverty with Microcredit: Experience in Bangladesh*. New York: Oxford University Press, 1998.

Kim, Kyoung-Jin. *Stewardship and Almsgiving in Luke's Theology*. Journal for the Study of the New Testament, Supplement Series. Sheffield: Sheffield Academic, 1998.

Kirk, Andrew. *God's Word for a Complex World*. Basingstoke: Marshall Pickering, 1987.

———. *Liberation Theology: An Evangelical View from the Third World*. Atlanta: John Knox, 1979.

Kittel, Gerhard, and Gerhard Friedrich, eds. *Theological Dictionary of the New Testament*. Translated by Geoffrey W. Bromiley. 10 vols. Grand Rapids: Eerdmans, 1974.

Klein, William W., et al. *Introduction to Biblical Interpretation*. Dallas: Word, 1993.

Klinken, Jaap van. *Diakonia: Mutual Helping with Justice and Compassion*. Grand Rapids: Eerdmans, 1989.

Klostermann, Erich. *Das Lukasevangelium*. Handbuch zum Neuen Testament. 2nd ed. Tübingen: Mohr/Siebeck, 1929.

Knight, George W. III. *The Pastoral Epistles: A Commentary on the Greek Text*. NIGTC. Grand Rapids: Eerdmans, 1992.

Knowling, R. J. *The Acts of the Apostles*. EGT. Edited by W. Robertson Nicoll. New York: Armstrong, 1902.

Knox, John. *Chapters in a Life of Paul*. Rev. ed. Edited by Douglas R. Hare. Macon: Mercer University Press, 1987.

Koehler, Ludwig, and Walter Baumgartner. *Lexicon in Veteris Testamenti libros*. 2nd ed. Leiden: Brill, 1958.

Koehler, Ludwig, Walter Baumgartner, and J. J. Stamm. *The Hebrew and Aramaic Lexicon of the Old Testament*. 4 vols. Translated and edited under the supervision of M. E. J. Richardson. Leiden: Brill, 1994–1999.

Köstenberger, Andreas J. *John*. BECNT. Edited by Robert W. Yarbrough and Robert H. Stein. Grand Rapids: Baker Academic, 2004.
Kraus, Annie. "The Sin of Folly." In *Standing Before God: Studies on Prayer in Scriptures and in Tradition with Essays*, edited by Asher Finkel and Lawrence Frizzell. New York: Ktav, 1981.
Lachs, Samuel T. *A Rabbinic Commentary on the New Testament: The Gospels of Matthew, Mark, and Luke*. Hoboken: Ktav, 1987.
Lane, William L. *Hebrews*. 2 vols. WBC. Dallas: Word, 1991.
Larkin, William J. *Culture and Biblical Hermeneutics: Interpreting and Applying the Authoritative Word in a Relativistic Age*. Grand Rapids: Baker, 1988.
———. "Luke's Use of the Old Testament in Luke 22–23." PhD dissertation, University of Durham, 1974.
Lasor, William S., et al. *Old Testament Survey: The Message, Form, and Background of the Old Testament*. 2nd ed. Grand Rapids: Eerdmans, 1996.
Lea, Thomas D., and Hayne P. Griffin. *1, 2 Timothy, Titus*. NAC. Nashville: Broadman & Holman, 1992.
Leaney, A. R. C. *A Commentary on the Gospel According to St. Luke*. Harper's New Testament Commentaries. New York: Harper, 1958.
Lenski, Gerhard E. *Power and Privilege: A Theory of Social Stratification*. 2nd ed. Chapel Hill: University of North Carolina Press, 1984.
Lightfoot, John. *Horæ Hebraicæ et Talmudicæ: Hebrew and Talmudical Exercitations Upon the Gospels, the Acts, Some Chapters of St. Paul's Epistle to the Romans, and the First Epistle to the Corinthians*. 4 vols. New ed. Oxford: Oxford University Press: 1859.
Lincoln, Andrew T. *Ephesians*. WBC. Dallas: Word, 1990.
Lingenfelter, Judith E. "The Impact of Cultural Bias on Ministry Strategies to Help the Poor." Paper presented at the AERDO conference. Scottsdale, AZ, 1996.
———. "Why Do We Argue over How to Help the Poor?" *Missiology* 26.2 (April 1998) 155–66.
Lingenfelter, Sherwood. *Agents of Transformation*. Grand Rapids: Baker, 1996.
———. *Transforming Culture*. Grand Rapids: Baker, 1998.
Llewellyn, Jennifer J., and Robert Howse. "Restorative Justice: A Conceptual Framework." Law Commission of Canada. No pages. Accessed 18 September 2003. Online: http://www.lcc.gc.ca/en/themes/sr/rj/howse/howse_main.asp.
Logan, Robert E., and Larry Short. *Mobilizing for Compassion: Moving People into Ministry*. Grand Rapids: Revell, 1994.
Longenecker, Richard N. *Galatians*. WBC. Dallas: Word, 1990.
Luce, H. K. *The Gospel according to St. Luke*. Cambridge Greek Testament. Edited by A. Nairne. Cambridge: Cambridge University Press, 1936.
Lüdemann, Gerd. *Paul, Apostle to the Gentiles: Studies in Chronology*. Translated by E. Stanley Jones. Philadelphia: Fortress, 1984.
MacIntyre, Alasdair C. *After Virtue: A Study in Moral Theory*. 3rd ed. Notre Dame: University of Notre Dame Press, 2007.
———. *A Short History of Ethics*. New York: Macmillan, 1966.
———. *Whose Justice? Whose Rationality?* Notre Dame: University of Notre Dame Press, 1988.
Malina, Bruce J. "Interpreting the Bible with Anthropology: The Case of the Poor and the Rich." *Listening* 21 (1986) 148–59.

———. *The New Testament World: Insights from Cultural Anthropology*. 3rd ed. Louisville: Westminster John Knox, 2001.

———. "Wealth and Poverty in the New Testament and Its World." *Int* 41.4 (October 1987) 354–67.

Manson, Thomas W. *The Sayings of Jesus: As Recorded in the Gospels According to St. Matthew and St. Luke*. London: SCM, 1975.

Marshall, I. Howard. *Beyond the Bible: Moving from Scripture to Theology*. Grand Rapids: Baker, 2004.

———. *The Epistles of John*. NICNT. Grand Rapids: Eerdmans, 1978.

———. *The Gospel of Luke: A Commentary on the Greek Text*. NIGTC. Grand Rapids: Eerdmans, 1978.

———. *New Testament Theology: Many Witnesses, One Gospel*. Downers Grove: InterVarsity, 2004.

Martens, Elmer. "Old Testament Theology since Walter C. Kaiser, Jr." *JETS* 50.4 (December 2007) 688–90.

Martin, Ralph P. *2 Corinthians*. WBC. Dallas: Word, 1986.

———. *James*. WBC. Dallas: Word, 1988.

Marx, Karl, and Friedrich Engels. "Kritik des Gothaer Programms." In *Werke 19*, 13–32. Berlin: Dietz, 1962.

McGovern, Arthur F. *Liberation Theology and Its Critics: Toward an Assessment*. Maryknoll: Orbis, 1989.

McKinion, Steven A., ed. *Isaiah 1–39*. Ancient Christian Commentary on Scripture: Old Testament. Edited by Thomas C. Oden. Downers Grove: InterVarsity, 2004.

McNeill, Donald P., et al. *Compassion: A Reflection on the Christian Life*. Garden City: Image, 1983.

McQuilkin, Robertson. *An Introduction to Biblical Ethics*. 2nd ed. Wheaton: Tyndale, 1989.

———. *Understanding and Applying the Bible*. Rev. ed. Chicago: Moody, 1992.

Mealand, David L. *Poverty and Expectation in the Gospels*. London: SPCK, 1980.

Meeks, Wayne A. *The Moral World of the First Christians*. Philadelphia: Westminster, 1986.

Merrill, Eugene H. *Deuteronomy*. NAC. Nashville: Broadman & Holman, 1994.

Metzger, Bruce M. *A Textual Commentary on the Greek New Testament*. 2nd ed. Stuttgart: Deutsche Bibelgesellschaft, 1994.

Meyer, Heinrich A. W. *Critical and Exegetical Hand-Book to the Gospels of Mark and Luke*. New York: Funk & Wagnalls, 1884.

Meyers, Eric M. "The Cultural Setting of Galilee: The Case of Regionalism and Early Judaism." In *Aufstieg und Niedergang der römischen Welt: Geschichte und Kultur Roms im Spiegel der neueren Forschung*, series 2, vol. 19/1, edited by H. Temporini and W. Haase, 686–702. Berlin: Walter de Gruyter, 1979.

———. "Galilean Regionalism: A Reappraisal." In *Approaches to Ancient Judaism*, edited by William S. Green, 5:115–31. Missoula: Scholars Press, 1978.

———. "Galilean Regionalism as a Factor in Historical Reconstruction." *Bulletin of the American Schools of Oriental Research* 221 (February 1976) 93–101.

Miller, Darrow L. *Discipling Nations: The Power of Truth to Transform Cultures*. Seattle: YWAM Publishing, 1998.

Miller, Darrow L., ed. *Worldview and Development: The Power of Truth to Transform Poverty*. Scottsdale: Food for the Hungry International, 1993.

Miller, Keith. *The Scent of Love*. Waco: Word, 1983.

Miller, William, and Kathleen Jackson. *Practical Psychology for Pastors*. Englewood Cliffs: Prentice Hall, 1995.
Miranda, José Porfirio. *Marx and the Bible: A Critique of the Philosophy of Oppression*. Maryknoll: Orbis, 1974.
MkNelly, Barbara, and Christopher Dunford. "Impact of Credit with Education on Mothers and Their Young Children's Nutrition: Lower Pra Rural Bank Credit with Education Program in Ghana." In *Freedom from Hunger Research Paper No. 4*, 1–61. Davis: Freedom from Hunger, 1998.
M'Neile, Alan H. *The Gospel According to Saint Matthew*. London: Macmillan, 1915.
Moffatt, James. *The Revelation of St. John the Divine*. EGT. Edited by W. Robertson Nicoll. New York: Armstrong, 1910.
Moltmann, Jürgen. *Theologie der Hoffnung. Untersuchungen zur Begründung und zu den Konsequenzen einer christlichen Eschatologie*. Munich: Chr. Kaiser, 1969.
Moo, Douglas J. *The Epistle to the Romans*. NICNT. Grand Rapids: Eerdmans, 1996.
Moore, G. E. *Principia Ethica*. New York: Cambridge University Press, 1903.
Morris, Leon. *The Book of Revelation: An Introduction and Commentary*. TNTC. Rev. ed. Grand Rapids: Eerdmans, 1987.
———. *The Gospel According to Matthew*. The Pillar New Testament Commentary. Grand Rapids: Eerdmans, 1992.
———. *Luke: An Introduction and Commentary*. TNTC. Rev. ed. Grand Rapids: Eerdmans, 1988.
———. *Testaments of Love: A Study of Love in the Bible*. Grand Rapids: Eerdmans, 1981.
Motyer, J. Alec. *The Prophecy of Isaiah: An Introduction & Commentary*. Downers Grove: InterVarsity, 1993.
Moulton, James H., and George Milligan. *The Vocabulary of the Greek Testament: Illustrated from the Papyri and Other Non-Literary Sources*. London: Hodder and Stoughton, 1929.
Mounce, Robert H. *The Book of Revelation*. NICNT. Rev. ed. Grand Rapids: Eerdmans, 1998.
———. *Romans*. NAC. Nashville: Broadman & Holman, 1995.
Mounce, William D. *Pastoral Epistles*. WBC. Dallas: Word, 2000.
Murphey, Dwight D. *Liberal Thought in Modern America*. Lanham: University Press of America, 1987.
Murphy, Rowland E. *Proverbs*. WBC. Dallas: Word, 1998.
Murray, John. *Collected Writings of John Murray*. Edinburgh: Banner of Truth Trust, 1976.
———. *Principles of Conduct: Aspects of Biblical Ethics*. Grand Rapids: Eerdmans, 1957.
Murray, Joyce. "Liberation for Communion in the Soteriology of Gustavo Gutierrez." *TS* 59.1 (March 1998) 51–59.
Nägelsbach, Carl W. E. *The Prophet Isaiah*. A Commentary on the Holy Scriptures: Critical, Doctrinal, and Homiletical, with Special Reference to Ministers and Students. Edited by Johann Peter Lange and Philip Schaff. Translated by Samuel T. Lowrie and Dunlop Moore. New York: Charles Scribner's Sons, 1878.
Nardoni, Enrique. *Rise Up, O Judge: A Study of Justice in the Biblical World*. Translated by Seán Charles Martin. Peabody: Hendrickson, 2004.
Nash, Ronald H. *Poverty and Wealth: The Christian Debate over Capitalism*. Wheaton: Crossway, 1987.
———. *Poverty and Wealth: Why Socialism Doesn't Work*. Richardson: Probe, 1992.

———. *Social Justice and the Christian Church*. Milford: Mott, 1983.

———. *Why the Left Is Not Right: the Religious Left: Who They Are and What They Believe*. Grand Rapids: Zondervan, 1996.

Nash, Ronald H., ed. *Liberation Theology*. Milford: Mott, 1984.

Nessan, Craig L. *Orthopraxis or Heresy*. Atlanta: Scholars Press, 1989.

Nestle, Eberhard, et al. *Novum Testamentum Graece*. 27th ed. Stuttgart: Deutsche Bibelgesellschaft, 1993.

Neusner, Jacob, ed. *The Talmud of the Land of Israel: A Preliminary Translation and Explanation: Sanhedrin and Makkot*. Chicago Studies in the History of Judaism. Chicago: University of Chicago Press, 1984.

Newbigin, Lesslie. *The Good Shepherd: Meditations on Christian Ministry in Today's World*. Madras: Christian Literature Society, 1977.

Niebuhr, Reinhold. *An Interpretation of Christian Ethics*. New York: Seabury, 1979.

Nijf, Onno M. van. *The Civic World of Professional Associations in the Roman East*. Dutch Monographs on Ancient History and Archaeology. Amsterdam: J. C. Gieben, 1997.

Nineham, Dennis E. *Saint Mark*. Baltimore: Penguin, 1968.

Noell, Edd S. "A 'Marketless World?' An Examination of Wealth and Exchange in the Gospels and First-Century Palestine." *Journal of Markets & Morality* 10.1 (Spring 2007) 85–114.

Nolland, John. *The Gospel of Matthew: A Commentary on the Greek Text*. NIGTC. Grand Rapids: Eerdmans, 2005.

———. *Luke*. 3 vols. WBC. Dallas: Word, 1989.

Nouwen, Henri. *Out of Solitude: Three Meditations on the Christian Life*. Notre Dame: Ave Maria, 1974.

———. *The Wounded Healer: Ministry in Contemporary Society*. New York: Image, 1990.

Novak, Michael. *The Catholic Ethic and the Spirit of Capitalism*. New York: Free Press, 1993.

———. *The Spirit of Democratic Capitalism*. Lanham: Madison, 1991.

———. *Will It Liberate? Questions About Liberation Theology*. New York: Paulist, 1986.

Nozick, Robert. *Anarchy, State, and Utopia*. New ed. Oxford: Blackwell, 2001.

Nunez C., Emilio A. *Liberation Theology*. Philadelphia: Fortress, 1985.

Nunez C., Emilio A., and William David Taylor. *Crisis and Hope in Latin America: An Evangelical Perspective*. Chicago: Moody, 1989.

Oakman, Douglas E. "The Ancient Economy." In *The Social Sciences and New Testament Interpretation*, edited by Richard L. Rohrbaugh. Peabody: Hendrickson, 1996.

———. "The Ancient Economy in the Bible." *Biblical Theology Bulletin* 21.1 (February 1991) 34–39.

———. *Jesus and the Economic Questions of His Day*. Studies in the Bible and Early Christianity. Lewiston: Edwin Mellen, 1986.

O'Brien, Peter T. *The Epistle to the Philippians: A Commentary on the Greek Text*. NIGTC. Grand Rapids: Eerdmans, 1991.

———. *The Letter to the Ephesians*. The Pillar New Testament Commentary. Grand Rapids: Eerdmans, 1999.

O'Donovan, Oliver. *The Desire of the Nations: Rediscovering the Roots of Political Theology*. Cambridge: Cambridge University Press, 1999.

———. *The Ways of Judgment: The Bampton Lectures*. Grand Rapids: Eerdmans, 2005.

Olasky, Marvin. *Renewing American Compassion: How Compassion for the Needy Can Turn Ordinary Citizens into Heroes*. New York: Free Press, 1996.

———. *The Tragedy of American Compassion*. Washington: Regnery, 1992.
Ondari, William O. "Poverty and Wealth: A Christian Perspective." In *Christ in the Classroom* 28, 343–62. Silver Spring: Institute for Christian Teaching, 2001.
Orr, James, ed. *The International Standard Bible Encyclopedia*. Grand Rapids: Eerdmans, 1956.
Osborne, Grant R. *The Hermeneutical Spiral: A Comprehensive Introduction to Biblical Interpretation*. Downers Grove: InterVarsity, 1991.
———. *Revelation*. BECNT. Edited by Robert W. Yarbrough and Robert H. Stein. Grand Rapids: Baker Academic, 2002.
Oswalt, John N. *The Book of Isaiah*. NICOT. Grand Rapids: Eerdmans, 1986.
Outka, Gene H. *Agape: An Ethical Analysis*. New Haven: Yale University Press, 1972.
Pannenberg, Wolfhart. *Anthropologie in theologischer Perspektive*. Göttingen: Vandenhoeck & Ruprecht, 1983.
Pastor, Jack. *Land and Economy in Ancient Palestine*. London: Routledge, 1997.
Pao, David W., and Eckhard J. Schnabel. "Luke." In *Commentary on the New Testament Use of the Old Testament*, edited by Gregory K. Beale and D. A. Carson, 251–414. Grand Rapids: Baker Academic, 2007.
Pauli, Christian W. H. *The Chaldee Paraphrase on the Prophet Isaiah*. London: London Society's House, 1871.
Phillips, Elaine A. "The Tilted Balance: Early Rabbinic Perceptions of God's Justice." *Bulletin for Biblical Research* 14.2 (2004) 223–40.
Pilgrim, Walter E. *Good News to the Poor: Wealth and Poverty in Luke–Acts*. Minneapolis: Augsburg, 1981.
Piper, John. *"Love Your Enemies": Jesus' Love Command in the Synoptic Gospels and in the Early Christian Paraenesis: A History of the Tradition and Interpretation of Its Uses*. Grand Rapids: Baker, 1991.
Pitt, Mark M., and Shahidur R. Khandker. "Household and Intrahousehold Impact of the Grameen Bank and Similar Targeted Credit Programs in Bangladesh." In *World Bank Discussion Papers 320*. Washington: World Bank, 1996.
Plantinga, Cornelius, Jr. "The Sinner and the Fool." *First Things* 46 (October 1994) 24–29.
Plato. *The Republic*. Translated by Desmond Lee. New York: Penguin, 1974.
Pleket, Harry W. "Urban Elites and Business in the Greek Part of the Roman Empire." In *Trade in the Ancient Economy*, edited by Peter Garnsey, Keith Hopkins, and C. R. Whittaker. Berkeley: University of California Press, 1983.
———. "Urban Elites and the Economy in the Greek Cities of the Roman Empire." *Münsterische Beiträge zur antiken Handelsgeschichte* 3.1 (1984) 3–36.
Plumb, Ralph E. "Toward a Theology of Mercy: Integrating Relief and Christian Witness." International Conference on NGO's, Humanitarian Relief, and Complex Emergencies. Langley, BC, 1997.
Plummer, Alfred. *A Critical and Exegetical Commentary on the Gospel according to St. Luke*. ICC. 5th ed. New York: Charles Scribner's Sons, 1896.
———. *A Critical and Exegetical Commentary on the Second Epistle of St. Paul to the Corinthians*. ICC. New York: Charles Scribner's Sons, 1956.
———. *An Exegetical Commentary on the Gospel according to St. Matthew*. 2nd ed. London: Elliot Stock, 1910.
Plummer, Alfred, et al. *Revelation*. The Pulpit Commentary. Edited by H. D. M. Spence and Joseph S. Exell. London: Funk & Wagnalls, n.d.
Pojman, Louis P. *Justice: An Anthology*. Upper Saddle River: Pearson, 2006.

Pojman, Louis P., and Owen McLeod, eds. *What Do We Deserve? A Reader on Justice and Desert*. New York: Oxford University Press, 1999.
Pokorný, Petr. "Die soziale Strategie in den lukanischen Schriften." *CV* 34.1 (1992) 9–19.
Polanyi, Karl. *The Great Transformation*. New York: Farrar & Rinehart, 1944.
———. *Primitive, Archaic, and Modern Economies: Essays of Karl Polanyi*. Garden City: Anchor, 1968.
Polanyi, Karl, Conrad M. Arensberg, and Harry W. Pearson, eds. *Trade and Market in the Early Empires: Economies in History and Theory*. New York: Free Press, 1957.
Polhill, John B. *Acts*. NAC. Nashville: Broadman & Holman, 1992.
Pope, Stephen J. "Proper and Improper Partiality and the Preferential Option for the Poor." *TS* 54.2 (June 1993) 242–71.
Porter, Stanley E. "The Message of the Book of Job: Job 42:7b as Key to Interpretation?" *Evangelical Quarterly* 63 (October 1991) 291–304.
Pouderon, Bernard, et al. *Aristide: Apologie*. Sources chrétiennes. Paris: Cerf, 2003.
Radant, Kenneth G. "Headcovering, Holy Kisses, Hierarchy, and Homosexuality: How Do We Discern What It Means to Obey Biblical Directives? A Truth-in-Context Model." Paper presented at the annual meeting of the Evangelical Theological Society. San Diego, CA, 15 November 2007.
Rahlfs, Alfred, ed. *Septuaginta: With Morphology*. Stuttgart: Deutsche Bibelgesellschaft, 1996.
Rashi (Rabbi Shlomo Yitzhaki). *Commentary on the Tanakh*. No pages. Accessed 18 May 2010. Online: http://www.chabad.org/library/bible_cdo/aid/15963/showrashi/true.
Rauschenbusch, Walter. *Christianity and the Social Crisis*. New York: Macmillan, 1907.
———. *Christianizing the Social Order*. New York: Macmillan, 1919.
———. *The Social Principles of Jesus*. New York: Association Press, 1916.
———. *A Theology for the Social Gospel*. New York: Abingdon, 1917.
Rawlinson, George. *Isaiah*. 2 vols. The Pulpit Commentary. Edited by H. D. M. Spence and Joseph S. Exell. New York: Funk & Wagnalls, n.d.
Rawls, John. *Lectures on the History of Moral Philosophy*. Edited by Barbara Herman. Cambridge: Harvard University Press, 2000.
———. *Political Liberalism*. New York: Columbia University Press, 1993.
———. *A Theory of Justice*. Oxford: Oxford University Press, 1973.
Regnerus, Mark D., et al. "Who Gives to the Poor? The Influence of Religious Tradition and Political Location on the Personal Generosity of Americans Toward the Poor." *Journal for the Scientific Study of Religion* 37.3 (September 1998) 481–93.
Reiling, J., and J. L. Swellengrebel. *A Handbook on the Gospel of Luke*. United Bible Society Handbook Series. New York: United Bible Societies, 1993.
Renan, Joseph Ernest. *Vie de Jésus*. Histoire des origines du christianisme. Paris: Michel Lévy Frères, 1863.
Rendall, Frederic. *The Epistle to the Galatians*. EGT. Edited by W. Robertson Nicoll. New York: Armstrong, 1903.
Rhodes, Ron. "Christian Revolution in Latin America: The Changing Face of Liberation Theology." *Christian Research Journal*. No pages. Accessed 26 November 2001. Online: http://home.earthlink.net/~ronrhodes/Liberation.html.
Rich, Arthur. *Etika Hospodářství*. Vol. 1. Translated by Karel Floss et al. Prague: Oikoymenh, 1994.
———. *Etika Hospodářství*. Vol. 2. Translated by Břetislav Horyna. Prague: Oikoymenh, 1994.

Richards, John, et al. *Helping the Poor: A Qualified Case for "Workfare."* Toronto: C. D. Howe Institute, 1995.

Richardson, Cyril C. *Early Christian Fathers*. The Library of Christian Classics. Philadelphia: Westminster, 1953.

Richardson, Kurt A. *James*. NAC. Nashville: Broadman & Holman, 1997.

Ridderbos, Jan. *Isaiah*. Bible Student's Commentary. Grand Rapids: Regency Reference Library, 1985.

Robertson, Archibald, and Alfred Plummer. *A Critical and Exegetical Commentary on the First Epistle of St. Paul to the Corinthians*. ICC. 2nd ed. New York: Charles Scribner's Sons, 1961.

Ropes, James H. *A Critical and Exegetical Commentary on the Epistle of St. James*. ICC. New York: Charles Scribner's Sons, 1916.

Ross, W. D. *The Right and the Good*. New York: Oxford University Press, 1930.

Rostovtzeff, Mikhail I. *A History of the Ancient World: The Orient and Greece*. Translated by J. D. Duff. New York: Biblo & Tannen, 1926.

———. *The Social and Economic History of the Hellenistic World*. Oxford: Clarendon, 1941.

———. *The Social and Economic History of the Roman Empire*. 2 vols. Edited by P. M. Fraser. Oxford: Clarendon, 1957.

Sanders, Ed P. "On the Question of Fulfilling the Law in Paul and Rabbinic Judaism." In *Donum Gentilicum: New Testament Studies in Honour of David Daube*, edited by C. K. Barrett, E. Bammel, and W. D. Davies. Oxford: Clarendon, 1978.

———. *Paul and Palestinian Judaism: A Comparison in Patterns of Religion*. London: SCM, 1977.

Sayre-McCord, Geoffrey, ed. *Essays on Moral Realism*. Ithaca: Cornell University Press, 1988.

Schnackenburg, Rudolf. *The Gospel of Matthew*. Translated by Robert R. Barr. Grand Rapids: Eerdmans, 2002.

———. *Das Johannesevangelium*. 2nd ed. Freiburg: Herder, 1971.

Schottroff, Luise, and Wolfgang Stegemann. *Jesus and the Hope of the Poor*. Translated by Matthew J. O'Connell. Maryknoll: Orbis, 1986.

———. *Jesus von Nazareth: Hoffnung der Armen*. Stuttgart: Kohlhammer, 1978.

Schrage, Wolfgang. *Der erste Brief an die Korinther*. 4 vols. Evangelisch-katholischer Kommentar zum Neuen Testament. Vluyn: Neukirchener Verlag, 1999.

———. *The Ethics of the New Testament*. Translated by David E. Green. Philadelphia: Fortress, 1988.

Schreiner, Thomas R. *Romans*. BECNT. Edited by Robert W. Yarbrough and Robert H. Stein. Grand Rapids: Baker Academic, 1998.

Schweizer, Eduard. *The Good News According to Luke*. Translated by David E. Green. Atlanta: John Knox, 1984.

Scott, James C. *The Moral Economy of the Peasant: Rebellion and Subsistence in Southeast Asia*. New Haven: Yale University Press, 1976.

Seccombe, David P. *Possessions and the Poor in Luke–Acts*. Studien zum Neuen Testament und seiner Umwelt. Linz: Fuchs, 1982.

Segundo, Juan Luis. *Liberation of Theology*. Maryknoll: Orbis, 1976.

Seim, Brian, ed. *Moved with Compassion*. Belleville: Essence, 2000.

Seitz, Christopher R. *Isaiah 1–39*. Interpretation. Louisville: Westminster John Knox, 1993.

Sharpe, Dores Robinson. *Walter Rauschenbusch*. New York: Macmillan, 1942.
Sider, Ronald J. *Good News and Good Works: A Theology of the Whole Gospel*. Grand Rapids: Baker, 1999.
———. *Lifestyle in the Eighties: An Evangelical Commitment to Simple Lifestyle*. Exeter: Paternoster, 1982.
———. *Rich Christians in an Age of Hunger: Moving from Affluence to Generosity*. 5th rev. ed. Dallas: Word, 1997.
Sider, Ronald J., ed. *The Chicago Declaration*. Carol Stream: Creation House, 1974.
Sigmund, Paul E. *Liberation Theology at the Crossroads: Democracy or Revolution?* New York: Oxford University Press, 1990.
Siker, Jeffrey S. *Scripture and Ethics: Twentieth-Century Portraits*. New York: Oxford University Press, 1997.
Silva, Moisés. *Philippians*. BECNT. 2nd ed. Edited by Robert W. Yarbrough and Robert H. Stein. Grand Rapids: Baker Academic, 2005.
———. "The Place of Historical Reconstruction in New Testament Criticism." In *Hermeneutics, Authority, and Canon*, edited by D. A. Carson and John D. Woodbridge, 105–33. Grand Rapids: Baker, 1995.
Skinner, John. *The Book of the Prophet Isaiah: Chapters 1–39*. The Cambridge Bible for Schools and Colleges. Edited by A. F. Kirkpatrick. Cambridge: University Press, 1896.
Smalley, Stephen S. *1, 2, 3 John*. WBC. Dallas: Word, 1984.
Smith, Christian. *The Emergence of Liberation Theology: Radical Religion and Social Movement*. Chicago: University of Chicago Press, 1991.
Smith, Gary V. *Isaiah*. 2 vols. NAC. Nashville: Broadman & Holman, 2009.
Smith, James E. *The Books of History*. Old Testament Survey Series. Joplin: College Press, 1995.
Sobrino, Jon. *The Principle of Mercy: Taking the Crucified People from the Cross*. Maryknoll: Orbis, 1994.
———. *The True Church and the Poor*. Maryknoll: Orbis, 1984.
Social Action Commission of the Evangelical Fellowship of Canada. "Good News to the Poor." Pages 1–10. Accessed 4 April 2001. Online: http://www.efc-canada.com/na/docs/poverty.htm.
Solomon, Robert C., and Mark C. Murphy, eds. *What Is Justice? Classical and Contemporary Readings*. 2nd ed. Oxford: Oxford University Press, 2000.
Spence, Henry D. M. St. *Luke*. 2 vols. The Pulpit Commentary. Edited by H. D. M. Spence and Joseph S. Exell. Grand Rapids: Eerdmans, 1950.
Stambaugh, John E., and David L. Balch. *The New Testament in Its Social Environment*. Philadelphia: Westminster, 1986.
Stassen, Glen H., and David P. Gushee. *Kingdom Ethics: Following Jesus in Contemporary Context*. Downers Grove: InterVarsity, 2003.
Statistics Canada. *Low Income Cut-Offs for 2006 and Low Income Measures for 2005*. Income Research Paper Series. Ottawa: Minister of Industry, 2007.
———. *Low Income Lines, 2008–2009*. Income Research Paper Series. Ottawa: Minister of Industry, 2010.
Stein, Robert H. "Is Our Reading the Bible the Same as the Original Audience's Hearing It? A Case Study in the Gospel of Mark." *JETS* 46.1 (March 2003) 63–78.
———. *Luke*. NAC. Nashville: Broadman & Holman, 1993.
Sterba, James P., ed. *Morality in Practice*. 5th ed. Belmont: Wadsworth, 1997.

Strack, Hermann L., and Paul Billerbeck. *Kommentar zum Neuen Testament aus Talmud und Midrasch.* 5 vols. 3rd ed. Munich: C. H. Beck, 1956.
Strelan, John G. "Burden-Bearing and the Law of Christ: A Re-Examination of Galatians 6:2." *JBL* 94.2 (June 1975) 266–76.
Swanson, James. *Dictionary of Biblical Languages with Semantic Domains: Hebrew (Old Testament).* Electronic ed. Oak Harbor: Logos Research Systems, 1997.
Swartley, Willard M. *Slavery, Sabbath, War, and Women: Case Issues in Biblical Interpretation.* Scottdale: Herald, 1983.
Sweeney, Marvin A. *Isaiah 1–39: With an Introduction to Prophetic Literature.* The Forms of the Old Testament Literature. Grand Rapids: Eerdmans, 1996.
Targum Jonathan to the Prophets. Comprehensive Aramaic Lexicon. Cincinnati: Hebrew Union College, 2005.
Targum Lexicon. Comprehensive Aramaic Lexicon. Cincinnati: Hebrew Union College, 2004.
Targumic Toseftot to the Prophets. Comprehensive Aramaic Lexicon. Cincinnati: Hebrew Union College, 2005.
The Ante-Nicene Fathers. 10 vols. Edited by Alexander Roberts and James Donaldson. 1885–1887. Repr. Peabody: Hendrickson, 1994.
The Nicene and Post-Nicene Fathers, Series 1. 14 vols. Edited by Philip Schaff. 1886–1889. Repr. Peabody: Hendrickson, 1994.
Theissen, Gerd. *The Religion of the Earliest Churches: Creating a Symbolic World.* Translated by John Bowden. Minneapolis: Fortress, 1999.
———. *The Social Setting of Pauline Christianity: Essays on Corinth.* Translated by John H. Schütz. Philadelphia: Fortress, 1982.
Thiselton, Anthony C. *The First Epistle to the Corinthians: A Commentary on the Greek Text.* NIGTC. Grand Rapids: Eerdmans, 2000.
Thompson, Augustus C. *Moravian Missions: Twelve Lectures.* New York: Charles Scribner's Sons, 1882.
Thompson, Michael, et al. *Cultural Theory.* Political Cultures Series. Boulder: Westview, 1990.
Thurén, Jukka. *Das Lobopfer der Hebräer: Studien zum Aufbau und Anliegen von Hebräerbrief 13.* Åbo: Academiae Aboensis, 1973.
Todd, Helen. *Women at the Center: Grameen Bank Borrowers after One Decade.* Colorado: Westview, 1996.
Topel, L. John. *Children of a Compassionate God: A Theological Exegesis of Luke 6:20–49.* Collegeville: Liturgical, 2001.
Trost, Travis D. "Pilate, Revolution, and Jesus." MTS thesis, Associated Canadian Theological Schools at Trinity Western University, 1998.
Truesdale, Albert L., Jr., and Steve Weber. *Evangelism and Social Redemption.* Kansas City: Beacon Hill, 1987.
Turner, David L. *The Gospel of Matthew.* Cornerstone Biblical Commentary. Edited by Philip W. Comfort. Carol Stream: Tyndale, 2006.
United Nations. "Universal Declaration of Human Rights." General Assembly resolution 217 A (III), United Nations Document A/810 at 71 (10 December 1948).
Urbach, Ephraim E. *The Sages: Their Concepts and Beliefs.* 2nd ed. Jerusalem: Magnes, 1979.
VanGemeren, Willem A., ed. *New International Dictionary of Old Testament Theology and Exegesis.* 5 vols. Grand Rapids: Zondervan, 1997.

Veerman, Dave. *How to Apply the Bible*. Grand Rapids: Baker, 1993.
Verbruggen, Jan L. "Of Muzzles and Oxen: Deuteronomy 25:4 and 1 Corinthians 9:9." *JETS* 49.4 (December 2006) 699–711.
Villafane, Eldin. *Seek the Peace of the City: Reflections on Urban Ministry*. Grand Rapids: Eerdmans, 1995.
Volf, Miroslav. *Exclusion and Embrace: A Theological Exploration of Identity, Otherness, and Reconciliation*. Nashville: Abingdon, 1996.
———. "Exclusion and Embrace: Theological Reflections in the Wake of 'Ethnic Cleansing.'" *CV* 35 (1993) 263–87.
Vööbus, Arthur. *The Didascalia Apostolorum in Syriac*. Corpus Scriptorum Christianorum Orientalium: Scriptores Syri. Waversebaan: Secrétariat du Corpus SCO, 1979.
Waldow, H. Eberhard von. "Social Responsibility and Social Structure in Early Israel." *Catholic Biblical Quarterly* 32 (April 1970) 182–204.
Wallis, Jim. *Who Speaks for God?* New York: Delacorte, 1996.
Walsh, Gary. "Evangelicals and the Poor." No pages. Accessed 4 April 2001. Online: http://www.efc-canada.com/garyw2.htm.
Waltzing, Jean-Pierre. *Étude historique sur les corporations professionnelles chez les Romains depuis les origines jusqu'à la chute de l'Empire d'Occident*. 4 vols. Louvain: Peeters, 1895–1900.
Warden, Duane. "The Rich and Poor in James: Implications for Institutionalized Partiality." *JETS* 43.2 (June 2000) 247–57.
Watts, John D. W. *Isaiah*. 2 vols. WBC. Dallas: Word, 2005.
Webb, William J. *Slaves, Women & Homosexuals: Exploring the Hermeneutics of Cultural Analysis*. Grand Rapids: InterVarsity, 2001.
Weston, Anthony. *A 21st Century Ethical Toolbox*. New York: Oxford University Press, 2001.
Wheeler, Sondra E. *Wealth as Peril and Obligation: The New Testament on Possessions*. Grand Rapids: Eerdmans, 1995.
White, Newport J. D. *Titus*. EGT. Edited by W. Robertson Nicoll. New York: Armstrong, 1910.
Widyapranawa, Samuel H. *The Lord Is Savior: Faith in National Crisis: A Commentary on the Book of Isaiah 1–39*. International Theological Commentary. Grand Rapids: Eerdmans, 1990.
Wigram, George V. *The Englishman's Hebrew and Chaldee Concordance of the Old Testament*. 3rd ed. London: Samuel Bagster, 1866.
Wilberforce, William. *A Practical View of the Prevailing Religious System of Professed Christians in the Higher and Middle Classes in this Country, Contrasted with Real Christianity*. London: Fisher, Fisher and Jackson, 1839.
Wildberger, Hans. *Isaiah 28–39*. Continental Commentary. Translated by Thomas H. Trapp. Minneapolis: Fortress, 2002.
Wilkins, Michael J. *Matthew*. The NIV Application Commentary. Grand Rapids: Zondervan, 2004.
Williams, A. Lukyn. *St. Matthew*. 2 vols. The Pulpit Commentary. Edited by H. D. M. Spence and Joseph S. Exell. London: Funk & Wagnalls, 1913.
Williams, David J. *Acts*. NIBCNT. Edited by W. W. Gasque. Peabody: Hendrickson, 1990.
Williams, Garry J. "Penal Substitution: A Response to Recent Criticisms." *JETS* 50.1 (March 2007) 71–86.

Winter, Ralph D., and Steven C. Hawthorne. *Perspectives on the World Christian Movement: A Reader.* Rev. ed. Pasadena: William Carey Library, 1992.

Witherington, Ben III. *The Acts of the Apostles: A Socio-Rhetorical Commentary.* Grand Rapids: Eerdmans, 1998.

Wogaman, J. Philip, and Douglas M. Strong, eds. *Readings in Christian Ethics: A Historical Sourcebook.* Louisville: Westminster John Knox, 1996.

Wolterstorff, Nicholas. *Divine Discourse: Philosophical Reflections on the Claim that God Speaks.* Cambridge: Cambridge University Press, 1995.

———. "How Social Justice Got to Me and Why It Never Left." *Journal of the American Academy of Religion* 76.3 (September 2008) 664–79.

———. "Justice and Peace." In *New Dictionary of Christian Ethics and Pastoral Theology*, edited by David Atkinson et al., 15–21 Downers Grove: InterVarsity, 1995.

———. *Justice: Rights and Wrongs.* Princeton: Princeton University Press, 2007.

———. "The Unity Behind the Canon." In *One Scripture or Many? Canon from Biblical, Theological and Philosophical Perspectives*, edited by Christine Helmer and Christof Landmesser, 217–33. Oxford: Oxford University Press, 2004.

———. *Until Justice and Peace Embrace.* Grand Rapids: Eerdmans, 1983.

World Bank. *World Development Report 1990: Poverty.* New York: Oxford University Press, 1990.

World Vision. "Compassion and Fatigue." The Washington Forum, 1996.

Wright, Christopher J. H. *An Eye for an Eye: The Place of Old Testament Ethics Today.* Downers Grove: InterVarsity, 1983.

———. *God's People in God's Land: Family, Land, and Property in the Old Testament.* Grand Rapids: Eerdmans, 1990.

———. *Old Testament Ethics for the People of God.* Downers Grove: InterVarsity, 2004.

———. *Walking in the Ways of the Lord: The Ethical Authority of the Old Testament.* Downers Grove: InterVarsity, 1995.

Wuthnow, Robert. *Acts of Compassion: Caring for Others and Helping Ourselves.* Princeton: Princeton University Press, 1991.

Wuthnow, Robert, ed. *Rethinking Materialism: Perspectives on the Spiritual Dimension of Economic Behavior.* Grand Rapids: Eerdmans, 1995.

Yoder, John H. *The Politics of Jesus: Vicit Agnus Noster.* 2nd ed. Grand Rapids: Eerdmans, 1994.

———. *The Priestly Kingdom: Social Ethics as Gospel.* Notre Dame: University of Notre Dame Press, 1985.

Young, Edward J. *The Book of Isaiah: The English Text, with Introduction, Exposition, and Notes.* 3 vols. Grand Rapids: Eerdmans, 2001.

Young, E. M. "'Fulfill the Law of Christ': An Examination of Galatians 6:2." *Studia biblica et theologica* 7 (1977) 31–42.

Yunus, Muhammad. "The Grameen Bank." *Scientific American* 281.5 (November 1999) 114–19.

Zahn, Theodor von. *Das Evangelium des Lukas.* Kommentar zum Neuen Testament. 4th ed. Wuppertal: Brockhaus, 1988.

Zaman, Hassan. *Assessing the Poverty and Vulnerability Impact of Micro-Credit in Bangladesh: A Case Study of BRAC.* Washington: World Bank, 2000.

Index of Names

Abraham, 114, 182, 283, 299, 302, 316
Achtemeier, Paul, 126n5, 202, 203
Adler, Alfred, 34
Agabus, 135
Agrippa II, King, 183, 183n117
Allison, Dale, 102n31
Ananias, 176
Andrew, 171n100, 217
Aristides, 157n73
Aristophanes, 47, 47n22
Aristotle, 36, 36n46, 41
Artemis (Greek goddess), 10
Assmann, Hugo, 26
Augustine, 287
Augustus, 156n70
Aune, David, 189n132

Bahnsen, Greg, 42n59, 59n1
Balz, Horst, 48
Barnabas, 135, 175, 176, 282
Barrett, C. K., 175–76n106
Barth, Karl, 60, 67
Basil of Caesarea, 266
Batten, Samuel Z., 24
Ben Sira, 321
Bernstein, Basil, 31
Besnier, Niko, 86, 97
Bhumibol, King of Thailand, 266
Binswanger, Ludwig, 34
Bloch, Ernst, 30
Blomberg, Craig, 102, 102n33, 142n33, 144, 152n58, 170n97, 199, 201, 301, 302, 303, 327, 340n140
Bock, Darrell, 156n70, 299n33, 310

Bonino, José Míguez, 26
Boss, Medard, 34
"The Brotherhood for the Kingdom," 25
Brown, Colin, 48, 246n4
Bruce, F. F., 159
Brueggemann, Walter, 314n84
Brunner, Emil, 30
Bultmann, Rudolf K., 112, 113, 125n4, 127
Burakumin, 279
Burridge, Richard, 61, 65, 97n14, 208n195

Caesar, Tiberius, 259n23
Calvin, John, 101–2, 159–60n80, 184n121, 198, 258, 312n78
Caputo, John, 111
Carson, D. A., 102
Cataplus, 307
Chamoïs, Setme, 306
Cladden, Washington, 24
Claerbaut, David, 45
Claudius, 292
Clement, 52n46
Coenen, Lothar, 47n21
Corban, 221n222, 281n7
Cornelius, 128, 129
Cyril of Alexandria, 313n81

Dalits, 1, 279
Danker, Frederick W., 48
David, King, 183n115
Davies, William, 102n31
Delitzsch, Franz, 320n102
Derrett, Duncan, 260n27

Derrida, Jacques, 38
Diana (Roman goddess), 10
Dives, 307n59
Dorcas, 131, 225
Douglas, Mary, 31

Elijah, 100, 116
Eliphaz, 322
Elizabeth, 109
Elizabeth II, Queen of England, 266
Ellis, Richard, 31
Esler, Philip, 48, 50, 246n4
Euodia, 100
Eysenck, Hans, 34

Fabry, Heinz-Josef, 315, 315n91
Feast of Booths, 78, 219n213
Feast of Unleavened Bread, 78
Feast of Weeks, 78, 219n213
Feinberg, Joel, 41n56
Finegan, Edward, 86, 97
Finley, Moses, 73n35
First Quest for the historical Jesus, 3
Fitzmyer, Joseph, 260n27
Fletcher, Joseph, 38n51, 83n74
Foster, George M., 74n38
France, Richard, 142–43n35, 145n43
Frankl, Viktor, 34
Freedman, David Noel, 48
Freud, Anna, 34
Freud, Sigmund, 34
Freyne, Sean, 75n41
Friedman, Milton, 22
Fromm, Erich, 34

Gallus, 307
Gates, Bill, 266
Geneva Bible of 1587, 313n81
Gesenius, Wilhelm, 313, 313n82
Gleaner Societies, 276–77, 308
God, 3, 4, 7, 8, 8n5, 9, 25–27, 33, 38, 38n52, 51, 51n38, 53, 62, 64, 65, 75, 77, 77n54, 79n64, 81, 84, 92, 93, 93n5, 94–96, 98, 99, 100, 102, 103, 103n35, 104, 104n36, 105, 105n38, 106, 108–10, 112–16, 116n74, 125, 128, 129, 137, 138, 139, 144, 151n57, 152n60, 157n72, 161, 163, 181, 184–87, 190–94, 194n142, 195, 208–9, 209n196, 216, 220, 224, 228n238, 236, 244, 250, 263, 266, 267, 272, 272n43, 281n7, 293, 296, 301, 301n36, 302, 310, 314n83, 322, 340
Gospel of Luke, 244
Gray, Sherman, 142n34
Green, Joel, 54–55, 56, 126n5, 202, 203
Günther, Walther, 338n138
Gustafson, James, 62n16
Gutiérrez, Gustavo, 26–27, 272, 273

Habel, Norman, 321n104
Hagner, Donald, 101, 199, 201
Hamel, Gildas, 74n38, 183n115, 183n117
Hanson, K. C., 73n34, 75, 76–77, 78, 79n62, 80, 81, 134n16, 202, 203, 333
Harland, Philip, 73n33, 74
Hauck, Friedrich, 48n23
Hawtrey, Kim, 17–18
Hayek, Friedrich, 22
Hays, J. Daniel, 61
Hays, Richard, xv, xvn1, 7, 9, 61–62, 62n16, 66, 66n24, 68, 82, 328
Hegel, Georg Wilhelm Friedrich, 25
Helen of Troy, 1, 2, 10, 270, 276, 297
Herod, 173
Hock, Ronald, 307n58
Hoekema, Anthony, 23, 25
Horney, Karen, 34
Hus, Jan, 246n4

Index of Names

Ignatius, 195n145, 223n227
Iscariot, Judas, 130, 131

Jairus, 55
James, 186, 224, 224n231, 228, 228n238, 237n251, 274, 335
Jeremias, Joachim, 305
Jerusalem church, 282
Jesus, 43n1, 49, 50, 53–55, 55n54, 55n55, 56, 64–67, 75–77, 77n52, 78–79, 79–80, 79n63, 79n64, 80, 81, 81n71, 97n14, 100, 100n22, 103, 103n35, 105n39, 108, 109, 113, 115, 116, 116n74, 124, 126–30, 130n10, 130n11, 131, 137, 140, 142n33, 143n37, 144, 145, 145n43, 145n44, 146n48, 147, 148, 150, 156, 157, 157n73, 160, 162, 163, 165, 166, 166n90, 167–69, 170n99, 171, 171n100, 172, 172n101, 173, 174, 179, 180n110, 181–82n113, 181n111, 183n115, 183n120, 186, 188n132, 190, 191, 191n138, 195, 196, 197, 200n164, 201n166, 202–4, 206, 208, 209, 209n197, 210–13, 215–18, 221n222, 226, 230n242, 231, 232, 232n246, 233, 234, 242, 246–48, 253, 257, 259n23, 261, 262, 263, 265, 268, 272, 274, 276, 284, 287, 288, 292, 296, 296n28, 297, 298, 299n31, 300, 301, 302n41, 303–5, 307, 319, 322, 324, 325, 329n129, 340
"Joanna the wife of Chuza," 55, 173
Job, 320–21, 322–23, 322n110, 326, 327, 339
John the Baptist, 21, 65, 109, 149, 152, 178n108, 234–35

Johnson, Luke, 54, 54n50
Jose, Rabbi, 200n163
Joseph, 109, 175, 310n70
Joseph of Arimathea, 54, 55, 171, 172, 246
Judah, Rabbi, 200n163
Jung, Carl, 34

Kaiser, Walter, 59, 61
Keil, Carl, 320n102
Kelsey, David, 9, 9n8
Kierkegaard, Søren, 83
Kittel, Gerhard, 48
KJV of 1611, 313n81
Knight, George, 221n222

Lachs, Samuel, 196n148
Law and the Prophets, 321
Lazarus, 53, 70, 81n71, 114, 166, 169, 170n97, 182, 184, 184n123, 189, 192, 246, 263, 263n31, 264, 265, 268, 272, 273, 277, 280n6, 281, 283, 298–301, 301n36, 302, 303n43, 304–9, 309n64, 317, 319, 323, 325–27, 327n125, 329, 331
Lightfoot, John, 196n147
Lingenfelter, Judith, 33
Longenecker, Richard, 154n68
Luce, H. K., 300n34
Lucian, 307
Luke (Disciple), 55, 174n102, 204, 234n247, 235n249, 322, 322n110
Lutherbibel of 1545, 313n81
Lydia, 176, 177

MacIntyre, Alasdair, 61
Malina, Bruce, 52, 53, 73n35, 166n89, 265n35, 289
Manson, Thomas, 146n48
Mark, 171n100, 179

Marshall, I. Howard, 184n123, 299n33, 302n41, 306n54, 309n65
Martens, Elmer, 86n79
Martha, 166, 246
Martin, Ralph, 134n15, 139n26, 162n83, 260n24
Marx, Karl, 21-22, 26, 39
Mary, 55, 109, 129, 166, 189, 246
Maslow, Abraham, 34
Matthew, 168n92, 179, 201, 208
May, Rollo, 34
Medusa, 1, 2, 10, 23, 270
Megapenthes, 307
Menippus, 307n59
Mennonite Gleaner Societies, 276-77, 308
Meyers, Eric, 75n41
Micyllus, 307
Milligan, George, 48
Miranda, José Porfirio, 26
M'Neile, Alan, 196
Moffatt, James, 159, 189n132, 313
Moltmann, Jürgen, 27, 30
Moo, Douglas, 59
Morris, Leon, 102
Moses, 99, 114, 182, 184, 283, 298, 299, 303, 321, 323
Moulton, James H., 48
Mounce, William, 222

Naaman, 235n249
Nägelsbach, Carl, 312-13, 314
Nicodemus, 172n101
Nicomachean Ethics, 36n46
Niebuhr, Reinhold, 43n1
Noell, Edd, 75, 77n53, 80, 81
Nolland, John, 78n60, 184n123, 191n137, 206n189, 246n4, 260
Novak, Michael, 27, 74
Nozick, Robert, 20

Oakman, Douglas, 73n34, 75, 76-77, 78, 79n62, 80, 81, 134n16, 202, 203, 333
O'Donovan, Oliver, 40n55, 42
Oswalt, John, 314

Pannenberg, Wolfhart, 30
Pao, David, 301n35
Pastor, Jack, 282n9
Paul, 51, 51n39, 101, 105, 105n39, 108, 109, 113, 114, 125, 131-34, 134n16, 135, 136-38, 139n27, 151, 154-56, 156n71, 157n73, 158, 159, 177, 178, 178n108, 186n128, 193, 204, 209, 227, 231, 242n2, 257, 258n21, 267, 293, 322
Peter, Simon, 131, 167, 168n92, 171n100, 179, 210, 217, 225, 233, 322
Pharisaic school of Hillel, 304, 304n45
Pharisaic school of Shammai, 304, 304n45
Philip, 217, 218
Phoebe, 215
Plato, 41, 112
Plutus, 47n22
The Politics of Jesus (Yoder), 66
Polycarp, 195n145

Rahlfs, Alfred, 316n93
Rashi (Rabbi Shlomo Yitzhaki), 316
Rauschenbusch, Walter, 24, 25, 270
Rawlinson, George, 313n80
Rawls, John, 20-21, 22-23
Regnerus, Mark, 15n1
Renan, Ernest, 298, 298n30
Ritschl, Albrecht, 24
Rogers, Carl, 34
Rorty, Richard, 24

Index of Names

Sanders, E. P., 59n1
Sapphira, 176
Schnackenburg, Rudolf, 101
Schneider, Gerhard, 48
Schreiner, Thomas, 209n198
Schweitzer, Albert, 3
Scott, James C., 74n38
Seccombe, David, 55–56, 309
Segundo, Juan Luis, 26
Sider, Ronald, 23, 27, 27n25
Sikkink, David, 15n1
Simon the Pharisee, 55
Si-Osiris, 306, 307
Siren, 2, 10, 23, 270
Skinner, Burrhus F., 34
Slim, Carlos, 266
Smith, Christian, 15n1
Social Action Commission of the Evangelical Fellowship of Canada, 46
Socrates, 112
Solomon, King, 163
Spence, Henry, 306n54
Stählin, Gustav, 157
Stein, Robert, 260n27, 301n35, 310
Strelan, John, 140
Susanna, 173
Swanson, James, 314n83, 315
Sweeney, Marvin, 311n73
Syntyche, 100

Tabitha, 123, 129, 131, 161, 225, 255, 286, 308, 332
Targum Jonathan, 316
Theologie der Hoffnung (Theology of Hope) (Moltmann), 27
A Theology of Liberation (Gutiérrez), 26
Thompson, Marianne, 126n5, 202, 203

Thompson, Michael, 31
Timothy, 99n21
Titus, 132
Topel, John, 205
Turner, David, 102
Tyrrell, George, 3

United Nations, 291
Universal Declaration of Human Rights, 44
Until Justice and Peace Embrace (Wolterstorff), 28

Volf, Miroslav, xvi, 39, 272n43

Watson, John, 34
Watts, John, 311–12n75
Widyapranawa, Samuel, 314n85
Wildavsky, Aaron, 31
Wildberger, Hans, 314n84
Wilkins, Michael, 102
Williams, David, 156n70
Wisdom of Solomon, 315n90
Wolpe, Joseph, 34
Wolterstorff, Nicholas, xvi, 10–11, 23, 28, 28n27, 29–30, 38n52, 41n56, 42, 44, 45, 56, 98, 107, 111n61, 123n3, 150, 218, 224, 239, 274, 312–13, 335n135
Wright, Christopher, 28, 61
Wycliffe, John, 246n4
Wycliffe Bible of 1395, 313n81

Yoder, John Howard, 66, 66n25, 67
Young, Edward, 314n85, 315n92

Zaccheus, 54, 55, 246
Zacharias, 109
Zahn, Theodor von, 184n121
Zarephath, 100, 116, 235n249

Index of Scripture

OLD TESTAMENT

Genesis
1–3	27
14:14	316

Exodus
1–3	27
12:48	283n10
16:16	133
16:18	133
20:12	221n222
21:10	28
21:24–25	200
22:21–24	219, 310
22:22–24	96
22:24	92n3
22:26–27	200

Leviticus
18–19	59
19:9–10	225
19:15	37, 228, 263n30, 272n42
19:17–18	71
19:18	228, 272n42
23:22	225
25:10–15	234
25:25	93
25:28–33	234
25:35	17, 201n167
25:35–37	205
25:40	234
25:50–54	234
27:17–24	234

Numbers
30:2	7
36:4	234

Deuteronomy
1:17	37
5:16	221n222
6:25	309n66
10:18–19	64
14:28–29	219, 324
14:29	324n116, 325n121
15:1–3	325
15:4	51, 175
15:7–8	205
15:7–11	198, 323–24, 325n121, 326
15:9	98, 196
15:11	324
15:12–18	325
16:1–17	78, 324
16:9–17	219
16:19	37
19:11–15	97
19:18–19	230
23:20	325n121
23:21	7
23:23	7
23:24–25	225, 261–62, 262n29, 267
24:6–15	309
24:12–13	200
24:14–15	97

Deuteronomy (cont.)

24:14–17	283
24:15	98, 283
24:17–28	219
24:19	219, 325n121
24:19–22	225
24:20–22	219
26:12	323–24
26:12–13	219
27:19	219
28	104, 104n36
28:1–2	104n36
28:54–58	196
30:16	325n121
31:6–8	194n142

Joshua

6	100

1 Samuel

2:8	64

1 Kings

17:19	100

Esther

8:15	183n115

Job

1:3	320
1:6–12	322
5:13	322
20:19	323
22:4	322
22:5	219
22:5–11	322, 326
22:7	322, 326
22:7–9	327n124
22:9–11	219
24:3	219
24:3–11	323
24:12	219
24:19–21	219
29:7	323
29:11–12	96
29:11–27	323
29:12–14	219
29:16–17	219
31:9–10	320n102
31:16–17	219, 283
31:16–22	96
31:16–28	283n10, 319, 322, 326
31:18	326
31:19–20	326
31:32	321
31:38–40	320n102
39:2	322n110
41:11	322

Psalms

8:5–8	171
37:11	169n95
50:10	191
94:3	219
94:6	219
107:41	64
111:9	51
112	139n27
112:9	51, 138, 139n27
113:7–8	64
113:9	64
146:8	64

Proverbs

14:20	265
19:4	265
19:17	190
23:6	196
24:23	94
25:1	315n91
25:21–22	151
28:21	94
28:22	196
29:7	94
31:21–23	183n116
31:22	183n116

Isaiah

1:17	93, 219
1:19–20	219
1:23	219
1:27	10
3:15	312n77
5:8	339
10:1–2	219
10:2	312n77
32:1–5	311
32:5–7	311, 326
32:6	311, 313, 313n82, 314, 315, 315n91, 316, 317, 322
32:7	317n97
49:8	235
56:6–7	79
58:3	310
58:4	310
58:6	234
58:6–10	309, 311, 326
58:11	310
61:1–2	234

Jeremiah

7:5–7	219
7:11	79
22:2–5	219
22:3	41n58

Ezekiel

16:49	222
18:1–3	318
18:4–18	317
18:12–18	317
18:19–20	318
22:2	219
22:6–7	219

Daniel

4:24	117
4:27	117

Hosea

12:8–11	189n132

Amos

5:24	3
6:1–7	310
6:8	310

Micah

6:8	310

Zechariah

7:9–10	219
7:10	283
8:16	7
13:7	146n48

Malachi

3:5	219, 283

APOCRYPHA

Tobit

2:14	125n4
4:7–10	196n149
12:9	125n4
14:11	125n4

Sirach

4:1–3	315
4:3	315
14:3–10	196n149
20:14–15	206
21:15	222

Baruch

5–9	125n4

NEW TESTAMENT

Matthew

1:19	109
3:15	109
4:19	166
5	113n72
5:3	169n95
5:5–6	169n95
5:6	113n71
5:7	113, 237, 286
5:8	113
5:10–12	169
5:12	169
5:19	146, 148, 163–64
5:20	169n95
5:27	266
5:38–42	198
5:39	7, 168
5:40	198
5:41	284n11
5:42	197–99, 201–4, 207, 208, 244, 253, 254n16, 256
5:43–45	271
5:43–48	199
5:44–48	238
5:45	208n195
5:46–47	201
5:48	208n195
6:1–4	10, 109, 125n4, 126, 127n8, 338
6:2–4	340
6:9–13	174
6:12	230n242
6:15	103, 103n35, 211
6:19–21	162, 164
6:19–34	164, 196
6:20	127–28
6:22–23	191n135, 196, 244
6:22–24	181
6:23	340
6:24	164
6:24–34	162
6:25	164
6:25–32	53
6:25–34	137
6:26	164
6:32	188n131
6:33	169n95
7:1–2	208, 209n197
7:7–11	79, 285
7:9	79n63
7:11	79n63
7:12	285
7:28–29	164
8:5–13	65
8:8	282
8:20	171
8:21–22	221n222
8:22	221n222
9:2–8	233
9:9	166
9:13	237
9:18–26	65
9:20–22	233
9:27	115
9:36	116n76
10:5–6	144, 215
10:8	232n246
10:9–10	156n70, 164, 165
10:10	165, 231, 257
10:12–14	165
10:14	144
10:29–31	79
10:37	221n222
10:40–42	144, 145n43, 147, 214, 243
10:41	214–15
10:41–42	144
10:42	142, 145, 147, 214
11:4–5	233, 235
11:11	145n44, 148
11:25	143
12:1	226, 261
12:7	226, 237
12:12–13	242

Matthew (cont.)

12:18	234, 235
12:40–50	168
12:48–49	142n33
12:50	168
13:10–15	77n54
13:13–15	116n76
13:22	187, 188
13:44–46	164n87
13:52	55n55
13:54–58	116, 233
13:57	116n74
14:15–22	216, 218
15:3–6	221n222, 258
15:3–9	257–58
15:19	284–85n12
15:22	115
15:26–27	184
15:27	306n52
15:30–31	233
15:32	218
15:32–38	218
16:23	179
16:24–27	179
17:15	115
17:24–27	79
17:25	79n64
17:27	100
18	142, 144, 146, 148
18:1–5	148n53, 210, 211
18:4	145n44
18:4–5	212n206
18:5	142, 143, 147, 211, 214
18:6	19, 142, 143, 231
18:10	142
18:14	142
18:15	145–46
18:21–23	230n242
18:23–34	115, 230
18:25–35	103n35
18:27	116n76
18:33	6
18:35	103
19:12	168n93
19:14	211
19:18	284–85n12
19:18–19	229
19:21	210
19:21–22	127, 166
19:21–24	245
19:21–25	165, 166, 189
19:25	81
19:27	167, 168, 248
19:27–30	168, 209, 210, 248
19:28	168
19:29	168, 221n222
19:29–30	209n199
19:30	167
20:1–6	248n6
20:15	196
20:16	209n199
20:25–28	212, 213
20:26–28	288
20:30–34	232
21:12–13	78
21:13	79
21:14	233
23:2–4	259n23
23:11	288
23:11–12	213
23:14	219–20, 219n214, 260, 260n28, 271
23:23	237
23:23–25	236
24:3	77n52
24:45–46	259n23
24:45–51	77n52, 148n52
25	103
25:1–13	77n52
25:16	77
25:24	77
25:27	77
25:29	77
25:31–46	53, 101, 102–3, 140, 147, 155, 245, 249, 249n8, 250, 250n11, 253n15, 256, 264, 264n34, 281, 330, 337n137

Matthew (cont.)

25:35	151
25:36	76, 147, 224, 264
25:38	151
25:39	76, 147
25:40	143, 146–48, 212
25:43	147, 151
25:43–44	76, 264
25:44	151, 250
25:45	108, 146
26:6–13	129, 130
26:10	130
26:11	130n11, 198, 324
26:15	156n70
27:3–10	156n70
27:57	171, 172
28:10	142n33

Mark

1:19	166
1:29–30	171n100
1:33	171n100
1:40–42	232
2:23	226, 261
3:4–5	242
3:9–10	233
3:31–35	168
3:35	168
4:10–12	77n54
4:11–12	116n76
4:18–19	187, 188
4:19	188
4:24	208, 209
4:24–25	77n54
5:18–19	167
5:19	116, 233
5:22–43	65
5:25–34	233
5:26	233
6:1–6	235n249
6:8–9	164, 165
6:10	165
6:34	116n76
6:34–44	216, 218
7:9–13	221n222, 257–58, 281n7
7:21–23	229
7:22	195, 196
7:23	20, 195
7:24	171n100
7:27–28	184
7:28	266
8:33	179
8:34–37	179
8:38	179
9:28	171n100
9:33	171n100
9:34–37	143, 148n53, 210, 211
9:35	143, 288
9:36–37	214
9:37	143
9:41	214, 215, 243
9:42	19, 142, 145, 231
10:10	171n100
10:14–15	211
10:19	229, 284–85n12
10:19–23	245
10:21	81, 85, 166, 166n90, 210, 246
10:21–22	127
10:21–26	165, 166, 189
10:24	81, 143n37
10:26	81
10:28	167, 168, 248
10:28–31	168, 210, 248
10:29	168, 221n222
10:30	168
10:42–45	212, 213
10:43–45	288
10:44	213
10:47–48	115
11:15–17	78
11:17	79
11:25	6
12:15	100
12:38–40	219
12:40	260, 271
12:41–44	172

Mark (cont.)

12:42–43	49
12:44	49, 172, 250
14:3–9	129, 130
14:7	130n10, 130n11, 198, 242, 324
14:14	171n100
15:17	183n115
15:20	183n115
15:24	205
15:43	171, 172

Luke

1:6	109
1:46–55	55
1:52–53	298
1:53	189
1:58	114
1:72	115
2:34	298
3:11	53, 149, 152, 244, 245, 256, 330
3:12–13	229, 230, 260, 270
3:12–14	260–61, 271
3:14	178n108, 229, 230, 260, 270, 334
4:16–27	55
4:18	235n249
4:18–21	234, 235n249
4:23–27	116, 233, 235n249
4:24	116n74
4:25	116
5:17	55
5:27	166
5:29	168n92
6:1	226, 261
6:9–10	242
6:17	164
6:20	49, 163–64, 168, 272, 299n31
6:20–26	169n96
6:21	50
6:22–23	169, 299n31
6:23	169
6:24	169, 264
6:24–25	187, 298
6:24–26	55n54
6:27	239, 284n11
6:27–28	238
6:27–36	205, 207
6:29	198, 205, 242, 271
6:29–30	197, 205, 207, 208, 242n1, 253
6:29–36	338
6:30	198, 198n153, 205, 206, 207n193, 208, 242, 244, 256, 286n13
6:31	285–86
6:32–33	238
6:32–34	97n17, 206
6:32–35	201
6:34	206n189
6:34–35	204, 253, 256, 286
6:34–36	197, 242
6:36	85, 208, 208n195, 242, 286
6:37	103
6:38	197, 208, 209, 244
7:1	164
7:1–10	65
7:6	282
7:12–13	233
7:12–16	65
7:22	234, 235
7:28	145n44
7:36	55
7:37–38	55
7:50	299n31
8:1	55
8:1–3	131, 164, 166, 172, 173
8:2–3	248
8:3	55
8:12	299n31
8:14	188
8:18	209n197
8:19–21	168
8:21	168
8:38–39	167

Luke (*cont.*)

8:40–42	55
8:41–56	65
8:43–48	233
8:49–56	55
9:3	165
9:23–25	179
9:26	179
9:46–48	143, 148n53, 165, 210–12
9:48	143, 145n44, 214
9:58	171
9:59–60	221n222
9:60	221n222
10:1–4	246
10:4	165
10:5	165
10:7	246, 257
10:9	232n246
10:21	143
10:27	150
10:27–37	149, 237, 244
10:30	101
10:30–37	141
10:33	116n76, 150
10:34	101
10:35	101
10:36–37	150
10:37	6, 101, 115
10:38	167
11:1–4	174, 230n242
11:4	230n242
11:9–13	79
11:11	79n63
11:13	79n63
11:34–36	196, 244
11:39–42	236, 338
11:46	259n23, 287
12:6–7	79
12:11–12	65n19
12:13–21	169, 170, 190, 246, 263n31, 265n35, 268n39, 327n125
12:15	85, 263
12:20	263
12:21	164
12:22	170
12:22–34	127, 128, 163, 164, 170, 181, 192, 196, 338
12:24	164
12:26	146n49
12:29	164
12:30	188n131
12:32	164
12:33	54, 127n8, 164, 166, 170, 186, 196, 210, 244–47
12:33–34	164
12:42–43	259n23
13:19	234, 235
13:30	209n199, 248n6
14:12–14	52–53, 55, 150, 244, 245, 329
14:13	76, 109
14:14	109
14:26	221n222
14:33	170, 171
15:8	156n70
15:20	116n76
16:1–13	180, 181, 191n136, 195, 244, 265n35, 268n39
16:9	298, 340
16:10	146n49
16:11	340
16:11–12	340
16:13	164
16:14	181, 184, 184n124, 265, 298, 300, 304
16:15	181, 181n112, 184, 265
16:16–18	184
16:18	300, 304
16:19–31	53, 169, 182, 185, 189, 263, 264, 268, 276, 319, 332
16:20	70, 185n126
16:20–21	264n32
16:21	306, 306n52
16:24	114
16:25	169, 265, 298, 299, 306

Luke (*cont.*)

16:27–28	300
16:28–39	298
16:29	283, 321
16:30	185, 301
16:31	283, 298
17:1–2	231
17:2	19, 142, 145
17:3–4	6
17:13	115
18:1–5	220n215
18:7–8	113
18:16–17	211
18:18–25	55
18:20	229, 284–85n12
18:22	54, 127n8, 166, 210, 245–46
18:22–23	127
18:22–26	166, 189
18:26	81
18:28	167
18:28–30	168
18:29	168, 221n222, 247
19:2	166, 173
19:8	54
19:8–9	166, 173
19:11	77
19:13	77
19:17	146n49
19:21	77, 205
19:23	77
19:26	77
19:45–46	78
19:46	79
20:46–47	219
20:47	260, 271
21:1–4	172
21:2–3	49
21:4	49, 172
21:34	171, 188n131
22:24–27	213
22:26–27	288
22:27	213
22:31–32	322
22:35–36	173, 296n28
23:11	183n115
23:50–51	54, 55, 172
24:27	321
24:44	321

John

1:43	166
2:13–16	78
2:16	79
2:17	142n33
4:22	283
4:46–54	65
5:2–9	233
5:3	233
6:4–15	217, 218
6:5	218
6:6	218
6:26	156
6:26–27	116
6:27	156
6:28–29	156
9:1–23	126n5
11:5	166
11:11	166
11:31	167
12:3–8	129–30
12:8	130n11, 198, 324
13:14	213
13:29	130, 131, 201n168
13:34	64
13:34–35	238
15:12	64
15:20	66
19:2	183n115
19:5	183n115
19:38	166, 172

Acts

2:24	322n110
2:43–47	97
2:44–45	153
2:44–46	155, 175, 245
2:46	176n106

Acts (cont.)

3:2	201
3:2–6	156n70
3:2–8	233
4:32–37	175
4:34	51, 175–76n106
5:1–11	176, 247
6:1	153, 224, 225, 247, 254, 331
8:20	156n70
9:36	123, 129, 131, 161, 225, 242, 245, 254, 255, 286
9:39	161
9:39–41	123, 254
10:2	127–29
10:4	127, 128
10:28	282
10:31	127, 128
10:38	233, 242, 288
11:19–21	292
11:28	140, 292, 331
11:28–30	135, 249, 331
16:14–15	176, 177
16:35–39	271n40
19:19	156n70
20:33–35	156–58, 250–51, 263, 329
20:35	52–53, 76, 155, 157n73, 204, 251
21:8	247
21:9	247
24:17	111, 125, 131, 136, 249
26:22	321
28:23	321

Romans

1:17	109
1:28–29	195
1:31	237, 238
2:6–8	100
2:7	161, 242n2
2:10	161, 242n2
3:12	242n2
4:3–22	109
4:4	232
4:4–5	115
7:7–11	195
7:21	242n2
8:29	142n33
9:14–16	114
9:22–23	113
9:30–32	109
10:3	109
11:30–32	114
11:35	322
12:5	253, 256
12:8	114, 209, 253
12:9	236, 238
12:11	157, 158
12:13	150, 253
12:16	7, 227
12:17–21	271
12:19	64
12:20	53, 256
12:20–21	151, 244, 330
13:7	100
13:8	7, 230
13:8–10	237, 238
13:9	7, 195
13:9–10	229, 230
13:10	239
14:5	105
14:6	105
14:14	105n39
14:20	105n38
14:23	105
15:2	239, 286
15:25–27	136, 249
15:26	51, 134, 138, 138n25, 151, 154
15:27	131, 134n16, 135, 154, 293, 293n26
15:31	131–32, 293
16:2	215, 243

1 Corinthians

2:44–46	175
3:19	322

1 Corinthians (*cont.*)

4:3	146n49
5:9–11	192, 263, 336
5:11	336
5:13	336
6:1–8	271n40
6:2	146n49
6:7–10	192, 338
6:8–10	229
6:9	336
6:9–10	336
6:10	336
7:4	28
7:29–31	174, 175, 247
8:12–13	19
9:4–6	28
9:4–11	257
9:4–18	232, 257
9:5	247, 257
9:6	257
9:9	257n19
9:12	28
9:14	231–32, 257
9:15	232
9:18	28
10:24	286
11:21–22	154, 155, 245
11:26–27	154
11:29	154
11:33–34	154
12:23	262
12:25	279
12:28–30	232n246
13:1–3	177
13:3	177, 178, 247, 296n28, 341
13:4–6	238
13:6	239
14:1	238n253
15:9	146
16:1–3	132, 178
16:3	111
16:13–14	239

2 Corinthians

4:1	113
6:2	235
8–9	136n24, 138n25, 154
8:1	140
8:1–5	133
8:2	50, 293
8:2–5	137
8:6–7	111, 133
8:6–8	132
8:8	111
8:9	137
8:11–12	133
8:11–13	178, 247–48
8:11–15	178
8:13–15	133, 137, 293
8:14	51, 249, 293
8:15	133
8:19–20	137, 138
8:24	134
9:1	111, 138
9:5–6	134, 263
9:6	135
9:7	95, 111, 125, 135, 139n27, 249, 296
9:8	242, 293
9:8–11	51n38, 138, 161, 195, 244
9:9	51, 138
9:10	51
9:11	139n26
9:12	249
9:12–13	139
9:13	132, 151
11:9	224
12:13–14	224
12:14	177, 247
12:16	224

Galatians

2:10	154
5:6	239

Galatians (cont.)

5:13	239
5:13–14	288
5:19–21	336
5:21	336
5:22	195n146
6:1	140
6:2	139, 140
6:6	232
6:9–10	162, 242
6:10	148, 242, 256, 285, 288

Ephesians

2:4–5	114
2:8	115
2:8–9	115
2:10	161, 243
3:8	146
4:25	7, 253, 256
4:28	155, 158, 251, 297
5:3	195
5:5	195
5:6	195

Philippians

2:1–4	239
2:2	100
2:3–4	288
2:7	288
4:2	100
4:11–13	177, 178, 178n108, 247
4:14–17	155, 232
4:17–18	101
4:18	134

Colossians

3:5–6	193
3:9	7
3:12	237

1 Thessalonians

2:5	193n141
2:9	224
4:11–12	158, 248, 282
4:12	251
5:14	158, 251

2 Thessalonians

3:6	14, 252
3:6–13	159, 161, 242
3:6–15	251, 252, 271, 273, 274n44, 275
3:6–16	273
3:8	224, 251
3:10	252, 258
3:11	223, 255
3:13	251
3:14	261
3:14–15	278n4

1 Timothy

1:2	115
1:13	113
1:14	113
1:16	113
2:9–10	186n128
3:2–3	194, 195
3:8	195
5:3	254
5:3–16	94, 161, 219–20, 221, 254–55
5:4	258, 281n7
5:6	340
5:8	258, 281n7, 283
5:10	213, 222, 242, 288
5:13	223, 255
5:15	258
5:16	254, 255, 281n7
5:17	223
5:17–18	257
6:5–11	170n98, 193
6:8	53
6:11	236
6:17	189n132, 267

1 Timothy (*cont.*)

6:17–19	155, 161, 185–87, 195, 242, 244, 248, 286–87, 308
6:18	197, 242–43, 267, 327n124
6:19	267

2 Timothy

1:2	115
1:16	114, 115
1:18	113
2:19	236
3:2	278
3:16–17	xv
4:13	100

Titus

1:7–8	195
1:12–13	160, 252, 261
2:14	161, 243
3:5	115
3:8	161, 243
3:13–14	161–62, 242–43
3:14	287

Hebrews

2:11–12	142n33
4:16	113, 114
6:10	216
10:24	340
10:32–34	282
10:34	101, 116n76, 155, 215, 242, 271
13:1–3	215, 216, 243
13:2	243
13:3	273, 282
13:5	178n108
13:5–6	151n57, 170n98, 193, 194
13:16	151, 161, 242

James

1:9–11	186, 247
1:10	186n129
1:26	224n231
1:27	17, 219, 224, 224n231, 255, 282, 340
2:1–7	227
2:1–12	262, 272
2:4	186n129, 228n239, 262
2:5	227, 272
2:6	259, 270
2:6–7	231
2:8	228, 237n251, 272n42
2:8–12	228
2:9–11	237n251
2:12	237n251
2:13	103, 114, 115, 237, 286, 286n14
2:14–17	141, 149, 151, 152, 155, 237n251, 249, 250, 256, 281, 286n14, 330
2:15	53, 174, 245, 250, 252
2:15–16	249
2:18	250, 339
3:4	146n49
3:17	162, 228, 262
4	104–5
4:1–5	188n131, 194
4:4	104
4:11	104
4:13–16	104
4:13–17	186n129
4:17	104–5
5:1–6	186, 187, 230, 231, 258, 259, 260, 271, 335
5:4	270
5:5	222, 340
5:6	259, 270
5:11	322

1 Peter

1:3	114
1:18	156n70
2:10	113

1 Peter (*cont.*)

2:18–23	65n19
2:19–20	97n17
3:3	186n128

2 Peter

2:1	193n141

1 John

3:16	249–50
3:16–18	141, 149, 152, 155, 249, 250, 250n11, 256, 281
3:17	250, 253, 339
5:17	236, 338, 338n138

2 John

1:3	115

3 John

1:2	132, 178, 247

Jude

1:2	115
1:12	154, 245
1:21	113
1:22–23	6
1:23	114

Revelation

3:17–18	188
3:19	189n132

~

OTHER

1 Clement

38:2	52n46, 157n72

Gittin

52a–52b	260

Hagigah

2.77d	307

Sanhedrin

6.23c	307

www.ingramcontent.com/pod-product-compliance
Lightning Source LLC
Chambersburg PA
CBHW071230290426
44108CB00013B/1355